The Power of Corporate Networks

Corporate networks, the links between companies and their leaders, reflect a country's economic organization and its corporate governance system. Most research on corporate networks focuses on individual countries or particular time periods, however, making fruitful comparisons over longer periods of time difficult. This book provides a unique, long-term analysis of the rise, consolidation, decline, and occasional re-emergence of these networks in 14 countries across North and South America, Europe and Asia in the twentieth and early twenty-first centuries.

In this volume, the editors bring together the most internationally well-known specialists to investigate the long-term development of corporate networks. Using a combination of quantitative and qualitative research approaches, the authors describe the main developments and changes in the corporate network over time by focusing on important network indicators in benchmark years, and identify historical explanations for these developments. This unique, long-term perspective allows readers insight into how and why national corporate networks have evolved over time.

Thomas David is Professor of Economic and Social History at the University of Lausanne and Director of the College of Humanities at the Ecole Polytechnique Fédérale of Lausanne, Switzerland.

Gerarda Westerhuis is a researcher and lecturer at the Department of History and Art History (Utrecht University) and at Rotterdam School of Management (Erasmus University).

Routledge International Studies in Business History

Series editors: Ray Stokes and Matthias Kipping

1 **Management, Education and Competitiveness**
Europe, Japan and the United States
Edited by Rolv Petter Amdam

2 **The Development of Accounting in an International Context**
A Festschrift in Honour of R. H. Parker
T. E. Cooke and C. W. Nobes

3 **The Dynamics of the Modern Brewing Industry**
Edited by R. G. Wilson and T. R. Gourvish

4 **Religion, Business and Wealth in Modern Britain**
Edited by David Jeremy

5 **The Multinational Traders**
Geoffrey Jones

6 **The Americanisation of European Business**
Edited by Matthias Kipping and Ove Bjarnar

7 **Region and Strategy**
Business in Lancashire and Kansai 1890–1990
Douglas A. Farnie, David J. Jeremy, John F. Wilson, Nakaoka Tetsuro and Abe Takeshi

8 **Foreign Multinationals in the United States**
Management and Performance
Edited by Geoffrey Jones and Lina Galvez-Munoz

9 **Co-Operative Structures in Global Business**
A new approach to networks, technology transfer agreements, strategic alliances and agency relationships
Gordon H. Boyce

10 **German and Japanese Business in the Boom Years**
Transforming American management and technology models
Edited by Akira Kudo, Matthias Kipping and Harm G. Schröter

11 **Dutch Enterprise in the 20th Century**
Business Strategies in small open country
Keetie E. Sluyterman

12 **The Formative Period of American Capitalism**
A materialist interpretation
Daniel Gaido

13 **International Business and National War Interests**
Unilever Between Reich and Empire, 1939–45
Ben Wubs

14 **Narrating the Rise of Big Business in the USA**
How Economists Explain Standard Oil and Wal-Mart
Anne Mayhew

15 **Women and their money 1700–1950**
Essays on women and finance
Edited by Anne Laurence, Josephine Maltby and Janette Rutterford

16 **The Origins of Globalization**
Karl Moore and David Lewis

17 **The Foundations of Female Entrepreneurship**
Enterprise, Home and Household in London, c. 1800–1870
Alison C. Kay

18 **Innovation and Entrepreneurial Networks in Europe**
Edited by Paloma Fernández Pérez and Mary Rose

19 **Trademarks, Brands, and Competitiveness**
Edited by Teresa da Silva Lopes and Paul Duguid

20 **Technological Innovation in Retail Finance**
International Historical Perspectives
Edited by Bernardo Bátiz-Lazo, J. Carles Maixé-Altés and Paul Thomes

21 **Reappraising State-Owned Enterprise**
A Comparison of the UK and Italy
Edited by Franco Amatori, Robert Millward, and Pierangelo Toninelli

22 **The Dynamics of Big Business**
Structure, Strategy and Impact in Italy and Spain
Veronica Binda

23 **Family Multinationals**
Entrepreneurship, Governance, and Pathways to Internationalization
Edited by Christina Lubinski, Jeffrey Fear, and Paloma Fernández Pérez

24 **Organizing Global Technology Flows**
Institutions, Actors, and Processes
Edited by Pierre-Yves Donzé and Shigehiro Nishimura

25 **Tin and Global Capitalism**
A History of the Devil's Metal, 1850–2000
Edited by Mats Ingulstad, Andrew Perchard, and Espen Storli

26 **The Power of Corporate Networks**
A Comparative and Historical Perspective
Edited by Thomas David and Gerarda Westerhuis

The Power of Corporate Networks
A Comparative and Historical Perspective

Edited by
Thomas David and
Gerarda Westerhuis

NEW YORK AND LONDON

First published 2014
by Routledge
711 Third Avenue, New York, NY 10017

and by Routledge
2 Park Square, Milton Park, Abingdon, Oxon OX14 4RN

First issued in paperback 2018

Routledge is an imprint of the Taylor & Francis Group, an informa business

© 2014 Taylor & Francis

The right of the editors to be identified as the author of the editorial material, and of the authors for their individual chapters, has been asserted in accordance with sections 77 and 78 of the Copyright, Designs and Patents Act 1988.

All rights reserved. No part of this book may be reprinted or reproduced or utilized in any form or by any electronic, mechanical, or other means, now known or hereafter invented, including photocopying and recording, or in any information storage or retrieval system, without permission in writing from the publishers.

Trademark Notice: Product or corporate names may be trademarks or registered trademarks, and are used only for identification and explanation without intent to infringe.

Library of Congress Cataloging-in-Publication Data
The power of corporate networks : a comparative and historical perspective /
    edited by Thomas David and Gerarda Westerhuis.
       pages cm — (Routledge international studies in business history ; 26)
    Includes bibliographical references and index.
    1. Business networks—History.   2. Interorganizational relations—History.
 3. Corporations—History.   4. Corporate governance—History.   I. David,
Thomas, 1967–   II. Westerhuis, Gerarda, 1973–
    HD69.S8P694 2015
    338.8'7—dc23
    2014011531

ISBN 13: 978-1-138-34072-5 (pbk)
ISBN 13: 978-0-415-72974-1 (hbk)

Typeset in Sabon
Apex CoVantage, LLC

Contents

Figures and Tables	xi
Acknowledgments	xiii
Preface	xv
FRANS STOKMAN	

1 Comparing Corporate Networks in a Long-Term Perspective   1
    THOMAS DAVID AND GERARDA WESTERHUIS

PART I
Large Developed Economies

2 The Decline of the American Corporate Network, 1960–2010   31
    TODD SCHIFELING AND MARK S. MIZRUCHI

3 The Structure of Networks: The Transformation of UK Business, 1904–2010   48
    GERHARD SCHNYDER AND JOHN F. WILSON

4 The Corporate Network in Germany, 1896–2010   66
    PAUL WINDOLF

PART II
Small European Economies

5 The Dutch Corporate Network: Considering Its Persistence   89
    GERARDA WESTERHUIS

6 From National Cohesion to Transnationalization: The Changing Role of Banks in the Swiss Company Network, 1910–2010   107
STÉPHANIE GINALSKI, THOMAS DAVID AND ANDRÉ MACH

7 Austria Inc. under Strain, 1937–2008: The Fading Power of *Creditanstalt* Bank and the End of the Nationalized Industry   125
PHILIPP KOROM

PART III
State Capitalism?

8 Ebbs and Flows of French Capitalism   149
PIERRE FRANÇOIS AND CLAIRE LEMERCIER

9 Persistent and Stubborn: The State in Italian Capitalism, 1913–2001   169
ALBERTO RINALDI AND MICHELANGELO VASTA

PART IV
"Peripheral" Europe

10 Business Coalitions and Segmentation: Dynamics of the Portuguese Corporate Network   191
ÁLVARO FERREIRA DA SILVA AND PEDRO NEVES

11 Bulgarian Business Elite, 1900s–2000s   213
MARTIN IVANOV AND GEORGI GANEV

12 "From Dense to Loose?"—Corporate Networks and Interlocks in Finnish Business in the Twentieth Century   233
SUSANNA FELLMAN, KARI-MATTI PIILAHTI AND VALTTERI HÄRMÄLÄ

PART V
Developed Economies in Asia and Latin America

13 Longitudinal Study of Interlocking Directorates in Argentina and Foreign Firms' Integration into Local Capitalism, 1923–2000   257
ANDREA LLUCH AND ERICA SALVAJ

14 Between State Power and Familism: The Directorate Interlock
   Network in Taiwan throughout the Twentieth Century   276
   ZONG-RONG LEE AND THIJS A. VELEMA

15 Evolution of Corporate Networks in Twentieth Century Japan   296
   SATOSHI KOIBUCHI AND TETSUJI OKAZAKI

   Appendix I   305
   List of Contributors   331
   Index   335

Figures and Tables

FIGURES

1.1	The Average Degrees of the Corporate Networks of the 14 Countries (1900–2010)	13
2.1	Features of Top Ten Interlockers, 1962–2010	42
3.1	Network 'Depth' vs. Network 'Width'	54
3.2	Cumulated Degree of Financial Sector Firms among 10 Most Central Companies (% of Total)	57
3.3	Difference between Density Coefficients within and between Sectors	59
4.1	Ego-network of Deutsche Bank, 1914	70
4.2	Total Corporate Network—Germany, 1914	71
4.3	Network Density: Germany (G) and United States (US), 1896–2010	72
5.1	Percentage of Firms in Main Component, and in m-core, 1903–2008	92
5.2	Percentage Interlockers and Big Linkers, 1903–2008	93
6.1	Swiss Corporate Network's Density, 1910–2010	109
7.1	The Evolution of Simple and Multiple Personal Ties between the Largest 125 Austrian Companies, 1938–2008	128
7.2	Network Components of Austria Inc., 1949–1983	136
8.1	Pulsations in the French Network	150
9.1	Density and Isolated and Marginal Firms	174
9.2	Density of the Top 250 Companies in Some Selected Countries	175
10.1	Network Sociogram, 1925	198
10.2	Network Sociogram, 1973	203
10.3	Network Sociogram, 2010	208
12.1	The Interlocks between Companies in 1912	241

xii *Figures and Tables*

12.2	The Pattern of the 'Bank Spheres' in Finnish Big Business in 1984	245
12.3	Corporate Networks in Finland in 2004	247
13.1	Evolution of Percentages of Firms in Main Component vs. Isolated and Marginal Firms	259
13.2	Evolution of Number of Lines, 1923–2000	261
14.1	Shareholding Relationship between Early Taiwanese Publicly-owned Financial Institutions and Large Private Companies in 1969	286

TABLES

4.1	Interlocks between Banks and Non-financial Firms	76
4.2	Intra- and Inter-sectoral Density: Germany—United States, 1928	78
6.1	Inter- and Intra-sectoral Ties, Average Degree, 1910–2010	111
6.2	Main Affiliation of the Directors of the Three Largest Banks, 1910–2010 (in %)	112
7.1	General Structure of the Network, 1938–2008	129
9.1	Firms by Type of Interlocks	176
9.2	Interlocking Directorates Generated by the Top Ten Big Linkers, 1913–2001	178
10.1	Portuguese Big Business—Network Indicators	194
11.1	Cluster Fragmentation of the Business Elite, 1911–1946	219
11.2	Business Network Density (in %)	221
11.3	Assets of the Largest Bulgarian Companies, 1911–1946, as % of GDP	223
11.4	Explanatory Variables for Interlocking	224
11.5	Bulgarian Big Business Elite, 1989–2005	227
11.6	Levels of Business Connectivity in Bulgaria, 1994 and 2005, in %	228
12.1	Some Basic Figures about the Network of Companies	237
14.1	Descriptive Statistics Taiwan Directorate Interlock Network, 1941–2003	278
14.2	Directorate Interlocks in the Inner Circle of Directors and the Embeddedness of Public and Private Firms in the Directorate Interlock Network, 1962–2003	289
15.1	Cohesion Measures Based on Director Interlocking and Director Dispatching	302

Acknowledgments

This project started in 2008 during the Congress of the European Business History Association (EHBA) in Bergen. We discovered that we were not alone in working on networks of interlocking directorates from a historical perspective. A year later, at the EBHA congress in Milan, while enjoying a very pleasant evening of excellent Italian meals and wines, the decision was taken to launch this project. The ambience of this Milan evening encapsulates perfectly the wonderful atmosphere that has accompanied the years of work on the project.

During the next three years, we tried to gather researchers who were working on national corporate networks from a historical perspective. Some of them joined spontaneously during the conferences that were organized for the project, others were proposed by colleagues and some accepted our 'invitation' to participate!

In the beginning of the project, we wrote a white paper outlining the goals of the project, the research questions, theoretical framework, firm sample, benchmarks and methods, which was circulated among the participants. After harsh debates and long meetings, a consensus was reached. This process was very important because it gave a certain homogeneity to the chapters. After this, a further three years were necessary to finalize the project.

During these six years, the help of a number of people was important in the preparation of this project. First, all those who contributed the chapters—they agreed to comply with our exorbitant requests! Some colleagues agreed to comment on preliminary versions of the chapters, which were presented at various conferences. Their remarks, critiques and support were very important and we would like to extend thanks to Meindert Fennema, Frans Stokman, Kees van Veen and Eelke Heemskerk, who made comments during our first workshop at Utrecht University in November 2010, which was financed by the Netherlands Organisation for Scientific Research (NWO). At our second workshop at Lausanne University (UNIL) in 2012, the following people agreed to make comments on the different chapters of the book: Mary O'Sullivan, Phil Scranton, Matthias Kipping, Matthieu Leimgruber and Philipp Korom, and we extend our thanks to them. The second workshop was financed by the Swiss National Science

Foundation and the University of Lausanne. Some of the papers were also presented at the EBHA congresses and benefitted from comments from Joep Schenk (Milan 2009), Patrick Fridenson (Athens 2011) and Neil Rollings (Paris 2012), for which we are grateful. We also wish to thank Frédéric Rebmann and Steven Piguet, who helped us and some of our colleagues by gathering data for France and UK, as well as Stéphanie Ginalski, whose help and support has been invaluable during the last two years.

During the last phase—the editing of the book—some people and institutions were very helpful. Thanks to the support of the Collège des Humanités at l'Ecole Polytechnique Fédérale de Lausanne, Kate Forbes-Pitt was able to help us by undertaking language editing and manuscript compilation. Marion Beetschen and Yitang Lin also helped us in the final step of the edition of the manuscript. Within Routledge, we would like to thank Ray Stokes and Matthias Kipping, who edit the Routledge series, "International Studies in Business History", and the three anonymous referees of our book proposal. The data collected for the project are available on the website of the Centre for Global Economic History, at Utrecht University (see *http://www.cgeh.nl/power-corporate-networks-comparative-and-historical-perspective*). We are very grateful for the assistance of Sarah Carmichael (Utrecht University) for uploading all of the project information and data and putting it on the web.

The editors

Thomas David
Gerarda Westerhuis

Preface

As I argue in my forthcoming historical overview of policy networks (Stokman, forthcoming), the increasing analytic possibilities of social network analysis in the 1970s gave rise to a large number of network studies to investigate power centers. The many studies on elite and intercorporate networks are a prominent example of this. Social network analysis of joint membership in clubs and organizations started to reveal the duality of meeting places of political and economic elites. On the one hand, similar educational and social background, joint membership in a large number of elite organizations and leading positions in powerful organizations, like large corporations, revealed who belongs to the ruling elite (Domhoff 1967). On the other hand, social network analysis revealed the many links between seemingly independent organizations, providing access and giving influence to each other. The newly developed network analytic methods uncovered hidden power centers. Prominent examples are studies at the local level by Laumann and Pappi (1976) and at the national level by Mintz and Schwartz (1985). Later studies compared these American studies with similar studies in other countries, like the study of Networks of Corporate Power (Stokman, Ziegler, and Scott 1985). Almost all interlocking directorates' studies among the largest companies revealed that the banks were the spin in the center of these densely connected national networks.

Such studies were, therefore, able to reveal hidden power centers, but they were unable to specify their effects on policies. This is due to the fact that interests are not specified, but assumed. Whereas American scholars tended to interpret network power centers as homogeneous and interlocks as signs of shared interests, Marxist oriented researchers, like Fennema (1982), qualified this interpretation and emphasized that shared board membership (for example, two bankers within one board) may well imply competition. Moreover, the previously mentioned duality of interlocks as result of elite recruitment versus institutional link between corporations asked for longitudinal studies where stability of interlocks between corporations can be compared with career patterns of persons. Stokman et al. (1988) showed that both components are present and can be roughly specified by such a longitudinal study. More importantly was the revelation of a system of interlocking directorates, held together by a dense network of national 'network specialists', a group of persons, meeting one another at many places and consequently developing a strongly normative framework.

The present volume is unique in its scope by combining a comparative analysis between a large number of countries with a longitudinal analysis over the whole twentieth century. This implies that the comparative element between national corporate networks in studies like Networks of Corporate Power can be combined with the evolution of networks over time, not only for one country but also for all national networks together. This resulted in a number of very interesting new insights. The most important ones are that the present study shows how interests fundamentally change over time, not just for one or a few countries but for all, revealing dramatic, dynamic effects on these networks in certain periods. Whereas the studies in the 1970s and 1980s revealed national centers with national banks in the center, the present study reveals how these power centers developed in the late nineteenth and early twentieth century, but rapidly declined after 1990. The early industrial revolution primarily took place within the nation states; normative constraints still had to be established and resulted in the crisis of 1929, followed by a stabilization of dense national networks in the period after that, lasting until around 1990. Subsequently, however, globalization really broke through in the 1990s due to the fall of the Soviet system and the international market orientation of China. Global competition required international recruitment of corporate board members on the basis of American salary and bonus levels at the expense of national elite recruitment and resulting interlocks between national companies. But this increased the playing field of the financial sector, as well, and gave them freedom of operation without the confinement within the national business elites. Network theory and studies reveal time and time again that dense trust networks sustain normative behavior. The decline of the dense national networks resulted in less normative constraints in business and particularly in its national centers. It is likely one of the reasons why banks could exploit this loss of normative control for increasing their own profits by unethical practices, resulting in the financial crisis of 2005.

Frans N. Stokman
*Honorary Professor of Social
Science Research Methodology,
University of Groningen*

REFERENCES

Domhoff, G. William. 1967. *Who rules America?* Englewood Cliffs, NJ: Prentice-Hall.
Fennema, Meindert. 1982. *International Networks of Banks and Industry.* The Hague: Martinus Nijhoff Publishers.

Laumann, Edward O., and Franz U. Pappi. 1976. *Networks of Collective Action. A Perspective on Community Influence Systems.* New York: Academic Press.

Mintz, Beth, and Michael Schwartz. 1985. *The Power Structure of American Business.* Chicago: University of Chicago Press.

Stokman, Frans N., Rolf Ziegler, and John Scott, eds. 1985. *Networks of Corporate Power. A Comparative Analysis of Ten Countries.* Cambridge: Polity Press.

Stokman, Frans N., Jelle van der Knoop, and Frans W. Wasseur. 1988. "Interlocks in The Netherlands: Stability and Careers in the Period 1960–1980." *Social Networks* 10: 183–208.

Stokman, Frans N. 2014, forthcoming. *Policy Networks: History, Encyclopedia of Social Network Analysis and Mining.* New York: Springer Science and Business Media.

1 Comparing Corporate Networks in a Long-Term Perspective[1]

Thomas David and Gerarda Westerhuis

1. INTRODUCTION

In 1912, the Pujo Committee was created by the US Congress to investigate the activities of bankers and financiers of Wall Street, the so-called Money Trust. Based partly on the affiliations of 18 selected financial institutions, the Committee came to the following conclusion about the power of this community:

> [. . .] the management of the finances of many of the great industrial and railroad corporations of the country engaged in interstate commerce is rapidly concentrating in the hands of a few groups of financiers in the city of New York [. . .], and that these groups, by reason of their control over the funds of such corporations and the power to dictate the depositories of such funds, and by reason of their relations with the great life insurance companies [. . .], have secured domination over many of the leading national banks and other moneyed institutions and life insurance companies in the city of New York [. . .]. [And] that these institutions and their funds are being used to further the enterprises and increase the profits of these groups of individuals [. . .].
> (Pujo 1913, 4)

This quotation shows that corporate networks have been a concern for over a century. Corporate networks are formed by board interlocks (i.e., ties between companies created by directors sitting on more than one board). Networks can emerge because boards consist of executive and non-executive directors. The non-executives are recruited from other firms, or from financial, public or political institutions, often based on shared backgrounds, friendships or family ties (Scott 1991). Thus, a corporate network consists of firms and directors, also known as a two-mode network in social network analysis. Granovetter (1985) stated that economic action is embedded in social structure. Thus, individuals, being managers, bankers or politicians, are actors that operate within the structure of the corporate network; they can influence the structure, but they are also being constrained by it.

In this volume, we address the question of how corporate networks developed and changed over time, and we explain these changes. The chapters show that the way in which, and degree to which, corporate networks change depends on the organization of national institutions. To our knowledge, this is the first attempt to combine research on corporate networks of different countries in the long-term perspective. The literature on corporate networks is quite extensive. Evidence on how corporate networks develop is, however, mostly anecdotal, as the studies focus on individual countries and/or particular time periods. The few cross-sectional studies that make comparisons among different countries only take into account one or two benchmark years, and focus in particular on the very recent period. Often they try to categorize countries by defining archetypes (e.g., liberal market economies vs. coordinated market economies). Moreover, these studies seem to assume that networks are just there and that it is only the decline since the 1980s that needs to be explained. In so doing, these latter studies see globalization as the main explanatory factor for change. However, corporate networks have a much longer history. They have emerged, developed, and sometimes declined and emerged again, often for very different reasons and not just because of globalization.

We used a combination of a quantitative and qualitative research approach to answer our question as to how corporate networks developed and changed over time. This method allows us to describe, on the one hand, the main developments of the network over time by focusing on important network indicators in benchmark years. On the other hand, a qualitative, historical approach enables us to find explanations for these developments. It allows for exploring complexity and unraveling interdependence of variables. Moreover, it safeguards against overgeneralizations generating archetypes (Wadhwani and Bucheli 2014). We cover 14 countries on three continents, each covered in one chapter (the US, Great Britain, Germany, the Netherlands, Switzerland, Austria, France, Italy, Portugal, Bulgaria, Finland, Argentina, Japan and Taiwan), and adopt common benchmarks that cover the whole twentieth century and the first decade of the twenty-first century.

This introduction begins with a literature review followed by a discussion of our methodology and the data. Thereafter, we present a framework to understand the dynamics of corporate changes before putting forward a broad periodization of the evolution of corporate networks in 14 countries during the whole twentieth and early twenty-first centuries. We conclude by presenting the main issues of the book and by sketching some further research issues related to corporate networks.

2. LITERATURE REVIEW

Corporate networks are not a new phenomenon. They emerged with the Second Industrial Revolution and the appearance of modern corporations, and they have been discussed and analyzed since the late nineteenth century.

Views have obviously evolved over time with the evidence and methods available. Thus, in the late nineteenth century, the literature started with the concepts of control and power; however, as more research was conducted, other functions of corporate networks also came to the forefront: competition, cohesion and communication. As a result of technological developments, in the 1980s, it became possible to compare networks between countries, which led to new insights, most important being the significance of the institutional context. We will first summarize the literature based on the four different functions of corporate networks before moving to a discussion of the results and contributions of comparative research to the literature on corporate networks.

Functions of Corporate Networks

As the example of the Pujo Committee demonstrated, corporate networks had sparked the interest of politicians, as well as academia, as early as the late nineteenth and early twentieth century. This interest was especially generated by a general fear of the emergence of seemingly powerful groups of companies (trusts). From the beginning, the role of banks has been at the very heart of the study of networks. Brandeis' (1914) and Hilferding's (1910) famous analyses of the power of banks, both of whom—from different points of view—were very critical of the role of banks in modern capitalism, constitute very early examples of the study of board overlaps. Hence, the role of banks is to some extent the very reason why interlocking directorates became the subject of scientific studies in the first place.

The oldest approach to corporate interlocks was Hilferding's "finance capital model" (Scott 1985). The concept of finance capital developed by Hilferding (1910) designated a stage of capitalism where the financial capital controlled by banks and the industrial capital controlled by stock corporations merged and resulted in the formation of powerful groups of companies or trusts. The theory of "finance capital" was pushed a step further during the 1970s with the notion of the "bank-control model", which explicitly saw banks as the pinnacle of the decision-making hierarchy within a group of companies and as using this power in their own interest (Scott 1985). This model predicted that ties between banks and industrial companies were directed from banks to industrial companies, and thereby indicated the pre-eminence of banks. Banks sat on the boards of their debtors to monitor a firm's financial status and degree of risk (e.g., Zeitlin 1974; Helmers et al. 1975 for the Netherlands). Mintz and Schwartz (1985) went further by arguing that the model of financial hegemony provides a more comprehensive framework in order to understand corporate networks. According to this viewpoint, banks and insurance companies monopolize the flow of investment capital and, therefore, their directors and top executives determine the broad lines of corporate development for the whole economy.

Contrary to these accounts of 'bank control' or financial hegemony, some authors have argued that bankers' dominance over financial companies was merely a transient state in the evolution of modern capitalism. Thus, Paul Sweezy (1942) argued that Hilferding's theory referred precisely to the stage of capitalist evolution where banks were indeed dominant, but that banks' control has decreased thereafter. The later stage would hence be characterized by rather more reciprocal relationships between banks and industry, where coordination, not dominance, was the prevailing mode of interaction. Historians have found some empirical evidence that, at some point, the relations between banks and industrial companies were indeed more reciprocal, thus counterbalancing the banks' dominance (e.g., see Wellhöner 1989; Wixforth 1995 and Krenn 2008 for the German case).

Corporate networks do not only concern the relationships between banks and industries. Interlocks can also be useful as a channel for information and communication. A corporate network establishes a channel via which business and other information can be spread (Mizruchi 1996). Through corporate networks, information and transaction costs are lowered and privileged access to markets can be gained. Interesting in this respect is research showing that firms adopt takeover defenses (e.g., see Davis 1991 about the spread of the poison pill among US firms) or start acquiring firms (e.g., see Haunschild 1993 about interorganizational imitation focusing on acquisition between 1981 and 1990 in the US) when they are tied via directorship to firms that have already adopted these takeover defenses or have taken over firms. Interlocks might also give access to resources; for example, to capital in the form of loans.

A more negative connotation with interlocks stems from the impression that the effects of interlocks hinder the functioning of the market; in other words, that interlocks restrict competition. A well-known example is that of the US at the beginning of the twentieth century when the enormous number of interlocks within industries were being questioned, which ultimately resulted in the Clayton Act of 1914, section 8, prohibiting interlocks between firms that competed in the same markets. On the other hand, in Germany at the same time, the government gave cartels a legal framework in which interlocks between firms could exist (Windolf 2009).

In this perspective, networks can create a kind of moral control. They can be interpreted as an expression of cohesion within the economic elite and as a means to contribute to this group's social. Thus, in the principal-agency relationship between a company's directors and its capital suppliers, interlocks can become a kind of supervisory institution. Supervision of managers being one of the most important challenges for stock companies (Berle and Means 1932), interlocks can replace ownership as a mechanism of control. In this way, they help to reduce opportunistic behavior by imposing a certain code of ethics on the members of the business elite (Windolf 2009). Frequent meetings and acquaintance favor the conclusion of business deals and strengthen the cohesion of the elite's values and ethics.

Therefore, big linkers—directors with three or more board positions—play a very important role. They are often considered to constitute an 'inner circle' of the business elite, which is politically very influential, and defends not only interests of one single company but of the business elite as a social group (Useem 1984). From the perspective of the firm, reputable individuals can be beneficial. They will add prestige to the firm and give advice (for this legitimacy argument, see Mizruchi 1996, 276). From the individual perspective, having many board positions can have advantages, because it extends the individual's network of contacts, adds to its experience, and enhances its prestige.

Comparative Research

Since the 1960s, technical developments allowed for better modeling and visualization of the business relations between firms (e.g., graph theory). It became possible to compare networks between countries. One of the first (and now classic) books is the volume *Networks of Corporate Power: A Comparative Analysis of Ten Countries,* edited by Stokman, Ziegler and Scott (1985). The book focuses on Western European countries and the US. It was undertaken on a systematic and comparative basis. Moreover, it brought together American scholars, who were at that time at the forefront of the research on interlocking directorates, and European scholars. It thus stimulated research on business networks in Europe. Some general tendencies were found across all countries; in particular, the fact that large, national, domestic and public firms were the most interlocked corporations and transnational ties were mostly bi-national. Moreover, important differences were found among the 10 countries. In his conclusion, Rolf Ziegler draws attention to how striking these variations are (Ziegler 1985, 267). However, the book only deals with one year, viz. 1976, is largely descriptive in showing intercorporate relations at a specific moment and specific places and neglects the historical and cultural contexts. Moreover, it was published in 1985, before the major changes of the late 1980s and 1990s related to the globalization and financialization of the world economy.

Broadening Stokman et al.'s results, John Scott was one of the first to explain that differences in national institutional backgrounds might lead to different developments of corporate networks across countries. Relying on the extant literature outside Anglo-American countries, he revealed the importance of "cultural and historical embeddedness of personal, capital and commercial relations in business" (Scott 1991, 199). Thus, he distinguished among continental Europe, Anglo-American and Asian countries. The Anglo-American countries were, according to Scott, characterized by a combination of control through the constellation of interest and financial hegemony. Continental Europe could be divided into two groups. The first group consists of countries such as Germany, Austria, the Netherlands and Switzerland, where banks played an important role in the corporate networks. The other group is made up of countries such as France, Belgium and Italy, where investment holding companies were important and the state played an important role (France and Italy). Finally, Asian corporate networks "showed the importance of the state and of kinship as crucial differentiating factors" (Scott 1991, 199).

Many studies on corporate networks followed (see, for example, Cronin 2011 for a review). Most of these studies generally focus on one country and a short time period (e.g., Windolf and Beyer 1996; Vasta and Baccini 1997; Fohlin 1999; Okazaki, Michiru, and Kazuki 2005; Rinaldi and Vasta 2005; Tomka 2001; Windolf 2006, 2009; Heemskerk 2007). Other studies analyze the evolution of corporate networks in the long run but again on a national level (e.g., Mizruchi 1982; Scott and Griff 1984; Schnyder et al. 2005; De Jong, Röell, and Westerhuis 2010). There are a handful of studies that compare corporate networks in more than one benchmark year (Dritsas, Eigner, and Ottosson 1996; Musacchio and Read 2007; Windolf 2002, 2009) but they cover only a limited number of countries and a limited time span. Thus, most studies to date have focused on the national level or on a certain time period, and only very few studies adopted a comparative approach.

From the 1990s onwards, researchers started to analyze corporate networks again, diverging from the nationally oriented approach. Some of this new research had to do with the fact that networks in many countries started to decline, for which explanations were sought. Also, due to the ICT revolution, the techniques for analyzing networks had become much more sophisticated, enabling academics to reconsider earlier findings (see Cronin 2011, 44 for a presentation of the factors that underpinned the renewal of this research).[2] In contrast to the hereto rather descriptive approach, research on corporate networks moved toward a more analytical and explanatory approach. Intercorporate relations were more often placed in their historical and cultural context. Aguilera and Jackson noticed, however, that although it is known that institutions matter, comparative institutional analysis has still been scarce (Aguilera and Jackson 2003).

This new research was further stimulated by the seminal work of Hall and Soskice (2001) on the varieties of capitalism. They made a distinction between liberal market economies (LME) versus coordinated market economies (CME). In a LME, firms organize their activities mainly via markets and hierarchies, whereas in a CME, they are more dependent on non-market relations. In LMEs, firms turn to financial markets for investment capital and, therefore, transparency is important, and share prices are a primary yardstick of firms' performance. In contrast, in a CME, firms are financed by debt and banks play an important role. Close relations exists between banks and industrial companies. Reputation and trust, instead of share prices, are important measures for firms' performance.

These two rather dichotomous models led to publications showing that national systems do not neatly divide that way, in particular over time, but sometimes even at specific moments in time (Herrigel 2007; Wilkins et al. 2010). Business historians, among others, argued that market economies are not static and changed a great deal over the long twentieth century (for empirical studies, see Fellman et al. 2008; Wilkins et al. 2010; Sluyterman, forthcoming). Research on corporate networks also started challenging these stylized archetypes.

Thus, Kogut's edited book (2012), based on two benchmarks, enabled him to show, among other things, that the dichotomy between liberal market and coordinated market economies is more nuanced. The authors collected data on ownership and directorship ties for 22 countries around the world, and integrated two panels, the first for the period 1990–1995 and the second centered around 2000. The aim of the book is to explore "the interaction of corporate networks and exogenous shocks to identify different national responses to globalization" (Kogut 2012, 20). Among the numerous results of the book, two deserve particular emphasis. First, there are important differences between countries sharing an Anglo-Saxon heritage (US, UK and Canada). Conyon and Shipilov (2012, 75) stress that "there is no uniform Anglo-Saxon corporate governance" due partly to the different institutional histories of these countries. Second, behind these differences there are still continuities; in particular, the persistence of small worlds where firms within the corporate network are connected by short average path lengths and show a high degree of clustering.

Julian Cardenas (2012), in a recent article based on 2005 data on corporate networks of 12 countries, offers another typology than the one based on the varieties of capitalism literature. Using Fuzzy set Qualitative Comparative Analysis (FsQCA), Cardenas explains this typology by showing "the joint effect of financial systems, state intervention, ownership structure and economic internationalization in the formation of corporate networks" (Cardenas 2012, 315–316). He distinguishes two kinds of countries. In the first group, corporate networks can be characterized as being cohesive: the power structure is based on unity, concentration and control. The cohesive network in Italy, France, Germany and Spain is thus explained by the combination of bank-based financial structure, interventionist state, firms with blockholders and low economic internationalization. The networks of the second group of countries (Canada, Australia, Switzerland, the US and the UK) are called dispersed because they are fragmented, decentralized and have more single ties. The conjunction of non-interventionist state, market-based financial structure and widely-held corporations is responsible for the dispersed corporate network.

3. DATA AND METHODOLOGY

As sketched above, the past few years has seen some very stimulating research adopting a comparative approach on corporate networks. However, to date, these studies focused on a very short time span and were thus only partially able to tackle our main question: how have corporate networks developed and changed over time, and why? In order to answer this question, we combined a quantitative with a qualitative research strategy. This method allows us to describe, on the one hand, the structural changes of the network over time by focusing on important network indicators in benchmark years for the whole twentieth century and first decade of the twenty-first century. On the other hand, a qualitative, historical approach enables us to find explanations for these changes.

We chose this approach because we believe it will contribute to the understanding of developments of corporate networks in two ways. First, comparisons over time allow for analyzing changes. The impact on networks of multiple external pressures, such as globalization and financialization, and also war or economic depression, can only be understood by taking a long-run historical perspective. Second, in trying to explain dynamic and interdependent processes, the methods of history, especially contextualization and interpretation, are invaluable tools. The historical approach allows for the exploration of complexity and unraveling the interdependence of variables by tracing their interconnections over time. These methods of history also safeguard against overgeneralization producing archetypes (Wadhwani and Bucheli 2014; Jones and Khanna 2006). As a result of the broad scope, the book escapes from the developed European and/or Anglo-Saxon view, which has, to date, dominated the literature on corporate networks (for an exception, see Kogut 2012). We are able to revisit old debates in corporate networks literature, such as the interactions between the manufacturing and financial sectors. New topics that have hardly been discussed in the extant literature on corporate networks are also introduced, such as the role of state-owned enterprises, business groups, or multinationals (see also Cardenas 2012 and Kogut 2012). It should be stressed that our choice to focus on historical changes in the networks implies that we did not emphasize the effects of different types of corporate networks on economic performance (for a similar perspective on corporate networks, see Kogut 2012, where he makes a distinction between an evolutionary perspective (a 'because of' argument) vs. teleology (an 'in order to' argument)).

The quantitative part of our method requires standardization of data selection and network indicators across country cases and time. The chapters take into account a very long period covering the entire twentieth and early twenty-first centuries. We used eight benchmark years: 1913, 1928, 1938, 1958, 1973, 1983, 1993 and 2003. Moreover, the book covers 14 different countries—including less developed countries, as well as countries outside Europe and the US. We selected the top 125 joint-stock firms for small countries and top 250 for large countries on the basis of total assets, of which 25 and 50, respectively, are financial firms. These companies are both incorporated in a country and have their headquarters in the same country. The scale of the project limited the overall homogenization of data. Due to the number of countries and benchmarks, and differences in data and source availability among countries, some minor deviations from the general rules concerning the selection of companies and benchmarks were accepted. These deviations, however, did not undermine the relevance and results of the comparison.

Moreover, we defined common network indicators in order to make comparisons among countries and among the different benchmarks possible (see Appendix I and http://www.cgeh.nl/power-corporate-networks-comparative-and-historical-perspective for a detailed description for each country). Among the main networks' indicators, we selected density and average degree, which give an indication of the cohesion of the network. Density is "the number of lines in a network, expressed as a proportion of the maximum possible number of lines" (De Nooy, Mrvar, and Batagelj 2011, 322). Average degree— "the average degree of all vertices is the number of lines incident with them"—is a better measure of overall cohesion than density because it does not depend on network size, so average degree can be compared between networks of different sizes (De Nooy et al. 2011, 64). In addition to these overall measures of the network, we also looked at the individual nodes in the network by including indicators on intercompany and interpersonal networks. To measure intercompany connectedness, the top 10 firms according to degree centrality and betweenness centrality for each benchmark and for each country were selected (see Appendix I for definitions). To measure interpersonal networks, the top 10 big linkers were selected. By big linkers, we mean directors who hold three or more positions in the network.

4. A FRAMEWORK FOR ANALYZING CORPORATE NETWORKS

Based on the findings of the chapters in this volume, we developed a framework that helps us to detect relationships and processes over time. In other words, it helps to describe and explain changes in the development of corporate networks. The framework consists of three levels:

1. Macro level: the political and economic environment at the national level;
2. Meso level: the social structure of the network. Firms and their stakeholders act as economic agents but within the boundaries of the structure of the corporate network;
3. Micro level: the stakeholders within firms. Owners, managers and employees each have their own and sometimes conflicting interests.

Macro level

The macro level represents political and macro-economic aspects. Political aspects can be divided into politics and policies. During the twentieth century, different political regimes have been powerful. In the early twentieth century, in many countries, liberalism prevailed, characterized by *laissez faire*, whereas after World War II, many countries witnessed the rising intervention of the state in the economy. In the meantime, communism came to power in several countries. The 1970s and 1980s, especially with the regimes of Reagan and Thatcher, marked a clear break with the previous era, and coincided with neo-liberalism. At the same time, communist regimes broke down almost everywhere.

By policies, we refer to direct and indirect influence of the state via their 'strategies'. First, the state can own majority or minority stakes in companies. State owned enterprises (SOEs) are firms where the state has majority ownership and control, enabling it to influence the governance of the firm (on SOEs in a historical perspective, see Toninelli 2000). Control by the government can be exercised by appointing directors to the boards of these firms. A number of justifications for the emergence of 'state capitalism' can be given. For example, some justify the involvement of the state in the economy as a way to resolve market failures. One market failure refers to poorly developed financial markets, in which investments for firms are difficult to find. Another market failure stems from coordination problems. In this case, the state creates linkages between different parts of the production chain in order to promote complementary investments. Second, a more indirect way government can influence business is by the enactment of laws (banking laws, corporate laws or accounting laws), or by granting subsidies to private companies (Musacchio and Lazzarini 2012).

Apart from political aspects, this level consists of macro-economic developments, such as the degree of economic development or the openness of a country's economy. For example, the degree of a country's openness, which can be measured by export and import ratios and/or foreign direct investment (FDI) measures, has an influence on the internationalization of ownership and management.

Meso Level

The meso level refers to the corporate network. Here, non-financial firms and the financial sector interact due to personal ties between them. The different functions of interlocks have been discussed in Section 2. Here, we briefly summarize them using four modes of interaction: control, competition, cohesion and communication. Since the boards are the place where directors meet, discuss, and make important strategic decisions, banks, and also family firms or the state, often have a seat in the boards of the firms they have a controlling share in. In addition, creditors, who make financial investments in a firm, also want to have a position in the corporate board to safeguard their loans (*control model*). Interlocks among firms (in the same sector) can hinder *competition* and reinforce cartel agreements (see Windolf 2009 or Cortat 2009). Interestingly, business groups—which can loosely be defined as groups gathering legally independent firms operating across industries and bound together by formal and informal ties (Khanna and Yafeh 2007)—can be an alternative to cartels on the one hand, and mergers on the other. Also, by favoring frequent meetings and imposing a kind of moral code, interlocks can reinforce class *cohesion* within the elite. Lastly, interlocks function as a channel of *communication*, which can be important for the diffusion of information and practice.

To show how the macro level influences the meso level, consider the example by which the level of economic development has an influence on the role played by business groups. Contrary to countries that went through the initial phase of industrialization during the nineteenth and twentieth centuries, in late-industrializing economies, "the large business groups appeared in the early phase of industrial development, and those very groups have collectively and individually remained the prime and leading business organizations in the relevant economies up to the twenty-first century" (Colpan and Hikino 2010, 51). Whether these business groups favor interlocking between firms within the group and/or between groups, they will influence the characteristics of the corporate network (Brookfield et al. 2012; Colli and Vasta, forthcoming).

The corporate network is closely related to other institutions related to the capital, labor or product markets. The personal ties between firms (interlocking directorates) can overlap with other economic or social networks (e.g., supplier relations, cartel agreements, equity claims, social clubs, family ties). These multiplex networks (see Aguilera and Jackson 2003, 454) could strengthen collaboration or exacerbate competition among actors and thus influence the structure of corporate networks (for a very interesting illustration of these multiplex networks, see Pak 2013).

Micro Level

The micro level consists of the firm, in which three important stakeholders have their own interests: capital, management and labor. Capital consists of shareholders (or the owners of firms) and other stakeholders that make financial investments in the firm (the creditors, such as banks). In the extant literature, the distinction is often made between two types of ownership: dispersed and concentrated ownership. The US is a country where dispersed ownership prevails, whereas in Continental Europe, ownership is often concentrated in the hands of banks, the state or families. However, Aguilera and Jackson (2003, 450) stress that "less attention has been given to the fact that various types of capital (e.g., banks, pension funds, individuals, industrial companies, families, and so forth) possess different identities, interests, time horizons, and strategies". In other words, there is much more diversity than one might expect when analysis is based only on dispersed vs. concentrated ownership.

By management, we mean the managers of a firm who occupy strategic leadership positions and can exercise control over business activities. The background of these top managers (financial vs. technical education; internal vs. external career) can be very diverse, which can lead to different strategies or commitment: within the firm toward the other stakeholders and, when they sit on the board of the firm, toward other firms in the corporate network (Aguilera and Jackson 2003, 457 and further.)

Labor has been largely ignored by the literature on corporate networks even if, in some countries such as Germany, employees have access to the board through the system of co-determination (see Höpner and Müllenborn 2010 on Germany). Labor can have two strategies to influence decision-making in a firm and thus corporate networks: one of internal participation and another of external control through the threat of collective action. The choice of strategy depends on the power positions of the other stakeholders, and also on the institutions that govern the representation rights of labor (Aguilera and Jackson 2003, 454 and further.)

The interactions between capital, labor and management can be various. They can lead to different coalitions between these stakeholders, which will influence the structure of the corporate network. However, the interests of the three actors are also shaped by this network: the network can influence each stakeholder, and also structure stakeholder interactions by "triggering different conflicts, and supporting different types of coalitions among the three stakeholders" (Aguilera and Jackson 2003, 460). An example is a situation when managing directors gain so much power that they are able to use the firm to further their own interests rather than the interests of shareholders, also called management entrenchment. The managerial entrenchment theory states that directors adopt, for example, takeover defenses in order to increase their job security at shareholders' expense (Shleifer and Vishny 1989; DeAngelo and Rice 1983). There can also be situations where business elites get entrenched with political elites. According to economic entrenchment theory, a small group of business elites with influential access to politicians in power can hold oligarchic control over particular industries or over the economy (Rajan and Zingales 2003; Morck, Wolfenzon, and Yeung 2005). To maintain their privileged position, the elite will use its political connections to hinder institutional development. They use their influence to further their own interests at the expense of other firms and of the economy at large (Morck et al. 2005).

5. CORPORATE NETWORKS CHANGE AT DIFFERENT TIMES AND AT DIFFERENT PACES

Now that we have outlined the framework that we use as a tool to describe and explain changes in the corporate network, we will turn to our empirical findings for the 14 different countries studied. Not surprisingly, we found that the structure of corporate networks changed over time. Figure 1.1 distinguishes four broad periods: a rise of corporate networks from the late

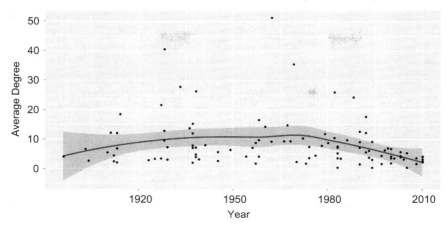

Figure 1.1 The Average Degrees of the Corporate Networks of the 14 Countries (1900–2010).

Source: For the average degrees of the corporate networks of the 14 countries of the book, see Appendix I.

Note: We plotted the moving average of the average degree as a function over time between 1900 and 2010. Then, we considered the four main temporal phases to investigate the relationship between the year and the average degree across countries. For each of the four temporal phases, we built a linear mixed effect regression using the year as linear predictor of the dependent variable referring the average degree. Given the nature of the test, the country identifier was taken into account as grouping factor. The statistical tests confirm our hypothesis that the average degree grows till 1929. Between 1929 and 1945, we cannot conclude anything from the data distribution. Between 1945 and 1980, the average degree distribution grows moderately. Finally, after 1980, it diminishes moderately until 2010.

nineteenth century to the late 1920s (roughly, 1890–1930); divergence during the 1930s and World War II; very slow growth from the 1950s to the 1970s; and a decline in almost all countries since the 1980s.

We will now elaborate on this periodization and explain why corporate networks change by taking into consideration the complexity of and interconnectedness with the institutional environment.

Late Nineteenth Century—End of 1920s

During this period, the emergence and rise of corporate networks can be observed for almost all countries. However, the national actors and institutions that explain this phenomenon are very different from one country to another. The process of industrialization played an important role in the emergence of corporate networks. The Second Industrial Revolution resulted, in many countries, in the creation of large firms—first in capital intensive industries, such as railroads—and their directors started to sit on multiple boards. Another feature of this period up to World War I was growing internationalization of business, leading some scholars to argue that this period could be described as the period of first globalization (O'Rourke and Williamson 1999; see McKeown 2007 for a critical view), whereas World War I can be seen as a critical juncture, as it triggered measures to protect national economies.

Besides the macro-economic environment, interactions between firms were influenced by political aspects. Thus, via legislation, the state can be seen as an important player in the emergence of national corporate networks. This can be illustrated by the divergent evolution of corporate networks in the US and Germany during the first decades of the twentieth century. At the end of the nineteenth century, a ruling by the German Supreme Court legalized cartel contracts and provided a stable legal framework for cartel organizations. This was in contrast to the situation in the US where the Sherman Act (1890) and the Clayton Act (1914) prohibited cartels and monopolies and outlawed direct interlocks between competitors. Capitalism and corporate networks in both countries started to diverge. In Germany, the density and centralization of the network increased in parallel with the growing degree of cartelization, whereas in the US, mergers were preferred to cartels, and the density of the network declined. Although cartels were not legalized in the UK, they seemed to play an important role in the British corporate network, reflected by strong intra-sector interlocks.

At the meso level, banks played an important role in the emergence of corporate networks in countries such as the US, Germany, Switzerland, Italy, Bulgaria, Portugal, Finland and the Netherlands. Depending on the country, they fulfilled different functions, either exercising control over other sectors, furthering or limiting competition and/or favoring the cohesion among business elites. They provided loans to firms to finance their growing activities, they owned share capital of firms, they underwrote securities issues and/or gave advice. For these reasons, bankers entered the corporate boardroom to protect their interests. The chapter on the Italian network is revealing for the light it sheds on the role of banks. The density of the Italian network peaked in 1927, when the influence of the larger banks (Banca Commerciale, Credito Italiano and Società Bancaria Italiana) on the nation's corporate system reached its apex. These banks, created in the 1890s, were the major cause underlying Italy's first big industrial spurt before World War I. The 1920s reinforced the position of these banks within the network. Because of the post-World War I crisis, many companies were unable to repay their debts to banks, which were forced to transform their 'frozen' loans into share capital and to become the real owners of many industrial companies.

Until recently, the literature on corporate networks saw this relationship as an instrument to exercise control. However, recent studies and some chapters in this book (see Switzerland, the Netherlands, and the UK for the later period) challenge this interpretation. They argue that relationships between banks and firms were reciprocal, where networks emerge because bankers sit on the boards of firms and boards of banks were meeting places for firms' directors. In this sense, coordination and cohesion, not control, was the prevailing mode of interaction.

In some countries, such as Argentina and to a lesser extent Japan, the absence of or minor role played by banks was substituted for, or complemented by, business groups during this period. In Argentina, for example, business groups served as connectors between foreign and local financial markets and contributed to the growing density of corporate networks during the interwar period. In France, business groups performed another function as they formed a substitute for forbidden cartels in order to coordinate economic activities. Yet another important actor in the emergence of the corporate network was the colonial firm. In Portugal and the Netherlands, colonial firms were often linked to trading houses, banks and transport companies, resulting in tight networks. We would like to emphasize this point as, with one or two exceptions, national studies on corporate networks neglect colonial firms and colonial interlocking directorates (for an exception, see Nobel and Fennema 2003).

In countries such as Finland, the Netherlands and Switzerland, corporate law limited the number of foreigners who could serve as board members. For example, at least half of board members had to be Finnish citizens according to the Finnish Company Act of 1864. Moreover, from the end of the nineteenth century, a growing concern about foreign and national threats emerged, respectively, the growing importance of foreign influence within the national economy and the increasing political weight of communist parties, as in Germany or Bulgaria. A focal feature of the structure of the Finnish corporate network before World War II was language and culture. It led to the emergence of two networks: a Swedish and a Finnish one. In this perspective, the rise of corporate networks can be interpreted as a protective device against foreign and national threats, which led to growing class cohesion among business elites.

On the micro level, the French case is also interesting. In this country, class cohesion was enhanced by the quest for legitimacy, which shaped the corporate network during the first decades of the twentieth century. Firms with high share capital, located in Paris and having certain seniority as listed firms, tend to be central in the network and share directors among themselves. This status logic—the status of an actor relies on the links he has with other actors—partly explains the increasing density of the French network during this period.

The 1930s and World War II

The development of national corporate networks followed very different paths. Some countries, such as the UK, Switzerland, France, Finland, Bulgaria and Argentina, continued to experience a densification of the corporate network during the Great Depression, whereas in other countries (the US,

Italy, the Netherlands, Germany, Portugal), the average degree of corporate networks declined, sometimes sharply.

In particular for these last countries, the Great Depression of the 1930s can be seen as a structural break with the past that had repercussions on corporate networks. During the 1930s, financial markets and the banking sector, in particular, encountered many difficulties. This era also saw a decreasing internationalization of the economy. In order to cope with these difficulties, governments increased their intervention in the economy.

The decline of the average degree in these countries was the result of the diminishing interlocks between banks and manufacturing firms. In some countries, banking laws prohibited or regulated the financial participation of banks in industries, which may explain the decline in interlocks. Italy, Portugal, Germany and the US belong to the group of countries in which laws played an active role in the decline of the corporate network. These laws led to a diminution of interlocks between the financial sector and industry, to less control and more competition between these two sectors and/or, in some cases, to a limitation of the number of big linkers who played an important role in the cohesion of the network. In Italy in 1936, a new banking law was introduced imposing a clear-cut separation between banks and industry. Banks were allowed to extend only short-term credit, while their share participations in non-financial companies were strictly limited. In Portugal, a new law was adopted in 1935 that limited banks' long-term loans and investment in other firms. In the US, the Glass-Steagall Act of 1933, which required the separation of commercial and investment banking, resulted in less tight relations between financial and nonfinancial firms. In Germany, a combination of two factors explains the sharp decline of the network during the 1930s. First, in 1931, the German government introduced a corporate law that prohibited any person to have more than 20 board positions. Second, political factors played a role, too. After the Nazi regime came to power in 1933, they expelled Jewish directors—many of them big linkers during the 1920s—from their board positions.

Up to the 1930s, the state thus influenced corporate networks in an indirect way by enacting laws or granting subsidies to private firms, whereas during the Great Depression, governments also began to have a more direct impact through state-owned enterprises. In Finland, the state had come to occupy a rather important position in business by the mid-1930s, and firms and ministries worked in close cooperation. In Italy, in addition to the banking law of 1936, the creation of the big state-owned holding, Iri, in 1933 was a turning point and helps to explain how the state took over the role of universal banks.

In some countries, it was not banking laws that put limits on the functioning of banks, but the banks themselves that chose new strategies. In the Netherlands, the decline in the cohesiveness of the network in the 1930s was not related to banking laws, but can be explained by the reaction of banks to the banking crisis of 1921–1922. After this crisis, the

Dutch banks returned to trade financing again, and they became reluctant to provide long-term credit to firms, at least until the 1960s.

Even if the chapters in this book are not particularly focused on World War II, we can see that, in some countries, the war had important consequences on the network, as illustrated by the cases of Austria and Japan. In Austria, the *Anschluss* (the Nazi occupation between 1938 and 1945) came with a process of 'Germanization' of Austrian industry and banking. This period also saw the establishment of large-scale enterprises, which was part of a modernization of the local economy subordinated to the needs and wants of the German war economy. At the same time, the Anschluss led to the exclusion of Jews and the confiscation of their property ('Aryanisation'). In Japan, during the war, the government restricted the rights of investors, in particular to lower income inequality and, thus, social tension.

Period 1945–1980

The post-World War II period witnessed a period of slow growth of average degree, which implies a consolidation of corporate networks in most countries. The period 1945 up to and including the 1970s was characterized by a long period of economic growth, also known as the 'golden age' (Eichengreen 2006), which began with the recovery from war damage. During this period, the internationalization of the economy remained rather low for many countries and state intervention increased during the whole period. Some scholars also characterized this period, for developed countries, as a period of corporatism, in which state, labor and employers cooperated. Finally, the Cold War also left its mark on this period.

For some countries, the aftermath of the war brought tremendous political changes that had a direct and lasting impact on the corporate networks. In Japan and Germany, the American occupation led to the introduction of laws that affected the network. The decline of German network density after World War II was the result of laws on the decartelization and deconcentration of German industry. In Japan, the Americans dissolved *zabaitsu* just after the war and thus reinforced the role of the banks—which, as we will see, had already begun to emerge during the war—within the corporate network. In both countries, these measures were adopted in order to limit communist influence.

Indeed, the postwar period saw the rise to power of communist parties in several countries around the world. This had important consequences for corporate networks. In Bulgaria, for example, enterprises were interlocked not through people but through the Communist Party and through the Plan. As none of these new linkages could be captured through social network analysis, the comparison of the structure of corporate networks during the Communist period with other periods is very difficult.

The aftermath of World War II also had an impact on colonial countries. In Taiwan, foreign occupation began in 1895 when Japan conquered the country. Until the 1930s, the Japanese focused on the development of Taiwanese agricultural base. However, from the 1930s up to Japan's defeat in 1945, the colonial government tried to foster industrialization of Taiwan through indirect interventions. After Taiwan became independent in 1947, the national government of Chiang Kai-Shek received all the assets of Japanese companies and transformed them into publicly-owned businesses, forming an important foundation for the corporate network of Taiwan, which would last for a long time.

At the meso level, banks played a central role within corporate networks during these three decades of economic growth. In the US, the Netherlands, Germany, Switzerland and Finland, banks kept their core position in corporate networks, whereas in the UK and Japan, they emerged as important actors only during or after World War II. In Japan, banks emerged as a substitute to capital markets. Japan thus shifted during this period from a market-based system to a bank-based one. Banks financed the recovery and economic growth, and created interlocks with other sectors. They thus contributed to the consolidation of corporate networks. In the UK, the increasing centrality of banks resulted, on the one hand, from anti-trust laws enacted after World War II, which made interlocking directorates among firms from the same sector increasingly problematic and, on the other hand, from the divorce between ownership and control, providing an opportunity for banks to offer their services to boards of directors.

At the meso level, business groups constituted a second actor, which was important within national corporate networks after World War II, even if they were already present in some countries, such as in France, before the war. This actor, often neglected in the extant literature on corporate networks, deserves special attention, as shown by the contrasting examples of Taiwan and Portugal. Both cases emphasize that some major features of business groups—differences in state participation, cross-ownership, or verticality—can profoundly influence the structure of corporate networks (see Brookfield 2012, 89 and further). In Taiwan, after World War II, close inter-group ties were relatively frequent, partly due to the role of the state, and these ties favored the increasing density of the network. In contrast, in Portugal, business groups became more exclusive during the 1950s and 1960s. The focus on intra-group ties resulted in decreasing corporate network integration and cohesion.

Besides banks and business groups, state ownership became important in some countries, as governments in France, Austria, Italy, Finland, Argentina and Taiwan nationalized some very important firms. In Austria, the nationalization of firms was introduced in order to deprive the Allies of control of important sectors of the economy and to guarantee full employment. It even went so far that, in 1956, the Austrian government enacted a law that representatives of political parties should sit on the boards of SOEs. In Finland, the number of state companies grew and they became more closely tied to state bureaucracy due to increasing trade with the

Soviet Union, in which trade agreements were conducted at the highest political level. The government took an active role both in conducting this trade and in the state companies, thus strengthening the ties between private companies, SOEs and the political elite. The creation of SOEs did not lead to the emergence of a network of public firms isolated from private firms. On the contrary, in Italy, France, Austria, Taiwan and Finland, SOEs were almost always integrated in the core of the network and participated in the consolidation of corporate networks by being closely interconnected to private companies. Argentina is the only exception. In this country, the insular behavior of SOEs resulted from frequent overhauls of their boards related to the volatile political and economic context. This environment also explains the shifting role of MNEs within the Argentinean corporate network after World War II.

On the micro level, some contributions to the book (see, for example, Westerhuis or Ginalski, David and Mach this volume) describe how the use of takeover defenses, which empowered managers relative to shareholders—or of other instruments, which protect the owners against foreign or minority shareholders—can be seen as an important reason for the consolidation of the network, also enforcing class cohesion. In the Netherlands and the US, the then prevailing countervailing forces of corporatism (shareholders, managers and employees) led to a kind of legitimation of the network. In Portugal, corporatist institutions of the *Estade Novo* had the opposite effects. They tried to "rule competition and promote cooperation between business interests, as well as between businessmen and workers. They constituted an alternative mechanism of business coordination toward corporate networks, explaining why the density decreased even below the already lower levels of network integration existing until the 1930s." (See Da Silva and Neves this volume, 204.) (On the differences of corporatism in developed and peripheral countries, see Schmitter 1979.)

1980s–Twenty-First Century

In almost all countries, the corporate network has experienced a slight degree of erosion since the 1980s, a decline that accelerated during the 1990s. Some chapters in this book confirm this periodization, whereas others show a different periodization and argue that the processes behind the decline were much more complicated than the process of globalization put forward by most scholars.

From the 1980s onward, the world economy experienced tremendous changes. There is a shift to be seen from Keynesian political economy characterized by state intervention to neoliberal policies, whereby market forces were held to be all important and should be allowed to prevail and the role of the state should be marginal. This change resulted in a wave of privatizations and deregulation. The ascension to power of Ronald Reagan in the US and Margaret Thatcher in the UK is often seen as the starting point of this transformation. Related to this development was the growing internationalization of markets. This globalization concerned labor, capital, and goods and services. According to the extant literature, these changes profoundly affected the structure of corporate networks.

Scholars, mainly basing themselves on the US case (e.g., Davis and Mizruchi 1999; Davis 2009), argue that the most important explanatory factor for the disintegration of national networks since the 1980s has been a conscious strategic choice of disengagement from industrial companies on the part of the banks. This changing strategy was closely linked to macro-level developments: the effects of globalization and financial deregulation deeply affected the banks' activities.

However, the evolution of corporate networks was not similar in all countries, partly due to changes at the macro level. Some countries experienced a much earlier decline of the network. Italy, for example, not only experienced an earlier erosion of its corporate network (since the 1970s) than other industrialized nations, but its drivers also seem to have been different: the major cause of the disentangling of the corporate network in Italy seems to have been the changing role of SOEs and their disconnection from private companies. In Argentina, the diminution of the number of interlocking directorates began even earlier (during the 1960s) and was partly related to changing state economic policies. In contrast, other countries experienced an increase in average degree during the last decades. In Portugal, this surprising evolution can be explained by the nationalizations of 1975. The resulting SOEs did not interlock among themselves, nor with private firms, which led to a sharp decline of the average degree of the corporate network. However, since the end of the 1980s, a process of privatization and of economic liberalization, closely related to European integration, occurred. The banking sector, which was privatized during the 1990s, started to play a key role in the re-emergence of the network. The justification of the decline should also be elaborated on. The chapter on the US emphasizes that other factors at the meso level, rather than changing strategies of banks, explain the decline of the US network, in particular the business-led neutralization of the countervailing forces of government and organized labor. The political successes of business in eviscerating the power of organized labor during the 1970s and 1980s partly contributed to the decline.

The decline could hide changes in the function of corporate networks, which are very different among countries. The UK example brings forward the contrasting evolution of the network depth and width—the fact that simple ties persist and actually become more numerous while strong ties decline during the same period. This could indicate a move from a more control-based network toward a more diffuse network that may promote coordination. In France, the important loss of density (the overall density halved between 1990 and 2000) meant a strengthening of the core-periphery, status-based structure of the network. The density of ties within the core remained high, whereas firms in the periphery established fewer connections among them, resulting in a more isolated periphery.

The decline could also mean that new networks are replacing traditional national corporate networks. On the one hand, in Bulgaria, the very low density of corporate networks during the post-communist period could be explained by the fact that directors of big companies were not connected through interlocks but through alternative social networks. This could be a deliberate strategy of Bulgarian elites to hide their business connections as much as possible. On the other hand, in small and open countries, such as Finland, the Netherlands and Switzerland, the internationalization of boards led to less interlocks as foreign directors were less integrated into the national business elite.

On the micro level, another explanation for the decline, put forward in the literature, is the increasing focus of firms on shareholder value (on this notion, see Lazonick and O'Sullivan 2000). This focus resulted, among other outcomes, in the professionalization and shrinking of boards. It means that the number of big linkers diminished within the networks of many countries, which could also explain the decline of the networks (Beyer and Hopner 2003; Heemskerk 2007; David et al. 2014). However, the increasing focus on shareholder value by firms as an explanation for the decline is more complex. The Dutch case shows, by looking at the micro level, how the distance between the discourse emphasizing the importance of shareholder value on the one hand and the implementation of practical instruments on the other (*decoupling*) led to the relative persistence of the network, despite external forces such as globalization. An important reason for this decoupling was what is termed 'management entrenchment'. In Argentina, the corporate network crumbled during the last decade of the twentieth century due to privatization. The resulting ownership structure changes imply important modifications at the micro level. Contrary to previous periods, MNEs that benefitted from these privatizations did not choose professionals or well-connected managers to sit on their boards. Legal concerns due to new regulations regarding directors' liability seem to have undermined the social status and prestige conferred to big linkers, which explains the decreasing number of interlocking directorates during this decade.

6. MAIN CONCLUSIONS AND FURTHER RESEARCH

We argue that because of a focus in the literature on stylized archetypes, much less attention has been paid to institutional changes and the complexity of these changes. By comparing structural characteristics of institutions across countries and sometimes over short time periods, similarities and differences have been recognized in the extant literature. However, using this approach, changes are not really explained and, when they are, they tend to be explained only as a response to exogenous 'shocks', such as depressions, wars and globalization. We agree that institutional change within countries can be triggered by exogenous shocks as they put pressure on countries to (re)act. But there is more to it, we argue. The chapters in this volume show that national corporate networks react very differently to external structural breaks; some networks changed earlier and/or more profoundly than others. We relate these differences to differences in national institutions. Based on the findings in the chapters, we developed a framework consisting of three interrelated levels. First, the macro level—the political (which can be divided into politics and policies) and macro-economic environment (degree of economic development, for example)—directly or indirectly influences the corporate network. Second, the interrelationships (control, competition, cohesion and communication) at the meso level affect the structure and features of interlocking directorates. Finally, the relations among the three most important stakeholders (capital, management, labor) at the micro level of the firm also shape the corporate network. Building on the empirical findings, we showed that these three levels interact and influence each other, and that it is these interactions and influences that together explain why national corporate networks react differently to major external pressures. We conclude from this that these three levels should be taken into account when studying and explaining changes in corporate networks. In particular, more attention should be paid to the micro level of corporate networks. Some chapters in this book touched on it, but more research definitely should be encouraged (see below for suggestions for future research on the micro level).

By adopting a comparative and historical approach, this book brings three new elements to the existing literature on corporate networks. First, the chapters add a new perspective to the debate on the role of banks within corporate networks, which until now has been conducted in ahistorical fashion and focused on developed countries (the US, the UK and Germany). The relation between industry and banks was often one of reciprocal coordination instead of bank control. Second, the state can have a direct and/or indirect influence on corporate networks through state-owned enterprises or through its political economy and the enactment of laws. Third, in some time periods and/or in some countries, banks and/or the state can be replaced by other institutions in the network, institutions that have been neglected by the literature, such as business groups, family firms, colonial enterprises and multinationals (for the role of family firms within corporate networks, see also Ginalski 2012). These actors can be a substitute for the role of the state or the banks within corporate networks, or they can have a complementary function.

We hope that this book will stimulate further research on corporate networks in a comparative and historical perspective. Two avenues of research seem particularly promising: the sociology of elites and transnational networks. First, we argue that more attention must be paid to agency in order to explain the evolution of corporate networks (see also David et al. 2009; Mizruchi 2013). In fact, change must ultimately be explained by varying preferences of the people who govern the firms (Jackson 2010). In this sense, interlocks are not only a reaction to a new environment or structural breaks, but also the result of changing corporate strategies toward interlocks. Research on corporate networks should thus put more emphasis on the micro level by, for example, taking into consideration the mechanisms of elite recruitment and of elite coordination other than corporate networks. Moreover, the notion of economic elites should be broadened and not restricted solely to managers (Savage and Williams 2008) or to males (on the position of women within corporate networks in the Netherlands, see Heemskerk and Fennema 2014). Finally, new methodological devices should be put forward. For example, network analysis should be combined with other techniques, such as multiple correspondence analyses, in order to study the actors of the networks (Bühlmann, David, and Mach 2012; Toninelli and Vasta 2014).

Second, future research on interlocking directorates should go beyond the comparative approach and integrate the interaction between the objects of comparison (Werner and Zimmermann 2006). In this sense, the issue of transnational networks is promising. Indeed, an important debate concerning the transnationalization of economic elites developed during the last decade (Carroll and Fennema 2002; Kentor and Jang 2004; Carroll 2010; Veen and Kratzer 2011; Burris and Staples 2012; Murray and Scott 2012; Heemskerk 2013). These studies used either the interorganizational perspective—in other words, they see networks as networks of firms connected via common directors—or the interpersonal perspective. This latter approach looks at networks as networks of directors connected via shared board membership and implies that more research should be done into the background, more specifically on the nationality, of the directors. However, this debate on transnational elites covers only the recent period. This is unfortunate because portions of the business elites and thus of corporate networks could be considered as transnational or cosmopolitan already on the eve of World War I (Wagner 2007; Jones 2006; Schnyder et al. 2005). By examining big linkers (i.e., directors that occupy several seats on the boards of the largest companies) in the twentieth and twenty-first centuries, and by linking the national databases that form the core of this book, new contributions to this debate could be made. We hope that this book will stimulate the adoption of a long-term and comparative perspective in new research on corporate networks.

NOTES

1. We would like to thank Pierre Eichenberger, Stéphanie Ginalski, Matthias Kipping, André Mach and Gerhard Schnyder for very helpful comments on previous versions of the Introduction, Sarah Carmichael for her corrections of our English and Andrea Mazzei for his help with Figure 1.

2. Some scholars work on modeling network dynamics. These statistical models are increasingly being used for interlocking directorates' studies, as well (Heemskerk and Struijs 2012; Snijders 2011; the Siena webpage: http://www.stats.ox.ac.uk/~snijders/siena/).

REFERENCES

Aguilera, Ruth V., and Gregory Jackson. 2003. "The Cross-National Diversity of Corporate Governance: Dimensions and Determinants." *The Academy of Management Review* 28 (3): 447–465.

Berle, Adolf A., and Gardiner C. Means. 1932. *The Modern Corporation and Private Property.* New York: Macmillan.

Beyer, Jürgen, and Martin Höpner. 2003. "The Disintegration of Organised Capitalism: German Corporate Governance in the 1990s." *West European Politics* 26 (4): 179–198.

Brandeis, Louis D. 1914. *Other People's Money: And how the Bankers Use It.* New York: F.A. Stokes.

Brookfield, Jon, Sea-Jing Chang, Israel Drori, Shmuel Ellis, Sergio Lazzarini, Jordan I. Siegel, and Juan Pablo von Bernath Bardina. 2012. "Liberalization, Network Dynamics, and Business Groups." In *The Small Worlds of Corporate Governance,* edited by Bruce Kogut. 77–116. Cambridge: MIT Press.

Bühlmann, Felix, Thomas David, and André Mach. 2012. "The Swiss Business Elite (1980–2000): How the Changing Composition of the Elite Explains the Decline of the Swiss Company Network." *Economy and Society* 41 (2): 199–226.

Burris, Val, and Clifford L. Staples. 2012. "In Search of a Transnational Capitalist Class: Alternative Methods for Comparing Director Interlocks within and between Nations and Regions." *International Journal of Comparative Sociology,* 53 (4): 323–342.

Cárdenas, Julián. 2012. "Varieties of Corporate Networks: Network Analysis and FsQCA." *International Journal of Comparative Sociology* 53 (4): 298–323.

Carroll, William. 2010. *The Making of a Transnational Capitalist Class.* London: Zed Books.

Carroll, William K., and Meindert Fennema. 2002. "Is There a Transnational Business Community?" *International Sociology* 17 (3): 393–419.

Colli, Andrea, and Michelangelo Vasta. Forthcoming. "Large and Entangled: Italian Business Groups in the Long Run." *Business History.*

Colpan, Asli M., and Takashi Hikino. 2010. "Foundations of Business Groups: Towards an Integrated Framework." In *Oxford Handbook of Business Groups,* edited by Asli M. Colpan, Takashi Hikino, and James R. Lincoln, 15–66. Oxford: Oxford University Press.

Conyon, Martin, and Andrew Shipilov. 2012. "Is There an Anglo-Saxon Model? Historical and Social Network Accounts of the Differences in Ownership and Control in the UK, Canada and the U.S." In *The Small Worlds of Corporate Governance,* edited by Bruce Kogut, 53–76. Cambridge: MIT Press.

Cortat, Alain. 2009. *Un cartel parfait. Réseaux, R&D et profits dans l'industrie suisse des câbles.* Neuchâtel: Alphil.

Cronin, Bruce. 2011. "Networks of Corporate Power Revisited." *Procedia—Social and Behavioral Sciences* 10: 43–51.

David, Thomas, Stéphanie Ginalski, Frédéric Rebmann, and Gerhard Schnyder. 2009. "The Swiss Business Elite between 1980–2000: Declining Cohesion, Changing Educational Profile and Growing Internationalization." In *European Economic Elites. Between a New Spirit of Capitalism and the Erosion of State Socialism,* edited by C. Boyer and F. Sattler, 197–220. Berlin: Duncker & Humblot.

David, Thomas, Martin Lupold, André Mach, and Gerhard Schnyder. 2014. *De la 'Forteresse des Alpes' à la valeur actionnariale: Histoire de la gouvernance d'entreprise suisse au 20ᵉ siècle*. Zurich: Seismo.
Davis, Gerald F. 1991. "Agents without Principles? The Spread of the Poison Pill through the Intercorporate Network." *Administrative Science Quarterly* 36: 583–613.
Davis, Gerald F. 2009. *Managed by the Markets: How Finance Re-Shaped America*. New York: Oxford University Press.
Davis, Gerald F., and Mark Mizruchi. 1999. "The Money Center Cannot Hold: Commercial Banks in the U.S. System of Corporate Governance." *Administrative Science Quarterly* 44 (2): 215–239.
DeAngelo, Harry, and Edward M Rice. 1983. "Antitakeover Charter Amendments and Stockholder Wealth." *Journal of Financial Economics* 11: 329–359.
De Jong, Abe, Ailsa Röell, and Gerarda Westerhuis. 2010. "Changing National Business Systems: Corporate Governance and Financing in the Netherlands, 1945–2005." *Business History Review* 84: 773–798.
De Nooy, Wouter, Andrej Mrvar, and Vladimir Batagelj. 2011. *Exploratory Social Network Analysis with Pajek*. New York: Cambridge University Press.
Dritsas, Margrit, Peter Eigner, and Jan Ottosson. 1996. "Big Business' Networks in Three Interwar Economies: Austria, Greece and Sweden." *Financial History Review* 3: 175–195.
Eichengreen, Barry. 2006. *The European Economy since 1945: Coordinated Capitalism and Beyond*. Princeton: Princeton University Press.
Fellman, Susanna, Martin Iversen, Hans Sjögren, and Lars Thue. 2008. *Creating Nordic Capitalism: The Development of a Competitive Periphery*. Palgrave Macmillan.
Fohlin, Caroline. 1999. "The Rise of Interlocking Directorates in Imperial Germany." *Economic History Review* (2): 307–333.
Ginalkski, Stéphanie. 2012. "Du capitalisme familial au capitalisme financier: le cas de l'industrie suisse des machines et métaux au 20e siècle." PhD Thesis. Université de Lausanne.
Granovetter, Mark. 1985. "Economic Action and Social Structure: the Problem of Embeddedness." *American Journal of Sociology* 91: 481–510.
Hall, Peter A., and David Soskice. 2001. *Varieties of Capitalism: the Institutional Foundation of Comparative Advantage*. Oxford: Oxford University Press.
Haunschild, Pamela R. 1993. "Interorganizational Imitation: the Impact of Interlocks on Corporate Acquisition Activity." *Administrative Science Quarterly* 38: 564–592.
Heemskerk, Eelke M. 2007. *The Decline of the Corporate Community. Network Dynamics of the Dutch Business Elite*. Amsterdam: Amsterdam University Press.
Heemskerk, Eelke M. 2013. "The Rise of the European Corporate Elite: Evidence from the Network of Interlocking Directorates." *Economy & Society* 42 (1): 74–101.
Heemskerk, Eelke M., and Meindert Fennema. 2014. "Women on Board: Female Board Membership as a Form of Elite Democratization." *Enterprise & Society* 15 (2): 252–284.
Heemskerk, Eelke M., and Ferdi Struijs. 2012. "How Network Effects Determine the Evolution of the Network of Interlocking Directorates." *Paper Presented at the 28th EGOS Colloquium, Helsinki*.
Helmers, H. M., R. J. Mokken, R. C. Plijter, and F. N. Stokman. 1975. *Graven naar macht: op zoek naar de kern van de Nederlandse economie*. Amsterdam: Van Gennep.
Herrigel, Gary. 2007. "A New Wave in the History of Corporate Governance." *Enterprise & Society* 8 (3): 475–488.

Hilferding, Rudolf. 1968 [1910]. *Das Finanzkapital. Eine Studie über die jüngste Entwicklung des Kapitalismus*. Frankfurt am Main: Europäische Verlagsanstalt.
Höpner, Martin, and Tim Müllenborn. 2010. "Mitbestimmung im Unternehmensvergleich: ein Konzept zur Messung des Einflusspotenzials der Arbeitnehmervertreter im mitbestimmten Aufsichtsrat." *MPIfG Discussion Paper* 10/3. Cologne: Max-Planck-Institut für Gesellschaftsforschung.
Jackson, Gregory. 2010. "Actors and Institutions." In *Oxford Handbook of Comparative Institutional Analysis*, edited by John Campbell, Colin Crouch, Glenn Morgan, and Richard Whitley, 63–86. Oxford: Oxford University Press.
Jones, Geoffrey. 2006. "The End of Nationality? Global Firms and Borderless Worlds." *Zeitschrift für Unternehmensgeschichte* 51 (2): 149–166.
Jones, Geoffrey, and Tarun Khanna. 2006. "Bringing History (back) into International Business." *Journal of International Business Studies* 37: 453–468.
Khanna, Tarun, and Yishay Yafeh. 2007. "Business Groups in Emerging Markets: Paragons or Parasites?" *Journal of Economic Literature* XLV: 331–372.
Kentor, Jeffrey, and Yong Suk Jang. 2004. "Yes, There is a (Growing) Transnational Business Community: A Study of Global Interlocking Directorates 1983–98." *International Sociology* 19 (3): 355–68.
Kogut, Bruce. 2012. *The Small World of Corporate Governance*. Cambridge: MIT Press.
Krenn, Karoline. 2008. "Von der Macht der Banken zur Leitidee des deutschen Produktionsregimes: Bank-Industrie-Verflechtung am Beginn des 20. Jahrhunderts." *Zeitschrift für Unternehmensgeschichte* 53 (1): 70–99.
Lazonick, William, and Mary O'Sullivan. 2000. "Maximizing Shareholder Value: a New Ideology for Corporate Governance." *Economy and Society* 29: 13–35.
McKeown, Adam. 2007. "Periodizing Globalization." *History Workshop Journal* 63 (2): 218–230.
Mintz, Beth, and Michael Schwartz. 1985. *The Power Structure of American Business*. Chicago: University of Chicago Press.
Mizruchi, Mark S. 1982. *The American Corporate Network, 1904–1974*. Beverly Hills: Sage.
Mizruchi, Mark S. 1996. "What Do Interlocks Do? An Analysis, Critique, and Assessment of Research on Interlocking Directorates." *Annual Review of Sociology* 22: 271–298.
Mizruchi, Mark S. 2013. *The Fracturing of the American Corporate Elite*. Cambridge: Harvard University Press.
Morck, Randall, Daniel Wolfenzon, and Bernard Yeung. 2005. "Corporate Governance, Economic Entrenchment, and Growth," *Journal of Economic Literature* 43 (3): 655–720.
Murray, Georgina, and John Scott, eds. 2012. *Financial Elites and Transnational Business: Who Rules the World?* Northampton, MA: Edward Elgar Publishing.
Musacchio, Aldo, and Sergio G. Lazzarini. 2012. "Leviathan in Business: Varieties of State Capitalism and Their Implications for Economic Performance." *Harvard Business School Working Paper* No. 12–108, June 2012.
Musacchio, Aldo, and Ian Read. 2007. "Bankers, Industrialists, and Their Cliques: Elite Networks in Mexico and Brazil during Early Industrialization." *Enterprise & Society* 8 (4): 842–880.
Nobel, Joris, and Meindert Fennema. 2003. "Economische elites na de dekolonisatie van Nederlands-Indie: verlies van posities, desintegratie van netwerken, verschuiving van netwerken." In *Nederlandse elites in beeld: continuïteit en verandering*, edited by Meindert Fennema and Hubert Schijf. Amsterdam: Amsterdam University Press.
O'Rourke, Kevin, and Jeffrey G. Williamson. 1999. *Globalization and History. The Evolution of a Nineteenth-Century Atlantic Economy*. Cambridge: MIT Press.

Okazaki, Tetsuji, Sawada Michiru, and Yokoyama Kazuki. 2005. "Measuring the Extent and Implications of Director Interlocking in the Prewar Japanese Banking Industry." *Journal of Economic History* 65 (4): 1082–1115.
Pak, Susie J. 2013. *Gentlemen Bankers: The World of J.P. Morgan*. Harvard: Harvard University Press.
Pujo, Arsène. 1913. *Money Trust Investigation. Investigation of Financial and Monetary Conditions in the United States Under House Resolutions Nos. 429 and 504*. Part 1. Washington: Government Printing Office. https://fraser.stlouisfed.org/docs/historical/house/money_trust/montru_pt01.pdf.
Rajan, Raghuram G., and Luigi Zingales. 2003. "The Great Reversals: the Politics of Financial Development in the Twentieth Century." *Journal of Financial Economics* 69: 5–50.
Rinaldi, Alberto, and Michelangelo Vasta. 2005. "The Structure of Italian Capitalism, 1952–1972: New Evidence Using the Interlocking Directorates Techniques." *Financial History Review* 12: 173–198.
Savage, Mike, and Karel Williams. 2008. "Elites: Remembered in Capitalism and Forgotten by Social Sciences." *The Sociological Review* 56 (1): 1–24.
Schmitter, P. C. 1979. "Still the Century of Corporatism?" In *Trends Toward Corporatist Intermediation*, edited by P. C. Schmitter and G. Lehmbruch, 7–48. Beverly Hills.
Schnyder, Gerhard, Martin Lüpold, André Mach, and Thomas David. 2005. "The Rise and Decline of the Swiss Company Network during the 20th Century." *Travaux de Science Politique*, Nouvelle Série, no. 22. Université de Lausanne, Institut d'études politiques et internationales.
Scott, John. 1985. "Theoretical Framework and Research Design." In *Networks of Corporate Power. A Comparative Analysis of Ten Countries*, edited by Frans M. Stokman, Rolf Ziegler, and John Scott, 1–19. Cambridge: Polity Press.
Scott, John. 1991. "Networks of Corporate Power: a Comparative Assessment." *Annual Review of Sociology* 17: 181–203.
Scott, John, and Catherine Griff. 1984. *Directors of Industry: the British Corporate Network, 1904–1976*. Cambridge: Polity Press.
Shleifer, Andrei, and Robert W. Vishny. 1989. "Management Entrenchment. The Case of Manager Specific Investments." *Journal of Financial Economics* 25: 123–139.
Sluyterman, Keetie E. (ed.). Forthcoming. *Varieties of Capitalism and Business History. The Dutch Case*. New York, London: Routledge.
Snijders, Tom A. B. 2011. "Statistical Models for Social Networks." *Annual Review of Sociology* 37, 129–151.
Stokman, Frans N., Rolf Ziegler, and John Scott, eds. 1985. *Networks of Corporate Power. A Comparative Analysis of Ten Countries*. Cambridge: Polity Press.
Sweezy, Paul. 1956 [1942]. *The Theory of Capitalist Development: Principles of Marxian Political Economy*. Monthly Review Press.
Tomka, Bela. 2001. "Interlocking Directorates between Banks and Industrial Companies in Hungary at the Beginning of the Twentieth Century." *Business History* 43 (1): 25–42.
Toninelli, Pier Angelo, ed. 2000. *The Rise and Fall of State-Owned Enterprise in the Western World*. Cambridge: Cambridge University Press.
Toninelli, Pier Angelo, and Michelangelo Vasta. 2014. "Opening the Black Box of Entrepreneurship: the Italian Case in a Historical Perspective." *Business History* 56 (2): 161–186.
Useem, Michael. 1984. *The Inner Circle. Large Corporations and the Rise of Business Political Activity in the US and UK*. New York, Oxford: Oxford University Press.
Vasta, Michelangelo, and Alberto Baccini. 1997. "Banks and Industry in Italy, 1911–1936: New Evidence Using the Interlocking Directorates Technique." *Financial History Review* 4: 139–159.

Veen, Kees van, and Jan Kratzer. 2011. "National and International Interlocking Directorates within Europe: Corporate Networks within and among Fifteen European Countries." *Economy and Society* 40 (1): 1–25.

Wadhwani, R. Daniel, and Marcelo Bucheli. 2014. "The Future of the Past in Management and Organizational Studies." In *Organizations in time. History, Theory, Method*, edited by Marcelo Bucheli and R. Daniel Wadhwani, 3–32. Oxford University Press.

Wagner, Anne-Catherine. 2007. *Les classes sociales dans la mondialisation*. Paris: Découverte.

Wellhöner, Volker. 1989. *Grossbanken und Grossindustrie im Kaiserreich*. Göttingen.

Werner, Michael, and Bernard Zimmermann. 2006. "Beyond Comparison: Histoire Croisée and the Challenge of Reflexivity." *History and Theory* 45: 30–50.

Wilkins, Mira, Kathleen Thelen, Richard Whitley, Rory M. Miller, Cathie Jo Martin, V.R. Berghahn, Martin Jes Iversen, Gary Herrigel, and Jonathan Zeitlin. 2010. "Varieties of Capitalism" Roundtable. *Business History Review*, 84 (4): 637–674.

Windolf, Paul. 2002. *Corporate Networks in Europe and the United States*. Oxford: Oxford University Press.

Windolf, Paul. 2006. "Unternehmensverflechtung im organisierten Kapitalismus: Deutschland und die USA im Vergleich 1896–1938." *Zeitschrift für Unternehmensgeschichte* 51 (2): 191–222.

Windolf, Paul. 2009. "Coordination and Control in Corporate Networks: United States and Germany in Comparison, 1896–1938." *European Sociological Review* 25: 443–457.

Windolf, Paul, and Jurgen Beyer. 1996. "Co-operative Capitalism: Corporate Networks in Germany and Britain." *The British Journal of Sociology* 47: 205–231.

Wixforth, Harald. 1995. *Banken und Schwerindustrie in der Weimarer Republik*. Köln.

Zeitlin, Maurice. 1974. "Corporate Ownership and Control: The Large Corporation and the Capitalist Class." *American Journal of Sociology* 79 (5): 1073–1119.

Ziegler, Rolf. 1985. "Conclusion." In *Networks of Corporate Power: A Comparative Analysis of Ten Countries*, edited by Frans N. Stokman, Rolf Ziegler, and John Scott, 267–287. Cambridge: Polity Press.

Part I
Large Developed Economies

2. The Decline of the American Corporate Network, 1960–2010[1]

Todd Schifeling and Mark S. Mizruchi

1. INTRODUCTION

Corporations in the US have shared directors since as far back as 1816 (Bunting 1983). By the end of the nineteenth century, the vast majority of the largest American firms were connected into a single, continuous network through board of director ties. Through most of the twentieth century, this network exhibited a high level of stability. Across wars, economic crises, the rise and fall of various sectors, technological revolutions and the conglomeration mania of the 1960s, the density of the network persisted within a fairly narrow range. The network began to unravel in the 1980s, however, and the decline accelerated in the 1990s. There has been a nearly monotonic reduction in the density of the network since 1982. The path lengths between firms have either increased or have disappeared altogether. This decline, after a century of stability, has wide-ranging implications for the behavior of individual firms, the diffusion of corporate policies and practices, collective action by corporations, and the larger society. We argue in this chapter that the decline of the American corporate network has its roots in a series of events that occurred in the 1970s and 1980s: the business-led neutralization of the countervailing forces of government and organized labor; the resurgence of corporate shareholders, what Useem (1989) has called the "revolt of the corporate owners"; and the historic withdrawal of banking from its traditional role in the economy and, as a consequence, the network. We will suggest that these three interrelated factors inadvertently vaulted the network into a trajectory of decline.

The chapter proceeds as follows. First, we present our longitudinal dataset on the US corporate network. Second, we review the formation of the network and the subsequent long duration of stability. Third, we document the rapid deterioration of the network since the 1980s. Fourth, we present our arguments on the causes of decline. Finally, we conclude by discussing the implications of network decline for broader societal dynamics and for the broader literature on corporate networks.

2. DATA

We compiled a dataset of 250 large public American corporations for the years 1962 through 1994 in four-year intervals (except for 1970), followed by data for 1999, 2003, 2005 and 2010. In each panel, we include the 150 largest manufacturers; the 50 largest utilities, mining, transport and service firms; and the 50 largest financial firms on the basis of total assets. Network data were compiled from several sources reported in Davis, Yoo and Baker (2003) and Chu (2013). We calculated statistics on the composition of the sample, the density and cohesion of the corporate network, and the characteristics of the directors (see Appendix I).[2]

For the first half of the twentieth century, we draw on data reported in Mizruchi (1982). This information covers the networks of 167 leading companies, ranked by capitalization, at seven time points from 1904 to 1974.[3] Capitalization is defined as the book value of issued stock plus funded debt at par. Unreliable early data prohibited ranking by assets. The sample consisted of the largest 100 industrials, 25 transportation firms, 10 insurance companies and 20 commercial banks, plus 12 prominent investment banks for the years 1904, 1912, 1919, 1935, 1964, 1969 and 1974.

3. THE FIRST CENTURY

The American corporate network coalesced in the later years of the nineteenth century. In a study of ties among 20 banks, 25 railroads and 10 insurance companies, David Bunting (1983) found an increase in interlocks from 116 in 1871, to 204 in 1891, to 595 in 1912. In an analysis of cross-industry interlocks among 374 companies in 12 industries over the 20-year period from 1886 to 1905, William Roy (1983) found an increase from 149 interlocks between 1886 and 1892, to 207 between 1893 and 1897, to 649 between 1898 and 1905.

The rise of this network was dominated by the so-called 'robber barons', who operated primarily through railroads and financial institutions. After the Depression of 1893, corporate power became increasingly concentrated in the hands of financiers (Cochran and Miller 1942). The leading members of this group, which included J.P. Morgan of J.P. Morgan & Co., George F. Baker of the First National Bank of New York, James Stillman of the National City Bank, and Jacob H. Schiff of the investment bank Kuhn, Loeb & Co., provided the necessary capital for industrial growth. They also controlled their economic empires, in part by either personally sitting on the boards of multiple companies (Baker, for example, sat on the boards of 23 of the 166 firms in 1904), or by selecting the directors of those boards (Morgan admitted in his testimony at the Pujo Hearings in 1913 that he had approved the entire board of the newly-formed United States Steel Corporation in 1901).

The network that resulted from this activity was exceptionally dense by historical standards. In Mizruchi's (1982) dataset, the density of the network was 7.2% in 1904 and peaked at 7.6% in 1912, in the midst of the era of financial prominence. This latter year also saw a high point in the compactness of the network: within the main component, 91.2% of firms were within two steps of the most central firm, and 100% were within three steps.

The rise of this network attracted critics, however. In response to the perceived excesses of the period, Progressives and Populists attempted to place limits on the concentration of capital. The Sherman Antitrust Act of 1890 permitted the government to intervene in cases in which dominant individual firms used unfair practices to impede competition.[4] The Armstrong Investigation of 1905 and related legislation required insurance companies to divest from banks and trusts. These reforms limited the ability of managers and bankers to use the corporate network to control corporations and restrict competition, which was especially urgent due to the problem of high fixed costs leading to ruinous price competition. This pushed American business onto a path of mergers rather than cartels, and "competitive capitalism" rather than "cooperative capitalism" (Fligstein 1990; Windolf 2009). It was only with the Clayton Act of 1914, which outlawed direct interlocks between competitors, that the network itself was directly affected, however. In 1912, there were 124 interlocks between the banks in Mizruchi's dataset. By 1919, after the passage of the Clayton Act, only 19 such interlocks remained (Mizruchi 1982, 124).

In addition to the legal restrictions against interlocking, the early generation of financial titans, who often sat on multiple boards themselves, began to leave the network, either through death or retirement, and were not replaced with equally-connected directors. Twenty-seven directors held six or more directorships in 1912, but only 14 sat on six or more boards in 1919, and only three by 1935. The result of this decline in the number of multiple-board individuals was a sharp drop in network density. From a peak density of 7.6% in 1912, the level decreased to 5.6% in 1919 and to 4.0% in 1935. The percentage of firms in the main component that were within a two-step reach of the most central firm dropped from 91.2% in 1912, to 81.7% in 1919, to only 66.9% in 1935.

After the rapid changes of the 1912–1935 period, the American corporate network experienced more than a half-century of relative stability. Although Mizruchi's dataset contained a gap between 1935 and 1964, the three panels from this latter point—1964, 1969 and 1974—portrayed a network very similar to that of 1935, albeit more connected. The density, which had reached a low of 4.0 in 1935, increased to 4.4 in 1964 and 4.7 in 1969, before dropping to 4.2 in 1974. The two-step reach percentages also rebounded from the low of 66.9% in 1935, increasing to 75.7% in 1964 and 82.9% in 1969, before dropping to 70.1% in 1974.

Related analyses on different datasets confirm the stability of the American corporate network in the postwar period and extend this phenomenon into the early 1990s (Barnes and Ritter 2001; Davis, Yoo, and Baker 2003). Because density is affected by the size of the network (density tends to decrease as the number of nodes increases), the densities that we computed among the 250 firms are not directly comparable to those based on Mizruchi's networks of 167. Still, as Appendix I indicates, we continued to observe a high level of stability in these networks through 1994, with densities ranging from 2.9% in 1974 to 4.1% in 1982, and revealing no clear temporal trend. The average distance between any two firms also exhibited a relatively narrow range, between 2.75 and 3.09.

Interestingly, there was a sharp drop in network density in the 1970s (the network was relatively sparse in 1974 and 1978) before returning to a higher density level in 1982 (see also Mizruchi 1982; Barnes and Ritter 2001). The reasons for this low level of connectivity are unclear, but the 1970s were a period of considerable economic turmoil in American history, and American companies also mounted a major shift toward conservatism during that decade (we discuss both of these issues below). Under severe economic pressures, the tenure of the leaders of major corporations slid from an average of 8.7 years in the 1960s to 7.7 years in the 1970s.[5] These economic, demographic and political forces combined to weaken the network. By the early 1980s, network connectivity rebounded to new highs, however, indicating that the 1970s were a temporary deviation from a longer-term trend.

In addition to this system-level stability, the representation of sectors in the center of the network exhibited a high level of consistency during this period. From the formation of the network in the late 1800s into the early 1980s, financial institutions predominated among the most central firms (Mizruchi 1982; Davis and Mizruchi 1999). For the first 90 years of the twentieth century, financial firms represented approximately half of the 10 most central firms, despite representing only 20% of the firms in the network.

The durability of the network is even more remarkable given the scale of economic, political and technological change during the twentieth century. The network maintained its basic character through multiple wars, business cycles, increasing international competition, deregulation, and technological revolutions. The ownership of large corporations shifted over time as well, passing from individuals to institutions. By the early 1990s, institutional investors owned a majority of the shares in American corporations. This trend, along with increasing scrutiny from the investment community that included, among other things, the massive acquisition wave of the 1980s, shook the foundations of the management control of corporations (Useem 1996). Observing the consistent level of average distances among firms despite these destabilizing factors, Davis, Yoo and Baker concluded that local clustering and short path lengths are "an intrinsic property of the interlock network" (2003, 301).

4. THE UNRAVELING OF THE NETWORK

After more than half a century of stability, the American corporate network began to decline in the 1990s. As is evident in our data, the density of the network, which had fluctuated almost randomly around a mean of 3.6 from the early 1960s through the 1980s, declined precipitously after 1994 (see Appendix I). Density fell from 3.6% in 1994 to 2.7% in 1999, 2.2% in 2003, 2.1% in 2005 and 1.6% in 2010. The number of isolates, which had averaged 6.6 firms from 1978 to 1994, increased to 14 in 1999, 23 in 2005 and 29 in 2010, while the number of firms with two or fewer interlocks increased from 32 in 1994 to 73 in 2010. Within the main component, the average distance increased from 2.95 in 1994 to 4.04 in 2010.

Although there have been fluctuations in the network across its history, the slope of these changes in the post-1994 period and its consistency across consecutive panels is unprecedented. These findings have also been corroborated by other scholars. In an examination of approximately 250 leading firms drawn from both Standard & Poor's and Fortune lists at four different points from the 1960s through the mid-1990s, Barnes and Ritter (2001) found a 23% decline in network density between 1983 and 1995, the last year in their dataset. In a detailed analysis of the S&P 500 and 1500 networks, Chu (2013) documented the disappearance of heavily interlocked individuals and the subsequent decline in network connectivity from 1997 through 2010. Even Davis, Yoo and Baker (2003), who emphasized the continuity in network distances over time, reported a 14% decrease in the average degree of the main component from 1982 to 1999 for a network of Fortune firms.[6]

As suggested by the findings of Barnes and Ritter (2001), the decline of the American corporate network can be detected as far back as the 1980s. In our data, most measures indicate that 1982 was the high point of network connectivity. The density and average degree of the full network peaked at 4.1% and 10.3 ties in that year. The level of density began to decline in 1986, although it was only between 1994 and 1999 that a sharp decline becomes evident. In terms of average distance, 2.75 in 1982 was also the smallest that we observed. The average distance rose monotonically through the seven remaining panels, with a sharp jump again between 1994 and 1999.

The other network statistics show parallel patterns of decline. With the increasing sparseness of the network, betweenness centrality generally rose after 1982. The number of multiple ties had an earlier peak but also declined steadily after 1982. Other measures, including the number of isolates, diameter, average closeness centrality and the size of the 2-slice also reflected the decline in cohesion in the 1990s. Regardless of whether we date the decline from the 1980s or the 1990s, all of the measures point toward reduced connectivity over time.

With each decade, the *pace* of decline also accelerates. Density dropped 12% between 1982 and 1990, 25% between 1990 and 1999, and 41% between 1999 and 2010. Average distance increased 7% in the 1980s, 9% in the 1990s, and 26% in the first decade of the twenty-first century. The cumulative results are a 61% decrease in density and a 47% increase in average distance from 1982 to 2010.

In the remainder of this chapter, we attempt to account for the decline of the American corporate network after more than a half-century of stability. Drawing on the argument presented in detail by Mizruchi (2013), we focus on three factors.[7] First, we consider the defeat by corporate interests of the countervailing forces of organized labor and liberal government. Second, we examine the impact of the rise of activist stockholders. And third, we analyze the historic withdrawal of the banks from their traditional positions in the economy and the corporate network. We contend that all three of these factors are related, and that together they inadvertently led to the unraveling of the interlock network.

5. THE NEUTRALIZATION OF STATE AND LABOR PRESSURES

In the period immediately following World War II, two forces—a relatively active and highly legitimate state and a relatively powerful collection of labor unions—exerted a countervailing pressure on business (Galbraith 1952). The enormous military buildup during the war left the federal government with extensive power to intervene in the economy, and the heads of the leading corporations, as well as the general public, supported the idea that the government should actively promote the general public welfare. This perspective was enshrined in the Employment Act of 1946, which charged the federal government with maintaining high employment and price stability. Into the 1970s, policies initiated by Republican and Democratic administrations alike also sought to redress social and economic inequalities. Lyndon Johnson's Great Society programs, including Medicare, and Richard Nixon's groundbreaking environmental legislation and his proposals for universal health care all sought to increase well-being throughout the population, and all of these had the support of significant segments of the business community. Personal and corporate income taxes were also much more progressive at that time, and income and wealth were more equally distributed. The unions, meanwhile, wielded considerable power and, like the government, enjoyed a high level of support from the general public. They won steady raises, new fringe benefits and strengthened recognition in the decades immediately following the war.[8] The power of government and unions together operated to place limits on the actions of business.

The countervailing pressures of the state and organized labor also contributed to political moderation, as well as unity, among the leaders of large corporations (Mizruchi 2013). The Employment Act passed with the support of business leaders in both the Committee for Economic Development (CED) and US Chamber of Commerce (USCC) (Collins 1981). Acknowledging the power of unions, the extremely conservative National Association of Manufacturers (NAM) moderated its position to accept the right of unions to exist (Harris 1982). Leading business groups and corporate figures either grudgingly accepted the reality of organized labor and government intervention, as in the NAM's softening toward unions, or even promoted them, as in the support of the CED and USCC for the Employment Act. A focus on what the CED called "enlightened self-interest" emerged among the leading American corporations. This spirit was rooted in a long-term perspective, in which the idea was to align the interests of all three sectors—government, labor and business—in a manner similar to the corporatist approach in Western Europe (Streeck and Kenworthy 2005). As the principal organized proponent of this viewpoint, the CED developed a type of conservative Keynesianism, in which government efforts to encourage steady economic growth and high wages would promote the long-term interests of the business community and larger society (Collins 1981).

Just as large corporations' willingness to accept the role of government and labor contributed to the strength of those institutions, it also increased the legitimacy of business itself. The relatively strong state and labor movement helped ensure that economic prosperity would be widely shared. The taxes and wages paid by business helped to generate public support. However critical they might be of corporations, actors within government and organized labor were willing to accept the continuation of the existing form of corporate organization and leadership.

This system of mutual support would not last, however. The triadic balance collapsed under the economic pressures of the 1970s. Global competition increased due to the regrowth of postwar economies, as well as dramatic improvements in communication and transportation technologies (Whitman 1999). This competition combined with inflation, recession, and slow-downs in productivity and corporate profits to form a potent destabilizing shock, which was felt directly by American companies. Some observers believed this unprecedented confluence of problems represented an existential threat to business.[9] As reported earlier, executive tenure at major corporations began to decline. The persistent co-presence of high inflation and high unemployment, dubbed 'stagflation' during the 1970s, delegitimized the dominant Keynesian paradigm of the period, to which the American corporate elite had overwhelmingly subscribed (Barton 1985). This rendered corporate moderates increasingly unable to offer convincing solutions within the old framework.

In response to this predicament, business interests launched an extensive, and ultimately successful, attack on government regulation and organized labor (Vogel 1989). Corporate leaders formed new organizations, of which the Business Roundtable was the most important, and reinvigorated old ones like the USCC. Some of the first signs of success came during the early period of the Carter administration, when Democrats controlled the White House and both houses of Congress. After Carter assumed office in January 1977, consumer, environmental and labor activists were optimistic that the government would pass a series of bills that had been stymied by Republicans. To the shock of virtually all parties, including business, a full-scale mobilization by corporate interests succeeded in defeating a moderate labor law reform and new consumer and environmental regulations. The degree of business opposition to labor led United Auto Workers' president Douglas Fraser to protest that corporations were waging a "one-sided class war" (Shabecoff 1978, B4). Business was also able to turn President Carter's attempt to increase corporate taxes into a corporate tax cut (Ferguson and Rogers 1986, 100–102).

These early successes bloomed into major victories after Ronald Reagan became president in 1981. President Reagan famously stated in his inaugural address that "government is not the solution to our problem; government is the problem". Acting on this vision, he placed opponents of regulation in charge of agencies such as the Department of the Interior, Environmental Protection Agency, and Occupational Safety and Health Administration. These top-level administrators then attempted to place the agencies at the service of the businesses they were supposed to regulate. Reagan also created massive budget deficits through a combination of tax cuts and large increases in defense spending. The nature of the tax cuts, in which high earners received disproportionately large reductions, meant that income tax rates became significantly less progressive. The Reagan administration also threw the labor movement into disarray, first by crushing the air traffic controllers' union in 1981 and then with a series of hostile labor law rulings by the National Labor Relations Board. Combined with recession and global competition, the density and militancy of the US labor movement fell into a decline from which it has yet to recover.

Ironically, however, the neutralization of countervailing power that business had accomplished ultimately undermined the ability of corporations to act collectively to address their group-wide interests. Having achieved virtually all of their goals, there was no longer a need for corporations to organize politically. The first sign of this was evident in the negotiations surrounding President Reagan's 1982 tax increase. Faced with a spiraling deficit, Reagan pushed for and received an increase in business taxes, while protecting the individual tax cuts he favored. Large corporations were unable to unify and direct this legislation as they had for the tax reductions in the late 1970s. This early incapacity for collective action became even more evident in later years, as business was unable to agree on health care policy in the 1990s, and unable to mount a serious approach toward the deficit after the turn of the century.

Is there a relation between the apparent inability of the American corporate elite to engage in collective action and the declining connectivity of the interlock network? One possible account is that the demise of countervailing forces reduced the incentives for executives to connect with one other, resulting in network decline. This is the converse of Georg Simmel's (1955) external threat/internal cohesion hypothesis. Managers may have created ties through venues like the interlock network in response to vigorous opposition; without these antagonists, managers may have had less interest in organizing (Useem 1984). More immediately, however, the defeat of state interventionism and unions exposed business to a new set of pressures that would have significant consequences for the interlock network.

6. THE REVOLT OF THE OWNERS

The elimination of the old relations among business, government and labor opened the door to new attacks on management. In the internecine conditions of the 1970s, the legitimacy of all three groups declined (Lipset and Schneider 1983). The dominant view of managers as professionals balancing the competing interests of workers, customers, owners, and communities withered (Khurana 2007). One trigger for this questioning of the role of management was the rise of agency theory (Manne 1965; Jensen and Meckling 1976). According to this perspective, corporations were 'legal fictions', simply a 'nexus of contracts' among individuals. The corporation existed for one primary reason: to increase the value of its shareholders' investment. Managers were viewed not as autonomous professionals with a specialized body of knowledge, but rather as "hired hands", in Khurana's phrase, whose job was to maximize shareholder value.

Share prices had declined during the 1970s, meaning that corporations' market values lagged below their accounting book values, rendering them vulnerable to takeover. This situation, combined with the Reagan administration's support for the Manne-Jensen-Meckling view of the corporation, led to a lenient attitude toward corporate acquisitions. The result was a wave of acquisitions in the 1980s, many of them hostile, which eliminated nearly one-third of the Fortune 500. This movement burst asunder the stability that the leading American corporations had experienced since the early twentieth century (see Chandler 1977, 503–513). The companies that did survive often had to streamline operations, adopt anti-takeover devices, and lobby state governments for restrictions on takeovers. These actions did ultimately help to slow hostile takeovers, but the relation between owners and managers had been durably restructured.

Since the 1980s, owners and financial analysts have closely monitored managers for their performance, defined almost exclusively in terms of shareholder value. Although there has been continued debate over the extent to which institutional stockholders exert pressure on firm managers, the latter have experienced increasing constraint from the investment community since the acquisition wave of the 1980s (Useem 1996). Analysts and ratings agencies have exerted similar pressures (Davis 2009). These groups have also worked to stigmatize the once prestigious practice of holding multiple directorships, which they view as impeding corporate oversight (Chu 2013). The pursuit of shareholder value also unleashed further rounds of acquisitions in the 1990s and beyond. The logic of shareholder value became so thoroughly institutionalized that managers themselves embraced it, despite its negative implications for their own status (Westphal and Zajac 1998; Khurana 2007). The significant increases in CEO pay during this time also facilitated managers' acceptance of the ideology.

Amid the ratcheting up of management oversight, average CEO tenure has declined sharply. Among sitting chief executives of Fortune firms, the mean number of years in office fell from 8.9 in 1981 to 6.2 in 2002, a decline of more than 30%. From 1960, the first year for which we have data, average CEO tenure was never this low, even during the 1970s, when many firms performed poorly.[10] Despite their increased compensation, corporate CEOs now face unprecedented pressures to focus on improving shareholder returns.

CEO turnover and acquisitions have direct negative consequences for the connectivity of the interlock network. The removal of a CEO typically results in the breaking of that executive's ties, since corporations prefer to have active (as opposed to retired) corporate officers as outsiders on their boards (Useem 1984). Even if some of the host firms invite the company's new CEO to join their board, the new member is unlikely to rebuild all of the firm's previous ties. Given the increased liability that outside directors face, as well as the concomitant devaluing of multiple board positions, the sheer number of ties is likely to continue to decline as individual CEOs are replaced or choose to retire. As CEO tenure declines, we should therefore expect to observe a further decline in network density. Although the samples of firm-years do not match exactly, we found a correlation of 0.92 between average CEO tenure and network density for 11 time points between 1962 and 2005.[11]

The removal of established companies via acquisition also contributed to the decline in density. There is a 'newness penalty' for a company's network degree, since it takes time to build corporate interlocks. For each panel in our dataset, the firms continuing from the previous panel have, on average, 3.4 more ties than entering firms. Acquisitions remove companies with more established connections and increase the number of new firms in the subsequent panel. The firms that fill these slots have typically spent less time at the top of the economy, and they are therefore generally less connected. In our dataset, acquired firms, on average, had 1.5 more connections than firms that entered the sample in the next panel. If we exclude the 1970s, when this difference reversed itself, the average difference is 2.6 ties. Although acquired firms are generally less connected than firms that are not acquired, they still provide more ties to the network than the firms that fill their vacancies. In this way, the waves of mergers and acquisitions since the 1980s have directly eroded the network.

7. THE DECLINE OF THE BANKS

From the formation of the American corporate interlock network in the late nineteenth century into the 1980s, the one continuous feature was the central position of financial institutions, especially commercial banks (Mizruchi 1982; Bunting 1983). From 1904 to 1982, financial institutions constituted well over half of the most central firms, despite constituting between 15 and 25% of the firms in the various datasets (Mizruchi 1982, 126; Mintz and Schwartz 1985, 157; Davis and Mizruchi 1999, 229). In our own data, commercial banks alone constituted approximately half of the ten most interlocked firms across seven panels from 1962 through 1990, while making up fewer than 20% of the firms in the sample (see Figure 2.1). The individual leading banks themselves exhibit a high level of stability. Four banks—First National City, Morgan, Chase Manhattan and Chemical—were among the ten most interlocked firms 89% of the time from 1962 to 1990. The quality of the bank interlocks was also impressive. Chase Manhattan's board, for example, included 14 Fortune 500 CEOs in 1982, and 43% of the largest 648 American firms were within a two-step reach of Chase (Davis and Mizruchi 1999, 218).

The central position of banks began to erode in the 1980s. Technological and regulatory changes led to a shift in the traditional bank business model. On the demand side, the increasing availability of low-cost information about borrowers reduced the informational advantages that banks had enjoyed. Eurobonds, commercial paper, and consumer lending by non-financial firms steadily reduced the market for lending by American commercial banks (Berger, Kashyap, and Scalise 1995, 64–65; Stearns and Mizruchi 1993, 290; Davis and Mizruchi 1999, 220; Krippner 2011, 35–36). On the supply side, the deregulation of interest rates in the 1980s increased the banks' cost toward their savers, which cut into the banks' profits (Berger, Kashyap, and Scalise 1995, 78–81).

Against the backdrop of mounting bank failures, shrinking shares of lending and financial assets, and dire claims about the demise of banking, the banks began to transform their commercial activities (Berger, Kashyap, and Scalise 1995, 67, 75, 82; James and Houston 1996, 8, 11; Davis and Mizruchi 1999, 221). Among their most important changes was a shift into fee-based activities such as currency swaps, derivatives, capital market services, securities underwriting and general financial advice, all of which had been the province of investment banks. Here again, innovation and deregulation contributed to the movement of banks away from their traditional business. The Glass-Steagall Act of 1933 had required the separation of commercial and investment banks.[12] As we moved into the 1980s, the banks slowly began to overcome this separation by developing new financial instruments and taking advantage of lax regulation. The commercial banks' increasing shift into investment-bank-like activities culminated with the passage of the Graham-Leach-Bliley Act of 1999, which officially revoked Glass-Steagall (Funk and Hirschman 2014). By that time, many of the leading commercial banks were using lending primarily as a means of attracting corporate customers for their more lucrative fee-based business (Mizruchi and Stearns 2001, 654).

The movement of commercial banks away from lending and toward the business model of investment banks had profound consequences for their position in the interlock network. As Davis and Mizruchi (1999) document, the network positions of the leading American banks declined sharply from 1982 to 1994 in terms of board size, interlocks and centrality. The banks that reduced their commercial and industrial lending were precisely those most likely to exhibit smaller board sizes and declining centrality over time. This suggests that the shift in the business activities of commercial banks is what accounted for the contraction of their networks (Davis and Mizruchi 1999, 232–234). With a reduced emphasis on lending, banks no longer sought the informational benefits of occupying central network positions. The networks of nonbanks also declined during this period, but at a considerably lower rate. The result was that for the first time, after a century of continuity and stability, the banks were no longer the most central firms in the network.

These changes also contributed to decline in the overall interlock network. With the departure of the banks from the center of the network, a vacuum emerged. In our dataset, network centralization fell 67% from 1982 to 1994 before stabilizing.[13] For every panel from 1962 to 1986, the most connected firm was a commercial bank, with a degree ranging from 39 to 53 ties. In the 1990s, non-financial firms rose to the top of the list, but the number of ties held by the most interlocked firm fell below 30 in 1999 and reached an all-time low of 16 ties in 2010 (shared by Marathon Oil and IBM), as shown in Figure 2.1. With the

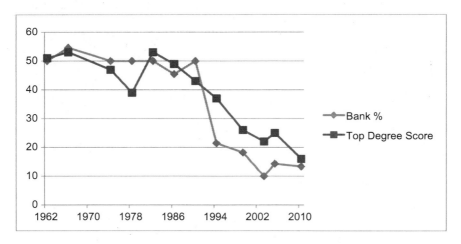

Figure 2.1 Features of Top Ten Interlockers, 1962–2010

restructuring of banks, non-financial firms took their place as the most central firms in the network, but these newcomers provided fewer connections. The virtual disappearance of individual super-connectors—no individual sat on more than four boards in 2010, whereas prior to 1999, fewer than five board seats would not have placed a director among the ten most interlocked individuals—greatly diminished the connectivity of the network (Chu 2013).[14] From 1990 to 2010, the average distance between any two firms in the main component rose 37%, while the density of the full network fell by 56%.

8. DISCUSSION

The American corporate network has entered an unprecedented phase in its history. After a tumultuous early period, the network had settled into a long duration of stability. Presidential administrations, economic cycles, wars, and industries came and went but the density and cohesiveness of the network fluctuated within a fairly narrow range for over half a century. The economic upheaval of the 1970s corresponded to a temporary dip in network connectivity, but it was the response of business to this crisis that pushed the network into a new trajectory of decline. The successful attack on government and unions had the unintended consequence of reducing the basis for future business cooperation and removing the old managerial justifications that had helped stabilize the corporate world. Without strong external challengers, managers withdrew from the corporate interlock network. Yet, without the equilibrating forces of a redistributive government and unions, managerial power could no longer be legitimated under the guise of professionals who balance the competing interests of owners, workers and communities. Owners and proponents of deregulation stepped into this void, challenging managerial prerogatives. This set off a wave of hostile takeovers in the 1980s and ultimately led to the institutionalization of shareholder value as the primary guiding principle of management. This, in turn, led to continued acquisitions, as well as increased scrutiny and constraint on managers. The result was not only a high level of instability in the interlock network, but a decline in connectivity, as well.

Deregulation and the rise of alternative financial instruments also led to a change in the traditional business models of commercial banks, while opening the door for them to move into other lines of business. Commercial banks chose to become more like investment banks, shifting their focus to fee-for-service activity, rather than traditional lending. As they did so, their boards also began to resemble those of investment banks, which led them to reduce their role as the meeting places for CEOs of Fortune 500 companies. This led to an unprecedented departure of banks from the center of the corporate network. The banks, in effect, abdicated their historic role as the meeting place for the leaders of major American firms. Again, the strategic actions of business had the inadvertent consequence of encouraging network decline.

The outcome of these processes has been an unraveling of the American corporate interlock network. Network decomposition began in the 1980s and has intensified over time. These changes are novel in both their extent and consistency.

Network decline has implications for both corporate behavior and business-society relations. Earlier analyses found that a well-connected network was an effective medium for diffusing strategic and political practices across corporations (Davis 1991; Mizruchi 1992). The decline of the network raises the question of whether the ties that exist continue to affect firm behavior in the ways that they did in earlier years. One recent study (Mizruchi, Stearns, and Marquis 2006) suggests that the effect of interlock ties on firm financial behavior declined between the early 1970s and the mid-1990s. As pressures from the financial community forced an increased conformity of behavior after the acquisition wave of the 1980s, firm decision making was less likely to diffuse through network connections. We are not suggesting that network ties no longer matter. There is continuing evidence that they do (see, for example, Mizruchi and Stearns 2001; Burris 2005; Dreiling and Darves 2011). Our findings do suggest the need to reexamine the extent to which firm practices diffuse through the network at all, or in a more heterogeneous fashion.[15]

The decline of the American corporate network is also both a cause and a consequence of changes in the relationship between corporations and society.[16] As we noted earlier, the vigorous actions by government and organized labor helped to create and promote a moderate and unified corporate elite, which, in turn, reinforced the strength of both unions and the state. The interlock network and the dominant position of financial institutions in this network also contributed to this dynamic. On one hand, the deterioration of the network undermined the existence of a moderate and unified elite. On the other hand, the fragmentation of the corporate elite may have reduced the incentives for corporate leaders to maintain a well-connected network.

The consequences of these changes are dramatic when we compare the positive contributions that American corporate leaders made to redressing major societal problems in the postwar period versus the absence of corporate leadership today. From roughly 1945 to the early 1970s, these leaders were vocal supporters of funding for education, expanded health care, and tax hikes to pay for wars and control deficits. In more recent years, there has been virtually no coordinated effort among business leaders to deal with an increasingly urgent set of issues confronting American society, including health care, education and the deficit. The reduced ability of directors to exchange ideas with one other and to adopt a broader perspective on the economy may be at least partly responsible for this loss of corporate leadership.

NOTES

1. We thank the conference organizers and participants, especially Thomas David and Mary O'Sullivan, for their excellent comments, and Jerry Davis and Johan Chu for providing the network data. Portions of this work were supported by the US National Science Foundation, grant SES-0922915.
2. Data on the directors were unavailable for 1962 and 1966.
3. The 1904 data consisted of only 166 firms. The data were originally collected by David Bunting and were supplemented by Mizruchi. See Mizruchi (1982, 33) for more details.
4. The Sherman Act was invoked in 1911 to break up Standard Oil, the jewel of John D. Rockefeller's empire, into a number of separate companies.
5. These figures are drawn from a sample of firms from all Fortune lists of the largest US firms from 1960 to 2007, sampling every five years. These lists expanded from 750 to 1,000 firms during this time period. Our data include both industrial and non-industrial firms and range from 183 to 595 firms per year.
6. In fairness to Davis, Yoo and Baker, at the time of their study, the trends that were evident a decade later were not as clear. It is therefore understandable that one could have interpreted the network as being highly stable.
7. See that work, especially chapters 6 and 7, for a more comprehensive list of sources.
8. This support did ebb on occasion, however. The wave of strikes following World War II created a public backlash against organized labor, which contributed to the Republicans taking control of both houses of Congress in the 1946 elections.
9. See, for example, the well-known 1971 letter by future Supreme Court Justice Lewis Powell, decrying opposition to the free-enterprise system and calling for a pro-business counteroffensive. The letter is available at http://reclaimdemocracy.org/powell_memo_lewis.
10. The unprecedented decline is even more noteworthy, considering the progressive removal of mandatory retirement policies and improvements in health. These two factors had curtailed CEO tenures to a considerable extent in the earlier time period.
11. Given the time-series nature of these data (albeit with at least four years between all data points), we tested for whether this coefficient is different from zero using an empirical generalized least squares model with the Prais-Winsten estimation technique. Despite only 11 observations, the T-statistic for our model was 6.51, $p < .001$.
12. Prior to Glass-Steagall, many commercial banks participated in securities underwriting, and many investment banks offered savings accounts.
13. We used the measure of centralization developed by Freeman (1979) and implemented in UCINET (Borgatti, Everett, and Freeman 2002).
14. The one exception to this was in 1978, when four board positions was the minimum among the top ten directors.
15. An alternative suggested by Chu is that elites may still form a cohesive network, but they have shifted their ties away from the public arena of corporate interlocks to more private forums like business associations or clubs (2013, 15). Additional research is necessary to investigate this possibility.
16. See Mizruchi (2013) for an extended discussion of this topic.

REFERENCES

Barnes, Roy C., and Emily R. Ritter. 2001. "Networks of Corporate Interlocking: 1962–1995." *Critical Sociology* 27: 192–220.

Barton, Allen H. 1985. "Determinants of Economic Attitudes in the American Business Elite." *American Journal of Sociology* 91: 54–87.

Berger, Allen N., Anil K. Kashyap, and Joseph M. Scalise. 1995. "The Transformation of the U.S. Banking Industry: What a Long, Strange Trip It's Been." *Brookings Papers on Economic Activity* 2: 55–201.

Borgatti, Stephen P., Martin G. Everett, and Lin C. Freeman. 2002. *Ucinet for Windows: Software for Social Network Analysis*. Harvard, MA: Analytic Technologies.

Bunting, David. 1983. "Origins of the American Corporate Network." *Social Science History* 7: 129–142.

Burris, Val. 2005. "Interlocking Directorates and Political Cohesion among Corporate Elites." *American Journal of Sociology* 111: 249–283.

Chandler, Alfred D., Jr. 1977. *The Visible Hand: The Managerial Revolution in American Business*. Cambridge: Harvard University Press.

Chu, Johan S. G. 2013. "Who Killed the Inner Circle? The Collapse of the American Corporate Interlock Network" (September 11). Accessed June 1, 2014. SSRN: http://ssrn.com/abstract=2061113 or http://dx.doi.org/10.2139/ssrn.2061113

Cochran, Thomas C., and William Miller. 1942. *The Age of Enterprise: A Social History of Industrial America*. New York: Macmillan.

Collins, Robert M. 1981. *The Business Response to Keynes, 1929–1964*. New York: Columbia University Press.

Davis, Gerald F. 1991. "Agents without Principles? The Spread of the Poison Pill through the Intercorporate Network." *Administrative Science Quarterly* 36: 583–613.

Davis, Gerald F. 2009. *Managed by the Markets: How Finance Re-Shaped America*. New York: Oxford University Press.

Davis, Gerald F., and Mark S. Mizruchi. 1999. "The Money Center Cannot Hold: Commercial Banks in the U.S. System of Corporate Governance." *Administrative Science Quarterly* 44: 215–239.

Davis, Gerald F., Mina Yoo, and Wayne E. Baker. 2003. "The Small World of the American Corporate Elite, 1982–2001." *Strategic Organization* 1: 301–326.

Dreiling, Michael, and Derek Darves. 2011. "Corporate Unity in American Trade Policy: A Network Analysis of Corporate-Dyad Political Action." *American Journal of Sociology* 116: 1514–1563.

Ferguson, Thomas, and Joel Rogers. 1986. *Right Turn: The Decline of the Democrats and the Future of American Politics*. New York: Hill and Wang.

Fligstein, Neil. 1990. *The Transformation of Corporate Control*. Cambridge: Harvard University Press.

Freeman, Linton C. 1979. "Centrality in Social Networks: Conceptual Clarification." *Social Networks* 1: 215–239.

Funk, Russell J., and Daniel Hirschman. 2014. "Derivatives and Deregulation: Financial Innovation and the Demise of Glass-Steagall." *Administrative Science Quarterly*. In press.

Galbraith, John Kenneth. 1952. *American Capitalism: The Concept of Countervailing Power*. Boston: Houghton Mifflin.

Harris, Howell John. 1982. *The Right to Manage: Industrial Relations Policies of American Business in the 1940s*. Madison: University of Wisconsin Press.

James, Christopher, and Joel Houston. 1996. "Evolution or Extinction? Where Are Banks Headed?" *Journal of Applied Corporate Finance* 9: 8–23.

Jensen, Michael C., and William H. Meckling. 1976. "Theory of the Firm: Managerial Behavior, Agency Costs and Ownership Structure." *Journal of Financial Economics* 3: 305–360.

Khurana, Rakesh. 2007. *From Higher Aims to Hired Hands: The Social Transformation of American Business Schools and the Unfulfilled Promise of Management as a Profession*. Princeton: Princeton University Press.

Krippner, Greta R. 2011. *Capitalizing on Crisis: The Political Origins of the Rise of Finance*. Cambridge: Harvard University Press.

Lipset, Seymour Martin, and William Schneider. 1983. *The Confidence Gap: Business, Labor, and Government in the Public Mind*. New York: Free Press.

Manne, Henry G. 1965. "Mergers and the Market for Corporate Control." *Journal of Political Economy* 73: 110–120.

Mintz, Beth, and Michael Schwartz. 1985. *The Power Structure of American Business*. Chicago: University of Chicago Press.

Mizruchi, Mark S. 1982. *The American Corporate Network, 1904–1974*. Beverly Hills: Sage.

Mizruchi, Mark S. 1992. *The Structure of Corporate Political Action: Interfirm Relations and their Consequences*. Cambridge: Harvard University Press.

Mizruchi, Mark S. 2013. *The Fracturing of the American Corporate Elite*. Cambridge: Harvard University Press.

Mizruchi, Mark S., and Linda Brewster Stearns. 2001. "Getting Deals Done: The Use of Social Networks in Bank Decision-Making." *American Sociological Review* 66: 647–671.

Mizruchi, Mark S., Linda Brewster Stearns, and Christopher Marquis. 2006. "The Conditional Nature of Embeddedness: A Study of Borrowing by Large U.S. Firms, 1973–1994." *American Sociological Review* 71: 310–333.

Roy, William G. 1983. "Interlocking Directorates and the Corporate Revolution." *Social Science History* 7: 143–164.

Shabecoff, Philip. 1978. "Auto Union Head Protests Role of Business, Quits Carter Panel." *New York Times*, July 20.

Simmel, Georg. 1955. *Conflict and the Web of Group Affiliations*. New York: Free Press.

Stearns, Linda Brewster, and Mark S. Mizruchi. 1993. "Corporate Financing: Social and Economic Determinants." In *Explorations in Economic Sociology*, edited by Richard Swedberg, 279–307. New York: Russell Sage Foundation.

Streeck, Wolfgang, and Lane Kenworthy. 2005. "Theories and Practices of Neocorporatism." In *The Handbook of Political Sociology*, edited by Thomas Janoski, Robert R. Alford, Alexander M. Hicks, and Mildred A. Schwartz, 441–460. New York: Cambridge University Press.

Useem, Michael. 1984. *The Inner Circle: Large Corporations and the Rise of Business Political Activity in the U.S. and U.K*. New York: Oxford University Press.

Useem, Michael. 1989. "Revolt of the Corporate Owners and the Demobilization of Business Political Action." *Critical Sociology* 16: 7–25.

Useem, Michael. 1996. *Investor Capitalism: How Money Managers are Changing the Face of Corporate America*. New York: Basic Books.

Vogel, David. 1989. *Fluctuating Fortunes: The Political Power of Business in America*. New York: Basic.

Westphal, James D., and Edward J. Zajac. 1998. "The Symbolic Management of Stockholders: Corporate Governance Reforms and Shareholder Reactions." *Administrative Science Quarterly* 43: 127–153.

Whitman, Marina V. N. 1999. *New World, New Rules: The Changing Role of the American Corporation*. Boston: Harvard Business School Press.

Windolf, Paul. 2009. "Coordination and Control in Corporate Networks: United States and Germany in Comparison, 1896–1938." *European Sociological Review* 25: 443–457.

3 The Structure of Networks
The Transformation of UK Business, 1904–2010

Gerhard Schnyder and John F. Wilson

1. INTRODUCTION

Over the course of the twentieth century, British business experienced some dramatic changes, especially among the largest firms that dominated both product and financial markets (Wilson 1995). While it is possible to discern distinct stages in this evolutionary process (Wilson and Thomson 2006), the most consistent feature was the divorce between control and ownership, often classified as the move from 'personal' to 'managerial' capitalism, a trend that Foreman-Peck and Hannah (2012) claim had already gathered extensive momentum by 1914. More recently, a further transformation has been observed and debated, indicating a move toward what has been called 'financial capitalism' (Tilba and Wilson 2012). These features of British business are reflected in the nature of ties that existed between British companies regarding shared members of the boards of directors (BoD). Indeed, intercompany networks created through interlocking directorates are an important aspect of a national business system and provide opportunities for collaboration among firms, thus potentially affecting companies' behaviors and strategies (Windolf 2002; Mizruchi 1996).

The relationship between financial and non-financial companies was—from its inception—a particularly important topic investigated by company network analysis (Brandeis 1914; Hilferding 1968 [1910]). In particular, many studies set out to investigate the 'bank hegemony thesis', which states that corporate networks are mainly used by banks to exercise control over other companies (Scott 1985). Given that one important feature of British capitalism over the last century concerns strong financial orientation, as measured by the contribution of the financial sector to total output, this chapter pays particular attention to the position of financial companies in the UK network. From a network perspective, a central position of banks in the interlocks network is usually considered as a necessary—but not sufficient—condition for bank hegemony (see Scott 1985).[1] Several previous studies have analyzed intercorporate networks in Britain, albeit usually over a limited period of time (cf. Windolf 2002; Conyon and Muldoon 2006; see Scott and Griff 1984). Regarding the role of the financial sector, previous studies of the UK network have found contradictory evidence. On the one hand, based on data for the mid-1970s, Scott (1987) has found evidence of an intimate relationship between financial and non-financial firms in Britain, with banks playing a pivotal role in these networks. He argued that financial institutions "were pivotal points in loose groupings of industrial, trading and financial enterprises . . . act[ing], in effect, as proxies for the wider financial community; they act as the guardians of the interests of the hegemonic financials". On the other hand, based on data for the early 1990s, Windolf (2002, 70) has rejected the 'bank hegemony' thesis for the UK, finding that while the UK banking sector receives many directors from other sectors, it does not send many to non-financial firms. Similarly, regarding the equity ownership network, Windolf (2002, 76) demonstrates intense interlocking between financial and non-financial firms, mainly because financial institutions (especially investment banks) have taken many equity positions in non-financial firms. However, he also shows that financial institutions do not appoint directors to the boards of the companies in which they hold stakes. Not only are the individual positions too small to warrant board representation, but also financial institutions have too many investments to send directors to each of these companies. This increases the autonomy of non-financial firms, especially toward their institutional shareholders, clearly contradicting the 'bank hegemony' thesis. Windolf concludes that the UK network—contrary to its German counterpart—is characterized neither by hierarchical power relations nor by relations of mutual control; rather, the British network in 1993 is diffuse and focused on—but not dominated by—the financial sector (Windolf 2002, 76).

Our longitudinal dataset allows us to show that Scott's and Windolf's contradictory findings may not be inconsistent, but rather reflect different phases of British capitalism. Indeed, based on a unique dataset, our study compares the network structure for nine benchmark years between 1904 and 2010, describing the changes in network topography using a series of measures of network connectivity and cohesiveness. This research demonstrates that while Scott's view on the central role of banks is supported for the period 1958 to 1983, the picture is quite different before and after this period. Thus, we find that bank centrality in the UK network did not emerge before World War II. Indeed, bank centrality was low for both pre-World War II years in our dataset (1904 and 1938), but had considerably increased by 1958. In addition, while the UK network was for several decades thereafter dominated by banks (see Scott and Griff 1984), in line with Windolf's (2002) findings, bank centrality has declined significantly since the 1980s. Indeed, the 1980s seem to mark a 'structural break' (Kogut 2012) in network evolution, in the sense that the traditional shape of the network changed fundamentally between the early 1980s and the early 1990s.

Using extensive research into British corporate networks and contextualizing this data within the historical literature, this chapter attempts to explain and interpret these changes. After looking in Section 2 at the data and methods employed to compile the database, Section 3 summarizes the network analysis results and evaluates the changes in network topography. This is followed in Section 4 by a contextual study that addresses how these changes reflect the broader transformation of British business since the early twentieth century, leading to some speculative and some clear conclusions that will stimulate more thought and research into this fascinating topic.

2. DATA AND METHOD

The dataset contains data on the composition of the boards of directors (BoD) of the 250 largest UK companies by net assets for nine benchmark years between 1904 and 2010 (1904, 1938, 1958, 1976, 1983, 1993, 1997, 2003 and 2010). The sample is composed of 50 financial firms and 200 non-financial firms, categorized according to the dominant sectoral activity of each firm. In order to compile this data, we relied partly on existing datasets,[2] as well as various archival sources, including stock exchange yearbooks, lists of largest companies provided by other scholars, commercial providers and annual reports. For certain years, it was not possible to locate sources that would have allowed us to compile a full sample of 250 firms. As a result, we only have 187 firms in 1958, 218 in 1983 and 247 in 2010. For 1993, we have 251 companies; for all other years, 250. By and large, however, the samples are of comparable size across our nine census dates.

As the aim of this chapter is to provide an overview of the general network trends in the UK since the early twentieth century, we use exploratory social network analysis (De Nooy, Mrvar, and Batagelj 2011) in order to describe and interpret general trends, rather than test any specific causal hypotheses. This analysis of network evolution will allow us to formulate in an inductive fashion some hypotheses that could be tested in future research. We have also used the Pajek software package in order to compute a series of indicators of network structure and coherence, as well as actor centrality measures. Overall, the analysis follows the methodology outlined in David and Westerhuis (2010).[3]

3. THE EVOLUTION OF THE BRITISH INTERLOCKING DIRECTORATES NETWORK

This section analyses and describes the transformation of the interlocking directorships network in light of more general transformations of British business. Indeed, while the chapter focuses on the changes in network structures, it also attempts to provide an original interpretation of the causality at work by drawing on the economic and business history literature.

General Measures of Network Topography

Density

The first general characteristic of a network is its overall 'density', i.e., how many ties there are. In this chapter, we use 'average degree'—namely, the average number of ties that each company in our sample has with other companies from the sample—because this measure is less sensitive than others to differences in sample size across different years (see Appendix I for details and definitions). This measure allows us to describe the evolution of the UK network in very general terms: in our first sample year (1904), the interlocks network was not yet very strongly integrated, as the average degree was low (2.5; i.e., each company had on average 2.5 ties with other companies among the top 250). However, a clear change took place over the next three decades because, by 1938, the network had become considerably denser, with each company having on average 4.7 ties. The density remained relatively stable over the next four decades, fluctuating between an average degree of 4.0 and 4.4. By 1983, however, a new phase would appear to have materialized, in that network density had dropped to 3.4, remaining at this relatively lower level over the next three decades, with the average degree oscillating around 3.5 (i.e., substantially lower than during the post-war period up to the economic crisis of the 1970s). The exception in our dataset is 1997, for which year we obtain a degree above 4.3. It should be noted, however, that in international comparison terms, this remains a very low density level; even in comparison to other Anglo-Saxon economies, such as the US (see Windolf and Schifeling and Mizruchi this volume).

Distance

A second characteristic of the network is how 'far' or 'close' companies are from each other. Indeed, social networks are often interpreted as a 'social infrastructure' that allows information, practices, ideas or social values to be transferred from one network node (in this case, firms or directors) to the other (Davis 1991). The speed with which such a 'transfer' or 'diffusion' happens depends precisely on the 'distance' between firms (see Appendix I for a technical definition of our distance measure). This distance measure provides us with a notion of 'connectivity' across the network: namely, how close different nodes are to each other and, hence, how well connected the network is overall. Starting with 1904, our data reveals an average distance across the network of 10.2, indicating that network ties were sparse. From 1904 to 1938, there was a sharp fall in distance, reaching 3.4, demonstrating that network ties were increasing. Over the period up to 1976, distance remained stable, with values of between 3.1 and 3.5. In other words, during that period, two firms—or rather their boards—were, on average, separated by roughly two intermediaries. Since then, however, average distance has increased to between 3.5

and 4.0 for the three dates in the 1980s and 1990s. The two dates in the twenty-first century indicate a further increase to an average distance of between 4.0 and 4.4. This means that by the 2000s, two firms were, on average, separated by three intermediaries. This increase in the number of intermediaries can be interpreted as seriously affecting the diffusion of ideas and information through the network of British boards. Indeed, any type of 'exchange' through network ties (e.g., of ideas or information) would now have to pass through an additional intermediary, increasing the likelihood of disruption or distortion and making the exchange generally less direct and slower.

Overall, the average degree and average distance figures provide some evidence of a periodization of the evolution of the British network. It is clear that between 1904 and 1938, the network became not just denser, but also much more cohesive, as indicated by the dramatic drop in average distance from 10.2 to 3.4. The figures for the period 1938–1976 are consistent with a phase of relative stability in the network. From then on, however, the network's density and cohesiveness have declined. Based on average distance, we might distinguish the 1980s and 1990s from the 2000s, but overall, the figures indicate a gradual relative 'erosion' of the network since the 1970s.

Network Centralization

A further measure of network topography concerns its 'centralization', a complementary concept to network density. As Scott (2000, 89) puts it: "Density describes the general level of cohesion in a graph; centralization describes the extent to which this cohesion is organized around particular focal points" (we use the definition of centralization specified in Appendix I). Using two different measures of point centrality—'closeness centrality' and 'betweenness' centrality—we find that the network reached its maximal cohesion at different points, depending on which measure we use. In terms of 'closeness', the network was most centralized in 1938, which implies that the most central company was very 'close' to all other companies in the graph (the 'closeness' score for that year was 27.5%, a marked increase on the 1904 figure of 16.7%.) From that point on, our data shows a steady decline in 'closeness' centralization, indicating that the network became much more dispersed. The average 'closeness' score was 20.8% (standard deviation 4.21), with the minimum score of 13.7% reached in 2010.

Looking at the 'betweenness centralization', on the other hand, we find a different narrative. The network reached its highest level of centralization in 1983 (with a 'betweenness' score of 13.5%), indicating that at the time, the most central company possessed most 'brokerage power'. In this respect, it is vital to note that 'betweenness' measures to what extent a given point lies on the path between any pair of nodes in the network; 'betweenness centrality' measures essentially on how many paths between all pairs of nodes a given node lies. Substantively, this can be interpreted as conveying a certain 'brokerage power' to a node with high betweenness centrality, as the position on the path implies a certain control over exchanges between the two connected nodes. However, over the whole period, there is less clearly a pattern of either integration or disintegration of the network based on this measure of centralization. Indeed, the 'betweenness centralization' measure fluctuates markedly around the mean of 7.4% (the standard deviation is 3.0), but does not seem to indicate a clear trend. Besides the two peaks in 1938 (10.8%) and 1983 (13.5%), the 'betweenness centralization' is between 4.6% and 7.6%. The lowest scores were reached in 1904 (4.7%) and 2010 (4.6%).

These centralization measures indicate that the network integrated extensively between 1904 and 1938, but became much sparser over time, leading to an increased distance between reachable pairs and, hence, a less central position for the most networked firms. Yet, in terms of the network's structural properties regarding 'exchanges' or 'flows' along network lines, the role of the most central corporations does not seem to have declined systematically (as indicated by the 'betweenness score'). Arguably, this may be due to the fact that the UK corporate network has always been rather decentralized and diffuse (Windolf 2002), implying that the network structure would not allow any single company to control most of the 'flows' in the network. As a result, the decline in connectivity has affected the 'betweenness centralization' of the network to a lesser extent than the closeness.

Areas of Density: m-slices

The measures discussed so far describe in general terms the evolution of the network's overall structure since 1904. The next step in this analysis is to look into areas of particularly high density and/or cohesiveness. Such areas may reveal groups of companies that entertain particularly close relationships, which can help in developing a substantive interpretation of network ties. One way to identify particularly dense areas in the network is to look at so-called m-slices, which are groups of nodes (companies) that are linked together by lines of strength two or above (De Nooy et al. 2011; see Appendix I). In other words, they are groups of companies that share (directly or indirectly) two or more directors. The number of 2m-slices was highest in 1938, when 21 different 2m-slices can be identified. This number decreased over the next decades, reaching a minimum of nine in 1993, but increased again to reach fifteen in 2010. The recent increase in 2m-cores is somewhat counter-intuitive because the earlier reported measure of general network cohesion indicated a decline in the density and cohesiveness of the network during the 1990s and 2000s.

A second step is to look more closely at the largest 2m-core for each year. This measure reveals a trend that is comparable to the number of 2m-slices: an absolute maximum was reached in 1938, when the largest 2m-slice comprised 64 firms; i.e., more than a quarter of the sample firms were part of this group of strongly connected firms. As we shall see later, this reflects the nature of British corporate capitalism at that time, with a high level of cartelization featuring prominently in many sectors. However, the size of the largest 2m-slice declined steadily over the following decades because by 1997, the largest 2m-slice was a simple dyad. At the same time, the number increased once again since then to four in 2000 and fourteen in 2010. The most central firms in the largest 2m-slice in 2010 were Standard Chartered (four strong ties), a universal bank, and Astrazeneca (three), a bi-national chemical-pharmaceutical company that resulted from the merger of the Swedish Astra AB and the British Zeneca Group PLC.

Figure 3.1 compares the proportion of firms that are part of a 2m-slice with the proportion of firms that are part of the network; namely, those firms that have at least one tie. In other words, the figure compares the strong ties with simple ties—an exercise that yields some interesting results. As mentioned earlier, the number of firms in groupings linked together with strong ties has declined continuously since 1938 until 2000. On the other hand, the number of firms integrated in the network through simple ties has steadily—albeit, moderately—increased over the same period of time. Thus, the proportion of firms that were part of the network increased from 69.20% in 1904 to 91.91% in 2010. The distinction between simple ties and strong ties is important because it implies a substantive difference in the type of relationships between companies. De Nooy et al. (2011) suggest that multiple ties are less personal and more institutionalized than simple ones. They are hence indicators of a different type of relationships. In our case, the increasingly encompassing nature of the network indicates that we are not faced with a simple erosion of the network; rather, we are faced with the

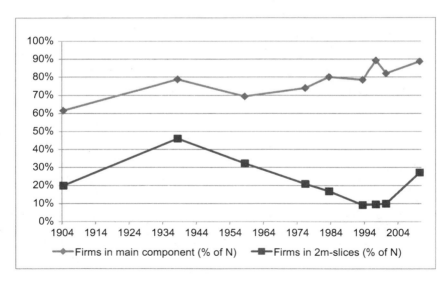

Figure 3.1 Network 'Depth' vs. Network 'Width'

emergence of a form of capitalism that is based on more diffuse and weaker, but nevertheless extensive, linkages across the business elite. In other words, paraphrasing the famous formulation by Karl Marx, one could say that the 'band of brothers' still exists, but has become somewhat more 'hostile', or at least distant.

Directors and Seats Distribution

So far, we have exclusively focused on characteristics of a network featuring links between companies. However, given that the company network is a two-mode network, where we have both companies and individuals, we can also look at the second mode featuring directors that actually constitute the network ties. In other words, we now turn to analyzing a network where individual directors constitute the nodes, and ties exist between directors who sit on the same board(s).

The proportion of directors that were 'big linkers'—i.e., individuals with three or more board seats—is a simple measure that allows us to explore the question of the depth and width of the network. In the literature, such individuals are expected to be particularly powerful and esteemed, representing the interests not only of a given company, but of the business elite as a whole (Nollert 2005).

It appears that between 1904 and 1938, the proportion of big linkers increased, indicating that the network was well integrated. Indeed, by 1938, one in three interlockers was a 'big linker',[4] sitting on the board of three or more companies, constituting the highest value throughout the century. This ratio remained at a very high level over the next four decades, with roughly one out of three interlockers being a 'big linker'. As with the other metrics of network integration used earlier, this measure dropped considerably during the 1980s and 1990s, when only one in four interlockers held more than two seats. The two data points in the 2000s hint at a further decline, with less than one in five interlockers being a 'big linker'.

The evolution of the proportion of simple interlockers, 'big linkers' and 'very big linkers'[5] shows some interesting features. We observe a relative stability in the proportion of all three categories of interlockers between 1958 and 1976, following which there was a slight decline in the proportion of 'big linkers' and a significant decline in the proportion of 'very big linkers' between 1976 and 1983. The proportion of simple interlockers, on the other hand, increased over the period 1983–2010 (from 7.2% to 10.4% in 2000 and 19.9% in 2010). The number of 'very big linkers' declined throughout the period 1983–2010, to reach extremely low absolute numbers: by 2000, only one 'very big linker' can be identified, while by 2010, there was no individual with five or more seats. The number of 'big linkers' seems rather stable until 2000, but increased over the next decade, reaching 4.4% (up from 2.4% 10 years earlier).

Overall, the distribution of seats confirms that the UK company network has not only become less centralized around particular individuals, but also is much more diffuse. It does not follow, however, that the network is disintegrating, in that the number of interlockers remains relatively stable. Nevertheless, we can conclude that the nature of the network has changed, as 'big linkers' and 'very big linkers' have become relatively less common. To illustrate this further, if we look at the absolute number of 'very big linkers', we find that while there were eighteen individuals with five or more seats on the boards of our 250 companies in 1938, when the network reached its peak, by 1958, there were eight, and in 1976, eleven. This group of people holding between five and seven seats certainly constitutes potentially the core of a cohesive business elite, but given their paltry numbers, it is clear that the core was extremely small.

Overall, the findings presented in this section hint at a change in the nature of the network, away from one in which companies had relatively strong links toward a more diffuse structure in which more interlockers have a limited number of positions. Our findings lend support to theories of interlocking directorates that see such links as a means of promoting 'class cohesion' among the business elite (Scott 1985). On the other hand, they do not support theories that see interlocks mainly as an instrument of particular firms to control others, or of different firms creating closely linked business groups, as in the case of the German *Konzern* (Windolf 2002). Indeed, at least since the 1980s, the ties are too sparse and weak to allow us to conclude that they may serve a 'control' purpose, an issue we can now turn to assess in greater detail by looking specifically at the role of financial companies.

Banks and the Network

Different scholars see interlocks between banks and industrial companies as instruments that banks use to extract rents from non-financial firms (Fitch and Oppenheimer 1970). While such a radical interpretation of bank-industry ties may be exaggerated, it seems undeniable that banks have played a pivotal role in the intercompany networks of many advanced capitalist countries (cf. for the US, Davis and Mizruchi 1999; for Germany, Höpner and Krempel 2004; for the UK, Scott and Griff 1984; for Switzerland, Schnyder et al. 2005). One indicator of bank dominance is the relative propensity of banks to interlock. In order to measure this propensity, we have calculated the cumulated degree of the top 10 most central companies[6] for each year, dividing the cumulated degree of financial sector companies in this ranking by the total figure (see Figure 3.2). The results demonstrate that there was a phase in British capitalism when banks were by far the most pivotal 'players' in the interlocking network. Indeed, between roughly 1958 and 1983, a large majority of the most central companies were from the financial sector, accounting for between 74% and 84% of the ties of the top 10 most central companies. This

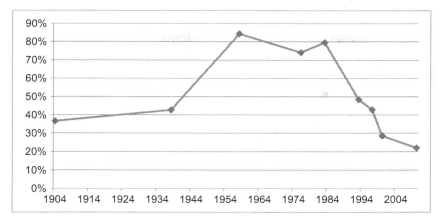

Figure 3.2 Cumulated Degree of Financial Sector Firms among 10 Most Central Companies (% of Total)

'dominance',[7] however, declined rapidly after the 1980s because by 1993, banks and insurance companies accounted for only 48% of the ties created by the 10 most central companies. This decline can help to explain in part the different conclusions that Scott (1985) and Windolf (2002) reach, given that they studied different periods. The proportion also continued to decline over the next two decades, reaching 22% in 2010, which is markedly lower than even at the beginning of the twentieth century.

Looking beyond the top 10 ranking, we find that among the cumulated number of ties created by the firms of a given sector, the financial industry does not have a particular propensity to interlock. While banks dominate the ranking of the most central firms during most years in the sample, if we divide the degree of the financial sector by the number of companies in this sector, the financial sector's propensity to interlock is actually the lowest across all sectors. Thus, each financial company creates on average across all years only .38 ties, a proportion that remains stable over time (with a minimum of .24 in 1904 and a maximum of .45 in 1976 and 2010). This compares to average degrees by other sectors of 1.68 in the metal industry, 1.01 among railroads, 1.29 among chemicals companies, 1.82 in mining, .75 in machinery, .80 in retail, .93 in construction and 1.64 in textiles. At the same time, one should stress that the difference between the centrality ranking of the most central firms and the average degree of individual sectors shows that while the financial industry as a whole does not show any particularly strong propensity to interlock, individual companies from this sector do. This implies that a handful of financial sector companies are very central to the network, while there is also a large number of financial sector companies that interlock only very little or not at all.

To conclude this section, our results show that the strong network integration between 1904 and 1938 observed earlier was not the result of an increasing propensity to interlock by banks. Indeed, the banks' relative centrality remained rather low in 1938 and banks started to dominate the ranking only in our first post-war benchmark year (1958). We can conclude that the phase of integration between 1904 and 1938 was due to increasing interlocking among non-financial firms, rather than between financial and non-financial firms, while 'bank-centeredness' only emerged after World War II when the increasing centrality of banks was presumably also helped by an increasing focus on anti-trust laws that made interlocking among non-financial firms from the same sector increasingly problematic.

Intra- and Inter-Sectoral Ties

The analysis of inter- and intra-sectoral ties creates an opportunity to shed further light on the question of financial sector centrality. First, we classified different sectors using two-digit US Standard Industrial Classification (SIC) codes, but combining several SIC codes into one group where this seemed justified.[8] We then calculated intra- and inter-sector standardized network density scores for each year using the calculations suggested by Windolf (2002), providing a measure of the number of ties compared to the number of companies in each of the sectors concerned.

Generally speaking, the sectoral analysis reveals that the network integration between 1904 and 1938 was in no small measure due to an increasing number of interlocks within similar sectors, rather than a result of an increase in interlocks between sectors. This hints at a tendency during this period for companies to coordinate activities within sectors, which came close to cartelization arrangements. However, after 1938, intra-sectoral interlocking declined in important ways, reaching a low point in 1976 when the average intra-sectoral density score was just 5.5 (compared to 39.4 in 1958 and 75.9 in 1938). Over the next 30 years, as Figure 3.3 illustrates, the score increased again, albeit at a very low level compared to the pre-World War II period (to 5.3 in 1983, 7.9 in 1993, 10.9 in 2000 and 17.5 in 2010).

At the same time, one should stress that the inter-sector densities—the frequency of interlocking across sectors—increased over the whole period, indicating a trend away from cartelistic, competition-restraining networks toward a network whose main purpose, or at least function, seems more to have been one of coordination across sectors rather than within them. The steep decline in intra-sectoral interlocking might certainly at least partly be explained by the adoption after World War II of the first modern competition law. On the other hand, the recent increase in intra-sector interlocking is surprising, given the anti-trust law reforms of the late-1990s and early-2000s. As we shall see in the next section, this could well have been attributable to changes in board composition, as opposed to having any link with anti-trust laws.

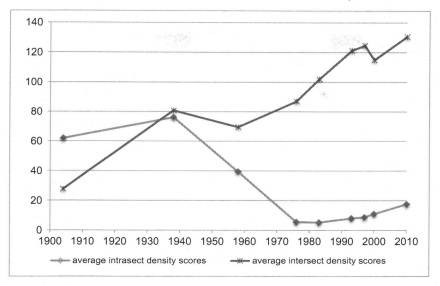

Figure 3.3 Difference between Density Coefficients within and between Sectors
Note: Coefficients defined following Windolf 2002

If we look at the number of sectors where the intra-sector density scores were larger than the inter-sector ones, we find that between 1904 and 1958, intra-sector interlocking (a sign of cartelization) was common, with between 65% and 80% of the intra-sectoral scores being larger than inter-sectoral ones. However, by 1976, the proportion had plummeted to 31%, a level at which it remained over the next three decades: 25% in 1983, 30% in 1993, 27% in 1997 and 34% in 2000, with a slight increase to 42% in 2010.

Finally, if we look at the intra-sector interlocking among financial services firms, we find a similar trend toward more interlocking between 1904 and 1958 (from 21.6% intra-sectoral density in 1904 to 33.8% in 1938 and 38.1% in 1958), with a steep decline thereafter until 2000 (33.6% in 1976, 31.5% in 1983, 11.4% in 1993 and 11.6% in 1997). Between 2000 and 2010, the trend has reverted for the first time since 1958, as we can observe a slight increase in intra-sector interlocks in the financial industry (from 10.4% to 12.1%), a trend that could well be due to an increase in interbank collaboration in the wake of the financial crisis of 2007–2008.

4. DISCUSSION

Our data shows that the UK network has changed in nature several times during the period under analysis. The first phase was one of network integration, starting from a very sparse network in 1904. By 1938, according to most measures, the network had reached its apogee. The lack of more data points during the first half of the twentieth century make it impossible to tell when exactly network integration peaked, but it appears that the UK network emerged during the first three decades of the twentieth century. Interestingly, and contrary to other countries (Schnyder et al. 2005), this first phase of integration was not due to an increasingly central position of banks, but rather to intra-sectoral interlocking, hinting at practices of coordination or even cartelization within different industries. Indeed, the period from 1930 to 1960 can be described as the high-water mark of British cartel activity, with trade associations having established a series of oligopolistic controls over almost all markets, especially during the 1930s when protectionist measures were adopted and domestic markets became the exclusive preserve of British firms. This situation prevailed until the late-1950s, contradicting claims that the UK was dominated by liberal trade laws (Wilson 1995, 155–157). While an anti-trust law was enacted in 1948, this was ineffective and required significant reform in the mid-1950s, while an increasingly free-trade stance was taken by the 1960s, significantly undermining the power trade associations had exerted over the previous three decades.

The post-war years (1958, 1976 and 1983) reveal relative stability in the network, while, in UK terms, achieving a high level of integration. It was also during this period that we observe a high level of centrality of banks in the British company network. At the same time as bank centrality increased, however, intra-sectoral interlocking declined strongly, in particular in non-financial sectors. Indeed, intra-sectoral ties have been continuously eroded since the 1950s, while inter-sectoral ones have increased in number. The pre-World War II intra-sectoral network was hence replaced by a post-war bank-centered network that lasted roughly from 1958 to 1983, coinciding thus quite closely to the Fordist period. In part at least, the growing centrality of banks reflected the increasing divorce between control and ownership across large-scale British business, providing an opportunity for financial institutions to offer their services to boards of directors (Wilson 1995, 192–193). At the same time, it is important to stress that between the 1940s and early-1980s, British banks were much more interested in domestic markets, given the limitations imposed on international financial activity during that era (Larson et al. 2011). Either side of the period 1958 to 1982, banks were not particularly central to the network, indicating that 'bank dominance' (or, at least, 'bank centrality') was a temporally limited historical configuration in Britain, rather than the universal phenomenon claimed by Scott and Griff (1984). Indeed, our data clearly show that Scott's observations about banks being the lynchpins of the UK network is certainly not applicable to the period spanning the first decades of the twentieth century (1900 to late 1930s) and the last decades of the century (1990s—2000s). The era of 'finance capitalism' had coincided in Britain with the retreat of banks from inter-corporate networks. By the 2000s, the most central companies were no longer banks but retailers and infrastructure companies, changing markedly the nature of British corporate networks.

Of course, the phenomenon of declining bank centrality is well documented for a series of OECD countries, but it seems particularly significant in the UK, given its substantial financial sector. While it goes beyond the scope of this chapter to explain these trends, drawing on findings from other countries (Davis and Mizruchi 1999), it seems plausible that the change in banking strategies away from traditional lending toward financial-market based activities, as well as the non-financial companies' increasing use of financial markets rather than bank loans for corporate finance, has contributed to this trend (Larson et al. 2011). At the same time, just as with US and German banks (Davis and Mizruchi 1999, Höpner and Krempel 2004), major UK banks have experienced dramatic strategic changes over the last decades, an issue that requires much further research in explaining network structures.

Having noted this 'retreat' of banks in the 1980s, it is equally important to stress that this did not lead to any diminution in the extent of the network. Specifically, we find a marked decline in multiple ties among firms—i.e., the network's depth—in that fewer firms were connected through two or more shared directors in the 1990s and 2000s than was the case in earlier years. On the other hand, the size of the network's 'main component' (the largest sub-group of firms sharing at least one director with at least one other company) has increased through the period under analysis. This implies that while ties among firms are less strong, more firms are potentially able to 'reach' each other through network ties, indicating that the network's 'width' has increased. Simple ties—as opposed to multiple ones—have been interpreted as a tool for coordination and communication among firms, rather than being a control tool (Carroll and Fennema 2002). This trend could be interpreted as a move away from a form of capitalism that is based on strong personal ties among members of the business elite (as expressed in strong ties between companies) to a form of capitalism where the business elite is still connected, but ties have become looser and less personal.

In parallel to the weakening of ties, a second important phenomenon that becomes clear from our data relates to the changing distribution of mandates among the directors in our dataset. While we observed a marked decline in the number of 'very big linkers' over the last three decades, this is partly compensated by an increasing number of directors sitting on two or three boards. In other words, over the years, more directors have become interlockers, but fewer hold large numbers of seats. This hints at a broader cause of the changing network structure that goes beyond banking strategies, in that the contrasting evolution of 'width' and 'depth' of the network can be better explained by linking this with the professionalization of the work of boards of directors and claims of greater shareholder activism in relation to the corporate governance movement that considers interlocks as a source of conflict of interests and collusion.[9]

Somewhat paradoxically, however, the corporate governance movement could also have favored the increase in the number of individuals with two or three seats. In this respect, the 1992 Cadbury Report encouraged boards to appoint a certain proportion of independent outside directors to their boards (non-executive directors, or NEDs). By their very nature, NEDs are prone to sit on more than one board, creating—somewhat paradoxically, given the shareholder movement's aversion to interlocks—more interlocks between firms (see Ferraro et al. 2012). This can help to explain why overall interlocks have increased in recent years, as companies are striving to appoint outsiders as NEDs. Similarly, the disappearance of 'very big linkers' could be a result of the corporate governance movement and the related professionalization of boards, a process that imposed such an onerous time commitment on directors that it has become impossible for people to accept a large number of seats (Wilson and Thomson 2006).

5. CONCLUSION

Taken together, our findings hint at different changes in the nature of British capitalism during the twentieth century. First, we can identify the emergence of a phase of a more coordinated form of capitalism between 1904 and 1938, during which period ties across companies from the same sector were relatively strong. Second, this was followed after World War II by a phase of stability and bank centrality. Third, more recently, we can detect a decline in strong ties, reflecting the emergence of a more strongly market- and competition-based type of capitalism in Britain, where strong linkages between firms no longer have a role to play, largely probably because of the tighter anti-trust laws. This is supported by the continuous decline in intra-sector interlocking. The recent changes have further reinforced a central characteristic of the UK network: namely, that its structure is relatively diffuse with few areas where strong control exists. This distinguishes the UK network from other countries such as Germany, where the interlock network reflects the existence of certain business groups (the combine, or *Konzern*) and particularly strong levels of connectivity (Windolf 2002). Arguably, in the UK, there were some—albeit comparatively few—such areas during the twentieth century, but they have recently been considerably weakened by both anti-trust laws and intense foreign competition in a liberal market. This implies that—at least, in this respect—the UK has become even more characteristic of the Anglo-Saxon brand of capitalism, where relationships between firms are based on competition, rather than coordination and control (Windolf 2002; Hall and Soskice 2001). Yet, it should also be noted that the increasing width of the network provides an interesting caveat to the story of network decline, in that there remains a more coordinated form of capitalism. Of course, theoretically, these interlock ties could still provide potential for closer coordination across firms, or at least perform a more diffuse 'class cohesion' function. This function contrasts with more strongly integrated networks that would rather hint at a control function. To be sure, while an international comparison of the level of 'coordinative capacity' of the British network may seem limited, our data demonstrates that the 'social infrastructure' of coordination through network ties was still in place in 2012. Further research is needed in order to confirm our interpretations of the dynamics that our exploratory analysis has revealed. In particular, a more detailed analysis of the relations between sectors and of strategic changes in the banking sector will help improve our understanding of the changes we have observed. Further research is also needed into the marked decline of the 'very big linkers' at the same time that the number of 'simple' interlockers increased. In particular, the link between these trends and the shareholder movement of the 1980s and 1990s requires further investigation.

NOTES

1. Necessary because board representation is seen as a crucial instrument to exercise control over firm-level decision-making. Not sufficient because centrality can be a sign of large numbers of outgoing ties (the bank sending directors to other companies) or large numbers of incoming ties (the bank boards are populated with non-financial firms' directors). The latter situation is rather a case of bank weakness than bank control.
2. We are grateful to Martin Conyon for providing us his dataset for 1997 and 2000, to Gerarda Westerhuis for the data from the Stokman project for 1976 and to John Scott and Paul Windolf for the 1904 and 1938 data. Philip Kern provided invaluable research assistance, not only collecting the data, but also transforming, completing and 'cleaning up' the sets. A detailed documentation of data sources used is available at http://www.cgeh.nl/power-corporate-networks-comparative-and-historical-perspective.
3. A full description of these methodologies is provided on the website that accompanies the book.
4. On average, there are 2,249 directors per year in our database, 287 or 12.8% of which are interlockers (holding two or more board seats).
5. Following the usual conventions, we designate as 'big linkers' individuals with three or more mandates among the sample companies. 'Very big linkers' are individuals with five or more seats.
6. Given that several companies can have the same degree, the ranking contains actually more than 10 firms for most years. For 2010, it only contains 9 because a large number of firms would have held joint 10th place (with a degree of 9). We, therefore, decide to limit the ranking to the top 9.
7. Again, it should be noted that 'dominance' refers in this context purely to the dominance in the table of most central firms. At this stage, our data does not allow us to distinguish between the banks in-degree and out-degree (i.e., the number of ties that are due to receiving directors versus the number of ties created by sending bankers to the boards of other companies).
8. For example, we combined SIC 13 and 29 into one broader category called 'oil/gas extraction and refining' because these sectors were mainly dominated by large vertically integrated firms. Details of our classification can be found on the project web page, http://www.cgeh.nl/power-corporate-networks-comparative-and-historical-perspective.
9. See Tilba (2011) for insights into the UK corporate governance movement.

REFERENCES

Brandeis, Louis D. 1914. *Other People's Money: And how the Bankers Use It.* New York: F.A. Stokes.

Carroll, William K., and Meindert Fennema 2002. "Is There a Transnational Business Community?" *International Sociology* 17: 393–419.

Conyon, Martin J., and Mark R. Muldoon 2006. "The Small World of Corporate Boards." *Journal of Business Finance & Accounting* 33: 1321–1343.

David, Thomas, and Gerarda Westerhuis. 2010. "Corporate Networks in the 20th Century: Structural Changes and Comparisons. White Paper." Unpublished manuscript.

Davis, Gerald F. 1991. "Agents without Principles? The Spread of the Poison Pill through the Intercorporate Network." *Administrative Science Quarterly* 36: 583–613.

Davis, Gerald F., and Mark S. Mizruchi. 1999. "The Money Center Cannot Hold: Commercial Banks in the U.S. System of Corporate Governance." *Administrative Science Quarterly* 44: 215–239.

De Nooy, Wouter, Andrej Mrvar, and Vladimir Batagelj. 2011. *Exploratory Social Network Analysis with Pajek.* 2nd ed. Cambridge: Cambridge University Press.

Ferraro, Fabrizio, Gerhard Schnyder, Eelke Heemskerk, Raffaele Corrado, and Nathalie Del Vecchio. 2012. "Structural Breaks and Governance Networks in Western Europe." In *The Small Worlds of Corporate Governance,* edited by Bruce Kogut, 151–182. Cambridge, MA: MIT Press.

Fitch, Robert, and Mary Oppenheimer. 1970. "Who Rules the Corporations?" *Socialist Revolution* 1 (Jul.-Aug.): 73–103.

Foreman-Peck, James, and Leslie Hannah. 2012. "Some Consequences of the Early Twentieth Century Divorce of Ownership and Control." CIRJE Discussion Paper.

Hall, Peter A., and David W. Soskice. 2001. *Varieties of Capitalism: The Institutional Foundations of Comparative Advantage.* Oxford, New York: Oxford University Press.

Hilferding, Rudolf. 1968 [1910]. *Das Finanzkapital. Eine Studie über die jüngste Entwicklung des Kapitalismus.* Frankfurt am Main: Europäische Verlagsanstalt.

Höpner, Martin, and Lothar Krempel. 2004. "The Politics of the German Company Network." *Competition & Change* 8: 339–356.

Kogut, Bruce. 2012. "The Small World of Corporate Governance: An Introduction." In *The Small Worlds of Corporate Governance,* edited by Bruce Kogut, 1–51. Cambridge, MA: MIT Press.

Larson, Mitchell J., Gerhard Schnyder, Gerarda Westerhuis, and John Wilson. 2011. "Strategic Responses to Global Challenges: The Case of European Banking, 1973–2000." *Business History* 53: 40–62.

Mizruchi, Mark S. 1996. "What Do Interlocks Do? An Analysis, Critique, and Assessment of Research on Interlocking Directorates." *Annual Review of Sociology* 22: 271–298.

Nollert, Michael. 2005. *Unternehmensverflechtungen in Westeuropa. Nationale und transnationale Netzwerke von Unternehmen, Aufsichtsräten und Managern.* Münster: Lit Verlag.

Schnyder, Gerhard, Martin Lüpold, Thomas David, and André Mach. 2005. "The Rise and Decline of the Swiss Company Network during the 20th Century." *Travaux de Science Politique* No. 22. Lausanne: IEPI University of Lausanne.

Scott, John. 1985. "Theoretical Framework and Research Design." In *Networks of Corporate Power. A Comparative Analysis of Ten Countries,* edited by Frans. N. Stokman, Rolf Ziegler, and John Scott, 1–19. Cambridge: Polity Press.

Scott, John. 1987. "Inter-Corporate Structure in Britain, the United States and Japan." *Shoken Keizai* 160: 51–64.

Scott, John. 2000. *Social Network Analysis. A Handbook.* London: Sage Publications.
Scott, John, and Catherine Griff. 1984. *The Directors of Industry. The British Corporate Network, 1904–76.* Cambridge and New York: Polity Press.
Tilba, Anna. 2011. "Pension Funds Investment Practice and Corporate Engagement." PhD dissertation, University of Liverpool.
Tilba, Anna, and John F. Wilson. 2012. "Corporate Ownership in the Era of Financial Capitalism: Accounts of Accountability within the Pension Fund Investment Chain." Paper presented at the IFSAM Conference, Limerick, IRL, June 26–29.
Wilson, John F. 1995. *British Business History, 1720–1994.* Manchester: Manchester University Press.
Wilson, John F., and Andrew Thomson. 2006. *The Making of Modern Management. British Management in Historical Perspective.* Oxford: Oxford University Press.
Windolf, Paul. 2002. *Corporate Networks in Europe and the United States.* Oxford: Oxford University Press.

4. The Corporate Network in Germany, 1896–2010

Paul Windolf

1. THE GERMAN PRODUCTION REGIME

The comparative analysis of economic institutions has been a long tradition in the social sciences. Schmoller (1906) compared the market structures in Germany and the US. He pointed out that the market structure in the US was shaped by an anarchic competition, while the market order in Germany was 'regulated' because of the cartelization of the German industry. Chandler (1990) emphasized the importance of economic institutions for the success of the large corporation. He presents Germany as an example of 'cooperative capitalism', while the US is the prototype of 'competitive capitalism'. He also refers to the central role of cartels for the coordination of market transactions in Germany.

In 1897, the German Supreme Court upheld the legality of cartel contracts and sentenced a disloyal member firm to pay the stipulated penalty for breach of contract.[1] This ruling legalized cartel contracts and provided a stable legal framework for cartel organizations for the next 50 years in Germany (Pohl 1979). The cartels and the dominant position of banks were the central institutions Hilferding (1915) had in mind when he described the German economy as a regime of 'organized capitalism'.

The German Supreme Court tried to balance two basic rights: freedom of trade (free competition) on the one hand, the right of the small producers to protect their trade and to secure their subsistence on the other hand. The Court ruled in favor of the small producer and substantiated its decision on the grounds that Thomson (1971) sets forth in his classic article on the 'Moral Economy'.[2]

In contrast, the Sherman Act (1890) defined cartels and monopolies as a 'conspiracy against the public' and as a criminal act that obstructs commerce. The market model that the American politicians had in mind when they voted for the Sherman Act was as a market order of *negative freedom;* any obstacle that stood in the way of free market exchange and unconstrained competition was to be removed.[3] The state sets the rules for the game, it has to guarantee a level playing field, but it does not interfere with the economy.

In their influential book on the 'varieties of capitalism', Hall and Soskice (2001) widened the comparative perspective by including a number of different economic institutions in their analysis, among them trade unions, the educational system, innovation systems and the welfare state. National market orders constitute a system of *functionally interdependent institutions*. These institutions differ systematically between, on the one hand, countries the authors label 'liberal market economies' (e.g., the US or UK) and, on the other hand, countries that belong to the group of 'coordinated market economies' (e.g., Germany or Switzerland).

Abelshauser (2001) provides a historical account of the German 'production regime'. He argues that many institutions in the German production regime were already created before World War I. The German Empire was a 'hot bed' of economic institutions that shaped the German production regime for the next hundred years. The restructuring of the German political economy in the late nineteenth century has frequently been misinterpreted as a 'backwards' step toward a more traditional economic order. Abelshauser (2001, 509) argues instead that it should be interpreted as an adaptation process of the economy on its way to a new knowledge and science-based industrial production. Among the central institutions that shaped the German production regime were non-competitive forms of market coordination (cartels, corporate networks), the revival and modernization of the apprenticeship system, the legalization of unions and the implementation of works councils (co-determination).

This article focuses on the analysis of one of these central institutions in Germany during the twentieth century: *corporate networks*. Networks among large corporations are created when a manager or director sits on the board of directors of *several* firms. These multiple directors offer their services as a 'go-between' to coordinate an exchange between large corporations; they provide information on technical and organizational innovations (Davis 1991). They may also control and discipline executive managers who fail to do their duties as trustees of the shareholders and employees. Multiple directors have access to confidential information; they influence the selection of top-managers and they vote on many issues of corporate governance. Therefore, corporate networks are more institutionalized than an informal club of alumni or a casual 'old boys" network; the decisions that multiple directors make as members of the board have legal consequences and may trigger claims for compensation.

The national corporate network is an important *economic institution* that provides an opportunity structure for the regulation of competition and the coordination of market exchange (cooperative capitalism). The network provides an institutional structure that may enable managers to follow long-term strategies and to choose cooperation instead of defection.

The structure of corporate networks—i.e., their density, centralization and the position of banks in the network—varies between countries. We have collected a sample of the 250 to 350 largest firms for several years during the twentieth century. This sample design provides empirical evidence to answer a number of questions; for example: Are there significant differences in the structure of corporate networks between Germany and the US? How does the structure of the networks evolve over time? What role do banks play in the corporate network (centrality)?

2. EXPLANATIONS

Institutional differences between nation states have been discussed in the scholarly literature for many years. At least three explanations have been offered for the varieties of institutions: (a) functional interdependence, (b) cultural inheritance and (c) economic development (modernization). A brief account of each will be presented in this section.

(a) Institutions evolve over time and become functionally interdependent in many ways. Hall and Soskice (2001, 17) emphasize the idea of institutional complementarities: "[. . .] two institutions can be said to be complementary if the presence (or efficiency) of one increases the returns from (or efficiency of) the other". Functional complementarities may solidify a process of path dependency. Economic actors cannot change a single institution without producing negative consequences for other institutions and, because actors cannot change everything at once, institutional structures become self-reinforcing. Institutional differences between countries persist over a long period; path dependency and institutional hysteresis[4] may even widen these differences over time. The central position of bankers in the corporate network and the importance of bank loans for industrial investments provide an example of functional complementarities in Germany. Banks granted long-term loans to large corporations (patient capital) and in exchange, bankers were offered a seat on the supervisory board of the debtor company.

In many cases, the network had a protective function. It sheltered producers against cut-throat competition (cartels), provided a control device for banks to monitor their debtors (bank loans) and protected the apprenticeship system and joint research and development ventures against free-riders (Thelen 2004). During the 1990s, the dense network between German banks and industrial firms protected the latter from hostile takeovers.

(b) Cultural patterns play an important role in the structural analysis of corporate networks in Asian countries. Business groups in Korea (chaebol), Japan (keiretsu) and China (qiyejituan) are examples of corporate networks of particularly high density and centralization.[5] Member firms coordinate their behavior, exchange employees, provide loans for industrial investments and form joint ventures for research and development.

Nakane (1970) argues that group cohesion is a cultural pattern that is reproduced in different subsystems of the Japanese society and is an important feature in understanding how economic and political institutions in Japan function. A similar argument is put forward by Biggart and Hamilton (1997, 37): "Asian economies espouse different institutional logics from those of Western economies, logics rooted in connectedness and relationships". In a comparative study on the 'origins of non-liberal capitalism', Streeck (2001, 2) argues that the strength of Rhineland capitalism is rooted in its "capacity to mobilize noneconomic social ties, non-competitive cooperation, collective obligations, and moral commitments in support of economic efficiency".

Explanations based on differences in cultural patterns underline the importance of social cohesion for economic performance. Dense social networks have the advantage of supporting deferred reciprocity in economic exchange; a service may be delivered today in the expectation that it will be reciprocated sometime in the future. Dense networks erect barriers against defection and 'free-riding', as network members have the capability for monitoring and sanctioning their members. The empirical evidence presented in Section 4 shows that the German corporate network had a particularly high density in the interwar period, when the country was hit by a series of political and economic crises.

(c) Two countries that have attained different levels of modernization and economic development have different systems of economic institutions. Institutions that are efficient for a backward nation trying to catch up may not be efficient for a mature economy that produces at the forefront of technology (Abramovitz 1986). For example, in relatively 'backward' nations, the allocation of financial resources are not channeled through financial markets, but are frequently distributed by a cartel of banks or the state (Gerschenkron 1962).

Katz (1998) argues that the dense corporate networks between Japanese firms (keiretsu) were efficient during the stage of economic development and the process of catching up. Once Japan had reached the stage of a mature economy, these networks became inefficient; an obstacle in the way of Japanese corporations adapting to a global economy. A similar argument has been made for the business groups in Korea (chaebols) and for the corporate networks in Germany ('Germany Inc.').[6]

The explanations for the varieties of institutions across different countries briefly outlined above are not mutually exclusive. Culturally specific institutions that provided a competitive advantage during the stage of economic development may become inefficient when a country has reached the stage of economic maturity. Path dependency and institutional hysteresis may prevent actors from adapting institutions to a changing environment. An alternative view claims, however, that there is not *one* but *several* ways to organize an efficient economy. Corporate networks that regulate competition and enable firms to benefit from a *cooperation rent* may be as efficient as a highly competitive market that produces high transaction costs (e.g., opportunism, financial crises).

3. MICRO/MACRO PERSPECTIVE

Corporations are free to create their own *ego-network* and to get connected to other corporations of their choice. The structure of ego-networks might be explained by organizational strategies; firms try to get connected to other firms to reduce their resource dependency (e.g., an interlock between an aluminum company and a power station). Many industrial firms co-opt bank directors to get access to financial resources (Mizruchi 1996). Figure 4.1 provides an example of the ego-network of the *Deutsche Bank* in 1914. Each dot represents a German corporation to which *Deutsche Bank* was connected. A director of *Deutsche Bank* had a seat on the supervisory board of, for instance, *Mannesmann, Siemens, Allianz, Accumulatoren Fabrik* and eight large coal mining corporations.[7]

The structure of an ego-network is determined by the decisions of individual firms. The structure of the *entire* network, however, cannot be controlled by any individual or company. In 1914, the corporate network created among 250 German companies comprised a total of 4,572 relationships (Figure 4.2). The *structure* of these relationships—meaning, the density, the level of centralization and the redundancy of the network (percentage of multiple ties)—lay beyond the control of any one person or organization.

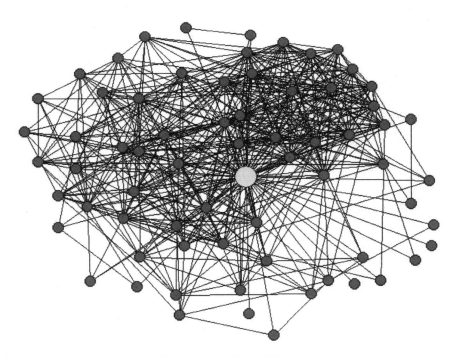

Figure 4.1 Ego-network of *Deutsche Bank*, 1914[8]

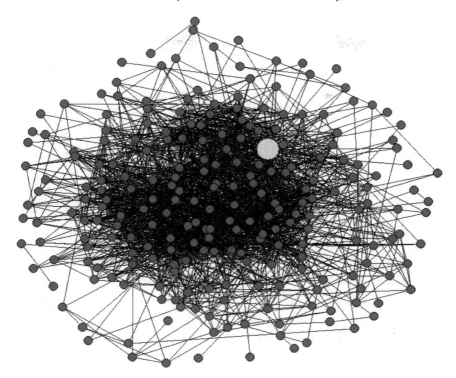

Figure 4.2 Total Corporate Network—Germany, 1914[9]

The structure was influenced by the legal framework (e.g., cartel laws), by traditions and cultural patterns (e.g., degree of social cohesion), by the development of the national economy (e.g., relative backwardness) and the geographical and sectoral distribution of large corporations (e.g., location of headquarters of many large corporations in New York or Berlin).

The difference between ego-networks—the micro-perspective—and the structure of the total national network—the macro-perspective—has important implications for the analysis and type of explanations one can offer. In the first case, we argue in terms of strategies and interests of individual actors, the actors being organizations or managers (Koenig, Gogel, and Sonquist 1979). In the second case, we look at the structure of the total network in which the individual company is embedded.

The structure of the national network is an example of what Durkheim (1950, 7) has called a 'social fact'. He points out that social facts "acquire a body, a tangible form, and constitute a reality in their own right, quite distinct from the individual facts which produce it". Figure 4.2 provides an example; ego-networks are created by individual actors but are embedded in a large encompassing structure that is out of the control of individual actors.

The following analysis does not examine the micro-perspective of individual actors or companies. It focuses on parameters that characterize the structure of the total network. In Section 4, the density of the network over the period 1896–2010 is analyzed. In Section 5, we look at the particular position German banks had in the network. In Section 6, *intra*-sectoral ties are analyzed, which complemented the cartel organization before 1938 and replaced it after World War II.

4. DENSITY OF THE CORPORATE NETWORK

Figure 4.3 presents the network density for Germany and the US for the twentieth century. Data are available for the following sample years: 1896, 1914, 1928, 1934, 1938, 1976, 1992 and 2010.[10] In Germany, network density was particularly high during the period 1914–1938; after World War II, it is in permanent decline until, at the beginning of the twenty-first century, the German corporate network has disintegrated almost completely.

The Corporate Network Up to World War II

At the turn of the nineteenth/twentieth century, the density of the German network was still lower than that of the US network; by 1914, the density was significantly higher in Germany, reaching its highest level in 1928 (16.2%). The period before 1914 was a period of take-off and consolidation. Many firms became public corporations listed on the stock exchange. They were connected to each other by directors with many board positions.[11]

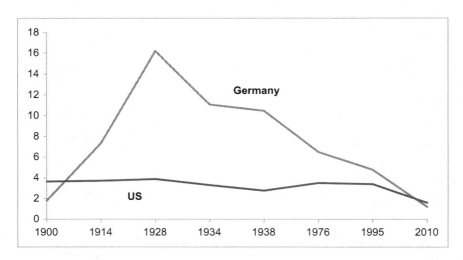

Figure 4.3 Network Density: Germany (G) and United States (US), 1896–2010

Why was the network density so high in Germany in 1928? It never again reached this high level later in the century, and neither France nor the US had a corporate network of such high density in any year during the twentieth century. There are two possible explanations.

During the 1920s, the network became *concentrated* on a small group of German managers who were repeatedly nominated to sit on the supervisory boards of large German firms.[12] In 1896, the top 15 German big linkers had, on average, 5.7 positions in the network; in 1928, they had, on average, 23.8 positions. The larger the number of positions held by the big linkers, the higher the density of the network.[13] If we eliminate the 15 top big linkers from the German network in 1928, the number of ties in the national network would be reduced by 37%.[14] In the US, the top 15 big linkers had, on average, 8.3 positions in 1900 and 8.6 positions in 1928. This small difference corresponds to the small difference in density in Figure 4.3. So, while there was a sharp increase in network density *and* in the average number of positions of the big linkers in Germany, there was hardly any change in the US.[15]

A second explanation for the high density in 1928 refers to specific historical circumstances in Germany. After World War I, German corporations lost all subsidiaries they owned in the countries of their former enemies; the German economy went through a hyper-inflation (1923) that destroyed the wealth of the middle class and depreciated the equity capital of banks. The French army occupied the industrial center of Germany (Ruhrgebiet) in 1923, and as a result, many large corporations were forced to move their headquarters out of the *Ruhrgebiet* to the northern/southern parts of Germany (Jeannesson 1996). The high density of the corporate network at the end of the 1920s may be interpreted as a *protective* device against an external enemy (the French army) and an internal one (the communist party).

Between 1928 and 1934, the network density declined from 16.2% to 11.1%. Two explanations may be offered for this decline. First, in reaction to the banking crisis of 1930/1931, the German government passed a law that limited the number of supervisory board positions.[16] This made it illegal for any person to hold more than 20 supervisory board positions. It was shown that network density strongly increases with the increasing number of positions a big linker is able to accumulate. Accordingly, the density is reduced when directors are forced to reduce the number of positions. The average number of positions the top 15 big linkers held in large German corporations declined from 23.8 (1928) to 18.3 (1934).

Second, before 1914 up to the late 1920s, many German big linkers were of Jewish origin, among them Jacob Goldschmidt (47 positions), Paul Silverberg (25 positions) and Georg Solmssen (21 positions). After the Nazi regime came to power in 1933, Jewish directors were ousted from their management and supervisory board positions, with many of them immigrating to the US or Switzerland. The liquidation of the German Jewish economic elite in 1933/1934 also reduced the network density (Windolf 2011).

The Corporate Network After World War II

In February 1947, the British and US occupation powers issued laws on the decartelization and deconcentration of German industry. "By the end of 1948 over 1,100 cartel agreements were formally terminated" (Wells 2002, 154). However, it took almost 10 years before the West German Parliament passed an antitrust law.[17] The antitrust law was one of the most controversial economic regulations in West Germany in the 1950s. Many German managers and entrepreneurs vehemently opposed the antitrust law, accusing antitrust of being a violation of the freedom of contract.[18]

Figure 4.3 shows that the density of the corporate network declined substantially after World War II. The first year for which data are available is 1976. Network density was about 6.5% and, by 1992, it had declined further to 4.8%, less than half of what it had been in 1938. It was still, however, significantly higher than in the US (3.4%). The decline of network density after World War II was a spillover effect of the antitrust legislation and of the deconcentration process of the 1950s in Germany.

Finally, by 2010, network density had declined even further to 1.1%, making the density of the German corporate network lower than the density of the US network (1.6%) in 2010. The density of the German network was also lower than in the late nineteenth century. The globalization of the economy and a change in corporate governance rules are important factors in the explanation of this decline.

During the twentieth century, the corporate network was a *national* network. It was a coordination instrument and a protective device for the large indigenous corporations producing in Germany. Globalization has changed this stable environment; in many large German corporations, more than 50% of the workforce is employed outside of Germany (e.g., *Siemens, Deutsche Bank*). A *national* network is no longer useful for the coordination of market exchange.

The globalization of financial markets has also changed the ownership structure of public corporations in Germany. In many large corporations, institutional owners (investment, pension and hedge funds) hold the majority of shares. They exercise a strong influence on the corporate governance of the firm. Section 5.4.5 of the *German Corporate Governance Code* stipulates that members of the management board should not take on more than *three* positions on the supervisory board of other corporations. The regulatory approach of the Code is similar to that in the US: managers are required to 'comply or explain'. Managers who hold more than three positions on the supervisory board of other corporations have to 'explain' why they are represented on so many boards. In our data set for 2010, none of the German managers held more than four board positions, thus complying with the corporate governance code.[19] It has been shown that in 1928, the top big linkers created almost 40% of all interlocks in the network. By 2010, however, big linkers had completely disappeared from the supervisory boards of large German corporations.

5. BANKS IN THE CORPORATE NETWORK

The position of bankers in the network and the influence they are able to exercise on non-financial firms have always been a central issue in debates over the power of banks. Even before World War I, Hilferding (1955, 445) maintained that the spheres of industrial, commercial and financial capital, which had once been distinctly separate from one another, were already under the joint command of high finance. This was an early statement of the *bank hegemony hypothesis* that was reformulated by Kotz (1978) in an influential book. Mintz and Schwartz (1985) argued that banks undeniably occupy a central position in the corporate network, but that this is not necessarily evidence of dominance or hegemony that banks supposedly exercise over industrial firms.

In this section, the position of banks in the corporate network is analyzed for Germany and the US. The analysis is limited to the network of *directed* interlocks;[20] i.e., the network of executive managers. If the *executive* directors of a bank sit on the board of non-financial firms, these interlocks are called the outdegree of the bank. If the *executive* managers of non-financial firms sit on the board of a bank, these interlocks are called the indegree of the bank. In 1928, each German bank had, on average, 8.3 directed ties to non-financial firms (outdegree). In the same year, each German bank had 2.1 industrial managers sitting on its supervisory board (indegree; see Table 4.1).

The *outdegree* of a bank is a proxy for the influence the bank is able to exercise over non-financial firms. Bank directors who sit on the boards of many industrial firms have a chance to influence their strategies and to monitor the level of risk-taking of these firms. However, this argument also applies to the bank itself; the indegree of a bank is a proxy for the influence non-financial firms are able to exercise over the bank.[21] Industrial managers who sit on the board of a bank have the opportunity to get loans with favorable conditions. In 1928, each US bank had, on average, 3.1 industrial managers sitting on its board (see Table 4.1).

Tarr (1966) examined several banks in Chicago that declared bankruptcy between 1893 and 1905. He discovered that local entrepreneurs sitting on the board of banks (*indegree*) actually 'plundered' the banks: "In 1893, the Chemical National Bank failed and subsequent examination revealed that most of its funds had been loaned to its directors and stockholders, often on poor security or signature alone. . . . [In December 1905,] the Chicago National, the Home Savings, and the Equitable Trust Company had failed". Cause for the bankruptcy was "Walsh's grossly excessive loans to his own enterprises and those of his banks' directors" (Tarr 1966, 451). Walsh was the CEO of these three banks.

We have calculated the ratio of outdegree/indegree (Table 4.1). In 1914, the average outdegree of German banks was 5.7; their average indegree was 0.8; the ratio of these two figures is 7.1. This figure means that for

76 *Paul Windolf*

Table 4.1 Interlocks between Banks and Non-financial Firms

Germany	1900	1914	1928	1938	1992	2010
Outdegree: Banks → non-financials	2.5	5.7	8.3	6.2	6.8	0.5
Indegree: Non-financials → banks	0.4	0.8	2.1	1.9	2.1	0.3
Ratio: Outdegree/indegree	6.3	7.1	3.9	3.3	3.3	1.6
United States						
Outdegree: Banks → non-financials	3.4	3.7	5.2	4.5	1.3	*
Indegree: Non-financials → banks	1.3	1.6	3.1	2.0	2.0	*
Ratio: Outdegree/indegree	2.7	2.3	1.7	2.3	0.6	*

*Data not available. Figures are calculated from the matrix of directed (primary) interlocks.

every industrial manager sitting on the supervisory board of a German bank, there were 7.1 bank managers sitting on the supervisory board of an industrial firm. German banks sent many more executive directors to the supervisory boards of non-financial firms than they received industrial managers to sit on their own supervisory boards. In the US, the ratio outdegree/indegree is lower for all sample years. In 1992, the US banks had an average outdegree of 1.3 and an indegree of 2.0. This means that there were more industrial managers on bank boards than bankers on the boards of non-financial firms (ratio: 0.6).

In Germany, non-financial firms were meeting places for bank directors (high outdegree). In the US, banks were meeting places for managers from industrial firms, as the banks co-opted many managers from non-financial firms to sit on their boards (high indegree).

How can the differences in the network structure between banks and industry in the two countries be explained? There are institutional differences between Germany and the US that influence the relationship between the financial sector and industrial firms, among them the structure of the national banking system (universal banks), the different types of financing (debt versus equity) and the distribution of risk among different market actors.

(a) In the US, the *concentration* of the industrial sector was much higher than that of the financial sector. The trusts controlled large parts of the American industry, while the financial sector was *fragmented* and the activities of financial institutions were confined to the state level. For example, in 1914, the largest steel company in Germany was the *Friedrich Krupp AG,* and in the US, it was the *United States Steel Corporation.* The largest bank in Germany was the *Deutsche Bank;* its counterpart in the US was the *National City Bank of New York.* The equity capital of the *Deutsche Bank* was approximately equal to that of *Krupp AG* (250:215 Mio RM), while the equity capital of the *United States Steel Corporation* was nearly 35 times higher than that of *National City Bank*. The largest American bank in New York had equity capital totaling no more than $25 million.[22]

American investment banks were financial intermediaries that sold securities (stock and bonds) for large corporations on the financial markets. The banks themselves would not have been able to cover the capital needs of big American corporations from their own resources. State regulation prevented the US banks from growing into large universal banks.[23] In contrast, in Germany, the universal banks controlled relatively large financial funds that enabled them to provide long-term loans to industrial firms for investment purposes.

If the manager of a debtor company sits on the supervisory board of the creditor bank, this relationship is prone to opportunism on the part of the debtor. German banks had mixed feelings about co-opting managers of debtor companies to sit on their supervisory boards. The debtors were good customers of the bank, but the bank was also aware of the vicious incentives inherent in such interlocks.[24]

(b) The distribution of entrepreneurial risk differed between the two countries. German banks that granted long-term loans to industrial firms took over part of the entrepreneurial risk (patient capital). They tried to get a seat on the supervisory board of the debtor company in order to monitor its management. US banks sold securities to the public. The investors who bought these securities were the ultimate risk bearers. The bank was not liable when a corporation went bankrupt whose securities it had floated. The bank could only lose its reputation.

In the US, the middle class was able[25] and willing to take over part of the entrepreneurial risk of the second industrialization. The culture of Puritanism and the tradition of an immigrant population have shaped the attitude toward risk in the US. In Germany, the bourgeoisie was not willing to invest in risky industrial securities. The bourgeoisie preferred to buy government bonds, which were erroneously perceived as being risk-free assets.

A final remark refers to the sample year 2010. Table 4.1 shows that the average outdegree of German banks had dropped from 6.8 in 1992 to 0.5 in 2010. In 1992, *Deutsche Bank* had an outdegree of 47, i.e., the executive directors of *Deutsche Bank* held positions on the supervisory board of 47 non-financial firms.[26] In 2010, the outdegree of *Deutsche Bank* was five. These figures provide further evidence for the hypothesis that the disappearance of big linkers is an important cause for the reduced network density in 2010 (see Figure 4.3).

In the US, the influence and network centrality of banks had already declined by the early 1990s (Davis and Mizruchi 1999). In 1992, the average US bank had an outdegree of only 1.3 and an indegree of 2.0.

78 Paul Windolf

In other words, there were more industrial managers sitting on the board of banks than bankers holding seats on the boards of non-financial firms.

6. INTRA- AND INTER-SECTORAL INTERLOCKS

Interlocking directorates at the intra-sectoral level serve to regulate competition among potential competitors. In the US, this type of interlocking was legally prohibited by the Clayton Act (1914). In Germany, cartels were legalized by the Supreme Court and, therefore, intra-sectoral interlocks could develop to complement cartels.

For both Germany and the US, we have computed matrices that give the densities of the intra-sectoral network for each economic sector in the diagonal (interlocks between firms in the same industry) and the densities of the inter-sectoral network off-diagonal (interlocks between firms in different industries). Then, we have computed a block-model analysis to identify the group of sectors with the highest density. Table 4.2 shows a selection of industries, that is, the cells of the matrix with the highest

Table 4.2 Intra- and Inter-sectoral Density: Germany—United States, 1928

Panel A: Germany	1	2	3	4	5	6
1 Electrical industry	0.58	0.46	0.37	0.27	0.33	0.23
2 Steel	0.46	0.59	0.46	0.31	0.41	0.22
3 Mining	0.38	0.46	0.42	0.26	0.32	0.20
4 Chemical industry	0.27	0.29	0.24	0.40	0.23	0.21
5 Mechanical engineer.	0.32	0.39	0.31	0.23	0.31	0.22
6 Banks	0.25	0.24	0.22	0.24	0.24	0.29
Number of firms (N)	12	37	34	22	25	59

Panel B: United States	1	2	3	4	5
1 Power stations	0.72	0.04	0.03	0.23	0.05
2 Banks	0.04	0.05	0.08	0.05	0.09
3 Railways	0.03	0.07	0.16	0.04	0.04
4 Utilities	0.22	0.05	0.04	0.16	0.03
5 Electrical industry	0.06	0.07	0.04	0.03	0.13
Number of firms (N)	15	46	39	20	10

Note: Only cells with the highest density are shown in Table 4.2 (submatrices). Figures in the diagonal give *intra*-sectoral density (directed + undirected interlocks); figures off-diagonal give *inter*-sectoral density. N: Number of firms in each economic sector. Inter-sectoral density was computed as follows: number of ties/(N^2); intra-sectoral density: number of ties/[$N*(N-1)$]. Complete matrices are available on request from the author. The number of firms (N) also gives the size of the (intra-sectoral) network. This size varies considerably between industrial sectors. When (intra-sectoral) densities are compared, the different network size should be taken into account.

densities for 1928 for Germany and the US. In Germany, both the intra-sectoral and the inter-sectoral densities are relatively high. *Intra*-sectoral ties may be used as a coordination device to support the cartel organization in each industry. The *inter*-sectoral ties are often strategic alliances between companies that are functionally interdependent (vertical integration).

In the US, the highest *intra*-sectoral densities are found among power stations, utilities and railways. These companies are 'network specialists', which are regulated by special federal/national laws. However, the densities in each cell are considerably lower than those for Germany. For most industries in the US, the *intra*-sectoral densities are zero or close to zero.

Summarizing the results, we can say that in Germany, the intra-sectoral density was relatively high and increased steadily between 1896 and 1938. The corporate network was used—parallel to the cartels—as an instrument to coordinate the market (regulated competition). The relatively high inter-sectoral density in Germany between several sectors of heavy industry (coal, steel, chemical, mechanical engineering) indicates that the corporate network was either used as a substitute for vertical integration or became the precursor of a vertical combine. German banks were very well interconnected with the sectors of heavy industry, although they did not have the highest density when compared with other business sectors.

In 1992, the *intra*-sectoral densities were still high compared to the US, even though the figures are on a lower level. The German Parliament never passed a law corresponding to the US Clayton Act (1914) making interlocks between competing firms illegal. Coal mining, the oil industry, iron and steel, power stations and the chemical industry were among the sectors with the highest intra-sectoral densities. The financial sector (banking) had the highest *inter*-sectoral densities; in other words, it was closely connected with almost every other non-financial sector.[27]

7. CONCLUSIONS

Figure 4.3 (shown previously) presents panel data for the density of the German corporate network during the twentieth century. There seems to be no clear trend in the data. A change in density between sample years seems to be determined to a large extent by period-specific historical contingencies.

The period from the late nineteenth century to World War I was a take-off period for the corporate network in Germany. It was during these years that the central economic institutions of organized capitalism were created. During the 1920s, network density increased substantially, reaching a peak in 1928; the large German corporations were closely connected by many interlocks. It was argued that this dense network was probably a protective device against an external and internal threat. The density decreased thereafter but remained at a relatively high level during the 1930s, at least in comparison to the US. After World War II, the US occupation enforced the decartelization of German industry. The strong decline in network density was probably a spillover effect of the decartelization process. After the year 2000, we see the almost complete dissolution of the corporate network in Germany; the density falls below the level of 1896.

How can we explain the sharp decline of network density during the early twenty-first century? During the 1920s, when network density reached its highest level in Germany, there were no legal obstacles that prevented companies from coordinating their behavior. Also, there was no code that inhibited managers from accepting as many supervisory board positions as were offered to them. However, during the 1990s, the *closed* German corporate network and the cross-shareholdings of large corporations were made responsible for the weak economic performance of Germany and the high unemployment rate.[28] In 2000, the German company *Mannesmann* was taken over by *Vodafone*. This hostile takeover was perceived as a warning that signaled the end of solidarity in the network. A final blow for the network was the German Corporate Governance Code, which requires that no manager take on more than three positions on the supervisory board of other companies. This was the end of the big linker, who had typically held 10 or more positions in the network.

In Section 2, it was argued that functional interdependencies are important for the stability of the network. Bankers had many positions on the supervisory board of debtor companies to monitor their level of risk-taking. In the 1990s, however, new financial techniques allowed banks to sell off their loans (securitization of debt), and banks could buy credit insurance to protect themselves from credit losses (credit default swap). Therefore, there was no longer any need to send bank directors to sit on the supervisory boards of debtor companies; the banks had sold off the risk.

German banks used to control many proxy votes of large companies (Baums and Fraune 1995). Proxies provided block votes to banks and enabled them to get their directors elected to the supervisory boards. Bank directors not only monitored their customers, they also protected them against hostile takeovers. This changed when German banks entered the investment banking business; they were no longer interested in blocking hostile takeovers. On the contrary, they earned a lot of money by *promoting* takeovers. This is a further example that illustrates how the dissolution of functional interdependencies weakened the German corporate network (Höpner and Krempel 2004).

Many authors have argued that there is no 'one best way' to achieve economic efficiency, but that there are different models of capitalism. Systems of economic institutions vary among countries due to cultural differences and historical heritage (Hall and Soskice 2001; Chandler 1990). The rise of neoliberalism has put the issue of the *convergence* of national systems of capitalism on the agenda once again. The global integration of markets, the rise of the 'new economy' and the implementation of global standards of corporate governance have put pressure on governments and economic actors to adopt a neoliberal program of deregulation and to dismantle rent-seeking institutions. The corporate network is regarded as one of those rent-seeking institutions that should be replaced by free markets and unfettered competition.

Figure 4.3 shows that the density of the German corporate network continuously declined after World War II. By 2010, the network had been effectively dismantled and the difference between Germany and the US had disappeared. However, it would be premature to conclude that the economic institutions in Germany and the US have converged completely, even though we observe a *partial* convergence due to the deregulation of markets. At the same time, the re-regulation of financial markets may create new forms of national differences.

NOTES

1. See Entscheidungen des Reichsgerichts in Civilsachen, Vol. 38, Leipzig 1897, 155–162. See also Böhm (1948), who criticized the ruling of the Court.
2. Bork (1978, xi) criticizes the idea that a market order should protect the small producer: "[. . .] the sole consideration the judge must bear in mind, is the maximization of consumer welfare. The judge must not weigh against consumer welfare any other goal, such as the supposed social benefits of preserving small businesses against superior efficiency."
3. The notion of 'negative freedom' is defined in Berlin (2002, 169).
4. See Bourdieu (1979, 158, 361).
5. For Japan, see Gerlach (1992); Korea, Chang (2003); China, Redding (1996).
6. See Chang (2003); Adams (1994).
7. The history of the *Accumulatoren Fabrik* is analyzed in Chandler (1990, 402–408). The long-term relationship between *Deutsche Bank* and *Mannesmann* is reported in Strandmann (1978). See Ziegler (1998) for an analysis of the supervisory boards of large German corporations during the 1920s.
8. Degree: 68; 992 ties; density: 21.8%.
9. Large dot: Deutsche Bank embedded in the total corporate network; N = 250 companies; ties: 4,572; density: 7.34%.
10. The first sample year for Germany is 1896; 1900 is the first sample year for the US. Data for 1934 are available for Germany only. Data source for 1976: Stokman and Wasseur (1985, 31); cf. Ziegler (1984). Data source for the US for 2010: Schifeling and Mizruchi (this volume and Appendix I). For more detail, see *http://www.cgeh.nl/power-corporate-networks-comparative-and-historical-perspective*.
11. Carl Klönne (Deutsche Bank) was sitting on 20 supervisory boards; Walther Rathenau (AEG) had 19 board positions; Carl Fürstenberg (Berliner Handelsgesellschaft) had 18 board positions.
12. Here is a list of the five top linkers (number of positions in parentheses): J. Goldschmidt (47, banker), O. Schlitter (33, banker), L. Hagen (29, banker), P. Silverberg (25, only supervisory board) and A. Vögler (25, steel). In 1923, Louis

82 Paul Windolf

      Hagen was the chairman of a group of German bankers who tried to negotiate an agreement with the French occupation army (Jeannesson 1996, 66).
13. Oskar Schlitter had 33 positions in 1928. This banker created $(33*32)/2 = 528$ ties in the network. If he had accepted one additional position, the number of ties would have been $(34*33)/2 = 562$; $562 - 528 = 33$ additional ties.
14. The computation refers to the total sample size of 366 firms (isolated firms excluded). Matrix: symmetrized, not dichotomized.
15. Barnes and Ritter (2001, 206) have published a study on the corporate network in the US for the period 1962–1995. They show that during this period, 25% of all ties were created by directors holding *two* positions; however, 75% of ties were created by directors holding *three or more* positions. This confirms the argument that density increases with an increasing number of top big linkers holding many positions.
16. See Die aktienrechtlichen Vorschriften der Verordnung des Reichspräsidenten über Aktienrecht, Bankenaufsicht und über eine Steueramnestie, 19 Sept. 1931, RGBl I, 493.
17. Gesetz gegen Wettbewerbsbeschränkungen; the law came into force in January 1958.
18. See Nörr (1994, 200). Böhm (1956) discusses the question of whether the antitrust law violated the (West) German Constitution.
19. They held one executive position and three non-executive positions on different supervisory boards, or they held four non-executive positions on supervisory boards (professional supervisory board members).
20. If the executive manager of company A has a seat on the supervisory board of company B (external director), this manager creates a *directed* (primary) tie between companies A and B. If the same manager holds a third position as external director on the supervisory board of company C, a directed interlock is created between companies A and C. At the same time, an *undirected* (secondary) tie is created between companies B and C. The more positions a manager holds in a corporate network, the more *undirected* ties are created. In a corporate network, there are usually many more undirected (secondary) ties. For instance, in the German network (1914), there are 3,219 *undirected* interlocks and 543 *directed* interlocks.
21. A detailed analysis of the composition of the supervisory boards of German banks is given in Krenn (2012, 227–239).
22. *Sources*: Handbuch der deutschen Aktiengesellschaften (Hoppenstedt), Vol. 18 (1914); Poor's Manual of Industrials. New York: Poor's Railroad Manual Co., Vol. 1914/1915. Rand McNally Bankers Directory (Bankers Blue Book). New York: Rand McNally Co., Vol. 1914/1915.
23. The McFadden Act (1927) prohibited interstate branching; the Glass-Steagall Act (1933) enforced the separation of investment and commercial banking (Roe 1994).
24. The bankruptcy of the German firm *Nordwolle* in 1931 provides an example for this opportunism: C. Lahusen was CEO of *Nordwolle* and member of the supervisory board of *Darmstädter und Nationalbank*. This bank had granted a large loan to *Nordwolle*. However, Lahusen had falsified the balance sheet to get the loan from the *Darmstädter and Nationalbank* (Born 1967, 75–76).
25. GDP per capita in 1913 (in 1980 international $): Germany: 1907 $; US: 3771 $. The average income of a middle class household in the US was considerably higher than in Germany. *Source*: Maddison (1989, 113, 128), own computation.
26. In 1992, Dr. Ulrich Weiss and Hilmar Kopper were members of the management board and 'ambassadors' of *Deutsche Bank*. Each of them held positions on the supervisory board of seven other firms.

27. A detailed analysis of the inter-/intra-sectoral densities for 1992 is given in Windolf (2002, 71, Table 3.5).
28. 'Germany Inc.' (*Deutschland AG*) was frequently used as a shorthand term for the German corporate network. The early stage of its dissolution is analyzed in Beyer (2003).

REFERENCES

Abelshauser, Werner. 2001. "Umbruch und Persistenz: Das deutsche Produktionsregime in historischer Perspektive." *Geschichte und Gesellschaft* 27: 503–523.
Abramovitz, Moses. 1986. "Catching Up, Forging Ahead, and Falling Behind." *The Journal of Economic History* 46: 385–406.
Adams, Michael. 1994. "Die Usurpation von Aktionärsbefugnissen mittels Ringverflechtung in der 'Deutschland AG'." *Die Aktiengesellschaft* 4: 148–158.
Barnes, Roy, and Emily Ritter. 2001. "Networks of Corporate Interlocking 1962–1995." *Critical Sociology* 27: 192–220.
Baums, Theodor, and Christian Fraune. 1995. "Institutionelle Anleger und Publikumsgesellschaft." *Die Aktiengesellschaft* 40 (3): 97–112.
Beyer, Jürgen. 2003. "Deutschland AG a.D.: Deutsche Bank, Allianz und das Verflechtungszentrum des deutschen Kapitalismus." In *Alle Macht dem Markt? Fallstudien zur Abwicklung der Deutschland AG*, edited by Wolfgang Streeck and Martin Höpner, 118–146. Frankfurt: Campus.
Berlin, Isaiah. 2002. *Liberty*. Oxford: Oxford University Press.
Biggart, Nicole, and Gary Hamilton. 1997. "On the Limits of a Firm-Based Theory to Explain Business Networks." In *The Economic Organization of East Asian Capitalism*, edited by Marco Orrù, Nicole Woolsey, and Gary Hamilton, 33–54. London: Sage.
Böhm, Franz. 1948. "Das Reichsgericht und die Kartelle." *Ordo* 1: 197–213.
Böhm, Franz. 1956. "Verstößt ein gesetzliches Kartellverbot gegen das Grundgesetz?" *Wirtschaft und Wettbewerb* 6: 173–187.
Bork, Robert. 1978. *The Antitrust Paradox*. New York: Free Press.
Born, Karl. 1967. *Die deutsche Bankenkrise 1931*. München: Piper.
Bourdieu, Pierre. 1979. *La distinction*. Paris: Minuit.
Chandler, Alfred. 1990. *Scale and Scope*. Cambridge: Belknap Press.
Chang, Sea-Jin. 2003. *Financial Crisis and Transformation of Korean Business Groups*. Cambridge: Cambridge University Press.
Davis, Gerald. 1991. "Agents without Principles? The Spread of the Poison Pill through the Intercorporate Network." *Administrative Science Quarterly* 36: 583–613.
Davis, Gerald, and Mark Mizruchi. 1999. "The Money Center Cannot Hold: Commercial Banks in the U.S. System of Corporate Governance." *Administrative Science Quarterly* 44: 215–239.
Durkheim, Emil. 1950 [1894]. *The Rules of Sociological Method*. New York: Free Press.
Gerlach, Michael. 1992. *Alliance Capitalism: The Social Organization of Japanese Business*. Berkeley: University of California Press.
Gerschenkron, Alexander. 1962. *Economic Backwardness in Historical Perspective*. Cambridge: Belknap Press.
Hall, Peter, and David Soskice. 2001. *Varieties of Capitalism*. Oxford: Oxford University Press.
Hilferding, Rudolf. 1955 [1910]. *Das Finanzkapital*. Berlin: Dietz.

Hilferding, Rudolf. 1915. "Arbeitsgemeinschaft der Klassen?" *Der Kampf* 8: 321–329.
Höpner, Martin, and Lothar Krempel. 2004. "The Politics of the German Company Network." *Competition & Change* 8: 339–356.
Jeannesson, Stanislas. 1996. "Pourquoi la France a-t-elle occupé la Ruhr?" *Vingtième Siècle Revue d'Histoire* 51: 56–67.
Katz, Richard. 1998. *Japan the System that Soured: The Rise and Fall of the Japanese Economic Miracle.* New York: Sharpe.
Koenig, Thomas, Robert Gogel, and John Sonquist. 1979. "Models of the Significance of Interlocking Corporate Directorates." *American Journal of Economics and Sociology* 38: 173–186.
Kotz, David. 1978. *Bank Control of Large Corporations in the United States.* Berkeley: University of California Press.
Krenn, Karoline. 2012. *Alle Macht den Banken?* Wiesbaden: Springer.
Maddison, Angus. 1989. *The World Economy in the 20th Century.* Paris: OECD.
Mintz, Beth, and Michael Schwartz. 1985. *The Power Structure of American Business.* Chicago: University of Chicago Press.
Mizruchi, Mark. 1996. "What Do Interlocks Do? An Analysis, Critique, and Assessment of Research on Interlocking Directorates." *Annual Review of Sociology* 22: 271–298.
Nakane, Chie. 1970. *Japanese Society.* Berkeley: University of California Press.
Nörr, Knut. 1994. *Die Leiden des Privatrechts: Kartelle in Deutschland.* Tübingen: Mohr.
Pohl, Hans. 1979. "Die Entwicklung der Kartelle in Deutschland und die Diskussionen im Verein für Socialpolitik." In *Wissenschaft und Kodifikation des Privatrechts im 19. Jahrhundert,* Vol. IV, edited by Helmut Coing and Walter Wilhelm, 206–235. Frankfurt: Klostermann.
Redding, Gordon. 1996. "Weak Organizations and Strong Linkages: Managerial Ideology and Chinese Family Business Networks." In *Asian Business Networks,* edited by Gary Hamilton, 27–41. Berlin: Walter de Gruyter.
Roe, Mark. 1994. *Strong Managers, Weak Owners: The Political Roots of American Corporate Finance.* Princeton: Princeton University Press.
Schmoller, Gustav. 1906. "Das Verhältnis der Kartelle zum Staat." *Verhandlungen des Vereins für Socialpolitik* 116: 237–271.
Stokman, Frans, and Frans Wasseur. 1985. "National Networks in 1976: A Structural Comparison." In *Networks of Corporate Power,* edited by Frans Stokman, Rolf Ziegler, and John Scott, 20–44. Cambridge: Polity Press.
Strandmann, Pogge von. 1978. *Unternehmenspolitik und Unternehmensführung: Der Dialog zwischen Aufsichtsrat und Vorstand bei Mannesmann 1900 bis 1919.* Düsseldorf: Econ.
Streeck, Wolfgang. 2001. "Introduction: Explorations into the Origins of Nonliberal Capitalism in Germany and Japan." In *The Origins of Nonliberal Capitalism: Germany and Japan in Comparison,* edited by Wolfgang Streeck and Kozo Yamamura, 1–38. Ithaca: Cornell University Press.
Tarr, Joel. 1966. "J.R. Walsh of Chicago: A Case Study in Banking and Politics, 1881–1905." *Business History Review* 40: 451–466.
Thelen, Kathleen. 2004. *How Institutions Evolve: The Political Economy of Skills in Germany, Britain, the United States, and Japan.* Cambridge: Cambridge University Press.
Thomson, Edward. 1971. "The Moral Economy of the English Crowd in the Eighteenth Century." *Past and Present* 50: 76–136.
Wells, Wyatt. 2002. *Antitrust and the Formation of the Postwar World.* New York: Columbia University Press.
Windolf, Paul. 2002. *Corporate Networks in Europe and the United States.* Oxford: Oxford University Press.

Windolf, Paul. 2011. "The German-Jewish Economic Elite. 1900–1930." *Zeitschrift für Unternehmensgeschichte* 56: 135–162.

Ziegler, Dieter. 1998. "Die Aufsichtsräte der deutschen Aktiengesellschaften in den zwanziger Jahren: Eine empirische Untersuchung zum Problem der 'Bankenmacht'." *Zeitschrift für Unternehmensgeschichte* 43: 194–215.

Ziegler, Rolf. 1984. "Das Netz der Personen - und Kapitalverflechtungen deutscher und österreichischer Wirtschaftsunternehmen." *Kölner Zeitschrift für Soziologie und Sozialpsychologie* 36: 585–618.

Part II
Small European Economies

5 The Dutch Corporate Network
Considering Its Persistence

Gerarda Westerhuis

1. INTRODUCTION

This chapter explains the development of the Dutch corporate network of exchange-listed firms between 1903 and 2008. A number of sociologists and historians have already produced literature about the Dutch corporate network. Hubert Schijf analyzes the emergence of corporate elites in 1886 and 1902 (Schijf 1993, 1984). Joost Jonker, a business historian, shows that the increasing amount of bank lending to industrial firms in the period 1910–1920 was the reason for an increase in the amount of interlocks between banks and industry, which diminished once again following the banking crisis of 1921 (Jonker 1989). Helmers et al. (1975) describe the interlocks between Dutch firms in the 1960s, based on the largest 86 Dutch firms identified in 1969. The study put a strong emphasis on the finance-capital model as an explanation of the structure of the network. The decline of the network at the end of the twentieth century is analyzed by Eelke Heemskerk (2007) using three benchmark years: 1976, 1996 and 2001. Taken together, these studies give an indication of how the Dutch corporate network evolved over time, but a truly longitudinal study is still lacking. Heemskerk and Fennema's study of 2009 is an exception. They investigate the cohesion of the Dutch business elite during the twentieth century, focusing on the interpersonal perspective of the network. Their study is based on a different reading of data on board interlocks to those already mentioned. The disparity of the data in all of these studies, however, makes comparison between them over a long time period difficult, if not impossible. There is thus no narrative for the entire twentieth century (for an overview of the data, see Table 1 in Heemskerk and Fennema 2009, 817).

In contrast to Heemskerk and Fennema, we take an intercompany perspective analyzing only a sample of exchange-listed firms. We collected data for 10 benchmark years, extending the analyzed period by adding 2003 and 2008. By doing so, we are able to give a more nuanced picture of the decline of the network at the end of the twentieth century and beginning of the twenty-first century. Based on our data, the development of the Dutch corporate network can be divided into four main phases. Its emergence in the late nineteenth century was followed by a temporarily decline in the 1930s. After World War II, there was a consolidation phase, which was followed by a period that is characterized by a decline of the network's density. Contrary to the existing literature, our data show that the network persisted for a long time and that the decline really set in only very recently; in other words, only in the twenty-first century. Although the depth of the network diminished during the 1980s and 1990s, around 85% of the firms within the network remained connected until at least 2003. This is a remarkable development, since the Dutch economy was very open, showing relatively high export and import figures. The 50 largest Dutch firms became highly internationally orientated, in particular from the early 1970s onwards (Jong, Röell, and Westerhuis 2011). Because of the resulting internationalization of boards, one might assume that there would be a decline in the network, as foreigners often are less integrated with other Dutch firms. Since the 1980s, firms started to pay greater attention to shareholder value. This results in smaller boards (Heemskerk 2007), which, it is often argued, should lead to fewer connection possibilities within the network. Last, the changing strategies of banks, shifting from long-term lending to short-term investment banking due to processes of globalization and financialization, is also said to lead to a decline of the network's density (Heemskerk 2007, 68; see also Davis and Mizruchi 1999 for the US). How can we explain the paradox of a network that persisted at least until the early twenty-first century and these other simultaneous developments, which are often brought forward as most important explanations for the decline of national corporate networks in the extant literature? To understand this paradox, we take a historical perspective to trace the emergence and consolidation of the Dutch network.

When Dutch firms started to expand and had to rely increasingly on external financing, management and ownership began to separate, and management became subject to many disciplinary forces to ensure that it acted in the interests of shareholders. Since we focus only on exchange-listed firms, in theory, this process of separation should be reasonably clear (see, e.g., Berle and Means 1932; Jensen and Meckling 1976). However, during the twentieth century, Dutch directors succeeded in remaining rather powerful. Shleifer and Vishny (1989) describe this as a process in which managers counter disciplinary forces by entrenching themselves. Managerial entrenchment refers to a situation in which managing directors gain so much power that they are able to use the firm to further their own interests, rather than the interest of shareholders. In the literature, it has been said that directors with strong rights try to prevent the loss of their privileges (see, e.g., Rajan and Zingales 2003; Morck, Wolfenzon, and Yeung 2005). One way for directors to retain autonomy is through financing. The 'pecking order' theory states that for directors, there is a hierarchy of preferences, from retained earnings to debt to equity (Myers 1984; Myers and Majluf 1984). By retained earnings, they keep the highest form of autonomy, whereas by issuing shares, more outsiders will be able to cling to control. However, even when issuing shares, firms have options to frustrate the separation of ownership and management, by using takeover defenses, for example. The managerial entrenchment theory states that directors adopt takeover defenses in order to increase their job security at the shareholders' expense (Shleifer and Vishny 1989; DeAngelo and Rice 1983). In this chapter, we analyze how and why management entrenchment leads to the persistence of the network by focusing on corporate financing and on two types of takeover defenses: priority shares and structure regime.

In what follows, we first describe the data selection, as well as the periodization of the development of the Dutch corporate network in Section 2. In Sections 3, 4 and 5, we explain the emergence and temporary decline, consolidation and further decline of the network, respectively. The last section concludes.

2. THE EVOLUTION OF THE DUTCH CORPORATE NETWORK, 1903–2008

The network analysis is based on 10 benchmark years in the period 1903–2008. For each year, we picked the top 100 exchange-listed Dutch firms and the top 25 listed and non-listed banks.[1] The selection was made on the basis of total assets, except for the banks in the period up to 1958, in which the selection was based on the nominal value of equity capital. Dutch firms are characterized by a two-tier board system, which consists of a managing board and a supervisory board. The supervisory board involves non-executive directors. For each firm, we collected the names of the managing and supervisory directors in 10 benchmark years.[2] We gathered interlock data using *Van Oss Effectenboek* for the period 1903–1973, and annual reports for the period 1978–2008. Information of the banks' boards was selected by the *Financieel Adresboek* for the period 1903–1958, and annual reports for the period 1963–2008.

Using social network analysis, the following phases can be distinguished in the formation of the Dutch corporate network: emergence (until late 1920s), temporary decline (1930s), consolidation (1950s–1970s) and gradual decline (since 1980s, but only significantly since the beginning of the twenty-first century). The emergence of the network is reflected in an increase of average degree from around 6.5 in 1903 and 1913, to 9.4 in 1928, while the average distance between two companies decreased from 3 to only 2.5 during this time. An interruption of this development in the 1930s is shown by the drop of average degree to 7.0 in 1938, which is in sharp contrast to other small countries such as Switzerland, where the network remained integrated during this period. After World War II, the network consolidated again, when average degree increased to more than 9.0 in the 1950s and 1960s and the average distance between two companies stayed at around 2.5, only to increase to 2.8 in 1983. The number of isolated firms—in other words, firms without any connection—was low; 12 in 1958, 11 in 1968 and 13 in 1983.

The decline of the Dutch network is often dated around the 1980s. Based on average degree, this is not surprising. This measure gradually declined from 9.2 in 1968 to 7.0 in 1983, and the further from 6.0 in 1993 to 4.1 in 2003, and 1.5 in 2008. However, despite a decline in average degree, the corporate network still remained connected but with less depth. Only after 2003 does a substantial decline set in. This becomes apparent when we show the percentage of firms in the main component that reflect the connectedness of the network, together with line multiplicity for showing the depth of the network (see Figure 5.1). So, during the entire twentieth century, the Dutch network consisted of a large main component, meaning that 80% to 90% of all firms in the sample were connected to each other. In 2003, 85.2% of the firms were still connected in the main component, which is more than was the case at the beginning of the twentieth century (78.4% in 1903), and it was only in 2008 that this percentage declined significantly, to 50%. Also, the average distance between two companies remained below 3.0 until the 1990s, increasing to 3.7 in 2003 and 4.6 in 2008.

The m-cores technique is a way of analyzing a network based on line multiplicity; an m-core is a sub-network defined by the multiplicity of its lines. Figure 5.1 shows the 2m-cores sub-network, in which firms are connected by lines with a value of 2 or higher. The number of firms that were part of the 2m-core network peaked in the 1920s, 1950s and 1960s and started to decline in the 1980s, dropping sharply in 2003. Thus, while the

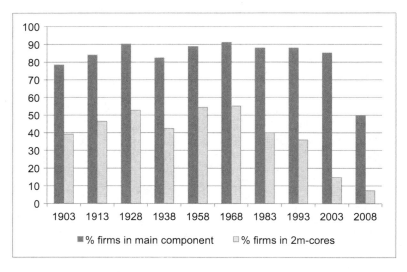

Figure 5.1 Percentage of Firms in Main Component, and in m-core, 1903–2008

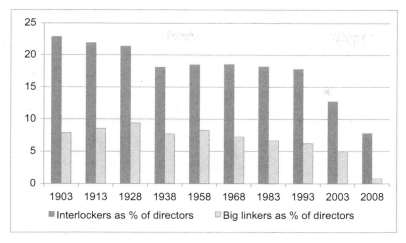

Figure 5.2 Percentage Interlockers and Big Linkers, 1903–2008

network still remained connected (85.2% of the firms in the main component), the depth of the connections became less substantial (compare this with Schnyder and Wilson this volume).

Interestingly, after World War II, the percentage of interlockers also remained reasonably constant up to 1998; around 18% of all directors connected two or more firms (see Figure 5.2). In 2003, there were still 12.8% of directors holding more than one board position, while 5.0% of them held more than three positions simultaneously—the 'big linkers'. This last figure had declined from 8.3% in 1958, but even more striking is the drop of this figure in 2008, in which only 0.8% were 'big linkers'. Therefore, the longitudinal data shows the persistence of the Dutch corporate network, which only declined substantially since the beginning of the twenty-first century. We will now move on to explain this relatively late decline by tracing the emergence and consolidation of the network over time.

3. EMERGENCE AND TEMPORARY WEAKENING OF THE NETWORK, 1890–1945

The Dutch economy experienced a period of rapid growth between 1890 and 1929. The liberals, who ran the country after 1848, interfered as little as possible in Dutch business and advocated the free market and *laissez faire* (Woltjer 1992). In this period of globalization characterized by integration between countries (Bordo, Taylor, and Williamson 2003), the Dutch economy was very open, without any protectionism. The import and export figures were, as a result, relatively high (Sluyterman 2005). The overseas colonies, especially the Dutch-Indies, were important for Dutch business.

At first, colonial business developed slowly, but at the end of the nineteenth century, it started to gain momentum, especially after 1870, when it was decided to open up the Dutch-Indies, allowing private entrepreneurs to do business. Consequently, many Dutch entrepreneurs started new businesses such as trading companies, banks and shipping lines, and many colonial firms became active in tobacco, sugar, coffee or tea.

At the beginning of the twentieth century, Dutch business was characterized by its small scale and the presence of family businesses and informal relations, but nevertheless, the Dutch economy started to flourish and industrialization began to take hold (Zanden and Van Riel 2000; Jonge 1968). The industrialization process and business with the Dutch-Indies were reflected in firms listed on the Amsterdam Exchange. This being the case, in the benchmark years 1903 and 1913, our sample is dominated by railway and tram companies that, because of capital-intensive infrastructural projects, needed large amounts of capital. Two more important groups were formed by colonial firms: (a) companies active in the former colony of Indonesia (Dutch Indies), such as the mining, tea, coffee, tobacco, sugar and rubber industries; and (b) companies active in export to the Dutch Indies, such as ship building and traffic, trade, aviation and banks (Nobel and Fennema 2003). While the sample of listed firms consists of few manufacturing firms in 1913, they are increasingly represented in the sample, especially after the late 1910s.

At the beginning of the twentieth century, Dutch companies were relatively small or medium sized compared to Germany or the US, but by 1930, this picture had changed (Bloemen, Kok, and van Zanden 1993). Large-scale enterprises became more important in the manufacturing industry, reflected by the presence of at least four Dutch multinationals: Royal Dutch Shell, Unilever, Philips and AKU. While, in 1906, people still tended to work for small firms (less than 10 employees) rather than for large firms (more than 200 employees), by 1939, 42% of those employed worked for large firms (Gerwen and Seegers 2003).

So, when Dutch industrialization began to take hold, large companies emerged and many new firms were created. Some of these were listed on the Amsterdam Stock Exchange. Private limited liability companies were required by the Commercial Code of 1838 to appoint a managing board. Supervisory boards, in which the members are comparable to the non-executive directors in a one-tier model, were not yet mandatory, but nevertheless, many firms had one. Directors took positions on the supervisory boards of other companies, which resulted in the emergence of a network of directors. At the end of the nineteenth century, this network consisted of a relatively small and closed group of international traders, ship-owners and bankers, dominated by the Amsterdam elites. Banks were not yet related to the manufacturing industry, but instead to the shipping and railway companies, which were the most capital-intensive firms (Schijf 1993; 1984).

It is important to note that the Dutch banking sector had developed differently from that in the UK or Germany. In the early twentieth century, Dutch banks were allowed to be active in securities, whereas in the UK, this activity was mainly limited to stockbrokers. Yet, Dutch banking activities were more narrowly defined than those of the German universal banks, which granted long-term loans to large industrial firms and were shareholders in these companies. Dutch banks were only rarely active in these types of financing in this early period; their principal activity was in trade finance. An important reason for the small scale of Dutch banking was the *prolongatiemarkt*, on which one could get short-term credit for a period of three months, using securities as collateral, and often the credit was prolonged automatically. Using this method, well-off citizens and entrepreneurs could invest their working capital. This system, in which intermediation by banks was unnecessary, functioned well until the 1910s (Jonker 1997) and caused the relatively late modernization of the Dutch banking sector.

This picture changed between 1910 and 1920, during which the connectedness between banks and manufacturing industry increased. This development is explained by an increase in lending by banks to industry, to finance the process of industrialization. Banks tried to obtain a position in the supervisory board of any firm to which they granted a loan, in order to oversee the firm's activities (Jonker 1989, 169). However, recent research shows that Dutch exchange-listed firms, of which the sample in this chapter comprise, hardly used long-term loans in order to finance activities, at least in the period before World War II (Westerhuis and de Jong 2014). After an initial public offering (IPO), companies preferred to finance themselves by retained earnings, preferred shares and/or bonds. Bonds and preferred shares, being fixed-income instruments, were popular financing instruments. This concerns the low degree of transparency that resulted from corporate accounts that were not always very clear or informative. Because of low transparency, external investors could not verify the level of profits to be paid out during this period. The firms also preferred the two financing instruments because they kept voting rights and power with the original owners. Banks, playing a very important role in underwriting issues, obtained positions in the firms' boards to represent the holders of these bonds and shares. In this capacity, they were not so much financiers granting loans as intermediaries giving advice and taking a representative role.

As a result of the growing underwriting activities of banks, they increasingly participated in syndicates—a group of banks that act jointly to loan money to a borrower or underwrite issues. The banks cooperated on a temporary basis, while at the same time being competitors. Interestingly, evidence from one of the largest banks, the *Nederlandsche Handel-Maatschappij* (NHM), suggests that managing directors themselves were active in syndicates, in which the bank took part, sometimes with significant amounts of money. Members of NHM's supervisory board viewed this behavior as normal and conventional; some of the supervisory directors even participated themselves (Graaf 2012, 148, 195). This is important because it provided another incentive for bankers to occupy a board position in firms in which they participated, to oversee their capital.

Yet another reason for the increase in the interlocking between banks and business was that firms were keen to have a banker on their boards (Kymmell 1996). Indeed, one can see that a couple of bankers, while not leaving their mark on economic developments, were quite important in diffusing innovations. During the course of the first decades of the twentieth century, characterized by globalization, many transatlantic investments were possible due to the personal transatlantic networks of intermediaries (Fear and Kobrak 2006). For the stock-broking business, it was important to be well-connected in financial centers such as London, Paris, Berlin and New York. Dutch directors of large banks and stockbrokers traveled abroad regularly in order to maintain contacts and build new relationships (Kymmell 1996). In this way, bankers became exposed to new financial developments and products, such as the use of preferred shares, which became widely spread in Dutch business, most likely on the advice of prominent bankers, such as Van Tienhoven (Westerhuis and de Jong 2014).

The decrease in the density of the network after the 1920s is explained in the literature by the reaction of the banks to the crisis that hit the Dutch banking sector in 1920 and 1921. After the banking crisis of 1921, the tight relationship between banks and industry was lessened, as banks that just recently had granted loans to industry strategically moved back, once again, to trade financing (Jonker 1989). It would only be in the 1960s that they would once again be involved in long- and medium-term credit loans. However, we have seen that our sample of listed firms hardly used these long-term banking loans. This being the case, the return of banks to trade financing is only part of the explanation for the decline in the 1930s. In fact, during the whole period, including that directly after the banking crisis, large banks kept a central position in the corporate network, some of them consistently appearing in the top 10 most central firms. Only in the 1930s, during the Great Depression, does the average degree of these banks diminish, and then only slightly. An important reason for the small decline is that preferred shares, which had been so widespread during the first decades of the twentieth century, became less popular as a financing instrument during the Great Depression. The fixed obligation to pay became a heavy burden for firms in times when they made less profit. In addition, firms started paying off bonds to reduce interest costs. With the diminishing use of these financing instruments, banks had fewer incentives to sit on corporate boards (Westerhuis and de Jong 2014).

Another important development was that the practice of NHM managing directors, as well as some supervisors, to participate actively in syndicates became less attractive after the Wall Street crash of 1929. After the crash, the risk that an issue would fail became larger, reducing the eagerness of directors to participate. In 1936, the supervisory board of NHM decided that the directors could only participate in syndicates when they had created first a reserve fund, while some of the supervisors required prohibition of participation completely (Graaf 2012, 291).

Despite fewer incentives for banks to have board positions in firms in the 1930s, they remained in the top 10 firms with highest degree. Among the big linkers with most positions we find many prominent bankers, individuals with well-known societal engagement. In a manner similar to that of the period before World War I, it is likely that these bankers were invited onto boards because of their knowledge of capital markets, new financial products and their relations to wealthy elites and thus to capital (Westerhuis and de Jong 2014).

4. CONSOLIDATION OF THE NETWORK, 1945–1980

After World War II, the development of the Dutch corporate network peaked again and it remained relatively cohesive during the 1950s, 1960s and 1970s, which coincided with a period of economic growth. Dutch firms were faced with two contrasting developments. First, in 1957, the Indonesian government decided to nationalize Dutch companies and sent many Dutch employees back to the Netherlands. Simultaneously, the Treaty of Rome was signed, which offered new opportunities for Dutch companies because of European economic integration in due time. Both of these events had major implications for Dutch business. The capital-intensive industries, such as shipbuilding, tram and railway companies and oil and mining industries, as well as the cultures active in the Dutch Indies, no longer dominated the exchange list. Instead, manufacturing companies started to become more important. Dutch business also became more internationally oriented, especially after the early 1970s, as foreign sales steadily increased (Jong, Sluyterman, and Westerhuis 2011).

Because of these developments, firms' demand for capital increased. While, in the 1950s, firms funded activities mainly through internal financing, possibly due to high profits, in the 1960s, they turned to banks more often. Dutch banks financed firms in the form of long-term loans and built long-term relations with business (Jong, Röell, and Westerhuis 2010). Consequently, during the 1960s and 1970s, Dutch manufacturing and financial companies formed tightly connected arrangements in which the financial companies occupied central positions. Helmers et al. (1975) describe the interlocks between large Dutch firms based on the largest 86 Dutch firms in 1969. They show that the overall network was rather dense in the 1960s because of banks starting to finance firms with long-term loans. In this way, the banks built long-term relations with Dutch business. Our analyses confirm these findings. Two banks, AMRO Bank and ABN Bank, formed by mergers in 1964, had the most connections with other companies; in 1978, AMRO Bank and ABN Bank had degree centralities of 34 and 33, respectively. Also, the *Maatschappij tot Financiering van National Herstel* (Dutch Recovery Bank) had a central position in the network. This bank was created in 1945 by the state, which held 50% of its shares, in cooperation with the commercial banks, cooperative banks and savings banks. It focused on long-term loans to industry, which were often guaranteed by the state. Only in the 1970s did its average degree diminish slightly. Executives of these large banks were popular as supervisory directors on corporate boards of manufacturing firms because of their knowledge of industry and financial markets. The banks themselves had large supervisory boards within which the most important clients held positions. However, the central role of banks is only part of the explanation for the consolidation of the network after World War II. The increasing use of takeover defenses, especially priority shares, enabled the network to persist over time, which was eventually formalized in 1971 with the structure regime. We will now elaborate further on this.

The network of personal ties between firms was strengthened by the increasing use of priority shares after World War II. Takeover defenses not only defended Dutch firms against hostile takeovers, but also substantially reduced shareholders' involvement in corporate affairs. Using priority shares, voting power about important decisions—such as binding nominations of supervisory and managing directors—became the prerogative of an exclusive group of shareholders; shareholders who represented only a minor part of the total capital of a firm.

One of the reasons for the increase in this type of takeover defense was that many family firms went public and issued their shares on the capital market, which was seen as a necessary step to increase their financial scope. Although new ownership was formally separated from management, many families still protected the former owner-manager using priority shares. The holders of these shares were very powerful because they had the authority of binding nominations of supervisory and managing directors. To illustrate the use of this type of priority shares, in 1970, 306 out of 346 firms (88.4%) had clauses of binding nominations in their charters (Cremers 1971). Executives found this justified because, as H.J. Hellema stated, "A well-connected action between the managers of a company is of vital importance for the company and even with the appointment of supervisory directors it is desirable to persuade oneself that the new supervisor is accepted by the managing board" (Hellema 1965, 10). The right of binding nominations, which was originally vested with the shareholders, was thus transferred to the managers. Using these priority shares, a group of top directors could effectively maintain themselves as a closed system of co-optation.

Simultaneously, the industrialization process, together with the rise of the lower and middle classes, put pressure on the idea of *laissez faire* (Zanden and Van Riel 2000). Its emancipation process had already begun in the interwar period and culminated after World War II, when corporatism was being institutionalized with the creation of the *Stichting van de Arbeid* in 1945 and the *Sociaal-Economische Raad* (SER) in 1950, an advisory body comprised of representatives of employer and employee organizations and the state (Nijhof and van den Berg 2012; Jaspers, Van Bavel, and Peet 2010). After institutionalization of labor, the next step for employees was to get a voice within firms.

Concurrently, and as a result of social developments, the general view of firms had changed. While in the corporate law of 1928, the firm was seen as a contract between shareholders; after World War II, it became increasingly viewed as a social structure of stakeholders, each with different interests (SER 1969; Hellema et al. 1965). This changing view was reflected in the way supervisory directors saw their own role within the firm. Indeed, while in the law of 1928, the role of supervisory directors was only marginally described; in practice, many firms had created a supervisory board to safeguard shareholders' interests. But, after World War II, supervisory directors perceived their role to be broader. W.C.L. van der Grinten, a prominent politician and law professor, argued that the supervisory board no longer functioned as the representative of capital, but that within large companies, supervisors were guided by the interests of the company as a whole. The shareholders' interests were among these, but they were not primary. From his own experience, he explained: "I am a supervisory director at various firms, but I don't feel myself, to be honest, a servant of the interest of capital or a servant of shareholders' interests" (Hellema et al. 1965).

Corporatism and the changed view of the firm as a nexus of stakeholders led to a debate about how firms should be managed, and what role labor, management and capital should have within firms. According to the employees, they should be able to influence firms' management to protect their own interests and to acknowledge their political awareness. The relatively low attendance of shareholders during the annual meetings increased the feeling among employees that the difference in the legal position between employees and shareholders did not square with the facts (about the evolving role of shareholders in Dutch business, see Jong, Röell, and Westerhuis, forthcoming). Before this period, many public limited companies had a strong personal and familial character, and their shareholders felt closely connected with the daily affairs of the firm. With the rise of 'big business', however, a new type of shareholder emerged who felt less related to the interests of the company. This shareholder was more an investor rather than a co-owner, whose goal was to get financial advantage via dividend and differences in exchange rates. This type of shareholder attended the shareholders' meetings less frequently (Boer 1957; SMO 1971). The relatively passive attitude of many shareholders gave the insiders (executives and supervisors) more power, and strengthened the employees in their argument that they should have equal rights.

All of these developments led, in 1960, to the creation of a public committee, headed by law professor Pieter J. Verdam, to discuss whether the legal form of companies should be changed. Particular attention was given to firms' management and supervision. However, the commission could not agree on the necessity to establish a supervisory director representing the employees, as was the case in Germany. A small majority was of the opinion that employees at large companies should elect at least one supervisory director, and two supervisors for a supervisory board consisting of five or more persons (Briede 1980). Since the committee was divided, the government asked the *Sociaal-Economische Raad* (SER) for advice. Although, at first, there was no consensus within the SER about the composition of supervisory boards and the role of employees, eventually, after unanimous advice was given in 1969, they reached a compromise. The SER proposed that supervisory directors appointed each other by co-optation, under the condition that the board was completely independent and neutral, meeting the following criteria: "the board should consist of wise people acting in the general interest" (SMO 1980). The shareholders' meeting and works council indeed received equal rights; both had the right to recommend a member for the board, the right to object and the right to veto a nomination (SMO 1980).

Based on this SER advice, in 1971, the state imposed the structured regime (structuurregime) on large companies, which stated that they were obliged to adopt a two-tier model consisting of a managing and a supervisory board. Members of the supervisory board were nominated on the basis of co-optation, which could also include former directors of the executive board. Though the law was intended to give more voice to employees, it did not go far enough to allow them to appoint a supervisory director. It is interesting that practices, such as co-optation, that were effectively already in use due to the custom of priority shares, were now formalized and institutionalized. One of the important rights that had originally rested with shareholders—appointment of executives and supervisors—had moved over to managers during the last decades, and this move was eventually formalized in corporate law in 1971. Co-optation within many firms was, therefore, practiced informally until 1971, and formally thereafter, resulting in a strong network that would last for a long time. Reputation and trust became critical for getting important positions, and it enabled executives and supervisors to strengthen their position.

5. COUNTERVAILING FORCES AT WORK, 1980–2008

In the western economies, the focus shifted back to the efficiency of the market in this period. These changes were first to be noticed in the US, where they were led by Ronald Reagan, and in the UK, where they were initiated by Margaret Thatcher. The state started to withdraw from business, and because of privatizations and deregulations, there was more room for entrepreneurship and the market. In the Netherlands, these changes occurred during the various administrations of Ruud Lubbers between 1982 and 1994. The Keynesian demand management and active support of business by the state no longer seemed the most effective way to achieve economic growth. An important incentive for the turn in state social-economic policies was the second oil crisis at the end of the 1970s. After the first one, the Dutch state had smoothed the consequences of the crisis with large investments. Banks were also still actively granting loans in the 1970s. The second oil crisis affected Dutch business harshly. Because interest rates rose, firms that had financed their expansions with borrowed money hit problems (Zanden 1997). In the beginning of the 1980s, many firms went bankrupt, among them large conglomerates that had long been considered infallible (Sluyterman 2005).

Dutch firms turned directly to the capital markets without interference of a bank (disintermediation). After the low returns on shares in the 1960s and 1970s, the boom on the stock market in 1983 increased turnover and market capitalization considerably. Subsequent favorable stock prices in the 1990s pushed firms further to the capital market. Also, international and institutional investors became more important financers of Dutch businesses (Jong, Röell, and Westerhuis 2010). The latter became important suppliers of capital, especially when they shifted their investment strategies from risk-adverse bonds to more risk-bearing (foreign) shares (Westerhuis and de Jong 2014). Two important consequences of these developments for our analysis were the changing strategies of banks and firms' increasing focus on the creation of shareholder value. It is to this that we now turn.

Because firms started to turn directly to the capital markets, surpassing the traditional role of the banks (disintermediation), Dutch banks were forced to change their strategies. They started combining commercial and investment banking. Long-lasting relations with industrial companies, which had been characteristic of commercial banking, was replaced by more short-lived contacts, during which banks had an advisory role on the basis of commissions and fees (Westerhuis 2008). The changing strategies of banks are often seen as an important factor in the decline of the corporate network. Heemskerk (2007) attributes the decline of the network from the 1980s onward to the changing strategies of banks, among other things, which shifted from long-term lending to short-term investment banking due to processes of globalization and financialization. Our analysis, however, shows that in the 1990s, banks and bankers were still well connected in the network, which is reflected by the top 10 firms and directors. This calls for further analysis.

Because external financing became more important, and simultaneously, (international and institutional) shareholders became more vocal, firms were forced to concentrate more on shareholder value. Targets were set for the share price in the short term. This focus was reflected in more firms paying dividends, and by firms buying back their own shares in order to 'hike' up the share price, a practice applied in particular in the 1990s. It also resulted in adjustments to the size and composition of the boards. The boards of Dutch firms became more international (Heemskerk and Fennema 2009). These foreigner directors often did not have connections with other firms and were thus less integrated with the Dutch corporate elites. Interestingly, however, large Dutch banks held back on international appointments for a long time and so were relatively late in appointing foreigners in their boards compared to non-financial firms. At ABN AMRO, this idea was first discussed in 1991 for the supervisory board. The bank's directors were afraid, however, that foreigners would not understand the bank's relation with typical Dutch institutions—institutions like the central bank and the central work council. It was also thought that the typical Dutch culture of meetings and gathering (*vergadercultuur*) would lead to misunderstandings. In 1996, two foreigners were appointed to the supervisory board of ABN AMRO, and only in 2000 were any foreigners appointed to the managing board (Westerhuis 2008). The late internationalization of boards might be one of the reasons why, in the 1990s, Dutch banks were still in the top 10 firms with the most ties.

Another consequence of the increasing focus on shareholder value should be diminishing board size. The size of the average managing board of non-financial firms decreased from 3.7 positions in 1968 to 2.9 in 1993, after which it increased slightly to 3.2 in 2003. At the same time, supervisory board size decreased with two positions on average, down from almost seven in 1968, and then to five positions in 2003. Interestingly, the managing boards of financial firms, while already on average larger than boards of non-financial firms, increased substantially in the same period, from 4.0 positions in 1968 to 5.3 in 1993, after which the number diminished to 4.7. The supervisory boards of financial firms were relatively large during the whole of the twentieth century, especially after the 1920s, and remained large with only a small decrease of one position between 1983 and 2003 (from 9.7 positions in 1983 to 8.7 in 2003). The decrease in board sizes of exchange-listed firms, then, was less substantial than one might expect.

The relatively large board sizes were often due to mergers. As Dutch firms (and banks in particular) were reluctant to send away directors and the principle of equality was important, when they merged, they often combined the boards into one. Then, only gradually would the size of the board decrease due to retirement. In 1990, when ABN and AMRO merged, its board size increased to 30 people in 1993 with 35 neighbors. In the next decade, its board size slowly diminished to 23 members in 1998 and 17 in 2003. Consequently, while in 1998 ABN AMRO still had the most neighbors (24), it is only in 2003 that the bank no longer features in the top 10. This can be seen as yet another reason why banks were so persistent in the center of the network.

The decline of the depth of the network in the 1990s can be attributed to changes to the composition and size of boards. However, the changes were not as profound as might be expected, which might be a reason for the persistence of the network into the twenty-first century. The remaining central positions of banks and bankers in the network, despite their changing strategies, formed an important part of this.

Yet another aspect is that the importance of shareholder value was not so self-evident, which had to do with directors trying to prevent losing privileges. This was reflected in the stressing of the importance of shareholder value in annual reports, while often different types of takeover defenses were still in use simultaneously (*decoupling*). Another example is that firms stated in the press that they had abandoned the structure regime, but at the same time, they adopted binding nominations as a takeover defense (see for prevailing use of takeover defenses by listed firms, *Volkskrant* 15 October 2013). Likewise, managing directors were, for a long time, quite reluctant to voluntarily reduce their number of board positions. This soon becomes apparent when one analyzes the implementation of two corporate governance codes; one in 1997 and another in 2004. Discussions about shareholder rights started at the end of the 1980s, leading to the creation of a committee that had to advise on the power balance between control and ownership in Dutch firms. Commission Peters, as the committee was called after its chairman, presented the first corporate governance code in 1997. This consisted of 40 recommendations, mostly based on self-regulation and better transparency (Westerhuis and de Jong 2014). As only few of these were implemented by Dutch firms, a new committee was formed in 2004, chaired by Tabaksblat. The code consisted of principles and provisions with which firms had to comply. If they did not, they had to explain their non-compliance in the annual report (Corporate Governance Code 2004). Apparently, the number of simultaneous board positions directors held was still perceived to be too high. Consequently, an important provision concerning the number of board positions was "a management board member may not be a member of the supervisory board of more than two listed companies. Nor may a management board member be the chairman of listed companies" (Corporate Governance Code 2004, II.1.7). Further, concerning supervisory boards, the code provided that the "number of supervisory boards of Dutch listed companies of which an individual may be a member shall be limited to such an extent that the proper performance of his duties is assured; the maximum number is five, for which purpose the chairmanship of a supervisory board counts double" (Corporate Governance Code 2004, III.3.4). Only after the Tabaksblat code did the numbers of interlocks between exchange-listed companies diminish substantially, which is reflected in our data of 2008.

6. CONCLUSIONS

This chapter has shown the development of the Dutch corporate network based on the 100 largest exchange-listed firms and the 25 largest financial firms in the twentieth and twenty-first centuries. It was revealed that the network persisted for a very long time and only declined significantly in the twenty-first century. We explain the long persistence with management entrenchment.

Managing directors obtained an entrenched position because of the way they financed their businesses. Using internal financing, and bonds and preferred shares, voting rights were kept with directors, and thus they were able to remain relatively autonomous. This power was further strengthened by the enormous use of priority shares, which created groups of directors who sustained themselves by co-optation. Corporatism after World War II legitimized this process and, eventually, it was even formalized by the structure regime of 1971, after which directors could nominate each other formally by co-optation. Because of management entrenchment, changes to improve shareholder rights since the 1980s were not so self-evident, so self-regulation was not followed by a reduction in the number of board positions. Only after provisions concerning the number of board positions that a director could hold simultaneously, which were formulated in the corporate governance code of 2004, did the network decline significantly.

Another explanation for the persistence of the Dutch network of listed firms is the central position that the banks consistently held in the network during the whole of the twentieth century. They held this position even in times when they were less connected with manufacturing firms via credit loans—that is, prior to the 1910s, during the 1930s and since the mid-1980s. Throughout, banks held a very central position in the network and bankers were active as important big linkers. Even when banks changed strategies after the 1980s to a more fee-based income, they remained central in the network. We explained this by the relatively large board sizes and relatively late internationalization of their boards. Further, the chapter showed that the control function of banking interlocks is only part of the story. Bankers sat on boards not only to oversee their credit loans, but also because of other interests. They represented bondholders and preferred shareholders on the boards and, as the bankers participated in syndicates themselves, safeguarded their own interests. It was also often the case that they were invited onto corporate boards because of their specific knowledge and expertise.

NOTES

1. Except for 1998: 22 banks, and 2003: 15 banks.
2. For a large project funded by NWO on the corporate governance and financing of Dutch business, we constructed a database with network data for the period 1903–2008 with five-year intervals (total of 20 benchmark years).

REFERENCES

Berle, Adolf A., and Gardiner C. Means. 1932. *The Modern Corporation and Private Property.* New York: Macmillan.

Bloemen, E., J. Kok, and J. L. van Zanden. 1993. "De vermogensontwikkeling van Nederlands grootste industriële bedrijven, 1913–1950." *Jaarboek voor de Geschiedenis van Bedrijf en Techniek* 10: 133–160.
Boer, Herman de. 1957. *De commissarisfunctie.* Amsterdam: De Bussy. Cited in SMO (Stichting Maatschappij en Onderneming). 1971. *Machtsverdeling in de naamlooze vennootschap.* Den Haag: SMO.
Bordo, Michael D., Alan M. Taylor, and Jeffrey G. Williamson. 2003. *Globalization in Historical Perspective.* Chicago: University of Chicago Press.
Briede, Johan W. 1980. "Inleiding." In *Een andere staat voor het commissariaat? Een rapport van het Overlegorgaan Vertrouwenscommissarissen over de toekomst van het commissariaat en een verslag van de daarover gevoerde discussie.* Scheveningen: SMO.
Cremers, J.H.F.J. 1971. *Prioriteitsaandelen.* Deventer: Kluwer.
Davis, Gerald F., and Mark Mizruchi. 1999. "The Money Center Cannot Hold: Commercial Banks in the U.S. System of Corporate Governance." *Administrative Science Quarterly* 44: 215–239.
DeAngelo, Harry, and Edward M. Rice. 1983. "Antitakeover Charter Amendments and Stockholder Wealth." *Journal of Financial Economics* 11: 329–359.
Fear, Jeffrey, and Christopher Kobrak. 2006. "Diverging Paths: Accounting for Corporate Governance in America and Germany." *Business History Review* 80 (2): 1–48.
Gerwen, Jacques van, and Co Seegers. 2003. "De industrialisatie van Nederland en het industriële grootbedrijf: beeld en werkelijkheid." *NEHA Jaarboek voor economische, bedrijfs en techniekgeschiedenis* 66: 138–171.
Graaf, Ton de. 2012. *Voor handel en maatschappij. Geschiedenis van de Nederlandsche Handel-Maatschappij, 1824–1964.* Amsterdam: Boom Publisher.
Heemskerk, Eelke M. 2007. *The Decline of the Corporate Community. Network Dynamics of the Dutch Business Elite.* Amsterdam: Amsterdam University Press.
Heemskerk, Eelke M., and Meindert Fennema. 2009. "Network dynamics of the Dutch Business Elite." *International Sociology* 24 (6): 807–832.
Hellema, Herman J., Willem C. L. van der Grinten, J.E.A.M. van Dijck. 1965. *De functie van commissaris in de naamloze vennootschap.* Amsterdam: FED.
Helmers, H. M., R. J. Mokken, R. C. Plijter, and F. N. Stokman. 1975. *Graven naar macht : op zoek naar de kern van de Nederlandse economie.* Amsterdam: Van Gennep.
Jaspers, Teun, Bas van Bavel, and Jan Peet, eds. 2010. *SER 1950–2010. Zestig jaar denkwerk voor draagvlak.* Amsterdam: Boom Publisher.
Jensen, Michael C., and William H. Meckling. 1976. "Theory of the Firm: Managerial Behaviour, Agency Costs and Ownership Structure." *Journal of Financial Economics* 3: 305–360.
Jong, Abe de, Ailsa Röell, and Gerarda Westerhuis. 2010. "Changing National Business Systems: Corporate Governance and Financing in the Netherlands, 1945–2005." *Business History Review* 84 (4): 773–799.
Jong, Abe de, Ailsa Röell, and Gerarda Westerhuis. Forthcoming. "The Evolving Role of Shareholders in Dutch Corporate Governance." In *Varieties of Capitalism and Business History: The Dutch Case,* edited by Keetie Sluyterman. London and New York: Routledge.
Jong, Abe de, Keetie Sluyterman, and Gerarda Westerhuis. 2011. "Strategic and Structural Responses to International Dynamics in the Open Dutch Economy, 1963–2003." *Business History* 53 (1): 63–84.
Jonge, J. A. de. 1968. *De industrialisatie in Nederland tussen 1850 en 1914.* Amsterdam: Scheltema & Holkema.
Jonker, Joost. 1989. "Waterdragers van het kapitalisme; nevenfuncties van Nederlandse bankiers en de verhouding tussen bankwezen en bedrijfsleven, 1910–1940." *Jaarboek voor de Geschiedenis van Bedrijf en Techniek* 6: 158–190.

Jonker, Joost. 1997. "The Alternative Road to Modernity: Banking and Currency, 1814–1914." In *A Financial History of The Netherlands*, edited by Marjolein 't Hart, Joost Jonker, and Jan Luiten van Zanden, 94–124. Cambridge: Cambridge University Press.

Kymmell, J. 1996. *Geschiedenis van de algemene banken in Nederland 1860–1914*, part IIB. Amsterdam: NIBE.

Morck, Randall, Daniel Wolfenzon, and Bernard Yeung. 2005. "Corporate Governance, Economic Entrenchment and Growth." In *Journal of Economic Literature* 43 (3): 655–720.

Myers, Stewart C. 1984. "The Capital Structure Puzzle." *Journal of Finance* 39: 575–592.

Myers, Stewart C., and Nicholas Majluf. 1984. "Corporate Financing and Investment Decisions: When Firms Have Information That Investors Do Not Have" *Journal of Financial Economics* 13: 187–221.

Nijhof, Erik, and Annette van den Berg. 2012. *Het menselijk kapitaal. Sociaal ondernemersbeleid in Nederland*. Amsterdam: Boom Publisher.

Nobel, Joris, and Meindert Fennema. 2003. "Economische elites na de dekolonisatie van Nederlands-Indie: verlies van posities, desintegratie van netwerken, verschuiving van netwerken." In *Nederlandse elites in beeld: continuïteit en verandering*, edited by Meindert Fennema and Hubert Schijf. Amsterdam: Amsterdam University Press.

Rajan, Raghuram G., and Luigi Zingales. 2003. "The Great Reversals: The Politics of Financial Development in the Twentieth Century" *Journal of Financial Economics* 69: 5–50.

Schijf, Hubert. 1984. "Economische netwerkelites rond 1900." In *Nederlandse elites in beeld*, edited by J. Dronkers and F. N. Stokman. Deventer: Van Loghum Slaterus.

Schijf, Hubert. 1993. *Netwerken van een financieel-economische elite: personele verbindingen in het Nederlandse bedrijfsleven aan het eind van de negentiende eeuw*. Amsterdam: Het Spinhuis.

SER (Sociaal-Economische Raad). 1969. *Advies inzake de herziening van het ondernemingsrecht*, no. 14. SER.

Shleifer, Andrei, and Robert W. Vishny. 1989. "Management Entrenchment. The Case of Manager Specific Investments." *Journal of Financial Economics* 25: 123–139.

Sluyterman, Keetie E. 2005. *Dutch Enterprise in the Twentieth Century. Business Strategies in a Small Open Economy*. London and New York: Routledge.

SMO (Stichting Maatschappij en Onderneming). 1971. *Machtsverdeling in de naamloze vennootschap*. Den Haag: SMO.

SMO (Stichting Maatschappij en Onderneming). 1980. *Een andere staat voor het commissariaat? Een rapport van het Overlegorgaan Vertrouwenscommissarissen over de toekomst van het commissariaat en een verslag van de daarover gevoerde discussie*. Scheveningen: SMO.

Volkskrant. 15 October 2013. "Nederlandse bedrijven sterk beschermd tegen belagers."

Westerhuis, Gerarda. 2008. *Conquering the American Market. ABN AMRO, Rabobank and Nationale-Nederlanden Working in a Different Business Environment, 1964–2005*. Amsterdam: Boom Publisher.

Westerhuis, Gerarda, and Abe de Jong. 2014. *Over geld en macht. De financiering en corporate governance van het Nederlands bedrijfsleven*. Amsterdam: Boom Publisher.

Woltjer, J. J. 1992. *Recent verleden: de Geschiedenis van Nederland in de twintigste eeuw*. Amsterdam: Balans.

Zanden, J. L. van. 1997. *The Economic History of the Netherlands 1914–1995*. London: Routledge.

Zanden, J. L. van, and Arthur Van Riel. 2000. *Nederland 1780–1914. Staat, instituties en economische ontwikkeling*. Amsterdam: Balans.

6 From National Cohesion to Transnationalization
The Changing Role of Banks in the Swiss Company Network, 1910–2010

Stéphanie Ginalski, Thomas David and André Mach

1. INTRODUCTION

From the very beginning of the study of interlocking directorates, the role of banks in the corporate network has been a defining issue. Two main interpretative models have been developed: the 'finance capital model' and the 'bank-control model' (Scott 1985, 6–9). The former—and older—model, inspired by the Marxist historian Hilferding (1910), postulated the formation of finance capital resulting from the unification of industrial and banking sectors. The latter, formulated during the 1970s, is one in which bankers claimed a seat on the board of directors of the firms that they were financing in order to oversee their investment. In this perspective, then, interlocks between banks and industrial firms are "both expressing and affecting this control" (Scott 1985, 8). This model is often applied to coordinated market economies, which are characterized by the strong involvement of banks in the industrial sector through lending.

Our chapter analyzes the long-term evolution of the Swiss company network, focusing on the role of banks and financial companies with regard to the industrial sector. We fill in a gap in two strands of existing literature on Switzerland that usually ignore each other: studies on interlocking directorates and studies on the financial center. First, the Swiss case is generally considered to be very similar to that of the German 'bank centered' corporate governance system, in which the largest banks occupy a central position in the corporate network. Out of the vast literature that exists in many countries on the history of intercompany networks, especially concerning the relation between banking and industry, only a handful of these studies concentrate on the Swiss case, and almost all of them use contemporary rather than historical data (see Schreiner 1984; Rusterholz 1985; Nollert 1998 and 2005; Loderer and Peyer 2002). These studies—as well as early findings by Giovanoli (1939) and Pollux (1944), who did not use formal network analysis—show that the banking sector occupies a central place in the network. However, they remain very descriptive and static. Only Schnyder et al. (2005) provide a long-term analysis of the Swiss company network. Second, due partly to difficulties in gaining access to the banks' archives, the literature on the Swiss financial center is incomplete, despite the importance of the financial sector to the Swiss economy and the existence of disproportionally large and powerful banks for a country the size of Switzerland (for a recent overview, see Guex and Mazbouri 2010). Some recent studies highlight the international role of Swiss banks and insurance, but studies that concentrate on the domestic activities of large banks, in particular their relations to Swiss industry, are rare (see Cassis and Tanner 1993). Moreover, most studies tend to focus on a short time-period (for a long-term perspective, see Straumann 2010; Mazbouri, Guex, and Lopez 2012).

As Schnyder et al. (2005) show, there are three main phases of the Swiss corporate network: emergence (1910–1930s), consolidation (1930s–1980) and decline of the ties (1980–2010). Our chapter highlights the major role of banks in these different phases. During the first two phases, banks were the backbone of the network. However, the reciprocal ties between the banking and the non-financial sectors at this time are more indicative of the 'class-cohesion model' than the bank-control model for the Swiss case. The 'class-cohesion model' presents interlocks as an expression of cohesion within the ruling class and as a means by which this unity is maintained and strengthened (Scott 1985, 11–12; see, e.g., Useem 1984). During the last 30 years, Swiss banks have played a major role in the weakening of the network as they disengaged from the boards of industrial companies. Three main factors explain this withdrawal: changing financial strategies, shareholder value orientation and internationalization.

2. DESCRIPTIVE CHARACTERISTICS OF THE SWISS COMPANY NETWORK, 1910–2010

We used a sample of the 100 largest Swiss companies for eight benchmark years in the twentieth and twenty-first centuries (1910, 1929, 1937, 1957, 1980, 1990, 2000 and 2010). We included the 25 most important firms in the financial sector (banks, insurance companies and financial companies) and the 75 largest industrial firms. For our network analysis, we derived the composition of the board of directors (BoD) and the main executive director(s) (1–4 people, depending on the year and the company) from different publications such as stock exchange manuals, financial yearbooks, annual reports of the firms and enterprises' monographs. The results of our network analysis are consistent with Schnyder et al. (2005). They allow us to distinguish three main phases in the long-term evolution of the inter-firm ties that we highlighted earlier: emergence, consolidation and decline. The first period, from 1910 to the 1930s, was characterized by the progressive integration of Swiss companies into a national network. Network density increased (see Figure 6.1 below), while the number of isolated and marginal firms decreased (see Appendix I). During this period, the network became quite cohesive; 89% of the firms were included in the main component in

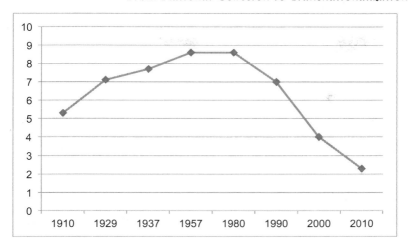

Figure 6.1 Swiss Corporate Network's Density, 1910–2010

Source: Database on Swiss elites during the twentieth century (www.unil.ch/elitessuisses)

1937. At this time, the average distance between two companies was only 2.49. This first phase corresponds to the consolidation of organized capitalism, which occurred at the end of the nineteenth century (for Switzerland, see Jost 1980 and Humair 2004).

The process of network integration continued during the following decades; ties grew denser and many peripheral firms became integrated until the beginning of the 1980s. At that time, only 6% of firms did not share a director with another company (as opposed to 11% in 1937, and 15% in 1910). This second phase could be considered as a period of consolidation. Ties became more inclusive as the percentage of connected firms increased slightly from the 1950s onwards.

The third and last phase is characterized by a very pronounced decline of inter-firm ties. Changes began in the 1980s, but the major transformations took place after this, during the two following decades. Density dropped from 7% in 1990 to only 4% in 2000, and then further to 2.3% in 2010. In 1980, a firm was linked to 8.5 other companies on average, to 7 in 1990, and 10 years later, the mean number of ties was only 4. Multiple ties, indicating more cohesive ties (De Nooy, Mrvar, and Batagelj 2005), also decreased sharply during that period. By the end of the twentieth century, the proportion of isolated and marginal firms was already higher than it was in 1910, and this process continued during the first decade of the twenty-first century. These results are consistent with the findings for other countries, such as the US (Davis and Mrizuchi 1999) and Germany (Beyer 2002; Höpner and Krempel 2003), which also show trends toward network dissolution. This evolution is closely linked to the internationalization of the economy and to deregulation of the financial markets.

110 *Stéphanie Ginalski et al.*

3. SWISS BANKS AND THE FORTRESS OF THE ALPS, 1910–1980

Two closely interrelated dynamics have contributed to the growing interlocking directorates among Swiss firms up to the 1980s. First, the 'autonomization' of Swiss companies from foreign influence after World War I led to the 'nationalization' of the boards of the firms. Second, the rise of the Swiss financial center, which also occurred after the war, led to stronger ties between Swiss banks and industrial companies. As a consequence, the Swiss corporate network grew denser and banks were very central within it.

Constitution of a National Network

Before World War I, interlocking directorates between the largest Swiss companies were mostly regionally based, and several representatives of important foreign companies—mainly German—sat on the boards of the firms. However, World War I led to a process of 'nationalization' of the boards of directors. Company law was revised in 1919, such that it required a majority of the board members in Swiss firms to be Swiss residents, and at least one administrator had to be a Swiss citizen. This regulation aimed to avoid the *Ueberfremdung* (a German term meaning 'overforeignization'— the fact or feeling of being swamped by foreigners) of Switzerland and preserve the national character of Swiss companies (see Lüpold 2010 for a detailed discussion). These new rules, which were included in the new Stock Corporation Law of 1936, resulted in the replacement of many foreign board members by Swiss administrators, and this contributed to growing interlocking directorates among Swiss firms at the national level.

Finance companies illustrate this 'autonomization' of Swiss firms from foreign influence. These were created at the end of the nineteenth century, performing three principal functions for industrial companies: provision of credit, means to raise capital and enabling expansion into new domestic and foreign markets (see Paquier 2001). They were particularly important in the electrical sector, which required considerable investment and in which only long-term capital investment brought return. These finance companies also functioned as intermediaries between large banks and industrial companies. As a consequence, they held a central position in the network. Four finance companies (*Elektrobank, Anlagewerte*, SFSIE and Motor-Columbus) were ranked in the top 10 of firms with high degree centrality, and three of them (SFSIE, *Elektrobank* and *Anlagewerte*) ranked in the top 10 betweenness centrality firms in 1910 (see Appendix I). Several of these finance companies began as joint ventures with foreign banks. *Elektrobank*, for example, was the result of collaboration between AEG (a German company from the energy sector), *Deutsche Bank* and *Crédit Suisse*, one of the largest Swiss banks, one of the largest Swiss banks.[1]

After World War I, due to precarious monetary conditions, German firms and banks were forced to sever their links with these financial firms, and so *Crédit Suisse* looked increasingly to team up with Swiss industrial enterprises. Segreto (1992) coined the term "from made in Germany to made in Switzerland" to characterize this shift. In this new set of circumstances, Swiss banks played a central role. In contrast to the difficulties experienced by German and French financial institutions in the immediate aftermath of World War I, the war and the 1920s marked the rise of the Swiss financial sector to that of a leading actor on the international scene (Mazbouri, Guex, and Lopez 2012). Swiss banks had three major 'trump cards'. First, capital was attracted by comparative financial freedom, such as a tax system that favored the holders of capital and bank secrecy laws. These conditions had existed since the beginning of the twentieth century but were further consolidated by the adoption of the Federal Law on Banks in 1934. Second, Swiss banks benefited from political stability and neutrality, circumstances that facilitated the inflow of foreign capital. Last, the stability of the Swiss franc was a major factor at a time characterized by the manifest instability of the international financial system. The growing importance of large banks led to their stronger involvement in Swiss industrial and financial companies; Swiss banks became major shareholders of financial companies in the electrical sector after the withdrawal of German investors (Segreto 1992, 347). This process contributed to a growing interlocking directorate within the financial sector during the interwar period (see Table 6.1). It is particularly noteworthy that the Swiss network had close ties between large banks and non-financial companies during most of the twentieth century; as shown in Table 6.1, these ties consistently increased until the 1980s. Interlocks within the financial sector, however, declined from the 1940s onwards, which contradicts the 'finance cartel' model proposed by Hilferding (1910).

There are two major consequences of the growing importance of Swiss banks for the Swiss corporate network. First, these banks held very central positions; the three main banks—UBS (*Union de banques suisses*), SBS (*Société de banque suisse*) and *Crédit Suisse*[2]—were consistently in the top 10 of firms with high degree centrality while financial companies lost their influence after World War I (see the Website). Second, banks played a crucial role in the constitution of a national network. At the beginning of the twentieth century, interconnections between firms were based largely on geographical proximity. The three main banks had, for example, strong

Table 6.1 Inter- and Intra-sectoral Ties, Average Degree, 1910–2010

	1910	1929	1937	1957	1980	1990	2000	2010
BANK – IND	2.7	3.9	3.8	3.9	4.1	3.5	1.6	0.8
BANK – BANK	3.0	4.2	4.6	2.7	2.2	1.7	1.0	0.8
IND – IND	2.6	2.9	3.6	5.4	5.2	4.2	2.8	1.8

BANK: Banks, financial institutions and insurance companies
IND: Industrial companies

112 Stéphanie Ginalski et al.

ties with companies from the city where they were incorporated; Basel for SBS (see Sarasin 1998), Zurich for *Crédit Suisse* and Winterthur for UBS. Some of these historical ties persisted right into the latest period of our study, but the importance of geographical proximity decreased over time as the banks increased their ties with industrial firms, including firms from the French part of the country, for example. The integration of regional elites at the national level during the interwar period was also supported by the growing role of powerful and highly representative peak-level business associations (for more details, see David et al. 2009; Ginalski 2012); the banks' economic power went together with their increasing political organization. The Swiss economy thus became more internally integrated, which led to the consolidation of a genuine national network that remained largely stable during the following decades.

Bank Centrality and Class Cohesion

As we have already shown, the links between the banks and non-financial companies became tighter between 1910 and 1980. In the bank-control model, these links could be seen as guaranteeing the lenders a certain degree of control over the companies in which they invest (Scott 1985). In the Swiss case, however, bank-industry ties were often mutual, with banks sending directors to the boards of other companies, but also receiving industrialists on their own boards. This being the case, the 'bank-control' hypothesis does not adequately describe the type of linking. If we look at the composition of the BoD of the three largest banks (UBS, *Crédit Suisse* and SBS) in order to identify the primary affiliation and/or occupation of the directors, we can indeed see that industrialists were well represented in all three (see Table 6.2).

Table 6.2 Main Affiliation of the Directors of the Three Largest Swiss Banks, 1910–2010 (in %)[3]

	1910	1929	1937	1957	1980	1990	2000	2010
N	39	66	57	66	62	70	24	26
Insiders	7.7	22.7	14.0	9.1	6.5	7.1	16.7	7.7
Outsiders	92.3	77.3	86.0	90.9	93.5	92.9	83.3	92.3
Other financial institutions	28.2	13.6	12.3	10.6	4.8	7.1	12.5	53.8
Insurance	2.6	3.0	7.0	7.6	4.8	4.3	12.5	15.4
Industries and services	28.2	27.3	33.3	50.0	62.9	57.1	37.5	15.4
Politicians/ Lawyers/ professors	15.4	22.7	22.8	19.7	17.7	17.1	20.8	7.7
Unknown	17.9	10.6	10.5	3.0	3.2	7.1	0.0	0.0
Total	100.0	100.0	100.0	100.0	100.0	100.0	100.0	100.0
Foreigners	10.3	0.0	0.0	0.0	1.6	2.8	20.8	61.5

Table 6.2 shows three interesting features in line with the general evolution of the company network between 1910 and 1980. First, the disappearance of foreign directors after World War I, related to the process of promoting Swiss nationals on Swiss firms that we have already described. This was only called into question during the 1990s, a matter to which we will return. Second, we can see a growing reluctance on the part of the banks to interlock among themselves. With the exception of SBS, which had private bankers on its board, there were few outside bankers on the boards of the two other major Swiss banks. Third, industrialists represented around 30% of those on the boards of banks between 1910 and 1937, rising to more than 50% during the period after World War II (for similar findings for Germany and England, see Krenn 2008 and Scott and Griff 1985). Why did industrialists sit on the boards of banks? In Germany, during the interwar period, this was determined by the size of the industrial enterprises (according to balance sheets and capital shares). Banks did not only lend, but also issued shares and bonds for industrial firms, especially large ones, and this was an important role. In turn, it became important for the large industrial firms to have representatives on the boards of the banks (Krenn 2008, 88–93). In Switzerland, during the main part of the century, shares and bonds issued by banks were also one source of financing for firms that, taken together with self-financing and loans, related banks to industries (on corporate finance in Switzerland during this period, see Lüpold 2010, chapter 8). Much as was the case in Germany, explanations for interlocking can also be found in a more sociological perspective; familial relations or that banks' boards were important meeting places for the Swiss elite, for example.

In short, the 'two-way' direction of the ties between banks and industrial companies confirms the central position of banks, but also hints at a more reciprocal relation between the banking and non-financial sectors. These reciprocal ties therefore allow us to relativize the bank-control model for the Swiss case and instead place greater emphasis on processes of cooperation, or coordination, that existed between these two sectors. For this reason, we prefer the 'class-cohesion' model,[4] a preference that is confirmed by the important ties within the industrial sector (see Table 6.1). The increasing social cohesion of the Swiss business elite throughout the twentieth century reached its peak during the 1980s, when most of the largest Swiss companies were integrated into a main component of the network. The consolidation of the national network reinforced the traditional model of Swiss corporate governance, which is characterized by the domination of a small category of insiders (for more details, see David et al., 2014). For a long time, this circle of insiders was extremely concentrated, comprised of managers of large companies and the largest banks, and historical shareholders (blockholders), who were often linked to the founding families (see Appendix I; on the importance of family firms within the network, see Ginalski 2012). This 'inner circle' (see Useem 1984) was also well represented in the major business associations and had many connections to the Federal Parliament[5]; it formed a coherent social group with shared values and a shared conception of the firm.

Despite strong criticisms from the left (especially during the 1930s and 1970s) and some tensions between its members, for many decades, the 'inner circle' was responsible for the preservation of the 'fortress of the Alps', a label often applied to Switzerland by international investors (Monks and Minow 1995, 320). In the context of a lax regulatory framework (company law and stock exchange regulations) that left ample room for maneuver in which companies could organize themselves, insiders—specifically, bankers and majority shareholders—showed a high capacity to find satisfactory solutions through mechanisms of self-regulation to stave off potentially destabilizing threats. These solutions contributed to the stability of the network. Indeed, the regulation of proxy voting by banks and the Gentlemen's Agreement of 1961 between the Swiss Bankers Association (SBA) and the major non-financial companies concerning the transferability of registered shares both serve as excellent examples of the high capacity of insiders to overcome their potential divisions and provide negotiated solutions that preserve their positions (for more details, see Mach et al. 2007). They also shed a new light on the role and function of banks in the corporate network.

Industrial companies generally made a deliberate choice to have a strong bank presence on their boards in order to facilitate the reciprocal arrangement. This co-optation allowed the company to integrate banks holding important numbers of proxy votes through clients who deposited their shares in the banks. Because of the banks' large shareholdings, the rules for proxy voting by banks were crucial in determining power relations during shareholder meetings and so within the firm (Schaad 1972; Commission des cartels 1979). The proxy voting system dated back to the beginning of the twentieth century, and was codified in directives of the SBA during the 1960s. Very often, the holders of safekeeping accounts gave the banks a 'general power of attorney', which allowed banks to have proxy votes during all shareholder meetings until the shareholder revoked such power of attorney. This general procuration gave the banks considerable leverage over decisions taken at the Annual General Meetings (AGMs), disadvantaging individual shareholders. It wasn't only the banks that profited from this situation. The companies profited from the proxy-voting system because the presence of the banks during their AGMs ensured that the meetings were quorate, rules set by the Stock Corporation Law to establish the validity of the AGM's decisions. Further, the banks most often voted with the board (Steinmann 1989, 93). As highlighted by Gautschi (1966, 194), a specialist of corporate law: "Representatives of banks [were] less often integrated [in the board of industrial companies] for their importance as lenders than because of the fact that they control[ed] voting rights of clients with shares deposited with the banks or voting rights of investment funds they control[ed]".

In addition, the 'Gentlemen's Agreement' of 1961 concerning the transferability of registered shares also illustrates the tendency and capacity for insiders to successfully act in their own self-interest (for more details, see Lüpold 2010, 864ff.). The Swiss Stock Corporation Law offered companies the option to issue shares in different categories (bearer shares and registered shares) and to limit the transferability of registered shares (a mechanism later called *Vinkulierung*, from the Latin word 'to bind'). This option could be used by historical blockholders to maintain control over their firms, even when they were no longer majority shareholders; shares that were '*vinkuliert*', or 'bound', could not be transferred from one shareholder to another without the consent of the company's board or management. *Vinkulierung* was especially useful in the systematic rejection of foreign investors. In 1957, a ruling of the Federal Tribunal (the Supreme Court in Switzerland) on the separation of the different rights appeared to endanger the functioning of *Vinkulierung*. As a reaction to this threat, in 1961, SBA, along with most of the largest Swiss firms from the industrial and service sectors, came to a 'Gentlemen's Agreement' concerning the transfer of 'bound' shares, which codified the tradability of these shares (published in Dufour and Hertig 1990, 789ff.). By entering into this agreement, the banks expressed their 'reluctant readiness' not to buy orders of registered shares if the buyer did not fulfill the requirements for registration fixed in the company's statutory rules. In exchange, the companies agreed to communicate regularly to the banks the conditions that a buyer of shares had to fulfill. So it was that, "in the name of the higher national interest" (a phrase used in the agreement), but also to prevent a 'politization' of the topic or a state intervention, the banks helped the companies to continue to refuse undesirable investors and notably foreigners.

The examples given of proxy voting and the Gentlemen's Agreement of 1961 indicate that banks often acted in the interests of the companies in which they held board seats, which did not always coincide with their own immediate interests. This is an important finding because, notwithstanding the centrality of banks in the network, it explains why the bank-control model is too radical a view to accurately characterize the Swiss case. In fact, the coordination mechanisms and the bulk-heading of Swiss firms against outside influence was one of the central features of Swiss organized capitalism during the largest part of the twentieth century—a feature that only started to erode during the 1990s. In short, interlocking directorates among Swiss companies, notably between industrial companies and banks, served primarily to protect Swiss firms from the unwanted influence of foreigners or, more generally, outsiders.

4. RECENT TRANSFORMATIONS OF THE NETWORK, 1990–2010: DISINTEGRATION AND TRANSNATIONALIZATION

The general cohesion measures show that the period 1990–2010 saw a general disintegration of the Swiss company network. These admittedly rather rough indicators, however, do not allow for an understanding of the nature of, or reasons for, the changes. It is important, therefore, to look at how the position of the individual companies within the network changed (see the website). The most striking observation concerns the position of the large banks. It is clear that from 1910 to 1990, the financial sector was overrepresented among the most central companies, but the centrality of banks began to decrease after 1990. In 1990, six of the thirteen most central companies belonged to the financial sector; in 2010, the first financial firm appeared at the tenth rank. The analysis of the big linkers confirms the decline of the central position of the financial sector.[6]

Table 6.1 (see Section 3) shows that the very clear decline in network integration from 1990 onwards was due, on the one hand, to the strong decreasing interrelations between banks and industry, which had constituted the backbone of the Swiss company network for the greatest part of the twentieth century, and on the other, to the decline in the links within the industrial sector. Three major interrelated factors contributed to the disintegration of the national company network from 1990 onwards, and in particular, to the diminution of the bank-industry ties: the changing financial strategies of large banks, shareholder value orientation of large banks and firms, and a sharp increase of foreigners among managers and directors.

The Changing Financial Strategy of Banks

The disinvestment of banks from their role in industrial companies is a feature that has been observed in several countries, and has been particularly pronounced in Switzerland. The major Swiss banks have undertaken considerable strategic re-orientations during the last 20 or so years and have become increasingly reluctant to engage in personal ties with non-financial companies. One factor that explains the decreasing number of interlocks between banks and non-financial companies is the process of concentration within the banking sector. For example, UBS and SBS between them were linked to 59 other companies in 1980 and 67 in 1990. After their merger in 1998, however, the new bank (named UBS) had only five ties in 2000, falling to two in 2010.[7] This important decrease was due in large part to the fact that the boards of the two banks were merged into one smaller board, reducing the potential number of interlocks. It would be misleading, however, to consider the decline in bank ties simply as an effect of this concentration. Indeed, it was also clearly a strategic re-orientation by the banks (Schnyder et al. 2005; Larson et al. 2011). What might be termed the 'securitization' of corporate finance induced the largest banks to develop their investment banking activities to the detriment of traditional credit practices (Davis and Mizruchi 1999; Plihon 1999; Beyer 2002; Davis 2009). Banks also faced increasing competition "from insurance companies for both household savings and newly created compulsory occupational retirement plan savings. As households increasingly turned away from the classic bank account, an important and—given Switzerland's low interest rates—cheap source for refinancing for banks started to dry up" (Larson et. al., 2011, 43). These two factors reduced the traditional (interest) incomes of banks and pushed them to seek and develop more profitable avenues, such as investment banking and asset management (see also Mazbouri et al. 2012 for the Swiss case).[8] One consequence of the strategic reorientation of major Swiss banks was their decreasing willingness to entertain close ties with industrial companies. In the investment banking sector, close ties to industrial firms were generally perceived as a conflict of interest, which called into question the credibility of the bank as an investment counselor. Consequently, the more Swiss banks expanded their activities into investment banking and asset management, the less they were inclined to represent themselves on the boards of industrial companies. Table 6.1 illustrates this trend; the average ties between banking and industrial sectors were reduced by a factor of five between 1980 and 2010 (from 4.1. to 0.8).

Shareholder Value Orientation of Large Companies

As in other European countries, from the 1990s onwards, Swiss banks and companies started to increasingly orient their strategies toward the satisfaction of minority shareholder interests. This is illustrated by increased transparency, simplification of the capital structure and the distribution of an increased part of the profits to shareholders (for more details, see Schnyder 2008 and David et al. 2014). Several aspects of a shareholder-oriented corporate strategy directly affected the coherence of the domestic company network. Shareholder activists called for a reduction in the size of BoDs because large boards were considered to be inefficient. This demand seems to have had an impact on the board size of Swiss firms; the mean board size of our 100 firms decreased from 11.5 in 1980 to 9.3 in 2010. Large firms saw larger reductions. Between 1988 and 2007, the size of the boards of the firms quoted at the SMI decreased from 14.6 seats to 10.1 (Volonte 2011, 29). For the three largest banks, the decrease was even more impressive. In 1980, *Crédit Suisse*, UBS and SBS had, between them, 62 seats in their BoDs; in 2010, only 26 seats remained between the two banks (UBS and SBS having merged, as stated earlier). The growing professionalization of the BoDs also contributed to the reduction in the number of interlocks. Indeed, according to the shareholder value ideology, the board members should invest a considerable amount of time in their mandate in order to be more efficient, and thus hold a limited number of seats in other companies (Heemskerk and Fennema 2009, 808). We do indeed observe a strong decrease in the accumulation of mandates among members of the largest Swiss firms. In 1980, 8% of them held three or more mandates, reducing to 4% in 2000 and 2% in 2010 (see Appendix I).

Another factor, linked to the new shareholder value strategy orientation discussed previously, was the restructuring and concentration process in different economic sectors in the 1990s and afterwards. Companies that had been implicated in mergers from 1990 onwards were eager to restructure in order to increase profitability—an obvious commitment to the creation of shareholder value. These companies were, therefore, among those that were most inclined to satisfy shareholders' interests and, as such, it is not surprising that they dramatically cut their ties with other companies. The merger between UBS and SBS, which was the result of six years of confrontation between UBS and Martin Ebner, is an instructive example (Schnyder 2008, 199ff.). Martin Ebner, a former employee of the private bank *Vontobel*, established the BZ Bank in 1985 and went on to also establish several investment companies called 'Visioning'. His investment strategy consisted of acquiring considerable stakes in the largest Swiss companies in order to impose new strategies that prioritized the increase of shareholder value (see Becher 1996). Despite the fact that Ebner did not manage to take the control of UBS, which was his main goal, the merger was a capitulation of the management of the 'old' UBS, and the new bank very soon implemented most of Ebner's demands.

At this time, large listed companies also increasingly financed their activities directly through the capital market. The proportion of bank loans as a source of finance for the enterprises quoted on the Swiss Market Index decreased from 55% to 31% between 1998 and 2006. Simultaneously, the equity ratio of these companies steadily increased (Schachtner 2009, 118–132). The expansion of direct financing was also illustrated by the impressive evolution of Swiss market capitalization since the beginning of the 1990s. This means that non-financial companies became less dependent on bank credit, which led to a decreasing need for bank representatives to sit on their BoDs.

The Transnationalization of the Boards of Directors

Since the 1980s, the increasing international expansion of Swiss companies went hand in hand with important changes in the composition of the BoDs and managers of the largest Swiss companies. Their sociological profile—in terms of nationality, education and career—underwent profound change (for an analysis of the managers sample, see Bühlmann, David, and Mach 2012). In particular, since 1980, there has been a large increase in the number of foreigners sitting on the BoDs of Swiss firms, rising from 3% in 1980 to 34% in 2010 (see also Volonte 2011, 37). This transnationalization has directly affected the structure of the national network, as foreign directors are less connected to other Swiss companies than Swiss directors. Again, the evolution of the largest banks provides a good illustration. Since the 1980s, in order to stay competitive at the international level and to become 'global players', large Swiss banks needed to obtain a critical size, which was not possible simply through internal growth. Therefore, acquisitions, mergers and strategic alliances in investment banking abroad, together with asset and wealth management, became important instruments in the banks' new strategic outlook (Schaub 1992, 243; Larson et al. 2011, 43–44). This affected both the ownership structure of the large banks, and the composition of their BoDs and management. The stronger presence of foreign institutional investors (notably, Anglo-Saxon or Asian investment funds following the 2008 financial crisis) and the importance of their foreign activities led to the recruitment of foreign directors. As shown in Table 6.2, the proportion of foreigners on the BoDs of the three largest banks increased strongly (from 1.5% in 1980 to more than 61% in 2010). This internationalization was illustrative of both the foreign expansion of the largest Swiss banks and the transformation of their activities. These foreigners came largely from other financial institutions (investment funds or insurance) and progressively replaced the Swiss representatives of industrial and service enterprises. Moreover, Swiss managers and owners also sat on the boards of foreign companies. Swiss large multinational companies seem particularly well integrated in transnational corporate networks (Carroll 2010, 163). We can thus hypothesize that the growing importance of interlocking directorates between large, international companies contributed to the decreasing importance of the domestic network.

At the management level, new foreign top managers also represent an increasingly high proportion (see Bühlmann et al. 2012). For example, Brady Dougan, the American CEO of *Crédit Suisse* in 2010, had a long work experience in Asia and the US. He had very few connections with Swiss politics and did not sit on the board of other Swiss firms. Thirty years earlier, Rainer E. Gut, who held the same position at *Crédit Suisse*, sat on the board of five other large Swiss firms and had very close connections with Swiss politics. What is more, he was part of virtually all Swiss networking organizations. He was a captain in the Swiss Army, sat on the committee of the powerful Swiss Bankers Association, and presided at the most important informal meeting of the Swiss business elite, the Rive Reine conference. Arguably, he was one of the best networked businessmen in Switzerland (Lüchinger and Nolmans 2003).

5. CONCLUSIONS

From the beginning of the twentieth century until the 1980s, the largest financial and industrial Swiss companies were progressively integrated into a dense inter-firm network at the national level. Two major factors contributed to the development of interlocking directorates: the 'autonomization' of Swiss companies from foreign influence and the internal integration of the Swiss economy. In this chapter, we focused on the central role of the banks in this evolution. After World War I, Swiss banks and financial companies developed increasing ties with industrial companies and systematically held the most central position in the network. An important turning point was the withdrawal of the German finance companies, which were very important in the electrical sector. This withdrawal led to the growing involvement of the Swiss banks. The role of the banks was then reinforced by the rise in importance of the Swiss financial sector as a leading international actor. As a consequence, banks became increasingly involved with Swiss industrial companies, an involvement that resulted in strong interlocks between the two sectors. The 'bank-control' model, however, does not apply to the Swiss case. We have shown that the ties between banks and industrial companies were often mutual. Not only did bankers sit on the boards of the firms they were financing or in which they held proxy votes, but industrialists also sat on the boards of banks. Between 1910 and 1980, this practice led to industrialists making up from 30% to 60% of the boards of the three largest banks. As a consequence, it is preferable to highlight the function of coordination of the company network and the social cohesion among the Swiss business elite as a whole. The regulation of proxy voting by banks and the 1961 'Gentlemen's Agreement' are highly representative of this cohesion.

From the 1980s onwards, the model in which corporate governance relied in large part on the banks was called into question. This led to a strong decline of the inter-firm network ties. By the end of the twentieth century, network density was even lower than it was before World War I. Three main factors contributed to this change in density. First, Swiss banks started to disinvest from their role in industrial companies, mainly because of the securitization of corporate finance. They also developed new activities, such as investment banking and bancassurance strategies. Second, Swiss banks and industrial firms started to reorient their strategies toward the satisfaction of minority shareholders. According to the shareholder value ideology, it is more efficient to reduce the size of the board and, above all, to limit the number of mandates held by a director. Third, growing internationalization contributed to the decline in interlocking directorates. Our results highlight the growing proportion of foreigners on the boards of large Swiss firms, foreigners who usually do not hold any other mandates in Swiss firms.

Did the decline of interlocking directorates among Swiss firms mean the end of coordination within the business elite? Concerning the recent decline of the American corporate network, Chu and Davis (2011, 18) show that this evolution:

> [. . .] may signal a shift in form but not the function of elite ties—the connections may still be happening, just not in the form of public company interlocks. Corporate interlocks may have served a functional purpose for elite cohesion, but the appeal of this particular mechanism

may have faded and other mechanisms may now connect the American elite. We should then look for burgeoning elite networks in other fora, such as private equity, non-profits, clubs, events or the equivalents of Facebook for the rich and famous.

The same argument might apply for Switzerland. If interlocks are less important than they were 30 years ago, new, more informal and transnational fora seem to favor class-cohesion within the business elite in Switzerland (on this topic, see Bühlmann et al. 2012).

NOTES

1. On the eve of World War I, *Elektrobank's* share capital was equivalent to that of the *Crédit Suisse*. On finance companies during the period 1890–1914, see Hertner (1987).
2. These three large banks played a key role in the development of the finance sector in Switzerland during the interwar period and largely dominated the Swiss banking sector throughout the twentieth century (Mazbouri et al. 2012).
3. Our calculation: It should be noted that certain persons had more than one affiliation (e.g. a business lawyer who was manager of a firm, a university professor who was also the member of a family of entrepreneurs, or private bankers who sat on the board of large banks); in such cases, we only took into account what we considered as the main affiliation. The category of other financial institutions includes other banks (in particular private banks during the first half of the 20th century), trading companies, and investment funds for the more recent period. Insiders refer to the top managers of the banks and to former top managers, who often continued to sit on the BoD (often as president) after their retirement as operative managers. Until 1937, the largest banks had several "*administrateur-délégués*" who were at the same time top managers of the banks and members of the BoD. In 1910, 2000 and 2010, there were only two large banks (CS and SBS in 1910 and CS and UBS in 2000 and 2010).
4. Yet, our data does not allow us to make any strong claim concerning the direction of links and the reasons for the evolution we observe, as we do not have any data on corporate finance.
5. Several multiple directors in our sample were at the same time members of the executive committee of the major business associations and/or members of Parliament.
6. We defined a big linker as a director who held three or more seats in the companies of our sample. Such directors can be expected to have a particularly important role in the economy, as they increase the cohesion of the business elite and may play the role of 'reputational intermediaries', increasing the trust in companies on which boards they sit (Nollert 2005; Windolf 2006).
7. The same holds true for the merger between Ciba-Geigy and Sandoz into Novartis. Whereas Ciba-Geigy and Sandoz cumulated 29 ties in 1990, the new company Novartis had, in 2000, merely 6 ties with other companies, and 3 in 2010.
8. The expansion of banking activity into the insurance business (bancassurance) was another strategy to meet these new challenges. Thus, *Crédit Suisse* incorporated *Wintherthur* Assurance in 1997. In the bancassurance strategy, financial services and insurance products needed to be as comprehensive as possible and available under the same roof. This strategy failed, however, and

the divestiture of Winterthur to AXA in 2006 signaled this failure. After that, the cooperation was limited to the development of agreements between insurance companies and financial service providers (on the bancassurance strategy, see Heemskerk and Schnyder 2005; Gantenbein 2008, 47).

REFERENCES

Becher, Jörg. 1996. *Das schnelle Geld: Martin Ebners Weg zur Macht*. Zürich: Bilanz ABC-Verlag.

Beyer, Jürgen. 2002. "Deutschland AG a.D: Deutsche Bank, Allianz und das Verflechtungszentrum grosser deutscher Unternehmen." MPIfG Working Paper 02 (4). Accessed March 12, 2012. http://www.mpifg.de/pu/workpap/wp02-4/wp02-4.html.

Bühlmann, Felix, Thomas David, and André Mach. 2012. "The Swiss Business Elite (1980–2000). How the Changing Composition of the Elite Explains the Decline of the Swiss Company Network." *Economy and Society* 41 (2): 199–226.

Carroll, William. 2010. *Corporate Power in a Globalizing World*. Rev. ed. Toronto: Oxford University Press.

Cassis, Youssef, and Jakob Tanner. 1993. *Banques et crédit en Suisse/Banken und Kredit in der Schweiz (1850–1930)*. Zürich: Chronos.

Chu, Johan S. G., and Gerald F. Davis. 2011. "Who Killed the Inner Circle? The Breakdown of the American Corporate Elite Network, 1999–2009." Paper 1. Accessed March 12, 2012. http://opensiuc.lib.siu.edu/pnconfs_2011/1.

Commission des cartels. 1979. *Die Konzentration im schweizerischen Bankgewerbe*. Bern.

David, Thomas, Stéphanie Ginalski, André Mach, and Frédéric Rebmann. 2009. "Networks of Coordination: Swiss Business Associations as an Intermediary between Business, Politics and Administration during the 20th Century." *Business and Politics* 11 (4): 1–38.

David, Thomas, André Mach, Martin Lüpold, and Gerhard Schnyder. 2014. *De la "forteresse des Alpes" à la valeur actionnariale: Histoire du gouvernement d'entreprise suisse au 20e siècle*. Zurich: Seismo.

Davis, Gerald. 2009. *Managed by the Markets. How Finance Re-Shaped America*. New York: Oxford University Press.

Davis, Gerald, and Mark Mizruchi. 1999. "The Money Center Cannot Hold: Commercial Banks in the US System of Corporate Governance." *Administrative Science Quarterly* 44 (2): 215–239.

De Nooy, Wouter, Andrej Mrvar, and Vladimir Batagelj. 2005. *Exploratory Social Network Analysis with Pajek*. New York: Cambridge University Press.

Dufour, Alfred, and Gérard Hertig. 1990. *Les prises de participation: l'exemple des offres publiques d'achat*. Lausanne: Payot.

Gantenbein, Marco. 2008. "Swiss Annuities and Life Insurance." In *Swiss Annuities and Life Insurance: Secure Returns, Asset Protection, and Privacy*, edited by Marco Gantenbein and Mario A. Mata. Hoboken: John Wiley.

Gautschi, Georg. 1966. Bericht und Vorschläge zu einer Revision des Schweizerischen Aktienrechts von 1936. Unpublished report, Archives Fédérales Suisses, E 4110 (B) 1989/197, vol. 32. Zürich.

Ginalski, Stéphanie. 2012. "Du capitalisme familial au capitalisme financier? Le cas de l'industrie Suisse des machines, de l'éléctrotechnique et de la métallurgie au 20e siècle." PhD dissertation, University of Lausanne.

Giovanoli, Fritz. 1939. *Libre Suisse, voici tes maîtres*. Zurich: Ed. Jean Christophe.

Guex, Sébastien, and Malik Mazbouri. 2010. "L'historiographie des banques et de la place financière suisse aux 19–20e siècles." *Traverse: Revue d'histoire* 1: 203–228.

Heemskerk, Eelke, and Meindert Fennema. 2009. "Network Dynamics of the Dutch Business Elite." *International Sociology* 24 (6): 807–832.

Heemskerk, Eelke, and Gerhard Schnyder. 2005. "Small States, International Pressures, and Interlocking Directorates: The Cases of Switzerland and the Netherlands." *European Management Review* 5 (1): 41–54.

Hertner, Peter. 1987. "Les sociétés financières suisses et le développement de l'industrie électrique jusqu'à la Première Guerre mondiale." In *Un siècle d'électricité dans le monde*, edited by Fabienne Cardot, 341–355. Paris: PUF.

Hilferding, Rudolf. 1910. *Le capitalisme financier. Etude sur le développement récent du capitalisme.* Paris: Ed. Minuit.

Höpner, Martin, and Lothar Krempel. 2003. The Politics of the German Company Network. MPIfG Working Paper 9. Accessed February 20, 2011. http://www.mpifg.de/pu/workpap/wp03-9/wp03-9.html.

Humair, Cédric. 2004. *Développement économique et Etat central (1815–1914). Un siècle de politique douanière au service des élites.* Bern: Peter Lang.

Jost, Hans-Ulrich. 1980. "Aperçus théoriques des relations entre l'Etat, l'économie et le capital entre 1870 et 1913. Le cas de la Suisse." *Bulletin du département d'histoire économique.* Geneva: Université de Genève.

Krenn, Karoline. 2008. "Von der 'Macht der Banken' zur Leitidee des deutschen Produktionsregimes: Bank-Industrie-Verflechtung am Beginn des 20. Jahrhunderts." *Zeitschrift für Unternehmensgeschichte* 53 (1): 70–99.

Larson, Mitchell, Gerhard Schnyder, Gerarda Westerhuis, and John Wilson. 2011. "Strategic Responses to Global Challenges: The Case of European Banking, 1973–2000." *Business History* 53 (1): 40–62.

Loderer, Claudio, and Urs Peyer. 2002. "Board Overlap, Seat Accumulation and Share Prices." *European Financial Management* 8 (2): 165–192.

Lüchinger, René, and Erik Nolmans. 2003. *Rainer E. Gut: Bankier der Macht. Anatomie einer Karriere.* Zürich: Bilanz Verlag.

Lüpold, Martin. 2010. "Der Ausbau der 'Festung Schweiz.' Aktienrecht und Corporate Governance in der Schweiz, 1881–1961." PhD dissertation, University of Zurich.

Mach, André, Gerhard Schnyder, Thomas David, and Martin Lüpold. 2007. "Transformations of Self-Regulation and New Public Regulations in the Field of Swiss Corporate Governance (1985–2002)." *World Political Science Review* 3 (2): 1–32.

Mazbouri, Malik, Sébastien Guex, and Rodrigo Lopez. 2012. "Finanzplatz Schweiz." In *Wirtschaftsgeschichte der Schweiz im 20. Jahrhundert*, edited by Patrick Halbeisen, Margrit Müller, and Béatrice Veyrassat, 467–518. Basel: Schwabe.

Monks, Robert, and Nell Minow. 1995. *Corporate Governance.* Cambridge: Blackwell Publishers.

Nollert, Michael. 1998. "Interlocking Directorates in Switzerland: a Network Analysis." *Revue suisse de sociologie* 24 (1): 31–58.

Nollert, Michael. 2005. *Unternehmensverflechtungen in Westeuropa.* Münster: Lit Verlag.

Paquier, Serge. 2001. "Swiss Holding Companies from the Mid-Nineteenth Century to the Early 1930s: The Forerunners and Subsequent Waves of Creations." *Financial History Review* 8: 163–182.

Plihon, Dominique. 1999. *Les banques: nouveaux enjeux, nouvelles stratégies.* Paris: La documentation française.

Pollux. 1944. *Trusts in der Schweiz. Die schweizerische Politik im Schlepptau der Hochfinanz.* Zurich: Association for Economic Studies.

Rusterholz, Peter. 1985. "The Banks in the Centre: Integration in Decentralized Switzerland." In *Networks of Corporate Power. A Comparative Analysis of Ten Countries*, edited by Frans M. Stokman, Rolf Ziegler, and John Scott, 131–147. Cambridge: Polity Press.

Sarasin, Philipp. 1998. *La ville des bourgeois. Elites et société urbaine à Bâle dans la deuxième moitié du XIXe siècle.* Paris, Montréal: L'Harmattan.

Schaad, Hans-Peter. 1972. *Das Depotstimmrecht der Banken nach schweizerischem und deutschem Recht.* Zurich: Schulthess.

Schachtner, Michael J. 2009. "Die Internationalisierung von Accounting Standards und deren Einfluss auf die Unternehemensfinanzierung: eine Analyse börsenkotierter Unternehmen in der Schweiz und in Deutschland." PhD dissertation, University of St. Gallen.

Schaub, Vera. 1992. *Konzernpolitik im Schweizer Bankbereich.* Bern: P. Haupt.

Schnyder, Gerhard. 2008. "Corporate Governance Reform in Switzerland: Law, Politics and the Social Organization of Business, 1965–2005." PhD dissertation, University of Lausanne.

Schnyder, Gerhard, Martin Lüpold, André Mach, and Thomas David. 2005. "The Rise and Decline of the Swiss Company Network During the 20th Century." IEPI Working Paper.

Schreiner, Jean-Paul. 1984. "Le capital financier et le réseau des liaisons personnelles entre les principales sociétés en Suisse." *Revue d'économie industrielle* 29: 78–95.

Scott, John. 1985. "Theoretical Framework and Research Design." In *Networks of Corporate Power. A Comparative Analysis of Ten Countries,* edited by Frans M. Stokman, Rolf Ziegler, and John Scott, 1–19. Cambridge: Polity Press.

Scott, John, and Catherine Griff. 1985. "Bank Spheres of Influence in the British Corporate Network." In *Networks of Corporate Power. A Comparative Analysis of Ten Countries,* edited by Frans M. Stokman, Rolf Ziegler, and John Scott, 20–44. Cambridge: Polity Press.

Segreto, Luciano. 1992. "Du Made in Germany au Made in Switzerland. Les sociétés financières suisses pour l'industrie électrique dans l'entre-deux-guerres." In *Electricité et électrification dans le monde,* edited by Monique Trédé, 347–367. Paris: PUF.

Steinmann, Markus. 1989. *Präventive Abwehrmaßnahmen zur Verhinderung unfreundlicher Übernahmen mit Mitteln des Aktienrechts.* Grüsch: Rüegger.

Straumann, Tobias. 2010. *Fixed Ideas of Money: Small States and Exchange Rate Regimes in Twentieth-Century Europe.* Cambridge and New York: Cambridge University Press.

Useem, Michael. 1984. *The Inner Circle. Large Corporations and the Rise of Business Political Activity in the US and UK.* New York, Oxford: Oxford University Press.

Volonte, Christophe. 2011. "Wie hat sich die Struktur des Verwaltungsrates schweizerischer Firmen in den beiden letzten Jahrzehnten verändert?" Accessed April 15, 2013. http://ssrn.com/abstract=1966329.

Windolf, Paul. 2006. "Unternehmensverflechtung im organisierten Kapitalismus: Deutschland und die USA im Vergleich 1896–1938." *Zeitschrift für Unternehmensgeschichte* 51 (2): 191–222.

7 Austria Inc. under Strain, 1937–2008
The Fading Power of *Creditanstalt* Bank and the End of the Nationalized Industry

Philipp Korom

1. INTRODUCTION

Austria Inc. (Ziegler, Bender, and Biehler 1985)—the tightly knit intercorporate network that facilitated control and coordination among companies in Austria—underwent a number of remarkable transformations during the twentieth century. After the bankruptcy of *Creditanstalt (CA)* in 1931 and its bail out by the state, banking concentration culminated in widespread bank industry relations that were part and parcel of the capitalist market economy of the young First Republic of Austria. Contrary to the widespread assumption that Germany was the home of universal banking, it can be argued to be found in a purer form under the Habsburg monarchy (Teichova 1994, 4). After the break-up of the monarchy, banks, especially CA, continued to hold large industrial clients.

The 'Germanization' of the Austrian economy reached its climax after the Anschluss of March 1938. Between 1938 and 1945, no single stone was left unturned in the Austrian shareholding structure. Austrian industrial enterprises were integrated into huge German banks, the 'Aryanisation' of Jewish-owned companies causing massive structural breaks.

After World War II, Austria Inc. was rebuilt from scratch. Rapid economic development and the nationalization of former German property and banks favored an unparalleled expansion of Austria Inc., which reached its peak in the 1960s and 1970s during the Second Republic. It formed the basis of an institutional framework consisting of a mixed economy containing strong elements of state intervention. Indeed, until the mid-1980s, Austria had one of the largest public sectors in Western Europe (Nowotny 1996). Following the international trend, moves toward privatization gathered momentum when major state-owned enterprises (SOEs) incurred significant losses in the 1980s. Because of their numerous industrial holdings, there were serious repercussions for both public banks—the CA and the *Länderbank* (Rathkolb 2010). The state set out to privatize large SOEs, though at first only partially; it was not until the late 1990s that SOEs were fully transferred to private ownership (Turnheim 2009). The ongoing process of privatization was one of the two main driving forces of the erosion of Austria Inc. The second force for declining cohesion can be located within the banking sector. Decreasing bank-industry relations, as well as mergers between leading Austrian banks, are at the root of many of the metamorphoses of Austria Inc. *CA*, the traditional backbone of the banking network, disappeared; in 1997, *CA* began a merger with Bank Austria, which later joined the Italian banking group *Unicredit* and disconnected from the remnants of the Austrian nationalized industry.

Despite major signs of erosion since the 1970s, parts of the network infrastructure are still in place today (Korom 2013). The resilience of this network is due partly to national business groups, among them the banking group *Raiffeisen*, that stepped into the power vacuum created by massive privatizations.

In what follows, the evolution of Austria Inc. will be traced in detail using an analysis of interlocking directorates between 1937 and 2011. The analysis relies on a notion of interlocking directorates as opportunity structures that allow for coordination between companies (Windolf 2006). The more disorganized the network becomes, the smaller the *potential* coordinative capacity of the economy. It is the exploration of such an infrastructure that allows us to identify critical junctures of economic development—i.e., periods of significant change—that are hypothesized to produce distinct legacies (Collier and Collier 1991, 27). This study does not limit itself to the description of changing macrostructures, but aims at reintroducing 'agency' into the study of intercorporate networks (Schnyder and Heemskerk 2008; Ferraro et al. 2012) by focusing on the changing strategies of companies *and* the state. It transpires that both are essential for understanding the evolution of Austria Inc. General interpretations of the pathways of the network that emerge from the data are examined on the basis of existing contributions on Austria Inc. (Eigner 1997a-c; Dritsas, Eigner, and Ottosson 1996; Morawetz 1985; Ziegler 1984; Ziegler et al. 1985).

2. DESCRIPTIVE CHARACTERISTICS OF THE AUSTRIAN CORPORATE NETWORK, 1937–2008

In (historical) social network studies, it is important to consider which actors to include, and in this chapter, a clear external definition of the boundaries is applied (the nominalist approach). The boundary of the set of the 125 largest companies was defined by four selection criteria as follows: the top 20 banks were defined in terms of assets itemized on balance sheets and the top 5 insurance companies were selected according to premium income; turnover (years 1983, 1992 and 2008) and total assets (years 1937, 1949, 1958 and 1967) were the basis for selection of the top 100 companies for all other (non-financial) sectors. Such a sampling strategy is close to that used in the most comprehensive investigation of intercorporate networks (Stokman, Ziegler, and Scott 1985). It deviates, however, from previous work that presumes nominal share capital as the best accounting indicator. A comparison of the results for the year 1937 with those presented in a study by Dritsas et al. (1996) that defined its sample by share capital shows that despite minor empirical differences, these two approaches lead to the same overall insights into the corporate structure. Foreign companies that are listed separately in the various editions of the *Finanzcompass* (1938–1968)[1] were generally not taken into account because it was not possible in every case to establish clearly whether business activities were located mainly inside or outside Austria.[2]

The *Wirtschafts-Trend-Zeitschriftenverlagsgesellschaft* regularly publishes a list of the largest companies (*Trend Top 500*) according to turnover, and it is on this that the study relies for samples between 1983 and 2008.[3] Information on the managers who sat on the executive (*Vorstand, Geschäftsführung*) or supervisory boards (*Aufsichtsrat*) of 'big business' was drawn either from the *Firmendatenbank Österreich* or various editions of the handbook *Österreich 2000,* both edited by the *Hoppenstedt-Verlag*. For all samples between 1937 and 1967, a sampling list was constructed by collecting and comparing the declared total assets of all registered companies. Again, the names of all managers (*Vorstände, Direktoren, Präsidenten, Verwaltungsräte*) were used for creating networks of interlocking directorates.[4]

As a complete historical sequence cannot be reconstructed, 'snapshots' of the evolution of Austria Inc. were taken. It was felt that the chosen points in time could provide information about whether the network developed via self-reinforcing sequences with limited change or underwent more dramatic reconfigurations. The first benchmark year, 1937, fleshes out the structure of the corporate network after the resolving of the CA crisis (Stiefel 1983) by heavy sacrifices of the state, which became its principal shareholder. By an "extensive writing off of advances, the cancelling of shares (lying in the portfolio of the CA) and the conversion of a part of the credits into new share capital" (Weber 1991, 24), the state started to steer CA and other banks in the reconstruction of dependent, indebted industrial companies. In 1949, the reconstruction of an economy shattered by World War II was in its infancy.[5] The public sector dominated the Austrian economy in 1949, 1958, 1968 and 1983. From the 1980s onwards, the nationalized industry increasingly required state subsidies and capital injections. Austria's large-scale privatization program started in October 1987, when shares in OMV, a monopoly belonging to the nationalized petroleum industry, began to be traded on the Vienna Stock Exchange. The benchmark year of 1992 captures a sequence during the 1990s, when a real 'wave' of privatization began to develop. The Austrian People's Party (ÖVP) formed a coalition with the nationalist Freedom Party (FPÖ) in 2000, which accelerated the pace of privatization (Obinger 2006). In 2008, the last benchmark year, the state had finally lost its substantial control over the economy.

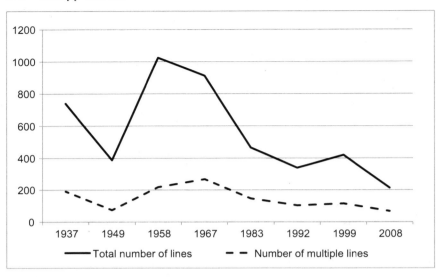

Figure 7.1 The Evolution of Simple and Multiple Personal Ties between the Largest 125 Austrian Companies, 1938–2008

Figure 7.1 reveals that, with the exception of disruptions caused by World War II, the development of Austria Inc. is marked by a period of continuous connective growth (1949–1958) followed by a period of decline (1958–2008; with the exception of 1999, which contradicts the general trend). The measures of network connectivity presented in Figure 7.1, all versus multiple interlocking directorates only, are not undisputed. Stinchcombe (1990, 381) argues, for example, that there exists no clear basis for the interpretation of interlocking directorates, as long as it is uncertain "what flows across the links, who decides on those flows in the light of what interest". The uniform manner in which thin (single-director) and thick (multiple-director) lines develop throughout the twentieth century, however, throws doubt on usual criticism, as thick lines allow a relatively unambiguous interpretation. These lines are indicators of "a hierarchy of control in place, or at least a formalized coordination of business strategies" (Carroll and Fennema 2002, 400). In the Austrian case, multiple interlocking directorates are mostly a secondary phenomenon that occurs alongside existing property relations. The two measures differ in total number per year, but follow the same trajectory, with the exception of the highest point that is either reached in 1959 (all lines) or 1968 (multiple lines only). If one takes a skeptical stance toward interlocking directorates, the heyday of Austrian corporate network could be attributed to the 1970s rather than the 1960s.[6] Whatever interpretation might be preferred, Figure 7.1 reveals that in later years, interlocks declined to such an extent that by 2008, the level during post-World War II was reached once again.

Table 7.1 General Structure of the Network, 1938–2008

	1937	1949	1958	1967	1983	1992	1999	2008
Number of firms (N)	125	125	125	125	125	125	125	125
Connected firms	111 (88.8%)	87 (69.6%)	115 (92.0%)	117 (93.6%)	90 (72.0%)	83 (66.4%)	99 (79.2%)	82 (65.6%)
Isolated firms	14 (11.2%)	38 (30.4%)	10 (8.0%)	8 (6.4%)	35 (28.0%)	42 (33.6)	26 (20.8%)	43 (34.4%)
Marginal firms	20 (16.0%)	21 (16.8%)	12 (9.6%)	13 (10.4%)	23 (18.4%)	19 (15.2%)	28 (22.4%)	19 (15.2%)
Isolated and marginal firms	34 (27.2%)	59 (47.2%)	22 (17.6%)	21 (16.8%)	58 (46.4%)	61 (48.8%)	54 (43.2%)	62 (49.6%)
Firms in the main component	107 (85.6%)	85 (68.0%)	115 (92.0%)	117 (93.6%)	88 (70.4%)	79 (63.2%)	88 (70.4%)	73 (58.4%)
Number of components	1	1	1	1	1	2	3	3

Note: For other indicators on the corporate network, see Appendix I.

130 *Philipp Korom*

A more detailed picture of changing corporate structures of Austria Inc. is revealed in Table 7.1. Looking more closely at the network, one sees that the number of connected firms, as well as the size of the largest component, reaches its climax in the 1970s (and not the 1960s). The proportion of firms embedded in the main component is an especially meaningful indicator for the connectedness of a network. As long as the majority of corporations are linked to each other, and not located in dozens of scattered smaller components, network decline is certainly not at the horizon.

Comparing elements of the microstructure, such as the number of connected and isolated firms, also suggests that 2010s represent historical lows. It is thus reasonable to suggest that today's network cohesion is even lower than it was in Austria's postwar economy.

Such a description of the evolution of Austria Inc., however, has one important caveat: interlocking directorates inform us only of the *potential* influence that corporate agents command. It is highly likely that structural network studies lead us, for example, to overestimate banks' influence. Take the example of Josef Joham, the former Generaldirektor of *Creditanstalt*. How likely is it that a banker has been an effective insider agent with respect to as many as 30 enterprises? The sheer number of accumulated directorships suggests that the actual exercise of bank power was restricted (Eigner 1997a, 93). Despite this reservation, Figure 7.1 and Table 7.1 summarize rather clear empirical evidence on the decline of the network macrostructure from the second half of the twentieth century onwards.

3. THE INTERWAR PERIOD AND THE ECONOMIC *ANSCHLUSS*, 1918–1944: FROM BANK-DOMINATION TO 'GERMANIZATION'

The downfall of the monarchy caused a fundamental rupture in the basic structure of the Austrian economy; the former core of a European great power found itself reduced to a small country. With the national revolutions of 1918, Austria, the 'leftover', was cut off from its supplies of food and raw materials, as well as its markets for industrial goods. As it became clear that all successor states would pursue protectionist policies with high tariffs and focus on neo-mercantilism in order to establish economic self-sufficiency, the conviction that the small state would not be able to survive became widespread among elites ('the state that nobody wanted').[7] The considerable assets of industrial capacity that the country still possessed were generally overlooked; in any case, these were underestimated (März and Szecsi 1981, 124). However, there were also enormous post-war losses. Nostrification legislation required that if a company's head office was located in Vienna but its operations were not, that the head office be moved to the states in which the company operated. In many cases, industrial conglomerates, typically steered by banks, ceased to exist. This, however, did not bring about an end to Vienna's role as a financial intermediary between Western investors and industrials in central and southeast Europe. "Foreign participations in the share capitals of the Viennese banks increased from 10.4 per cent in 1913 to 30.5 per cent in 1923" (Eigner 1997a, 102), a fact that was clearly mirrored by the multinational composition of managers sitting on the boards of Viennese banks in the 1920s. The continued impressive personal representation of these banks on Austrian industrial boards originated partly from the banks' strategy to force firms to repay credits by new share issues. "This policy of 'Veraktionierung', which was part of the common 'fight into assets', resulted in a huge holding of industrial equities at the end of the inflationary period [1922, PhK]" (Weber 1991, 21). In contrast to Germany, where in times of inflation, large-scale industries could emancipate themselves from banks, the rising need for credit in Austria led bank-industry relations to intensify (Eigner 1997b). It seems reasonable to suggest that the 'tally' of industrial directorships occupied by bankers was at its peak in the 1920s.

A crucial turning point in universal banking is usually associated with the crisis of *CA* in 1931, for which two main causes are identified in the literature. First, the bank suffered from the Great Depression, which hit its vast industrial portfolio and made many of its loans unrecoverable. Second, the merger with the bankrupt *Bodencreditanstalt* in 1929, Austria's second largest bank and industrial holding, led to additional losses.[8] To restore the capital of *CA*, the Austrian government entered into seemingly endless negotiations with a consortium of international investors that resulted in the Republic of Austria guaranteeing all of the bank's deposits and other liabilities. The withdrawal of many foreign deposits and the rescue by the state led to a so-called 'Austrification' of *CA*, "a bank which had a business volume of 635m sch. in 1932, in contrast to 1,400m sch. in 1929 and even 1,885m sch. in 1930" (Stiefel 1983, 428). As the *CA* merged with two other banks, the *Wiener Bank-Verein* and the *Niederösterreichische Escompte-Gesellschaft*, a financial colossus was established that one can claim dominated the Austrian economy—a claim that is supported by an analysis of interlocking directorates in the first benchmark of this study. By 1937, only four large Viennese banks were left: *Creditanstalt-Wiener Bankverein, Credit-Institut*, the branch office of the French *Länderbank* and *Mercurbank*, which was virtually a subsidiary of *Dresdner Bank*. After the dissolution of the Austro-Hungarian Empire, these banks did not limit their sphere of action to Austria and its industries but continued their business in the whole Danube region (Kernbauer, Marz, and Weber 1983, 365). In the same year, there were only 49 large enterprises with more than 1,000 employees operating in what we now call Austria. By European dimensions, there was only one big firm, namely the *Alpine Montangesellschaft* (Mathis 1990, 138). The *Creditanstalt-Wiener Bankverein*, with a degree centrality of 45,[9] was by far the most central company in the network of interlocking directorates. Every central industrial undertaking (degrees 25–37), whether belonging to such different branches such as steelworks (as in the case of *Schoeller-Bleckmann*) or electricity supply (as in the case of *Österreichische Kraftwerke*), had at least one director of *CA* on its board (*Verwaltungsrat*). As a consequence, the director-generals of CA can also be found among the leading 'big linkers' in 1937. As Dritsas et al. (1996, 183) point out, it was industrials interlocking with more than one bank on its boards (as, for example, *Alpine*) that were most likely to be found within the core of Austrian 'big business'. Generally, there was no significant 'Germanization' of the Austrian economy before the *Anschluss* of March 1938 (Matis and Weber 1992, 109). However, the two outposts of Nazi penetration of Austria, the German-controlled *Alpine* and *Siemens-Schuckert-Werke* could be seen to belong to the best-connected players in the network. The fact that, besides *CA*, no other domestic financial institution appeared among the best-connected companies clearly suggests a "one-bank system" (Teichova 1994, 8) with the giant *Creditanstalt*.

The Nazi occupation between 1938 and 1945 temporarily put an end to Austria Inc. In contrast to other annexed territories, Austria was treated as an integral part of the German *Reich*. Its resources of raw material (iron ore, magnesium, graphite), means of production and cheap labor force served the purpose of fulfilling the 'Four-Year Plan' by establishing a self-sufficient economy. The *Anschluss* came with a process of 'Germanization' of Austrian industry and banking that resulted in a radical change of property. The *CA* was first taken over by the Reich-owned holding, *VIAG*, and was later integrated into the *Deutsche Bank* (Matis and Weber 1992). The many interests of *CA* in industrial companies were transferred with the enlargement of the *Reichswerke* through acquisitions in the *Ostmark*. A company formation boom took place. Comprehensive investments were made to expand the Alpine water power stations. The capacity of steel production was increased by setting up the *Reichswerke Göring* in Upper Austria, later *VOEST,* which merged with the Styrian *Alpine-Montan AG* and *Lenzing* viscose plant, and the aluminum works were created at *Ranshofen* (Bardy 1994). The establishment of these and other large-scale enterprises were part of a modernization of the local economy, "albeit by a *dependent modernization of a quasi-colonial type,* subordinated to the needs and wants of the German war economy" (Weber 1997, 124). Despite the destruction and human loss of the bombing raids of World War II, the aforementioned companies were the 'pacemakers' of Austria's quickly expanding postwar economy (März and Szecsi 1981, 125). Besides this expansion-promoting tendency, the destructive one should not be omitted: the (economic) exclusion of Jews and the confiscation of their property. The 'Aryanisation' deprived Austria of its large Jewish middle class, as well as of many Jewish industrialists and bankers. "Also taking into account the 'Aryanisation' of more than 60,000 apartments, tens of thousands of work places and small businesses, to say nothing of furniture and other valuables, at least in Vienna, the expropriation of Jewish property amounted to a veritable socioeconomic 'revolution' of a magnitude the country had never experienced, either in 1918 or in 1848" (Botz 2006, 192).

4. THE PERIOD OF RECONSTRUCTION AND AUSTRIA'S 'ECONOMIC MIRACLE', 1945–80: THE STATE-DOMINATED NETWORK

The conditions for the reconstruction of Austrian industry were more difficult in 1945 than they had been after World War I. This time, there were not only heavy direct effects of war, but also occupation damages arising from the confiscation of industrial enterprises by the Soviets, the cost of 10 years' presence of Allied troops and the partition into zones of occupation until the State Treaty of 1955. Estimations of destruction that take into account the effects of post-war dismantling in the French and Soviet occupation zones assess the overall loss of machinery as at least 30% of the 1944 stock (Weber 1997, 123). Despite this disadvantageous starting position, Austria's economy grew faster than those of all other Organization for European Economic Cooperation (OEEC) countries by an average of 7.7% per annum (Matis 2003, 190)—a performance that has often been referred to as the 'Austrian economic miracle'. The main reasons for this impressive pace of recovery were the generous injections of investment capital from Marshall Plan aid funds and the post-war boom that spread to Austria.

The state came to play a key role in this 'success story', notably through the nationalization program. Among all major parties governing Austria after World War II, it was obvious that only by nationalizing the economy ('*Austrifizierung*') could the Allies be deprived of controlling important means of production, and full employment be guaranteed. By 1946, the First Law on Nationalization (*1. Verstaatlichungsgesetz*) had been passed. This law conveyed assets of the three largest joint-stock banks (*Creditanstalt-Bankverein, Länderbank, Österreichisches Credit-Institut*), as well as of numerous large-scale enterprises in the sectors mining, iron and steel, engineering and chemical and oil, to the Republic of Austria. In 1947, the Second Law on Nationalization (*2. Verstaatlichungsgesetz*) assigned electricity supply to state-owned utilities. These policy measures laid the foundation for a huge public sector that produced up to 25% of the gross national product until the end of the 1970s (Aiginger 2003). Objects of nationalization were not companies, but rather simply shares in firms. While the truly nationalized Austrian railways constituted a public body employing civil servants, nationalized industries and banks remained joint-stock companies organized according to Austrian company law (Weber 1994, 573). The 'direct connection' between the government's economic policy and the everyday business of state-owned industries was also rather loose. Neither the government nor any planning office or similar body established quantifiable goals for the industrial complex (Grünwald 1982, 143). There existed, however, intensive contacts between the government and the management of SOEs. The political bargaining over senior management positions in SOEs was so common that it was even written in law. The *Kompetenzgesetz* of 1956 established the requirement that personnel policy in SOEs had to be based on the strength of political parties in Parliament—a unique requirement found in no other country with a mixed economy (see da Silva and Neves, and Rinaldi and Vasta, this volume). This resulted in the proportional representation of parties (*Proporz*) on management boards:[10] "SOEs were reorganized after nearly every national election" (Stiefel 2000, 244). The government could urge managers not to reduce labor force extensively. However, due to the successful economic performance of SOEs until the late 1970s, managers on executive boards held a strong position vis-à-vis the shareholder meetings (Mathis 1995). In the case of banks, there was nearly no governmental control at all (Weber 1962, 200). The economy was, however, not completely free of political interferences. Van der Bellen (1977, 14) hints, for example, at economic planners affiliated to the conservative ÖVP party who sought to control the competition between private companies and the nationalized industries if the competition came down to innovation. When public companies intended to introduce large numbers of new products in a short time period, they were not capable of restructuring the production processes without financial support by the state. ÖVP politicians often feared that capital injections could create a monopolistic market that discriminated against private competitors, and thus often refused to encourage and finance innovatory techniques, processes or products.

What kind of imprint did the mixed economy in Austria place on the network of interlocking directorates? First, the nationalized *CA* continued to function as the neural system of Austria Inc. Given the underdeveloped capital market in the post-1945 period, it was up to big banks like *CA* to provide finance to key national companies, often regardless of whether there was any real profit in a lending transaction. Moreover, *CA* (and *Länderbank*) held shares in many industrial undertakings.[11] The banks' double role as lender and shareholder made them vulnerable to crisis of their companies, especially as they had to act in public interest and, therefore, could not let companies simply go bankrupt. *CA* did not only provide credit to industrial and commercial enterprises, but also held enterprises itself. From the middle of the 1970s onwards, however, the bank started to reduce its shareholdings. In 1983, *CA* held only multiple ties to six industrial undertakings (compared to ten in 1967): *Leykam-Mürztaler Papier u. Zellstoff, Maschinenfabrik Andritz, Semperit, Steyr-Daimler Puch, Treibacher Chemische Werke and Universale Bau*. In 1992, its bank-industry relations seem largely to have ceased.

The shape and connectivity of the public sector also transformed significantly over time. In order to detect these changes, networks can be decomposed into groups marked by multiconnectivity, which usually stand for collections of collaborating firms. The term multiconnectivity refers to k-components, in which all nodes are k-connected (Scott 2000, 110). K-components can take the form of 'Russian dolls', with increasingly cohesive groups nested inside each other. The most common example would be a group with a highly cohesive core, surrounded by a somewhat less cohesive periphery. The more 'dolls' are placed one inside the other, the higher the k-connectivity level. All components in Figure 7.2 are named after their most central companies. Numbers in italics stand for the connectivity level of the subgroup and numbers in bold indicate how many corporations a box encompasses. For overview purposes, interconnections among different business groups are *not* displayed in the figure.

In 1949, the greatest component encompassed 45 companies only, and was coordinated mainly by CA. Within this network, three dense semi-autonomous islands existed: the energy sector clustered around a company that specialized in extracting the hydropower potential of the Danube (*Donaukraftwerke*), the brewing business sector clustered around *Brauerei Schwechat* and a conglomerate of industrial companies to which the steel works of *Alpine Montangesellschaft* belonged. In 1958, 76 companies were connected to each other at a multiplicity level of two. CA still dominated the scene, but Austrian 'big business' also came to be managed by other players. Six companies belonged to the *Länderbank* concern, fifteen energy companies were steered by *Verbundgesellschaft* and ten other public companies held strong personal ties either to the brewery *Brauerei Schwechat* or *Gösser*. Ten years later, the corporate structure became even more subdivided; CA devolved power to the Austrian industry-holding stock corporation, *ÖIAG*,[12] which administered all investments of the Republic of Austria in nationalized companies. In the realm of nationalized organization, *Alpine Montangesellschaft* was key in the ongoing consolidation of Austrian heavy industry. Local cooperatives (*Genossenschaften*) formed a separate sphere within finance. Within the diverse industrial empire of CA, a densely connected manufacturing conglomerate around *Steyr-Daimler-Puch* emerged.

Morawetz (1985) and Ziegler (1984) analyzed Austria Inc. in the late 1970s from a network perspective. Their insights confirm most of the corporate structure that this study shows pertaining to 1983. *ÖIAG* and the two nationalized banks, *Creditanstalt* and *Länderbank*, together with their subsidiaries, formed distinguishable and only rarely overlapping clusters. The structure was determined by the principle *divide et impera*; Austria's indirectly nationalized enterprises were overseen by the nationalized banks *Länderbank* or *Creditanstalt*, whereas the directly nationalized ones were supervised by *ÖIAG*.[13] Integration of these circles of power in the 1970s were mainly due to the existence of two common meeting places (Ziegler 1984, 81): the joint venture of the three banks, *Österreichische*

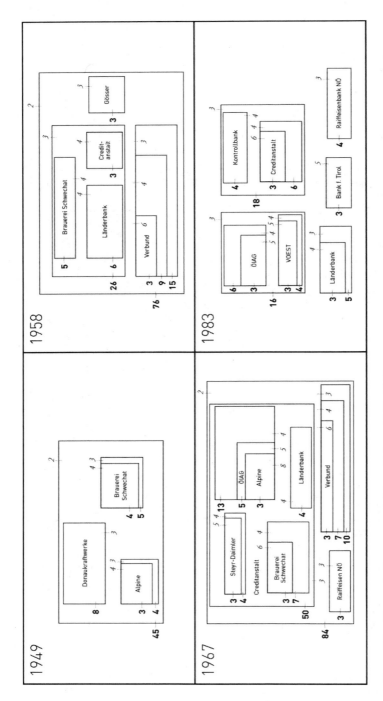

Figure 7.2 Network Components of Austria Inc., 1949–1983

Note: Components are shown at multiplicity levels from 2 to 10 that appear in italics. The size of components is given in bold type. Every component is named after its most central corporation.

Kontrollbank, which acted as a clearinghouse for banking, financing export and underwriting and the *ÖIAG* daughter and electrical engineering enterprise, *ELIN*, which split into subsidiaries and is therefore not to be found after 1983. Apart from the tripartite corporate network structure (*ÖIAG, Länderbank, Creditanstalt*) there were other blocs of power, too. *Investitionkredit* was founded in 1957 under the auspices of the World Bank and provided capital for the recovery of the Austrian economy, and *VOEST* merged with *Alpine Montangesellschaft*. The latter, with its 70,000 workers, became not only the symbol of Austrian state industry, but also one of the main causes of its downfall.

The analysis clearly reveals that, until the early 1980s, the corporate network was dominated by groups of affiliated companies. By making use of *ÖIAG* and large banks, the state could administer its interests through intermediaries. Such a corporate configuration facilitated the strategy to use public investment as an economic stimulus implemented to boost the economy ('Austro-Keynesianism') to a great extent. However, Austria Inc. started to crumble in the following years.

5. THE PERIOD OF PRIVATIZATION, 1980–2010: THE FADING OF THE STATE

In the middle of the 1980s, Austria still had one of the largest public sectors in Western Europe. Privatization projects were only considered when major state-owned companies incurred major losses that were caused by a worldwide steel crisis, an economic slump following the second oil shock and serious management errors. "Between 1981 and 1985 the two major steel firms, Voest-Alpine and VEW, had received 25 billions ATS (3.6 billions DM) in subsidies. In 1985 VOEST needed another 16 billions ATS while, for the first time, it announced plans of a mass lay-off from 34,500 to 25,000 people, to be achieved by 1990" (Hemerijck, Unger, and Visser 2000, 200). Additionally, *Intertrading*, a subsidiary of *VOEST*, announced enormous losses from speculation on international markets. In order to prevent the SOEs from becoming permanent subsidy recipients, the state set out to restructure the nationalized industry decisively. The poor performance of state-owned companies was just one of the causes of the government's reversal of the direction of its economic policy. Belke and Schneider (2006) mention these additional 'push factors': raising money in order to overcome problems related to the overflowing budget deficit, strong lobbying from national and international investment banks and a growing public support for the ideology, 'more market, less state'.

Between 1986 and 2006, major shares of large public companies were sold (Turnheim 2009). However, *ÖIAG* (and so, the government) always remained the largest shareholder with veto powers in the first rounds of privatization. It was only at the final stage in the 1990s that the companies were fully privatized. In 2012, ÖIAG's portfolio contained only the following listed companies: the Austrian postal service company (52.85% of shares); the international oil and gas company, OMV (31.5%); the largest communications company, *Telekom Austria* (28.42%); the mining company, *GKB-Bergbau* and the holding bank for publicly owned banks, *FIMBAG*. In any case, the Republic of Austria is still the majority shareholder in the largest electricity provider, *Verbund* (51%). The state and/or provinces own majorities in all smaller electricity companies, and Austrian Federal Railway (ÖBB) is still completely in public ownership. All in all, it is fair to say that the state has lost its substantial control over the economy even if the privatization process in Austria has not yet come to an end. A recent study points to further potential for privatization in the energy sector. Reducing shares to a blocking minority of 25% share acquisition in all electricity providers would imply an estimated return on sales between 3.2 and 6.3 billion Euros (Böheim, Handler, and Schratzenstraller 2010).

Besides large-scale privatizations, the unbundling of Austria Inc. was spurred by transformations in the banking sector. In 1991, *Länderbank, Kommerzialbank* and *Zentralsparkasse* merged to form *Bank Austria* and in 1997, the privatization of *CA* was announced—a bank that was clearly considered part of the conservative sphere of influence. *Bank Austria*—which is traditionally 'left-leaning'—made a takeover offer that was so generous that the government could not turn it down. That the bid was partly seen as a political gesture (Grubelnik 1998) indicates that the financial system was freeing itself from political attachments (Hofstätter and Korom 2012). All interests held by *CA* were transferred to *Bank Austria*, which decided to dissolve all industrial holdings in order to concentrate on the more profitable personal and commercial banking sector (Bruckner and Stickler 2000).

Austria Inc. was thus under enormous strain because of a 'pincer movement' (privatizations, end of the 'CA era'). Why did it not erode completely? Three reasons can be given. First, large companies in the service and energy sector remained in government hands. In companies like the Austrian Federal Railway (ÖBB); *Verbund*, Austria's largest electricity provider; the international oil and gas company, *OMV* and *Telekom Austria*, Leviathan (state capitalism) still acts as majority investor (Musacchio and Lazzarini 2014). Inter-linkages among these companies are important pillars of the corporate network in the twenty-first century. Second, the goal of the Austrian approach to privatization by the state (as opposed to privatization by state-owned banks) has been to downsize only moderately in terms of employment.[14] Even if maximizing the revenue was the main criteria for choosing among potential buyers, the strategic goal was to make sure that headquarters and employment opportunities would stay located in Austria ('national preference clause', Aiginger 2003). Maintaining a national core shareholder structure, in the case of *VOEST Alpine* for example, brought some stability to the changing corporate network.[15] Katzenstein (1985, 29) famously argued that small European states "adjust[ed] to economic change through a carefully calibrated balance of economic flexibility and political stability". He postulated several elements of 'domestic compensation' that could counter the harmful effects of liberalization and internationalization processes, such as employment and investment support, the size of the public sector, social welfare and industrial policy. Given the compensative effects that the continued national shareholder structure has on the erosion of Austria Inc., it seems plausible to argue that privatization in Austria was the product of a compromise centered on an ideology incorporating 'domestic compensation' (Katzenstein 1985).

Third, the power vacuum that was created by privatizations was filled by a new key player, the *Raiffeisen* bank group. Certainly, *Raiffeisen* does not share the large scope of the traditional *CA* concern; however, it functions as the new gravitational center of Austria Inc. (Korom 2013). In 2008, *Raiffeisen Zentralbank (RZB)* was the most central player, holding personal ties to 20 other companies. *Raiffeisen* originated from local cooperatives and is marked by a complex organizational structure. Today within *Raiffeisen*, 548 autonomous local banks are controlled by nine regional banks (that operate as universal banks), while the third tier constitutes *RZB*. *RZB* functions as the key link between banks located in Austria and *Raiffeisen Bank International*, with its network in CEE. *RZB* is currently Austria's largest holding company, owning shares in numerous enterprises such as the construction company, *Strabag;* the food companies, *Agrana* and *Leipnik;* the publishing house, *Kurier* and the insurance company, *Uniqua*. One of the eight central provincial banks, *Raiffeisen Oberösterreich*, is by far the most important local financier. It holds *inter alia* voting shares in the largest steel producing companies (*VOEST, AMAG*) that emerged in the course of privatizations.

The decline of Austria Inc. did not follow an even course over time. For the benchmark year 1999, our study reveals a temporary high of interlocks, which can be attributed principally to corporate restructuring following the merger between *CA* and *Bank Austria*. Between 1999 and 2008, the growth in network dismantling can be attributed to the end of a 13-year long SPÖ/ÖVP parliamentary majority and the coming about of a coalitional government between the conservative ÖVP and Haider's right-wing FPÖ (2000–2007) with the slogan, 'less state, more private' (Obinger 2006). Since ÖIAG reduced its stake in *Telekom Austria* to 25% in 2006, there has been a pause in this process and unpredictability surrounds the issue of whether further privatizations will occur.

6. CONCLUSION

The rise of Austria Inc. during the twentieth century was shaped principally by three major watersheds in Austrian economic history: first, the nationalization of *CA* in 1931 by the Austrian state, which feared its vulnerability, could start to ripple through other domestic and international institutes with devastating effects; second, the period of Nazi occupation that brought about a growth of large-scale enterprises at the detriment of small- and medium-size enterprises; and third, the transfer of a sizeable part of Austrian industry and the three major commercial banks, including *CA*, into governmental ownership after World War II.

Each critical juncture had a profound impact on subsequent patterns of change. In the post-World War I world, *CA* resumed its previous task of promoting industrial activity by providing long-term credit (mainly through the vehicle of 'credit on current account') in the whole Danubian Basin region. Its weakened constitution in the 1930s was but a "reflection of the shaky state of many of the industrial enterprises tied to the bank through the links of credit or capital relationships" (März and Weber 1983, 432). Making *CA* public property meant prolonging its central role as a capital provider for a further 50 years.

Without going further into the complex set of issues that are related to the question of whether Austrian's economic potential was really expanded between 1938 and 1945, there is a long lasting structural effect that has to be accounted for. By setting up large enterprises, the *Third Reich* changed the shape of Austria Inc. considerably (Eigner 1997c). It was, for example, the *Reichswerke Göring* in Linz—later *VOEST*—that was to become a key player in Austrian nationalized industry after 1945.

Last, but not least, it was the rise of a mixed economy that shaped the network of interlocking directorates. Throughout the second half of the twentieth century, the structure of Austria Inc. was mainly determined by the interlocking of the big nationalized financial and industrial corporations. As late as 1996, "the state and the banks were the largest ultimate shareholders in more than one fifth of the 600 largest corporations" (Gugler 1998, 288).

The decline of the Austrian intercorporate network was mainly triggered by the selling of the industrial undertakings of *CA*, the demise of the public sector, and the large-scale consolidation and internationalization of the banking system. All these changes form part of a more global transformation of the Austrian economic system that is guided by the rationale of 'less state, more market'.

However, despite the decline of bank-industry relations and the end of nationalized industries in Austria, the unbundling of the corporate network is not yet finished (Korom 2013). The strange 'non-death' of Austria Inc. can be explained by the chosen form of privatization: the Austrian government entrusted *ÖIAG* with complete or partial privatization. While undertaking this task, *ÖIAG* was asked not only to achieve the best possible price, but also to pay due regard to the interests of the Austrian people; i.e., to protect existing jobs. Policymakers were aware that the function of the network as a protective 'wall' against outsiders' interests would only remain intact if ownership continued to be concentrated in the hands of national actors. Consequently, in the wake of the privatization process, appropriations by Austrian groups were fostered by the government. In the many struggles over former SOEs (*Voestalpine, Constantia, Böhler Uddeholm, Lenzing*), national players like *Raiffeisen* became the winners. Only in some cases did privatization strengthen the position of foreign—mainly German—capital. The extent of internationalization in Austria is today below the level of Switzerland, where the intercorporate network has become truly transnationalized (see Ginalski, David and Mach, this volume). It is mainly because of this limited opening up to foreign investors that Austria Inc. continues to play a role in the twenty-first century.

NOTES

1. The years (e.g., 1938) indicated here are to be found in the title of the various handbooks (*Finanzcompass*) that served as data resources. However, one has to consider that all information always stems from the previous year.
2. Dritsas et al. (1996) revealed some different results, as they included the foreign dominated *Société Continentale de Gestion (Gesco)* and the *Allgemeine Versicherung-Gesellschaft Phönix* as companies with strong interest in the Austrian economy in their study.
3. Several omitted companies that clearly belong to Austrian 'big business', such as *ASFINAG* or *Merkur Warenhandels AG,* had to be added to the list. The Austrian National Bank (*Österreichische Nationalbank*) and Austria's state holding company (*Österreichische Industrieholding AG, ÖIAG*) were additionally included into the database in order to give an undistorted view of the public sector.
4. I am indebted to Özlem Cosen, Klaus Friedrich and Manfred Rohrer for their assistance in the data collection.
5. The rapid recovery from World War II is well documented. In 1946, indexes of industrial and agricultural production stood at less than half of prewar (1937). "Only three years later the 1937 level was reached; five years after that the peak level of the interwar period (1929) was surpassed" (März and Szecsi 1981, 126).
6. Considering the fact that "until the end of the 1970s, the world of the SOE seemed more or less in order" (Stiefel 2000, 249), and no large-scale program of privatization had been launched, such an interpretation seems much more plausible. After all, higher scores for simple personal ties and density (see Appendix I) in 1958 than in 1967 stem mostly from non-directional ties. For example, board member 1 forms an interlock between company A and company B. Sitting on the company B board is board member 2, who also sits on the board of company C. Thus, a secondary interlock is established between company A and C. It is well established that such coincidental interlocks can distort the analysis significantly (Mintz and Schwartz 1981, 98).
7. The journalist Hellmut Andics (1922–1998) expressed the sentiment that the 'rump state' Austria was not economically viable without its previous Hungarian agricultural sector and Bohemian industry of 1962 in his book entitled, *Der Staat, den keiner wollte* (*The State that nobody wanted*).
8. The conventional view holds that the *Creditanstalt* management was unaware of the troubles the merger involved. Recently, Aguado (2001) argued, however, that cross deposits were set up by Austrian Central Bank in order to compensate for taking over the insolvent bank.

9. Dritsas et al. (1996) report a degree centrality of 56, which results from a slightly different sampling strategy and size (see also footnote 2).
10. For the year 1976, Ziegler (1987) found a clear impact of political partisanship on the intercorporate network. Out of 57 big linkers, only six directors were non-partisan or their partisanship was unknown.
11. Acquisitions of shares occurred in the course of the classical banking business: a borrower found himself in financial distress. To save its credit engagement, a bank took over shares and gained more influence on its management.
12. ÖIAG had two predecessors. In 1956, ownership rights over public manufacturing firms were transferred from ministries to a holding company called *IBV* (*Industriebeteiligungsverwaltung*). Ten years later, *IBV* was replaced by *ÖIG* (*Österreichische Industrieverwaltungs-GmbH*), which was finally transformed into *ÖIAG* (*Österreichische Industrieholding AG*) in 1970.
13. As far as the enterprises coming under the First Nationalization Act were concerned, the situation was that the three nationalized banks came under the control of the Ministry of Finance, and the industries came under the jurisdiction of the Federal Ministry of Transport and Nationalized Industries. From 1956 onwards, there were several attempts to transfer the powers of the ministries to limited liability companies. In 1967, *Österreichische Industrieverwaltungs-AG* (*ÖIAG*, Austrian industry administration AG) was assigned the shares of the nationalized companies.
14. Privatization enacted by state-owned banks, such as in the cases of the tire maker, *Semperit* (which left Austria to produce in the Czech Republic), and *Steyr-Daimler-Puch* (shares were bought by the mogul Frank Stronach), led to significant labor shedding.
15. It should be mentioned in this context that, within the remnants of the nationalized industry party, patronage is still widespread. A recent study (Ennser-Jedenastik 2014) found that the partisan composition of managerial boards in SOEs still reflects the partisan composition of government in a proportional manner.

REFERENCES

Aguado, Iago G. 2001. "The Creditanstalt Crisis of 1931 and the Failure of the Austro-German Customs Union Project." *The Historical Journal* 44: 199–221.

Aiginger, Karl. 2003. "The Privatization Experiment in Austria." *Austrian Economic Quarterly* 4: 261–270.

Bardy, R. 1994. "Austria's Economy During the Second World War (A Survey)." In *The Economic Development of Austria since 1870*, edited by Herbert Matis, 529–538. Aldershot: Elgar.

Belke, Ansgar, and Friedrich Schneider. 2006. "Privatization in Austria: Some Theoretical Reasons and Performance Measures." In *Privatization experiences in the European Union*, edited by Marko Köthenbürger, Hans-Werner Sinn, and John Whalley, 89–116. Cambridge, MA: MIT Press.

Böheim, Michael, Heinz Handler, and Margit Schratzenstaller. 2010. "Optionen einer einnahmensbasierten Budgetkonsolidierung." *WIFO Monatsberichte* 3: 269–283.

Botz, Gerhard. 2006. "The Short- and Long-Term Effects of the Authoritarian Regime and of Nazism in Austria: the Burden of a 'Second Dictatorship'." In *Totalitarian and authoritarian regimes in Europe: legacies and lessons from the Twentieth Century*, edited by Jerzy W. Borejsza and Magdalena Hulas, 188–208. Cambridge, MA: MIT Press.

Bruckner, Bernulf, and Rudolf Stickler. 2000. *Österreichs Bankwirtschaft: Struktur, Wirtschaftlichkeit und internationaler Vergleich.* Wien: Orac.
Carroll, William K., and Meindert Fennema. 2002. "Is There a Transnational Business Community?" *International Sociology* 17: 393–419.
Collier, Ruth B., and David Collier. 1991. *Shaping the Political Arena: Critical Junctures, the Labor Movement, and Regime Dynamics in Latin America.* Princeton, NJ: Princeton University Press.
Dritsas, Margrit, Peter Eigner, and Jan Ottosson. 1996. "'Big Business' Networks in Three Interwar Economies: Austria, Greece and Sweden." *Financial History Review* 3: 175–195.
Eigner, Peter. 1997a. "Bank-Industry Networks: The Austrian Experience, 1895–1940." In *Rebuilding the Financial System in Central and Eastern Europe, 1918–1994,* edited by Philip L. Cottrell, 91–114. Aldershot: Ashgate.
Eigner, Peter. 1997b. "Die Konzentration der Entscheidungsmacht: die personellen Verflechtungen zwischen den Wiener Großbanken und Industriegesellschaften, 1895–1940." PhD dissertation, University of Vienna.
Eigner, Peter. 1997c. "The Ownership Structure of Austria's Big Business, 1895–1995." In *European Enterprise: Strategies of Adaptation and Renewal in the Twentieth Century,* edited by Margarita Dritsas and Terry R. Gourvish, 49–68. Athens: Trochalia Publications.
Ennser-Jedenastik, Laurenz. 2014. "Political Control and Managerial Survival in State-owned Enterprises." *Governance* 27: 135–161.
Ferraro, Fabrizio, Gerhard Schnyder, Eelke Heemskerk, Raffaele Corrado, and Nathalie Del Vecchio. 2012. "Structural Breaks and Governance Networks in Western Europe." In *The Small Worlds of Corporate Governance,* edited by Bruce M. Kogut, 151–182. Cambridge, MA: MIT Press.
Grubelnik, Klaus. 1998. *Die rote Krake: Eine Bank erobert Österreich.* Wien: Molden.
Grünwald, Oskar. 1982. "Austrian Industrial Structure and Industrial Policy." In *The Political Economy of Austria,* edited by Sven W. Arndt, 130–149. Washington, D.C: American Enterprise Institute for Public Policy Research.
Gugler, Klaus. "Corporate Ownership Structure in Austria." *Empirica* 25: 285–307.
Hemerijck, Anton, Brigitte Unger, and Jelle Visser. 2000. "How Small Countries Negotiate Change: Twenty-Five Years of Policy Adjustment in Austria, the Netherlands, and Belgium." In *Welfare and Work in the Open Economy,* edited by Fritz W. Scharpf and Vivien A. Schmidt, 175–263. Oxford: Oxford University Press.
Hofstätter, Lukas, and Philipp Korom. 2012. "Vom Austrokorporatismus zum Austrokapitalismus: Das Beispiel der Entbettung österreichischer Banken." In *Entfesselte Finanzmärkte: Soziologische Analysen des modernen Kapitalismus,* edited by Klaus Kraemer and Sebastian Nessel, 161–178. Frankfurt am Main: Campus.
Katzenstein, Peter J. 1985. *Small States in World Markets: Industrial Policy in Europe.* Ithaca: Cornell University Press.
Kernbauer, Hans, Eduard März, and Fritz Weber. 1983. "Die wirtschaftliche Entwicklung." In *Österreich, 1918–1938: Geschichte der Ersten Republik,* edited by Erika Weinzierl and Kurt Skalnik, 343–380. Graz: Styria.
Korom, Philipp. 2013. "Austria Inc. Forever? On the Stability of a Coordinated Corporate Network in Times of Privatization and Internationalization." *World Political Science Review* 9 (1): 357-375.
März, Eduard, and Maria Szecsi. 1981. "Austria's Economic Development, 1945–1978." In *Modern Austria,* edited by Kurt Steiner, Fritz Fellner, and Hubert Feichtlbauer, 123–140. Palo Alto, CA: Society for the Promotion of Science and Scholarship.
März, Eduard, and Fritz Weber. 1983. "Commentary." In *International Business and Central Europe, 1918–1939,* edited by Alice Teichova, 430–436. Leicester: Leicester University Press.

Mathis, Franz. 1990. *Big Business in Österreich II. Wachstum und Eigentumsstruktur der österreichischen Großunternehmen im 19. und 20. Jahrhundert.* Wien: Verlag für Geschichte und Politik.
Mathis, Franz. 1995. "Zwischen Lenkung und freiem Markt." In *Österreich in den Fünfzigern,* edited by Thomas Albrich, 169–180. Innsbruck: Österreichischer Studien Verlag.
Matis, Herbert. 2003. "Modern Austria." In *The Oxford Encyclopedia of Economic History,* edited by Joel Mokyr, 189–191. Oxford: Oxford University Press.
Matis, Herbert, and Fritz Weber. 1992. "Economic Anschluss and German Großmachtpolitik: The Take-Over of the Austrian Credit-Anstalt in 1938." In *European Industry and Banking between the Wars: A Review of Bank-Industry Relations,* edited by Philip L. Cottrell, Håkan Lindgren, and Alice Teichova, 109–126. Leicester: Leicester University Press.
Mintz, Beth, and Michael Schwartz. 1981. "The Structure of Intercorporate Unity in American Business." *Social Problems* 29: 87–103.
Morawetz, Inge. 1985. "Personelle Verflechtungen zwischen Großunternehmen und Banken in Österreich: Ergebnisse einer Netzwerkanalyse." *Österreichische Zeitschrift für Soziologie* 10: 73–84.
Musacchio, Aldo, and Sérgio G. Lazzarini. 2014. *Reinventing State Capitalism: Leviathan in Business. Brazil and Beyond.* Cambridge, MA: Harvard University Press.
Nowotny, Ewald. 1996. "Privatization in Austria: Causes and Consequences." *Annals of Public and Cooperative Economics* 67: 387–401.
Obinger, Herbert. 2006. "'Wir sind Voesterreicher': Bilanz der ÖVP/FPÖ-Privatisierungspolitik." In *Schwarz-blau: Eine Bilanz des 'Neu-Regierens',* edited by Emmerich Tálos, 154–169. Wien: Lit.
Rathkolb, Oliver. 2010. *The Paradoxical Republic: Austria, 1945–2005.* New York: Berghahn Books.
Schnyder, Gerhard, and Eelke M. Heemskerk. 2008. "Small States, International Pressures, and Interlocking Directorates: The Cases of Switzerland and the Netherlands." *European Management Review* 5: 41–54.
Scott, John. 2000. *Social Network Analysis. A Handbook.* London: Sage.
Stiefel, Dieter. 1983. "The Reconstruction of the Credit-Anstalt." In *International Business and Central Europe, 1918–1939,* edited by Alice Teichova, 415–430. Leicester: Leicester University Press.
Stiefel, Dieter. 2000. "Fifty Years of State-Owned Industry in Austria, 1946–1996." In *The Rise and Fall of State-Owned Enterprise in the Western World,* edited by Pier A. Toninelli, 237–252. Cambridge: Cambridge University Press.
Stinchcombe, Arthur L. 1990. "Weak Structural Data." *Contemporary Sociology* 19: 380–382.
Stokman, Frans N., Rolf Ziegler, and John Scott, eds. 1985. *Networks of Corporate Power: A Comparative Analysis of Ten Countries.* London: Polity Press.
Teichova, Alice. 1994. "Banking in Austria." In *Handbook on the History of European Banks,* edited by Manfred Pohl, 3–10. Aldershot: Elgar.
Turnheim, Georg. 2009. *Österreichs Verstaatlichte: Die Rolle des Staates bei der Entwicklung der österreichischen Industrie von 1918 bis 2008.* Wien: Manz.
Van der Bellen, Alexander. 1977. *Öffentliche Unternehmen zwischen Markt und Staat.* Köln: Kiepenheuer & Witsch.
Weber, Fritz. 1991. "Universal Banking in Interwar Central Europe." In *The Role of Banks in the Interwar Economy,* edited by Harold James, Håkan Lindgren, and Alice Teichova, 19–25. Cambridge: Cambridge University Press.
Weber, Fritz. 1994. "Austrian Nationalized Industry (1946–1986)." In *The Economic Development of Austria since 1870,* edited by Herbert Matis, 571–582. Aldershot: Elgar.

Weber, Fritz. 1997. "From Interwar Stagnation to Postwar Prosperity: Austria's Reconstruction after 1945." In *Central Europe in the Twentieth Century: An Economic History Perspective*, edited by Alice Teichova, 121–145. Aldershot: Ashgate.
Weber, Wilhelm. 1962. "State-Controlled Enterprise in Austria." *International Review of Administrative Sciences* 28: 192–205.
Windolf, Paul. 2006. "Unternehmensverflechtung im organisierten Kapitalismus: Deutschland und USA im Vergleich 1896–1938." *Zeitschrift für Unternehmensgeschichte* 51: 191–222.
Ziegler, Rolf. 1984. "Das Netz der Personen und Kapitalverflechtungen deutscher und österreichischer Wirtschaftsunternehmen." *Kölner Zeitschrift für Soziologie und Sozialpsychologie* 36: 557–584.
Ziegler, Rolf. 1987. "Besitzverhältnisse, Parteipräferenz und Personenverbindungen in der österreichischen Wirtschaft." *Österreichische Zeitschrift für Soziologie* 12: 81–92.
Ziegler, Rolf, Donald Bender, and Herman Biehler. 1985. "Austria Incorporated." In *Networks of Corporate Power: A Comparative Analysis of Ten Countries*, edited by Frans N. Stokman, Rolf Ziegler, and John Scott, 73–90. London: Polity Press.

Part III
State Capitalism?

8 Ebbs and Flows of French Capitalism

Pierre François and Claire Lemercier

1. INTRODUCTION

French interlocking directorates have not received much attention until recently, and few studies exist that put them into a historical perspective. The prolific school of French business history has produced excellent monographs, but few syntheses, and of these, few based on quantitative evidence. However, French capitalism has been thoroughly discussed in the business history and varieties of capitalism literatures. More generally, as in political history, it is often presented as the archetype of statism—beginning either with Louis XIV, Napoleon or the post-World War II governments. This focus on the role of the state in the economy often leads to the exclusion of France from other typologies of capitalism, especially in studies contrasting Anglo-Saxon and Rhineland varieties (Hall and Soskice 2001). French capitalism, revolving as it does around the state and family-led business groups (*groupes*), and perhaps lacking real big business in most sectors or real entrepreneurs (Landes 1949), is presumed not to have structures of its own. Its shape is seen solely as the product of external forces, those of politics and/or relationships between elite families.

The narrative that we present here is based on a study of the interlocks between the largest French firms listed on the Paris stock exchange from 1911 to 2000. It will not undermine the role of the state or that of families.[1] However, we will qualify more standard descriptions of French capitalism in two ways. First, we will discuss the usual understanding of the chronological development of French capitalism, or rather the lack thereof, and second, we will identify its underlying mechanisms. Our principal finding is that the general shape of the network remained remarkably stable from 1911 (or even before) to 2000. It was, however, subject to ebbs and flows, with two long periods of densification, each followed by moments of disruption (see Figure 8.1). It is impossible to make sense of both this enduring shape and these ebbs and flows if one takes a simplistic view of the Napoleonic or socialist state, or the backward-looking elite families. From the second half of the nineteenth century to the end of the 1930s, and then from the post-World War II period to the beginning of the 1990s,

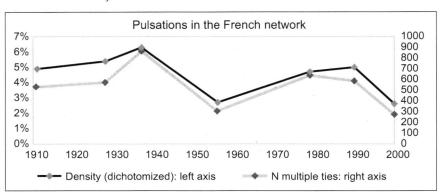

Figure 8.1 Pulsations in the French Network

the interlocking network underwent two similar phases of density growth, with the generation of many multiple interlocks between the largest French firms. Both of these periods were followed by a drastic drop in density, first around the time of World War II, and then again in the 1990s. We will see, however, that despite these impressive changes in density, the generative mechanisms of the network remained the same by and large, especially with regard to the hierarchy embedded within it. Two peculiarities of our dataset allow us to assert this. First, we were lucky enough to find a continuous source, which allowed us to use the same sampling and coding schemes for all dates, adding weight to our longitudinal comparisons. It should be noted that we are only looking at firms listed on the Paris stock exchange and that our definition of the largest firms is based on share capital. Second, our source and additional research allowed us to systematically gather information on firms (their age, location, etc.), as well as elements on the trajectories of interlockers, both of which are essential for our interpretation.

In this chapter, we specify the mechanisms underlying this tale of French capitalism. We believe that, in order to properly understand the roles of the state and elite families, we must see them as specific manifestations of three more general mechanisms. The first, and by far the most important, is based on status, with an interplay between the status hierarchy of firms and that of directors. The network is organized around a core of high-status firms. Lower-status firms are in the periphery of the network, but their directors do create some interlocks with the core. In addition, the shared demand to have a small set of high-status directors on various boards creates bridges in the network. The second mechanism is one of business group building; interlocks forge local solidarity without resorting to mergers or cartels. The third mechanism covers governance practices and principles, which change over time and influence the development of interlocks. These three mechanisms affect each firm individually and also are likely to generate the emergent overall structure that we uncovered. This chapter will describe the shifts that took place between 1911 and 2000 and present hypotheses regarding their causes. We conclude by summarizing what we have learned about the mechanisms that generate the enduring shape of this network.

2. 1911–1937: A STABLE STRUCTURE THAT SURVIVED WAR AND CRISIS

The structure of the 1911–1937 network is typical of that for the whole of the twentieth century. Both integrated and hierarchical, its integration relied on strong and increasing centralization. This is illustrated by the 30–40% of seats that were held by 'big linkers', for example. The interlocking network looks like a ball of yarn, with a disproportionately large core that is much denser than the surrounding layers. The inertia of this structure is all the more remarkable because it is not the product of political or economic stability.

Changing Actors in a Stable Structure

First, this stable structure was not caused by inertia in our sample of firms, and certainly not of directors. In contrast to smaller countries—Switzerland for example—we found significant turnover, with 57% of our 1928 firms not appearing in the 1911 sample and 36% of our 1937 firms absent in the 1928 sample, just nine years prior. That the structure endures through such change implies that new firms took over the same structural positions occupied by their predecessors at the previous observation point. Thus, many things may have changed among French firms and directors, but yet they interlocked in exactly the same way.

Second, this stability of the interlocking network occurred at a time of economic disruption. World War I (with battlefields covering several of the most industrial regions) was followed by the economic crisis that took hold in France from 1932 onwards and disrupted many parts of the economy, including the stock exchange. In addition, World War I led to new forms of state involvement in the economy and in the collective organization of businessmen, with the creation of the peak association, *Confédération générale de la production française*. Last, a Socialist-led administration was in power from 1936 to 1938, which, among other things, brought the railways under the exclusive control of the state (Daumas et al. 2010, 1287–1300).

These events inevitably changed business practices in France and also impacted which firms and individuals are found on the lists of the largest firms and interlockers. As a direct consequence of World War I, the *Crédit national* was created by special decree in 1919 in order to handle war reparations and to lend money to industrial SMEs. This new bank, a private corporation closely linked to the state, made it into the top 10 list in 1928 and was in first position in 1937, with an outstanding degree of 72. It is noticeable that a small number of newly created firms appear in the 1937 sample compared to that of 1928 or 1956, and this probably reflects the economic crisis. Finally, our lists of big linkers highlight the new role of business associations and think tanks. Two men appear in our top 10 lists in both 1928 and 1937; both were political leaders among businessmen. Ernest Mercier (1878–1935, at the top of both lists) created *Redressement français,* a think tank promoting modernization through planning. Henri de Peyerimhoff (1871–1953), like Mercier, was previously a high-ranking civil servant. He never became an executive but was the key man in the most influential business association, that of mechanical industries and mining (Beltran 2010, 468–470; Chatriot 2010, 543–545).

The French economy underwent major changes throughout this period, which can be observed in our results. Once again, this makes the overall stability of the whole network even more striking. The long-lasting structure emerged quite early on. Exploratory evidence on previous observation dates (1840, 1857 and 1883, based on samples of 120 firms (François and Lemercier 2012)) shows that it coalesced in the mid-nineteenth century, even before general incorporation laws. Thus, French firms started the process of interlocking directorates much earlier than others. Most studies of other countries describe this process as beginning only around 1900 (Carroll and Sapinski 2011, 181). This happened at a time when the role of boards was not well-defined and new businesses tried to attract investors by putting high-status names on their boards. The shape of the network that emerged at that time survived the loss of an industrial region to Germany, several financial crises, the legalization of business associations in 1884, the birth of new industries (e.g., automobile and electricity), as well as a world war and a global economic crisis.

The Logic of Status

Two primary mechanisms might explain how the network developed into such an integrated, hierarchical and stable shape. The first concerns what we call, after Podolny (2005), status logic. According to Podolny, the status of an actor relies on the links he or she has with other actors: links to prestigious and powerful actors give access to part of their prestige and power; links with more obscure actors, on the contrary, negatively affect status. In other words, in an uncertain world, the actors to whom I am linked send a signal about my worth. Taking into account such status logic makes more sense of the structure of our network than the alternative mechanisms that are typically highlighted in the interlocking directorates literature, such as the role of banks or the class-cohesion of the elite.

Therefore, the French case helps to develop an under-investigated part of this literature, alluded to by Mizruchi (1996, 276) as the "quest for legitimacy [...] By appointing individuals with ties to other important organizations, the firm signals to potential investors that it is a legitimate enterprise worthy of support". In our case, the logic of status is at play both for firms (sharing a director with a legitimate firm is important) and for the directors themselves (having a director whose personal trajectory brings them into the circle of the supposedly best and brightest is important).

With regard to firms, positions in the stable and increasingly centralized structure of the network were not randomly distributed. Inertia was also striking in this respect; in each period it is similar attributes that enable different firms to occupy similar positions in the network. Indeed, it is possible to extract a clear status hierarchy from our data. As will be seen, depending on the period, firms are seen to attain a high or low status on the basis of their sector, level of share capital, location in Paris and/or seniority as listed firms with high share capital. All of these elements apparently provide a form of legitimacy; they all denote a form of closeness to economic and/or political power. Therefore, an aggregate of these criteria is an indicator of the status of each firm. This attribute is so highly correlated with positions in the interlocking network that the shape of the network can almost be predicted using the status indicator alone. In all cases, high status is correlated both with centrality in the network and homophily among high-status firms. While these high-status firms preferred to share directors among themselves, some lower-status firms did succeed in establishing interlocks with them. In each cohort, a large number of firms have high status, as measured by at least one or two of the criteria, which is why our network has a disproportionately large core, but they are still clearly different from the lower-status firms in the periphery. This periphery is not made of isolated firms or small components, but simply of firms with fewer or weaker ties.

The status mechanism is well-illustrated in the 1911–1937 period. In the context of a highly skewed distribution of share capital, firms in the highest quartile had consistently higher average degrees (21 in 1937, compared to 11.1 for the lowest quartile). Firms without Parisian headquarters always had a much lower average degree, e.g., 11.4 in 1937, compared to 16.3 for Parisian firms. Finally, the centrality of firms already present in the sample for the previous observation point was consistently higher than that of newcomers, be they recently established firms, recently listed firms or firms that had recently increased their share capital. Parisian firms, large firms and those that were large and had been listed for some time were also significantly more homophilic than chance would allow.

The economic sector in which firms operated was involved in the same logic of status. Between 1911 and 1937, three economic sectors were both highly homophilic and more central than others: finance, energy and transportation/utilities. This was not entirely due to differences in the location, size or seniority of firms. Rather, it indicates that in the first half of the twentieth century, the core of the French interlocking network was composed of a mix of financial, transportation/utility and energy companies, with a tendency toward homophily within each of these sectors and many ties between them. It seems that the firms in these sectors were sought after in the same way that large or Parisian firms were: as potential sources of status signals based on interlocking. The fact that these firms were sought out by lower-status companies, and that some succeeded in interlocking with them, created a very integrated network; in the interwar period, more than 90% of firms were part of the main component.

How does this picture compare to classical descriptions of French capitalism? First, with the exception of *Crédit national,* these high-status, central firms had no particular ties with the state. From the firms' perspective, the state does not seem to play a central role in shaping the network prior to World War II. Second, the existence of this core of big, persistent, Parisian financial and non-financial firms qualifies traditional assumptions about feeble or late French big business—along the lines of Cassis's own qualification (2008). Not only did big listed firms exist, they were recognized as the center of developing French capitalism.

Status logic was not only at work for firms themselves, but also in their choice of directors. Who connected high-status firms among themselves and with the periphery? The choice of these 'network specialists'—the 'big linkers' who were deemed able to act as bridges between competitors or economic sectors, for example—was far from random. They were often the products of a well-known phenomenon in the sociology of the French elite: the continual reproduction of this elite through *grandes écoles* (selective higher education institutions), especially the *École Polytechnique* and, from 1945 onwards, the ENA (*École nationale d'administration*) (Bourdieu 1989; Maclean, Harvey, and Press 2006). Before the founding of the ENA, civil servants with legal-economic backgrounds who worked in specific offices and courts, primarily the *Conseil d'Etat* and the *inspection des finances,* played the same structural role. These schools were originally founded in order to train top management for public administration—especially that of the finance ministry, as well as mining and road and railway construction supervision. They produced a few dozen graduates each year, a dozen of which enter the top *corps* (special positions in the highest rank of administrative personnel). However, as early as the second half of the nineteenth century, many members of these *corps* left public administration after a few years in order to join firms. These moves from public administration to firms are called *pantouflage* (Charle 1987). The phenomenon is similar in some ways to the Japanese *amakudari* or the British tendency to name former diplomats as board members (Colignon and Usui 2003; Maclean et al. 2006, 189). Yet it is different because moves toward the French private sector are generally made early in a career, before the age of 40.

Take, for example, André Benac (1858–1937), who was a former ministerial staff member and senior officer in the finance ministry. He sat on the boards of many banks and railways and is in our top 10 lists for both 1911 and 1928. His profile and career is similar to that of Gérard Mestrallet (1949-), who is in our 2000 list—a graduate of *Polytechnique* and ENA, who has also acted as chairman of the European Roundtable of Industrialists.

This connecting role of the *pantoufleurs* prompts a reassessment of the role of the state in our network. Even though high-status firms had no specific connections with the state before World War II, the state did play a role in the status logic that we have outlined above; having a *pantoufleur* on a board was a source of prestige. This does not imply that public administration was implementing a deliberate policy aimed at implanting its own culture in the private sector. The moves of *pantoufleurs* were primarily due to individual and family strategies within the elite, which can be observed at the beginning of the twentieth, as well as in the twenty-first, century. Of course, this does not exclude the possibility that some form of culture was indeed exported from public administration to many firms; precisely what culture would depend on what was taught at elite schools and practiced in ministries. However, this culture cannot simply be characterized as 'statist'. More important for French interlocks is the general recognition of an elite of network specialists who create bridges in the network. Incidentally, these network specialists also often happen to have begun their careers in public administration, which contributed to their reputation of political influence and/or skills applicable in all types of firms and sectors.

Strong Ties Inside Business Groups

The status mechanism described above is certainly the one that most shaped the structure of the network. This mechanism does not work alone, however. It was combined with another, which created pockets of density within the network and pushed people who were not *pantoufleurs* and who performed bonding, not bridging, into our top 10 lists. The overall density and the prevalence of multiple interlocks (firms sharing two or more board members) in the French network places it somewhere between the so-called Anglo-Saxon and Rhineland models of capitalism. Its core-periphery structure differs from the latter, and it is also less dense, as there were no official cartels in interwar France, even though cartels and corporatism were very much under discussion from the end of the nineteenth century until World War II (Barjot 2010, 958–962; Denord 2010, 1018–1022).

At a more local level, however, we find network structures that look like those of Rhineland cartels, especially in the 1937 sample, which represents a high point in overall density. This density was mostly due to a sharp increase (+48%) in the number of multiple interlocks from 1928 to

1937; in 1937, 76% of our firms had at least one multiple interlock with another. The case of the electricity industry shows that concentration in this sector was achieved not through mergers, but rather by increasing both interlocks and ownership ties, which created business groups of varying elasticity. Such *groupes,* often deemed typical of France in the 1980s and 1990s (Swartz 1985), in fact began to thrive long before this. Compared with similar business groups in other contexts (Granovetter 1994), interlocks seem to play an important role in French *groupes,* complementary to that of ownership ties.

It was this kind of group-building logic that pushed Pierre Durand, Roger Durand and Robert Despres onto our list of top big linkers. They were all directors in the same six companies in the hydro-electricity sector in various French regions. In most cases, Pierre was the executive director and Roger and Robert were non-executive directors. All three were engineers (graduates of minor, non-elite schools). They were also, respectively, the son of, the son of a cousin of and the son-in-law of the founder of the *groupe.* They were also very active in business associations. If we look beyond our sample, in 1935, six members of their family held 84 positions in French boards among them (Vuillermot 2000). These were bonding, not bridging, big linkers.

Such *groupes* were used by some as a substitute for forbidden cartels in the quest for a more coordinated capitalism; they created local solidarity between firms. This cannot be compared to a pure merger, as the firms remained legally distinct and ownership bonds were often weak; neither can it be compared to cartelization, since they did not create 'co-opetition' in the entire electricity sector. *Groupes* competed with each other and were only linked via weaker, generally unique interlocks provided by network specialists.

3. 1937–1990: SHOCKS AND RECOVERY OF THE NETWORK

After the War: A Collapsed or Weakened Network?

Between our 1937 and 1956 observation points, changes in the French economy were even more significant than between 1911 and 1937. The war and the German occupation disrupted many economic sectors, and many entrepreneurs were killed or expropriated. At the same time, political changes affected the list of the biggest French firms and their interactions with the state. In the post-war period, state-owned monopolies of railways, Parisian public transportation, coal mining, electricity and gas production and distribution replaced many of the large old firms that played an important role at the core of the interlocking structure. Most insurance companies became state-owned at this time, as did a few large, symbolic firms such as the *Crédit national,* the central bank, the largest deposit banks and the automobile manufacturer, *Renault* (Chabanas and Vergeau 1996).

These events not only changed our list of firms (although not more than between 1911 and 1928), but also the density and structure of the interlocks. This change, however, did not take the form of a revolution, or of a collapse of the network. The 1956 structure looks very much like a less dense copy of the 1937 one, with multiple interlocks being the main missing element. The overall density dropped by more than half, but the main patterns remained. Very few firms were still excluded from the largest component, but many only had ties with one or two other companies. Only half of the firms still had multiple interlocks, and those that did had fewer than before; the number of multiple interlocks was almost divided by three. Most of the changes in the network were due either to the disruption of multiple interlocks or to the increased scarcity of ties between the core of high-status firms and the periphery.

Why did the network keep the same general structure? And why did it weaken? The general structure endured because the status logic continued to play a crucial role after the war. Parisian firms, as well as those with the highest share capital, those that were already in the 1937 sample and those in the most important sectors (finance and the mechanical and heavy industries, which now played the role that the transportation/utilities and energy sectors played before the war), were still significantly more homophilic than chance would allow. On average, the largest firms, as well as those that were in the 1937 sample, were also more central. Last, even though the density of interlocks dropped among firms that stayed in the sample from 1937 to 1956, it dropped less than that of the overall sample. Interlocks among firms with the highest status in French capitalism remained largely in place, although even they became scarcer. We do not claim that nothing happened regarding interlocks during the war and the post-war period, but the changes that occurred produced the same kind of structure that was in place before the war—albeit, a weaker version.

Prominent among the changes in the post-war period was the birth of a state-owned sector. However, this did not create a new mechanism shaping the network: state-owned firms followed on the pre-existing logics. The disappearance of private energy, transportation and utility firms, especially of locally dense structures such as the Durand electricity groupe, played a role in the loss of density of the interlocking network, specifically in the disruption of multiple interlocks. State-owned firms, however, took part in the reconstruction of a dense and centralized structure, as they exhibited a very significant homophily. Their average degree was similar to that of the sample, but with important internal differences. *Crédit national* was still the most connected French firm. Four other banks (including the central bank) and the national railway company were interlocked to between 10 and 20 other firms, both public and private. Therefore, the new state-owned sector did not give birth to a dual structure of interlocks (public firms on one side, private on the other) but, arguably, was part of an ongoing reconstruction of the previous shape of the network, as state-owned firms were prominent among the new cohort of high-status firms.

Thus, the status logic continued to play a role for firms after World War II, something also true for directors. Between 1937 and 1956, there was a clear generational change, even though few entrepreneurs were victims of political purges after 1945 (Joly 2010b, 1317–1321). However, even if some 1956 big linkers could be seen as new to the field, their career profiles often remained rooted in the exact same status logic that dominated before the war. Take Henri Lafond (1894–1963) as an example from our top 10 list. He held no seat in our 1937 sample and was part of the board of the state-owned electrical company in 1956; nevertheless, his career looks very much like that of *pantoufleurs* of the previous generations (Joly 2010a, 394–396). He was considered to be 'the Pope of the *corps des mines*', one of the most prestigious corps of Polytechnique graduates. He became the president of an investment bank, *Banque de l'Union parisienne*, was in charge of energy under the Vichy government from 1940 to 1942, then active in the peak business association after the war. He was an archetypical *pantoufleur*, but was not a friend of post-war Socialist or Gaullist governments.

In this way, status logic helps us understand why the structure of the network endured. But why did it weaken, apart from the effect of state monopolies? The disruption of interlocks, especially multiple ones, can be linked to changes in governance rules and practices that took place between 1937 and 1956. A 1940 law limiting the number of board positions for the same person to 8 threatened multiple interlocks, although this law was not always enforced (Joly 2009). More generally, the accumulation of board positions had been the subject of growing criticism both within and without the business community in the 1930s. The 'two hundred families', 'new feudal lords' and 'trusts' came under harsh criticism, which was directed at the owners of the central bank and those who accumulated economic and political positions and connections (Dard 2010, 1250–1253).

This shift in social and then legal norms might explain the drop in the percentage of positions held by big linkers and the fact that after it, our top 10 big linkers then each held 6 to 9 positions, and not 8 to 16 as they had done. This was also the time of the slow professionalization of the role of board members and of the *président-directeur général* (CEO), the single top executive position, which was becoming more common, whereas governance had been more collegial before the war. The time needed to adapt to these new governance schemes and to figure out how to interlock in this new context might account both for the diminished density of the network in 1956 and its new growth afterward.

1957–1990: Back to the Future

After getting shallower from 1937 to 1956, the network structure entered a new phase of densification and centralization that led to features in 1979 and 1990 that are strikingly similar to those of 1928. These processes are perhaps counter-intuitive, given at least two major changes that occurred during that time. First, a new economic crisis began just before 1979, which led to the near-complete disappearance of some economic sectors. The share of heavy industry gradually decreased, while that of consumer goods increased. While mechanical and electrical industries consistently represent one-fifth of our sample from 1956 to 2000, the shift in this period was initially toward electronics and, later, toward consulting firms. Construction and real estate firms were especially prevalent in 1979 and 1990. In this context, the turnover of firms in our sample is as high as before—approximately 60% for 20-year intervals and 40% for 10-year intervals. Second, a new Socialist-Communist government came to power in 1981 and brought a few dozen additional banks and a handful of industrial firms under state control. Even though most of these companies were returned to the private sector after the right won the elections of 1986 and 1993, our 1990 sample still includes the most state-owned firms (approximately 25). Despite these changes, however, the network kept its structure and became denser after 1956, although our indicators never again reach the peaks of 1937. It was as if, after a period of adaptation to the new governance structure and the new state monopolies, French capitalists fully returned to their pre-war logic; purely from a network perspective, the 1979 and 1990 samples cannot be distinguished from that of 1928.

The mechanisms that explain this new long-lasting period of densification and centralization are very much the same as those before World War II, especially the status logic. Between 1956 and 1990, the network continued to orbit around a large, dense center, surrounded by a looser periphery. What did change slightly, however, was the exact list of attributes that defined the high-status of a firm, with the changes observed in 1956 confirmed in both 1979 and 1990. State-owned firms were extremely homophilic, with an internal density of 16% to 18% in 1979 and 1990, as compared to 5% for the whole network—more than in any other high-status class of firms. They were also extremely central in the network, not disconnected in a separate component; their average degree was 17 to 19, as high as that of financial firms, compared to 12 for the whole network. Being state-owned, however, did not subject the firms to new mechanisms. This type of ownership was only one attribute of many high-status firms, the others still being an enduring presence among the largest listed firms, large share capital, location in Paris and activity in finance.

The position of financial firms is worth discussing. In previous cohorts, they could always be found in the core of the network; they were both central and homophilic. However, the 1979 and 1990 observation points are different in two respects. First, and contrary to the interwar period, no sector exhibited the same degree of homophily and centrality as the financial sector. Construction and real estate were the exception in 1979, but in fact, these firms can be understood as close to the financial sector; real estate companies (with profits coming primarily from rent) were often difficult to distinguish from leasing (*crédit-bail*) firms.

The second difference was the activity of the financial sector. In the first half of the century, there were many listed banks with large share capital, which played an important role in the core of the network. This changes from 1956 onwards, however. In that year, we find only approximately 20 banks in our sample, 15 in 1990 (half of them state-owned) and 10 in 2000. Mergers and acquisitions among the biggest banks created a dual structure, with smaller investment/merchant banks playing a key role in French capitalism, and often in the careers of our interlockers, but yet not appearing in our sample. What our samples do show, however, is the part played, very early on, by institutional investors: portfolio companies, leasing firms, etc. These represent a majority of our sample of financial firms from 1956 onwards. There were only 5 to 12 of them prior to 1956, and in 1937, the 12 institutional investors had a mean degree that was only modestly above average, well below that of banks. After 1956, however, and especially in 1979 and 1990, our population includes dozens of institutional investors, with an average degree of 17.3 in 1979 and 15.7 in 1990, very close to that of finance generally. These firms have diverse backgrounds. Some, such as *La Hénin*—founded in the nineteenth century—were longstanding members of the financial sector, and some were recently created real estate firms and state-controlled insurance companies. Others had moved to finance from declining economic sectors, such as *Pechelbronn* or the *Compagnie de navigation mixte*, or from an agricultural, commercial or industrial activity in the former colonies. The key role played by institutional investors, and finance generally, in the re-densification and re-centralization of the French interlocking network from 1956 onwards brings into question the standard narratives of financialization that describe it as an imported phenomenon occurring in the 1980s or after.

The return to the 1928 structure was based on the status logic, especially the role that state-owned and financial firms played within it. Along with companies' preferences for interlocking with high-status firms and for *pantoufleurs* as bridging big linkers, we also find local density and multiple interlocks based on the business group-building logic, just as we do in the interwar period. The right-wing government that prepared state-owned firms for their return to the private sector in the late 1980s deliberately strengthened this mechanism. It established *noyaux durs* (hard cores), i.e., complex webs of ownership ties and interlocking directorates that were supposed to protect French firms from foreign influence (Maclean et al. 2006, 185–188).

4. 1990–2000 AND BEYOND: TOWARD A DUAL FRENCH CAPITALISM?

In the 10-year interval between 1990 and 2000, the network arguably changed more than it did between 1937 and 1956. Spectacular changes in indicators, however, do not necessarily imply that entirely new mechanisms are at play, as had already been seen in 1956. In fact, some mechanisms simply seem to have become more radical. In the 1990s, the number of multiple interlocks halved once again. In 2000, more than 10% of the firms had ties with only one or two others, just like in 1956, but, unlike 1956, 20% were isolated, which was completely new. The overall density was thus halved, be it among financial firms, among non-financial firms or between financial and non-financial firms. However, unlike what happened between 1937 and 1956, this loss in density was anything but homogeneous. Many firms in the main component, and especially at its core, had more ties than before. If we focus on firms that were present in both the 1990 and 2000 samples, we actually find a modest increase in density among them. In other words, the loss of density of the network was not a symptom of the collapse of its core-periphery, status-based structure, but of its radicalization. This loss of density engendered a dual structure with a more isolated periphery, a phenomenon that can be explained by the same status logic that played such an important role throughout the twentieth century.

Changes in Finance

The enduring features of the network core were exacerbated in 2000. The density of ties not only remained high, homophily even increased in the case of state-owned firms, firms that were already in the 1990 sample and firms with the highest share capital. High-status firms reinforced ties among themselves, while densities in the periphery (e.g., among non-Parisian firms or firms with a low share capital) dropped to historic lows. The same was true for average degree centrality, with no less than 9.6 for the handful of state-owned firms that were still present, for example.

What changed was the precise position of finance. In 2000, financial firms lost the striking hegemony they had gained in the top centrality lists of 1979 and 1990. Accordingly, their average centrality of 8.8 in 2000 was only modestly above the 6.6 sample average (but still higher than that of any other sector). Homophily among them was still significantly higher than chance would allow, but it produced a limited internal density of 5.7%. This can be explained in part by the presence of a very peculiar structure, that of the Bolloré *groupe,* created, seemingly in the best interwar tradition, by complicated shareholding and interlocking bonds that united six firms of our sample into a quasi-clique of multiple ties. These included former colonial companies turned portfolio firms like the *Compagnie du Cambodge* and *Caoutchoucs de Padang*.

Apart from this peculiar situation, we find few weak ties among financial firms, unlike all of the previous observation points. Moreover, while the centrality of banks was slightly above that of institutional investors, homophily was centered on the latter; ties among banks produced a density of 2.2%, compared to 6.6% among institutional investors and

4.5% between banks and institutional investors. In 1990, the density among banks was 21.9% and only 9.2% among institutional investors. It was institutional investors, therefore, that kept the classical high-status position of the finance sector, while banks did not. The changing position of banks can be linked first and foremost to a redefinition of their tasks. Until the 1980s, their primary function was to directly provide firms with cash, and the control over the firm they gained by sitting on the board was of tremendous importance. From the 1990s onwards, their financing role was more embedded in market logic, and as such, was more anonymous and less direct; sitting on the board of many firms and directly controlling them was not as strategic as it used to be. Second, the position of banks also changed because of a decline in their homophily, which appears to indicate new relationships between banks, with interlocks no longer mitigating competition. Until the early 1990s, the banking sector, although not explicitly organized along the logic of a cartel, was collectively regulated in such a way that competitive dynamics were mitigated. The privatization of the banking sector and the gigantic mergers that took place in the sector in the late 1990s put an end to this internal regulation. After this, relationships between banks often turned into open warfare, such as the conflict between BNP and *Société Générale* in 1999. This behavior reduced, if not quashed, the homophilic logics that had prevailed until then.

A New, More Isolated Periphery

Despite these changes, high-status firms were generally still both homophilic and central in the network. However, lower-status firms established fewer interlocks with them, producing a more isolated periphery. To understand this shift, one has to keep in mind that the list of firms with the highest share capital changed at a much faster pace than before. In our 2000 sample, 60% of the firms included were not in the 1990 list, a change in 10 years that we only saw previously in 20-year intervals. New firms came from the same broad sectors as before, with a slight increase in the share of consumption goods, but in fact, the nature of these firms was quite different. Consulting and cleaning firms, for example, composed a significant part of our so-called mechanical sector (for want of a better category), and new activities appeared in the consumption goods sector: hotels, retailing firms, media groups and wines and spirits. Changes in the list of firms also exacerbated a tendency that had already been present since 1979: the inequalities in terms of share capital became huge. Between 1979 and 2000, the minimum share capital in our sample dropped by 37%, while the maximum was multiplied by 7.8; the Gini index rose from 0.48 to 0.79. While mergers and acquisitions created huge firms, companies with a different profile made their way into our sample and had an impact on the structure of the network.

Two categories with little overlap are worth mentioning here: family firms and non-Parisian firms. The former includes 33 family firms (13% of the sample) if we use a rough categorization, whereby family firms are those that name an individual or (more frequently) a family as their primary shareholder, whatever the percentage of shares held. Only one quarter of them were present in the 1990 sample, more than half produced consumer goods, their median share capital was well below average and their average degree was only 3.6, compared to 6.6 for the whole network; they were part of the sparsely linked periphery of lower-status firms. A good example is *Grand Marnier*, the famous producer of spirits, with 92% of its sales abroad. Three families each owned approximately 14% of the shares, with two members of the main shareholding family on the board, one being its chairman; no interlock with a firm in our sample was visible. The second category includes 46 firms in 2000 (18% of the sample); their headquarters were not located in Paris and they were not in the 1990 sample. Only six were also family firms, as defined previously. More than half of these firms produced consumer goods, their median share capital was below even that of family firms and so was their average degree (2.7). A good example is *Skis Rossignol*, the world leader in ski equipment, created in 1907, with headquarters in the Alps and no interlock in our sample.

Firms with the same profiles existed in the 1990 population, but they were much less numerous. If we use the same definitions, there were 11 family firms and 17 newly sampled non-Parisian firms. Even then, they tended already to have marginal positions in the network, with average degrees of 10.5 and 7.4, as compared to 12.5 for the whole sample, but few were completely isolated.

Something completely new happened in the 1990s: family and/or non-Parisian firms, often producing consumption goods and which had often existed for decades, suddenly entered the stock exchange and/or dramatically increased their share capital, probably on turning to export markets and/or buying foreign firms. They did not try—or, more plausibly, did not succeed—in choosing board members that would have allowed them to interlock with higher-status firms; the status logic excluded them from being connected to the center of the network. In 2000, their collective arrival produced a dual structure. It made observations of French interlocks all the more sensitive to sample size. Studies that focus on the 40 firms listed in the top stock exchange index, which is often the case, necessarily exclude the disconnected periphery. With a sample even larger than our own, Windolf (2002, 35–37) identified the dual structure already present in 1997. However, he interpreted this as comprising two separate classes of firms: an integrated public sector and isolated, family-led private firms criticizing state intervention. Our research provides a different account of this dualization. While state-owned firms generally had a high status, most of the firms in the core of the network were not under state control, and their directors generally did not advocate for state intervention.

Similar Big Linkers

The status logic can better explain the emergence of a dual structure. It also helps us gain a sound understanding of how this new structure could be accompanied by inertia in the profile of big linkers. In spite of the alleged internationalization of economic elites and changes in governance principles, *pantoufleurs* continued to be the most rewarded directors in the symbolic exchanges performed by interlocks. The status hierarchy was not upset by evolving practices of governance, which predated the 2001 law forbidding the accumulation of more than five board positions for one individual. Just as in the 1937–1956 period, we observe a decrease in average board size between 1990 (when it had returned to its interwar level of 12) and 2000 (10.4). This is partly due to the presence of more family firms with smaller boards (eight members on average), but it is, first and foremost, consistent with discussions in business associations and think tanks criticizing traditional governance (e.g., 'reciprocal' (multiple) interlocks) and praising the model of the 'independent director' (Maclean et al. 2006, 76–80). Triggered by international comparisons and by reports presenting new governance guidelines (e.g., the Viénot report in 1999), French firms, nonetheless, insisted on the necessity to adapt without strictly following UK or US models. Our results indicate a measure of success in this respect.

New governance guidelines probably played a role in the decrease in multiple interlocks. The big linkers, however, while they accumulated fewer positions than before, still had very similar profiles. Unlike what happened in smaller European countries (see Westerhuis or Ginalski, David and Mach this volume), France did not see a massive arrival of foreign directors. An exploratory study of interlockers in the 120 French firms with the highest market capitalization in 2009 shows that they very much resembled those of 1957 and 1979; if anything, *pantoufleurs* fared even better among them (François 2010). The status logic did not involve new (or foreign) profiles. Three names appear both in the 1990 and 2000 top lists, including that of Ernest-Antoine Seillière, who is the heir of one of the oldest French industrial families, a graduate of the ENA, has worked in several ministerial staffs and was president of the French peak business association from 1997 to 2005. As French elite schools aim precisely to produce graduates who are considered and, moreover, consider themselves to be excellent generalists floating above all interests and specialties (Boltanski and Bourdieu 1976), it is no wonder that changes in governance preferences that promoted the notion of 'independent' directors only reinforced their power as network specialists. While big linkers were less numerous and held fewer positions than before, their careers seem to have become even more standardized. Since these high-status directors tended to be associated with high-status firms, they could survive the dualization of the network structure.

5. CONCLUSION

We have recounted here a very French tale, which seems little influenced by external changes. The low point in density in 1956 is not to be found elsewhere and seems to be related to specifically French events (the creation of state monopolies) and processes (a change in views on governance). Foreign institutional investors did not drive the French financialization of 1957–1990. As for more recent changes, admittedly, they were influenced by international discussions on governance, but they still did not break the status logic we identify as central to the French network. Although the French interlocking network has become less dense and more dual, many of its distinctive characteristics still hold. These idiosyncrasies can be seen as both symptoms and consequences of a structure that, in spite of the shocks of World War II and the 1990s, has remained in place for more than 150 years.

This core-periphery structure, with its specific mix of density and hierarchy, has emerged from the coexistence of distinct mechanisms. The *governance logic* is certainly the most intuitive; when one changes the way boards are composed, the interlocking networks evolve mechanically. Still, this logic seems to have had little long-lasting influence on the structure. In retrospect, it only played an important role in the 1937–1956 period, where it can explain the weakening of the network. The *logic of business group building* had a more continual effect on the network, even though we exemplified it for only two specific moments: 1937 and 1990. This logic, which could either be set up by families or the government, has its roots in the creation of local solidarity networks based on interlocks, rather than ownership. However, the most important logic explaining the development of the French interlocking network from the mid-nineteenth century onwards is *status logic*. It has played a role in each and every period in several ways. High-status firms (as defined by different dimensions of status) tended to interlock with each other, lower-status firms tried to interlock with them and firms tried to put high-status directors on their board, a practice that created bridging network specialists who were often *pantoufleurs*. These three mechanisms prevailed throughout the twentieth century. Even the dramatic changes that occurred in the network in the 1940s and 1950s, and then again in the 1990s, were not caused by a weakening of these mechanisms; on the contrary, they can be explained by their continuing activation in a changing context. The two moments of disruption of the network did not, however, have the same causes. In the 1940s and 1950s, this disruption was mainly brought about by the new role of the state and changes in governance principles, while in the 1990s, the growth of firms was responsible for the radicalization of the core-periphery structure. At that time, the firms at the center of the network became bigger and bigger, and therefore, increasingly isolated from the smaller firms standing at the periphery. At the same time, this periphery was reshuffled by the arrival of firms that were previously much smaller, but which had gone public in order to sustain their spectacular growth.

It is only possible to tackle the peculiarities of French capitalism if we bring these three mechanisms together. In particular, the role of the state in forging this form of capitalism should be understood as only one part, among others, of the more general status logic. State-owned firms often were part of the high-status class, and high-status directors often were former civil servants. With this interpretation, French capitalism is not so much state capitalism as it is status capitalism—the state is not the cornerstone of French specific characteristics, but one version among others of a broader mechanism. Moreover, it is only through the combination of these three mechanisms that a proper understanding of the development of the network can be reached. The *pantoufleurs,* in the status logic, provide bridges between denser quasi-cliques that are created, in different sectors and at different times, by attempts at concentration by means other than ownership. Ties forged by business groups and status, acting together, produce a large and dense core. Shifting logics of governance only change the strength and density of these two kinds of ties, such that the network evolves, while its structure and underlying mechanisms endure.

NOTE

We would like to acknowledge the extremely valuable comments and suggestions from Jens Beckert, Valérie Boussard, Sylvain Brunier, Catherine Comet, Frank Dobbin, Hervé Dumez, Jean Finez, Olivier Godechot, Pierre-Cyrille Hautcœur, Hervé Joly, Paul Lagneau-Ymonet and Philip Scranton, as well as participants in the seminars and congresses where we presented this text, and the editors of this volume. The data collection has been funded by the *Direction Scientifique de Sciences Po*—further acknowledgments regarding data collection are in the online Appendix. Our English has been very efficiently polished by Annelies Fryberger.

1. For our indicators, sources and methods, including some results that were specifically produced by our methodology (e.g., tests of significance for homophily), see the Appendix and online appendices.

REFERENCES

Barjot, Dominique. 2010. "Cartels et ententes." In *Dictionnaire du patronat français,* edited by Jean-Claude Daumas, Alain Chatriot, Danièle Fraboulet, Patrick Fridenson, and Hervé Joly, 958–964, Paris: Flammarion.

Beltran, Alain. 2010. "Ernest Mercier 1878–1955." In *Dictionnaire du patronat français,* edited by Jean-Claude Daumas, Alain Chatriot, Danièle Fraboulet, Patrick Fridenson, and Hervé Joly, 468–470, Paris: Flammarion.

Boltanski, Luc, and Pierre Bourdieu. 1976. "La production de l'idéologie dominante." *Actes de la recherche en sciences sociales* 2 (2): 3–73.

Bourdieu, Pierre. 1989. *La noblesse d'État. Grandes écoles et esprit de corps*. Paris: Éditions de Minuit.
Carroll, William K., and Jean-Philippe Sapinski. 2011. "Corporate Elites and Intercorporate Networks." In *The SAGE Handbook of Social Network Analysis*, edited by John Scott and Peter J. Carrington, 180–194. London-Thousand Oaks: SAGE.
Cassis, Youssef. 2008. "Big Business." In *The Oxford Handbook of Business History*, edited by Geoffrey Jones and Jonathan Zeitlin, 171–193. Oxford: Oxford University Press.
Chabanas, Nicole, and Éric Vergeau. 1996. "Nationalisations et privatisations depuis 50 ans." *Insee première* 440: 1–4.
Charle, Christophe. 1987. "Le pantouflage en France (vers 1880-vers 1980)." *Annales. Économies, Sociétés, Civilisations* 42 (5): 1115–1137.
Chatriot, Alain. 2010. "Henri de Peyerimhoff 1871–1953." In *Dictionnaire du patronat français*, edited by Jean-Claude Daumas, Alain Chatriot, Danièle Fraboulet, Patrick Fridenson, and Hervé Joly, 543–545, Paris: Flammarion.
Colignon, Richard A., and Chikako Usui. 2003. *Amakudari. The Hidden Fabric of Japan's Economy*. Ithaca: Cornell University Press.
Dard, Olivier. 2010. "Des nouvelles féodalités aux 200 familles." In *Dictionnaire du patronat français*, edited by Jean-Claude Daumas, Alain Chatriot, Danièle Fraboulet, Patrick Fridenson, and Hervé Joly, 1250–1253, Paris: Flammarion.
Daumas, Jean-Claude, Alain Chatriot, Danièle Fraboulet, Patrick Fridenson, and Hervé Joly, eds. 2010. *Dictionnaire du patronat français*. Paris: Flammarion.
Denord, François. 2010. "Le corporatisme." In *Dictionnaire du patronat français*, edited by Jean-Claude Daumas, Alain Chatriot, Danièle Fraboulet, Patrick Fridenson, and Hervé Joly, 1018–1022, Paris: Flammarion.
François, Pierre. 2010. "Les guépards du capitalisme français? Structure de l'élite patronale et modes d'accès aux positions dominantes." Paper presented at the workshop "Les élites économiques en France," Université Paris Dauphine, November 4–5, 2010.
François, Pierre, and Claire Lemercier. 2012. "The Emerging Structure of French Capitalism. Interlocking Directorates among the French Largest Firms, 1840–1979." Paper presented at the European Social Science History Conference, Glasgow, April 11–14, 2012.
Granovetter, Mark. 1994. "Business Groups." In *The Handbook of Economic Sociology*, edited by Neil J. Smelser and Richard Swedberg, 453–476. Princeton: Princeton University Press.
Hall, Peter A., and David Soskice. 2001. *Varieties of Capitalism. The Institutional Foundations of Comparative Advantage*. Oxford-New York: Oxford University Press.
Joly, Hervé. 2009. "La direction des sociétés anonymes en France depuis le XIXe siècle : le droit entretient la confusion des pratiques." *Entreprises & Histoire* 57: 111–125.
Joly, Hervé. 2010a. "Henri Lafond 1984–1963." In *Dictionnaire du patronat français*, edited by Jean-Claude Daumas, Alain Chatriot, Danièle Fraboulet, Patrick Fridenson, and Hervé Joly, 394–396, Paris: Flammarion.
Joly, Hervé. 2010b. "L'épuration." In *Dictionnaire du patronat français*, edited by Jean-Claude Daumas, Alain Chatriot, Danièle Fraboulet, Patrick Fridenson, and Hervé Joly, 1317–1321, Paris: Flammarion.
Landes, David S. 1949. "French Entrepreneurship and Industrial Growth in the 19th Century." *Journal of Economic History* 9 (1): 45–61.
Maclean, Mairi, Charles Harvey, and Jon Press. 2006. *Business Elites and Corporate Governance in France and the UK*. New York: Palgrave.

Mizruchi, Mark S. 1996. "What Do Interlocks Do? An Analysis, Critique, and Assessment of Research on Interlocking Directorates." *Annual Review of Sociology* 22: 271–298.
Podolny, Joel. 2005. *Status Signals: A Sociological Study of Market Competition.* Princeton: Princeton University Press.
Swartz, David. 1985. "French Interlocking Directorships: Financial and Industrial Groups." In *Networks of Corporate Power: A Comparative Analysis of Ten Countries,* edited by Frans N. Stokman, Rolf Ziegler, and John Scott, 184–197. Cambridge: Polity Press.
Vuillermot, Catherine. 2000. "Pierre-Marie Durand, avoué lyonnais, roi de l'électricité." *Vingtième Siècle* 65 (1): 71–79.
Windolf, Paul. 2002. *Corporate Networks in Europe and the United States.* Oxford: Oxford University Press.

9 Persistent and Stubborn
The State in Italian Capitalism, 1913–2001[1]

Alberto Rinaldi and Michelangelo Vasta

1. INTRODUCTION

In the original formulation of varieties of capitalism (VOC), Italy, along with other Latin countries (e.g., France, Spain and Portugal), is grouped in an ambiguous position that deserves neither the label of liberal market economies (LMEs) nor that of coordinated market economies (CMEs) (Hall and Soskice 2001). These former nations seem to have been characterized above all by the central role of the state, which intervened more frequently and in a different way than in LMEs and CMEs. Thus, a third variety, 'state-influenced market economies' (SMEs), has been distinguished to account for the experience of these countries. In SMEs, the state plays a central role in coordinating inter-firm relations and shaping labor regulation (Schmidt 2002).

From the 1930s to the end of the twentieth century, Italy was a bank-based system, impaired by the inability of banks to own shares in non-financial firms. State actors in the form of both public agencies and state-owned banks provided coordination through formal and informal channels. Large-scale allocation of credit was authoritative and driven by political considerations. Corporate laws were consistent with a closed and highly coordinated system of finance. Protection of minority shareholders was nearly non-existent, ownership was extremely concentrated and the stock market underdeveloped (Deeg 2005). These structural characteristics of the Italian corporate system are among the most debated by both historians and economists.

Historians focus mainly on the 'macro-level' determinants of the structure of Italian capitalism and stress that economic growth was curbed by some traits that originated with Italy's unification and have been present since; for example, the limited size of the domestic market, the general shortage of capital and the lack of natural resources. As a consequence, only a few big companies could prosper, often enjoying state protection and monopolistic positions (Sereni 1966; Mori 1977; Bonelli 1978; Amatori and Colli 1999; Giannetti and Vasta 2006). State interventionism translated into 'political capitalism': entrepreneurs pursued growth not for economic reasons (economies of scale and scope), but to strengthen their bargaining power with politics (Amatori 2011).

Most of historiography holds that—in the face of such constraints—the creation of one of the largest state-owned sectors in the Western world in Italy was a way to provide those Gerschenkron-type 'substitutive factors' that were needed to catch up with more industrialized countries (Gerschenkron 1962). The action of state-owned enterprises (henceforth, SOEs) was restricted to those fields that the government considered strategic for the nation's economic development, and in which the private sector was reluctant to invest. This was particularly the case in such capital-intensive industries as steel, heavy engineering, energy, motorways and public utilities, whose expansion provided indispensable infrastructures for the growth of private initiatives in related sectors (Posner and Wolf 1967; Amatori 2000; Toninelli 2004).

Conversely, economists focus on the 'micro-level' foundations of the Italian corporate system. For example, following the 'new theory of the property rights' (Grossman and Hart 1986; Hart 1989; Hart and Moore 1990), a research group from the Bank of Italy shifted the analysis to the corporate governance system (Barca 1994; Barca et al. 1994). This approach explains high ownership concentration in Italian capitalism by the low level of shareholder protection and, more generally, the absence of appropriate rules for corporate governance.

A different approach focuses on technical change and considers innovation to be the main driver of economic growth. From this perspective, technology is considered to be the most powerful tool in order to provide a long-run periodization of the world economic history. Taking this view—starting from the concept of long waves triggered by specific technological breakthroughs conceived in term of Kondratiev cycles—notions such as 'technological paradigms' and 'general purpose technologies' have been used. These concepts overlap and represent the general frameworks within which different patterns of solutions to specific techno-economic problems are developed.[2] In light of this literature, some scholars hold that the characteristics of a given technology may require a particular institutional setting because its diffusion is largely determined by the context in which it takes place. However, it has also been suggested that technologies and institutions tend to adapt to each other and, thus, can be seen to follow a co-evolutionary pattern. According to this view, the passage from one technological paradigm to another can foster either a homogenization or an emergence of new viable idiosyncratic organizational forms, depending on the comparative institutional advantage of each nation. In turn, the system of corporate governance can affect the way in which new technologies evolve and are adopted, thereby regenerating institutional diversity, or in other words, VOC (Nelson 1994). Referring to this conceptual framework, Pagano and Trento (2003) propose an interpretation of the dynamics of the Italian capitalism based on complementarity between technology and its institutional setting.

Therefore, the creation of German-type universal banks in the last decade of the nineteenth century allowed Italy to catch up with the technological paradigm of the second Industrial Revolution. The early 1930s represented a turning point as, in order to face the Great Depression, in 1933, the fascist government created the *Istituto per la Ricostruzione Industriale* (Iri), which took over the universal banks and their industrial securities. The result was the substitution of the state for mixed banks as the linchpin of the system of financial intermediation (Toniolo 1980; Zamagni 1993). The boundaries of SOEs further expanded after World War II: Iri remained the main pillar of the system but a second pillar, the state energy super-holding, *Ente Nazionale Idrocarburi* (Eni), was founded in 1953 (Carnevali 2000). These two state holdings enabled Italy to catch up with the technological paradigm of the mass production during the 'Golden Age'. In the 1970s, the oil crisis and the advent of a new, ICT-based, technological paradigm resulted in a new scenario for Western economies. Italy was severely hit by this new situation. SOEs were increasingly burdened with special social objectives, such as prompting the industrialization of the backward South or rescuing ailing companies. The structure of the Italian corporate system changed noticeably between the 1970s and the 1980s: the new technological paradigm contributed both to the speeding up of the crisis of the SOEs and to the soaring of industrial districts and networks of small- and medium-sized enterprises. SOEs degenerated in the 1980s in the absence of a functioning political market that guaranteed democratic changes of parties in power and the erosion of the 'mission' culture of SOE managers (Barca and Trento 1997).

In the 1990s, massive privatizations reduced the weight of SOEs within Italian capitalism and opened up a new era of state entrepreneurship. Iri was dismantled and closed down in 2000. However, the state retained control of national champions in strategic sectors such as energy, aerospace and defense. Stock in these companies was also partially sold off to raise funds from private investors.

This chapter adds to previous research by analyzing the structure of the Italian corporate network, paying particular attention to the role of SOEs, in seven benchmark years covering the period 1913 to 2001. To undertake our analysis, we use a smaller sample of the top 250 companies, ranked by total assets, for each benchmark year. A particular focus is placed on the role of SOEs in the network. Network analysis, which has its origin in modern sociology, gained a significant place in social science in recent decades, including economics and, subsequently, economic and business history.[3] In our view, the use of network analysis can be especially suitable in highlighting both the macro- and micro-economic perspectives and, in particular, the relationship between the two approaches. Moreover, the use of the interlocking directorship technique can play a dual role by, on the one hand, complementing the traditional case-study method and, on the other, by allowing broad overviews of the social system under investigation.

This also aids in the verification of different theoretical approaches, such as studies in innovation economics. In some previous articles, we analyzed the structure of the Italian corporate network from 1952 to 1983 using a large sample of approximately 25,000 companies (Rinaldi and Vasta 2005, 2012). Our principal findings are that, in 1952 and 1960, the network, centered on the larger electrical companies, showed the highest cohesion. This center dissolved after the nationalization of the electricity industry in 1962, and in 1972, it had been replaced by a new and less cohesive network centering on financial intermediaries: banks, insurance and finance companies. SOEs and private companies were strongly interconnected and showed a high propensity to share board members. SOEs were well represented among the most central companies. The 1972–1983 period brought significant changes to the structure of the system. These included, on the one hand, a large decrease in the network's overall cohesion, and, on the other, a weakening of the ties between the private sector and SOEs, with the latter's marginalization from the center.

This chapter continues as follows: Section 2 describes the source utilized for this study. Section 3 describes the evolution of the structure of the network through the use of several indicators of network analysis. Section 4 provides an interpretation of the evolution of the Italian corporate network and, last, Section 5 concludes.

2. SOURCES AND DATA

For the benchmark years from 1913 to 1983, we selected the top 250 companies and their directors from Imita.db.[4] This dataset is the electronic version of *Notizie statistiche sulle principali società italiane per azioni*, edited by the *Associazione fra le Società Italiane per Azioni* (Assonime). As this publication ceased in 1984, for the benchmark year 2001, we selected the top 250 companies from *Le principali società italiane*, the annual report on Italian joint-stock companies, edited by *R&S-Mediobanca*. As this source does not report the names of the board members, we extracted them from *Infocamere*, a large dataset of *Unioncamere*, the association of the Italian chambers of commerce.[5]

3. GENERAL CHARACTERISTICS OF THE ITALIAN CORPORATE NETWORK

Descriptive Statistics of the Network

A brief analysis of the sample shows that the number of seats was highest in 1927 with 3,024 board positions and an average of 12.1 members per board.[6] The average size remained stable until 1972 at about 11–12 members per board, but then decreases with a minimum of 9.1 directors in 2001.

An important measure for the description of the system is the *cumulation ratio* (CR), that is, the average number of positions held by a single director. This, too, peaked in 1927. Then it decreased: first, only slightly from 1936 to 1960, but then substantially after 1972.

In 1913, none of the companies in the sample were state-owned. SOEs first appeared in 1927, when we find 17.[7] Their number increased in the subsequent benchmark years: there were 43 in 1936, 66 in 1960, 73 in 1972, reaching a maximum of 85 in 1983. What is probably the most striking is that their presence also remained substantial in 2001, with 56 companies out of 250, despite the massive privatizations of the 1990s.[8]

The classification of the Italian top 250 companies in industry also changed over time.[9] Manufacturing companies are consistently the most numerous. However, their number dropped from 101 to 85 between 1913 and 1927, then increased, reaching a maximum of 148 in 1972. They remained stable at 142 in 1983, but dropped to 111 in 2001. The biggest change, however, concerned the weight of the public utility companies. These were highly represented from 1913 to 1960, when they accounted for about one-quarter of all non-financials. They nearly disappeared in 1972 as a consequence of the nationalization of the electricity industry in 1962. In 1983, they were also nearly absent. Finally, they increased substantially in 2001 as a consequence of the massive privatizations of state-owned and municipal enterprises, and the take-off of the mobile telephone industry in the 1990s.

For a very long time, from 1927 to 1983, SOEs were concentrated principally among financials and manufacturing companies. Then, in 2001, after the privatization of Italian banks, SOEs disappeared from the financial sector and also reduced their weight in manufacturing. Now, SOEs are clustered primarily in the public utilities and services.

The Structure of the Network

For most of the period under investigation, the Italian corporate network consisted of a large main component that included about 90% of the firms of the sample.[10] However, after 1983, the proportion of the firms in the main component started to decline and, in 2001, dropped to 61.2%. In that year, the network appeared to be much more fragmented than it had been in the past, and—apart from isolated firms—there were another 11 small components in addition to the main one.

The number of isolated firms remained stable from 1913 to 1960, but then their number started to increase. The rise was slight in 1972 and 1983 but became much larger in 2001, when the number of isolated firms more than doubled—from 33 to 71 firms—compared with the previous benchmark year, and came to account for nearly 30% of total firms.

Marginal firms were stable from 1913 to 1960, and increased from 1972. Most of the surge occurred between 1960 and 1983, however, while from 1983 to 2001, marginal firms rose only slightly from 63 to 70.

We then calculated the number of ties (or lines) between companies and the number of multiple ties. Both the total number of lines and multiple lines reached a peak in 1927. Then, they remain stable between 1936 and 1960, diminishing considerably from 1972, with a minimum value in 2001.

The m-slice technique is a technique for analyzing a network based on line multiplicity; an m-slice is a sub-network defined by the multiplicity of its lines. We analyzed the 2-slices sub-network, in which firms have at least a double interlock with another firm. This index is important because it is argued that multiple ties are less personal and more institutional (De Nooy, Mrvar, and Batagelj 2006). In 1913, 158 out of 250 firms were part of the 2-slice. Their number rose to 187 in 1927 and remained very high and stable until 1960, with values around 180–190. Then, in 1972, this number started to decrease, dropping sharply in 2001 to 95.

The density of the network peaked in 1927, when the German-type universal banks had a pre-eminent position in the system. Then, in 1936 and 1960, it returned to values only slightly higher than those of 1913, and in 1972, the density started to decline. The fall was particularly strong in 1983 and 2001; that further signifies the loosening of the Italian corporate network in the two final benchmark years, just when the proportion of isolated and marginal firms surged substantially (see Figure 9.1).

Dynamics quite similar to that of the density are shown by all the other centrality and cohesiveness indicators. In other words, we have shown that the network reached its highest cohesiveness in 1927 and showed a massive decline starting from 1972, but this same peak can also be shown for diameter, average distance, average degree, degree centrality and closeness centrality.

The overall picture that emerges from all the connectivity indices, then, is a strong reduction in the overall cohesion of the Italian corporate network over time. This started after the nationalization of the electricity

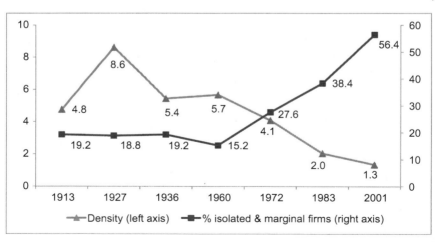

Figure 9.1 Density and Isolated and Marginal Firms

industry in 1962, became more severe between 1972 and 1983—in other words, during the crisis that followed the end of the 'Golden Age'—and was even sharper between 1983 and 2001, following the massive privatizations of the 1990s.

Comparing these characteristics to other countries, it can be seen that in the period prior to World War II, the density index in Italy seems to have followed much the same trend as in Germany, even if at lower values (see Figure 9.2). Then, Italy seems to have experienced a decline of its corporate network earlier than other advanced economies. In fact, for several other nations—such as the USA, Germany, Switzerland and the Netherlands—available studies show that corporate networks started to disentangle sometime after 1980, with the major changes taking place during the 1990s and 2000s (Davis and Mizruchi 1999; Höpner and Krempel 2002; Schnyder et al. 2005; David, Schnyder, and Westerhuis 2011).

The Links between Private Companies and SOEs

Private companies displayed a high propensity to be interlocked with other private companies for most of the period we investigated. In fact, the proportion of private companies linked to at least one other private company was about 90% from 1913 to 1961. Then, in 1972, it started to decrease. The decline was slight at first, but after 1983, became more pronounced (see Table 9.1).

What is most noticeable is the high proportion of private companies that were connected to SOEs. In 1927, more than a half of private companies were interlocked to at least one SOE. This number peaked in 1936,

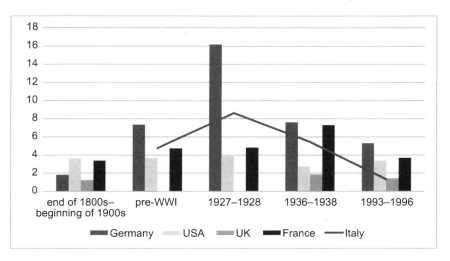

Figure 9.2 Density of the Top 250 Companies in Some Selected Countries*

* Data for France, Germany, USA and UK are drawn from Windolf (2010).

Table 9.1 Firms by Type of Interlocks

	1913 N.	1913 %	1927 N.	1927 %	1936 N.	1936 %	1960 N.	1960 %	1972 N.	1972 %	1983 N.	1983 %	2001 N.	2001 %
Total private firms	250	100	233	100	207	100	184	100	177	100	165	100	194	100
(1)	229	91.6	222	95.3	188	90.8	164	89.1	150	84.7	128	77.6	128	66.0
(2)	–	–	121	51.9	140	67.6	106	57.6	88	49.7	63	38.2	26	13.4
Total SOEs	–	–	17	100	43	100	66	100	73	100	85	100	56	100
(3)	–	–	12	70.6	38	88.4	65	98.5	73	100	80	94.1	39	69.6
(4)	–	–	14	82.4	38	88.4	57	86.4	56	76.7	37	43.5	19	33.9

(1) Private firms linked to at least another private firm.
(2) Private firms linked to at least one SOE.
(3) SOEs linked to at least another SOE.
(4) SOEs linked to at least one private firm.

immediately after the creation of Iri, with a value higher than two-thirds. Then, the corresponding value started to decline. Nevertheless, a strong interconnection between private companies and SOEs remained a prominent feature of the Italian corporate network until at least 1972, when half of private companies were still linked to SOEs. The two final benchmark years showed an increasing disconnection between private companies and SOEs. In fact, the proportion of private companies linked to at least one SOE dropped to 38% in 1983, and then plummeted to 13% in 2001.

In the same way, SOEs showed a high propensity to be interconnected to other SOEs from when the SOE system was created until 1983, with consistent values around 90%. This propensity then diminished and, by 2001, only 69% of SOEs were linked to at least one other SOE.

The links between SOEs and private companies are particularly interesting. From 1927 to 1972, more than three-quarters of SOEs were interlocked with at least one private company; in other words, the high cohesion of the Italian corporate network at that time was marked by a strong interconnection between the private sector and the SOE system. Then, a big change occurred: the proportion of SOEs linked to at least one private company fell to 43% in 1983, and to 34% in 2001. This drop highlights the disentangling of the Italian corporate network since the 1970s, which is characterized by the increasing disconnection of private companies and SOEs.

The Role of the Big Linkers

An analysis of the 'big linkers'—in our case, the 10 individuals who held the largest number of directorships in each benchmark year—can be very insightful. In capitalist countries, the big linkers perform an important function, one that ensures the cohesion of the system. These people are usually the business community's opinion leaders, the vehicle through which information is collected and spread among companies, as well as the principal channel connecting the business world and the political domain (Scott 1985).

We closely examined the interlocking directorships generated by the top 10 big linkers.[11] Table 9.2 shows that in each benchmark year, these individuals accounted for a very high proportion of total interlocking directorships, ranging from 21% in 1972 to 37% in 1960. In other words, the Italian corporate network was constituted to a large extent by the links generated by a handful of individuals, who played a dominant role in ensuring the cohesion of the whole system.

After the interwar period, big linkers showed a high propensity to achieve a high number of directorships in both private companies and SOEs, thereby functioning as big connectors between the privately-owned and state-owned sectors of the corporate system. In fact, we find that in 1927, when the SOE system was still very small, five of the top ten big linkers sat on the board of at least one SOE, as well as several private companies. The propensity of big linkers to hold directorships in both private companies and

178 *Alberto Rinaldi and Michelangelo Vasta*

Table 9.2 Interlocking Directorates Generated by the Top Ten Big Linkers, 1913–2001

	1913	1927	1936	1960	1972	1983	2001
(1) Total IDs	1,924	4,029	2,479	2,702	1,741	925	701
(2) IDs by the BL	516	1,450	767	999	535	201	235
2 / 1 (%)	26.8	36.0	30.9	37.0	30.7	21.7	33.5

SOEs further increased after the creation of Iri and remained very high until the early 1970s. In fact, in the benchmark years 1936, 1960 and 1972, eight of the top ten big linkers sat on the boards of at least one private company and at least one SOE. Thus, their directorships were not concentrated either completely in private companies or in SOEs.

A major change occurred in 1983, when no big linkers sat on the boards of both private companies and SOEs (there was only one in 2001). So, from the early 1980s onwards, nearly all of the big linkers held directorships exclusively in private companies or exclusively in SOEs. The decline of the Italian corporate networks and the increasing disconnection of the private sector from the SOEs seems, therefore, to have involved a change in the role of the top big linkers from connectors between the major state-owned and private enterprises to connectors only among the major private companies or only among the major SOEs.

Actor Centrality

In network analysis, it is presumed that central actors have better access to information, better opportunities to spread information and some 'power' with which they can coordinate the whole network. We use two measures to calculate the centrality of firms for the top 10 companies in each benchmark year: degree centrality and betweenness centrality.

Degree centrality is the simplest and most intuitive measure of actor centrality. It simply counts the number of actors to which an actor is tied. However, degree centrality is a local centrality measure and does not take into account the centrality of the neighbors to which an actor is linked. Therefore, an actor can have many neighbors but still be at the periphery of the network as a whole. This shortcoming is overcome by betweenness centrality. This measure is based on the idea that a firm is more central if it is more important as an intermediary in the communication network. So, for each actor, it calculates the number of shortest paths between any pairs of actors in the network that pass through this actor (De Nooy et al. 2005).

Regarding degree centrality, in 1913, the banking sector had the single most representations (4) among the most central companies (10).[12] The three larger universal banks (*Banca Commerciale*, *Credito Italiano* and *Società Bancaria Italiana*) and the *Banca d'Italia* (which, at that time, was still a privately-owned joint-stock company) played a central role in the system.

In 1927, the two larger universal banks were still at the top. Electrical companies had strengthened their position and now accounted for six of the top ten. In 1936, banks had lost their pre-eminent position, while the larger electrical companies and the two bigger insurance companies now occupied a central position. For the first time, three SOEs appeared among the top ten. The situation little changed in 1960, with four large electrical companies and two finance companies that were deeply involved in the electricity industry among the top ten.

The nationalization of the electricity industry in 1962 led to the disappearance of electrical companies from the top 10 in 1972. Manufacturing companies now made up a higher proportion: five out of ten. It is also possible to observe a larger presence of SOEs among the most central companies in 1972: four of the top ten companies. In 1983, the central role of manufacturing companies was further strengthened as they now accounted for seven of the top thirteen companies, while SOEs had dropped to three of the top thirteen.[13]

By contrast, in 2001, manufacturing companies had almost disappeared from the more central firms, with only the big aerospace and state-owned defense company, *Finmeccanica*, remaining. At this time, the most represented industries among the top ten companies were telecommunications and banks, with three presences each. To highlight their further marginalization from the center of the now weaker network, SOEs fell to two out of ten, despite their persistent presence among the largest companies in the sample (as we have seen, 15 out of 20 largest non-financials by total assets in 2001 were SOEs).

The betweenness centrality analysis shows very similar results to those obtained with degree centrality. The major difference concerns the place of SOEs in 1983, which are better represented according to the betweenness centrality measure (6 companies out of 10) than by degree centrality (3 out of 13). This might be a consequence of a change that may have occurred in the structure of the network between 1972 and 1983 with the passage from one large cohesive center that included both private companies and SOEs to two centers—one larger and private and the other smaller and state-owned—that are clearly disconnected one from the other. This would be consistent with the evidence found by Chiesi (1985) for 1976, using a different sample. It is possible that a smaller proportion of companies functioned as key channels of communication in the larger private center, which could explain the higher proportion of SOEs among the top 10 by betweenness centrality.

4. AN INTERPRETATION OF THE EVOLUTION OF THE ITALIAN CORPORATE NETWORK

We have seen that, in 1913, the Italian corporate network had a center based on the larger German-style universal banks that had been created in the 1890s. Gerschenkron (1962) singled out these banks as the major underlying cause of Italy's first big industrial growth in the 15 years prior to World War I. In his view, they provided financial support and managerial advice to the major companies, especially in the leading sectors of the second Industrial Revolution, such as steel, heavy engineering, electricity and motor vehicles.

In 1927, the center appears to have been enlarged and reached its highest connectivity. The post-World War I crisis had made it impossible for many companies to repay their debts to banks. So, the banks unwillingly transformed their 'frozen' loans into share capital and became the real owners of many industrial companies. In the 1920s, instead of selling their shares, the banks increased their stakes in order to sustain the stock exchange quotations (Confalonieri 1992, 1997). Thus, the two larger universal banks further strengthened their links with industry by superimposing interlocking directorships on share control relationships.

When the Great Depression struck, the entire system collapsed, and both the banks and their industrial clients had to be bailed out by the state. In 1933, the big state-owned holding, Iri, took over the universal banks and their industrial securities. In 1936, a new banking law imposed a clear-cut separation between banks and industry. Banks were allowed to practice only short-term credit, while their share participation in non-financial companies was strictly limited. At the same time, industrial credit was entrusted to newly created, specialized institutes (La Francesca 2004).

These changes had profound effects on the structure of the Italian corporate network. The former universal banks lost their pre-eminent position. By 1936, a new center had emerged, based on the larger electrical companies and, to a lesser extent, on the bigger insurance companies and SOEs. This new center remained in place until the electricity industry was nationalized in 1962. In fact, in the early 1960s, the Socialist Party had made the nationalization of the electricity industry a binding condition for its entry into a center-left governing coalition with the *Democrazia Cristiana*. In 1962, the Parliament passed the nationalization law and the new big state-owned agency, Enel, became Italy's sole electricity producer. The law required the state to give the former electrical-commercial companies a large sum in compensation for nationalization. The *raison d'etre* was that they could invest the compensation in new fast-growing industries, thereby boosting their growth. However, the former electrical-commercial companies failed to define a coherent strategy for the use of such funds and scattered them in many uncorrelated and unprofitable investments. As result, they suffered from heavy losses; most of them were taken over and by the end of the 1960s, had disappeared from the center of Italian capitalism (Bruno and Segreto 1996).

By 1972, a new center had emerged, which included several manufacturing companies allied to *Mediobanca*—Italy's sole merchant bank at that time—and a larger proportion of SOEs. So, by 1972, SOEs were placed in a prominent position at the center of a network that was still 'tight', and were strongly interconnected to private companies. The judicial instrument used by the state to intervene in the economy favored the intertwining of SOEs and private firms. In fact, organized according to public law and audited by a controller or auditor-general, but yet ruled by private law, state holdings in Italy had something of a 'double nature'. Within this framework, both the state (through one or more state-owned holdings) and private shareholders were present in the share capital of many SOEs, which were structured in multi-layered business groups thus favoring joint directors between SOEs and private companies (Colli, Rinaldi and Vasta, forthcoming).

In 1983, the cohesion of the network had sharply declined. Now, an unprecedented disconnection between the private sector and SOEs characterized a weaker network. Thus, Italy seems not only to have experienced an earlier erosion of its corporate network than other advanced economies—such as the USA, Germany, Switzerland and the Netherlands, where corporate networks started to disentangle after 1980 with the major changes taking place during the 1990s and the 2000s—but also the factors at work seem to have been different. In fact, in the other nations, the decline of the corporate networks was principally a consequence of a change in the strategy of banks. They disengaged from industrial companies as they moved away from traditional lending toward fee-based forms of business (Davis and Mizruchi 1999; Höpner and Krempel 2002; Schnyder et al. 2005; David, Schnyder and Westerhuis 2011). Conversely, the major cause of the disentangling of the Italian corporate network was the SOEs' changing role and their disconnection from private companies.

Somewhat paradoxically, this occurred when, at the beginning of the 1980s, the extension of the SOE sector was the largest in Italian history (Toninelli and Vasta 2010). In the face of the economic crisis of the 1970s, SOEs were given the mission of rescuing the larger private groups. SOEs bought private shareholders' minority stakes in those SOEs that were no longer paying dividends. Massive losses forced several SOEs to reduce their capital. In many cases, the subsequent capital increase was underwritten only by the state, so that recapitalization brought with it a substantial change in ownership structure for the SOEs involved, involving the almost total disappearance of private shareholders. This reduced the scope for generating interlocking directorships based on share relationships between SOEs and private companies (Bianchi 2002). These bailouts further worsened the SOEs' financial situation, making them more exposed to political pressure. As a consequence, in the 1970s, a new generation of managers that were more closely tied to the governing political parties surged to the front of the SOE system. After taking control of the SOEs, the governing political parties pushed them to grow larger without consideration of profit and loss. At the same time, partnerships and joint strategies with private companies were treated with suspicion because they could destabilize the balance of power between and within the political parties. Hence, party-controlled SOEs became less interested in recruiting private businessmen for their boards of directors. In addition, the affiliation of the new generation of SOE managers with political parties made private companies reluctant to appoint them to their own boards, lest they could become instruments for the parties to expand their influence on private business (Barca and Trento 1997; Amatori 2000).

Italy was led by government coalitions based on *Democrazia Cristiana* without interruption from 1945 to 1992. Between 1992 and 1994, a massive wave of scandals brought a major questioning of the legitimacy of the governing coalition and the demise of the Christian Democrats. In the political vacuum that arose, a series of governments headed by technocrats and supported by center-left coalitions ruled the country for most of the 1990s. These governments sought to reduce the role of the state in the economy, with the aim of cutting public deficits, tackling corruption and increasing the role of markets and competition in the economy in line with the logic of the European Single Market (Rangone and Solari 2012). So, in the 1990s, the massive losses suffered by many SOEs and an unsustainable sovereign debt drove Italy to carry out the largest privatization process in the Western world. In this process, Iri was dismantled and closed down. The stocks of other state-owned holdings, such as Eni, Enel and Finmeccanica, however, were only partially sold off to enable the state to retain a controlling stake (R&S-Mediobanca 2000). The privatizations in the 1990s reshaped and further weakened the Italian corporate network, which, in 2001, became even more disentangled with all the connectivity indicators showing their lowest values. The remaining SOEs were marginalized and moved away from the center of the system. Such a marginalization of SOEs probably reflected the transition to the third Industrial Revolution technological paradigm (ICT). In fact, the 1970s saw the rise of flexible networks of small and medium-sized firms that made use of computerized process-control technology in Italy (Piore and Sabel 1984). In larger private firms, the introduction of computer-based technology from the early 1980s onwards triggered the pursuit of higher organizational flexibility and the start of post-Fordist restructuring. This pushed firms to loosen the constraints that arose from their dense ties with SOEs. Among these was the sharing of board members.

In 2001, manufacturing companies also nearly disappeared from the more central firms. A new and smaller center had taken shape, based on some large insurance companies and the larger companies in the recently privatized sectors: telecommunications, public utilities and banks.

At the beginning of the twenty-first century, then, the structure of the weakened Italian corporate network seems to reflect an increasing dualism of the Italian corporate system and the different dynamics of its two components. On the one hand, there is the export-oriented sector. This sector consists principally of small- and medium-sized, privately-owned, manufacturing firms that operate in the 'Made in Italy' sectors: in other words, manufacturing personal and household goods—textiles, clothing, leather, footwear, wood, tiles, furniture, jewelry, cosmetics, musical instruments, toys and sports items—and light engineering, producing the machinery to manufacture the former. The share of this sector in the nation's economy increased after the 1970s, but the declining importance of the domestic market for its competitiveness seems to have decreased the importance of being entangled in a national corporate network. The most dynamic companies in this sector pursued dimensional growth and experienced accelerated internationalization. Therefore, they have been called 'pocket multinationals', although this label has been known to include a heterogeneous mass of companies.[14] Of the 296 Italian 'pocket multinationals' that were mapped by Colli (2002) in the late 1990s, 29 are included in our sample for 2001. These 29 'pocket multinationals' show a lower propensity to generate interlocking directorships than the other companies in the sample: 45% of pocket multinationals were isolated firms, as against 26% of the other firms in the sample. Also, the proportion of marginal firms was higher for pocket multinationals: 31% as compared to 28% for the other firms.

On the other hand, there is the sector serving the domestic market, within which most of the recently privatized companies—telecommunications, public utilities and banks, for example—operate: in other words, those whose weight in the national economy has diminished over the course of time but for which the integration in a national corporate network remains important. This can explain the weakening of the network as a whole and the monopolization of the center by companies operating in the latter sector.

5. CONCLUSIONS

This chapter has analyzed the structure of the Italian corporate network from 1913 to 2001, applying network analysis techniques to a sample of the top 250 companies, ranked by total assets, for seven benchmark years.

It has shown that the system was very cohesive from 1913 to 1960. The highest values were observed in 1927, when the influence of the larger German-type universal banks on the nation's corporate system reached its apex. Conversely, the cohesion of the system started to decrease in 1972, after the nationalization of the electricity industry and with the start of the transition from the technological paradigm of the second to that of the third Industrial Revolution. The disentangling of the network became sharper in 1983 and 2001, when the connectivity indexes plummeted to their lowest values. Moreover, multiple ties became scarcer and the inclusiveness of the network sharply declined alongside a strong increase of isolated firms.

This chapter has shown that a persistent and resilient presence of SOEs among the top 250 companies stands out as one of the major features of the Italian corporate system. This was still the case at the beginning of the twenty-first century, after Italy had carried out the largest privatization process in the Western world in the 1990s.

However, the relationship between private companies and SOEs changed over time. For a long time, from the 1920s to the early 1970s, a strong interconnection between private companies and SOEs was a distinguishing feature of the network. SOEs were well-represented within the most central firms and the numbering of positions on boards of both private companies and SOEs was a common practice among big linkers. The propensity of SOEs to generate interlocking directorships with private companies dates back to the birth of SOEs in the interwar period and was due to the nature of state intervention in the Italian economy that was conceived as a form of support to private entrepreneurship.

In the mid-1970s, the situation changed considerably. By 1983, SOEs and private enterprises had become much more disconnected. In 2001, the SOEs that still remained following the privatizations had been marginalized from the center of the system. The marginalization of SOEs probably reflected a broader strategy of the private sector. In fact, with post-Fordist restructuring and the advent of the ICT revolution, larger private enterprises started to pursue higher flexibility and reject the constraints derived from their dense ties with SOEs.

By comparison, Italy seems to have experienced an earlier decline of her corporate network than other advanced economies—the USA, Germany, Switzerland and the Netherlands, for example—where corporate networks started to disentangle after 1980 with the major changes taking place during the 1990s and 2000s. Also, the factors at work seem to have been different. In the other industrialized nations, the decline of the corporate networks was principally a consequence of a change in the strategy of banks, which disengaged from industrial companies as they moved away from traditional lending toward fee-based forms of business—in particular, investment banking. Conversely, in Italy, the major cause of the disentangling of the network was the disconnection of private companies from SOEs and the marginalization of the latter.

NOTES

1. We wish to thank the editors of this volume, Thomas David and Gerarda Westerhuis, as well as Pier Angelo Toninelli, who made many important suggestions at different stages of the research. Thanks are also due to Phil Scranton (discussant) and other participants in the conference, "Corporate networks in the 20th century: development and structural changes" (Lausanne, 27–28 August 2012) for their helpful comments. This work has relied on the use of Imita.db, a large dataset funded by Miur, the Italian Ministry for University and Scientific Research; on Infocamere, the large dataset of Unioncamere, the association of the Italian chambers of commerce; and on R&S-Mediobanca dataset on the Italian top companies. We thank the Chamber of Commerce of Modena for letting us have access to Infocamere, and R&S-Mediobanca for

providing precious information on balance sheets of the Italian firms. A special thank you is due to Fulvio Coltorti, head of R&S-Mediobanca, for his valuable and generous help. The usual disclaimer applies.
2. The notion of technological paradigm was proposed, within the neo-Schumpeterian approach, by Dosi (1982). The characteristics of these paradigms in historical perspectives were investigated by Freeman and Louçã (2001). The notion of general purpose technology (GPT) was introduced by Bresnahan and Trajtenberg (1995). For an updated discussion on these topics, see Dosi and Nelson (2010).
3. The necessity to introduce new methodologies and the opportunity to integrate much more economic, business and social history has been recently maintained in a very stimulating essay (Jones, van Leeuwen, and Broadberry 2013).
4. Imita.db is available online at http://imitadb.unisi.it.
5. For a detailed description of the sources and selection of our data, see our file, "Sources and Method", at http://www.cgeh.nl./power-corporate-networks-comparative-and-historical-perspective.
6. See our file, "Descriptive Statistics of the Network", at http://www.cgeh.nl./power-corporate-networks-comparative-and-historical-perspective.
7. We define 'state-owned enterprises' as those companies in which the state or state-controlled holding companies owned at least 20% of the share capital. The same threshold is used in the literature to identify participations that enable their holders to exert an 'effective' control (La Porta et al. 1999).
8. Perhaps it is striking that, in 2001, after Italy had gone through the largest privatizations in the Western world in the 1990s, 8 of the top 10 and 15 of the top 20 companies by total assets were state-owned.
9. See our file, "Classification in Industries", at http://www.cgeh.nl./power-corporate-networks-comparative-and-historical-perspective.
10. Data are reported in the Appendix to this volume and in our file, "The overall measures of the network", at http://www.cgeh.nl./power-corporate-networks-comparative-and-historical-perspective.
11. The list of the top 10 big linkers in each benchmark year is provided in our file, "Top Ten Big Linkers", at http://www.cgeh.nl./power-corporate-networks-comparative-and-historical-perspective.
12. The list of the 10 most central companies by degree centrality and betweenness centrality in each benchmark year is provided in our file, "Top Ten Firms", at http://www.cgeh.nl./power-corporate-networks-comparative-and-historical-perspective.
13. In 1983 and 2001, the actual number of more central companies by degree centrality was 13 and 11, respectively, instead of the 10 speculated, since in those years, some companies appear in 10th position with the same degree.
14. A recent evolution in Italian capitalism is the increasing weight of medium-sized enterprises (MSEs). This is the result of the process both of downsizing of the large companies (state-owned, privatized and private) and hierarchization *inside* the previously fragmented tissue of the industrial districts. Starting from the early 1990s, the increasing pressure of globalization determined a restructuring of many Italian industrial districts, with the rise of lead firms that pursued dimensional growth and experienced accelerated internationalization with the establishment of trade and production subsidiaries abroad. Most of these MSEs are specialized in niches, often global—for instance, machine tools and other durable goods, clothing, luxury goods and various branches of the so-called 'Made in Italy'. Because of their relative small size, as compared to multinationals operating and mass-production and high-tech industries, these Italian MSEs are defined as 'pocket multinationals' (Colli 2002).

REFERENCES

Amatori, Franco. 2000. "Beyond State and Market: Italy's Futile Search for a Third Way." In *The Rise and Fall of State-Owned Enterprises in the Western World*, edited by Pier Angelo Toninelli, 128–156. Cambridge: Cambridge University Press.
Amatori, Franco. 2011. "Entrepreneurial Typologies in the History of Industrial Italy: Reconsiderations." *Business History Review* 85: 151–180.
Amatori, Franco, and Andrea Colli. 1999. *Impresa e industria in Italia dall'Unità ad oggi*. Venice: Marsilio.
Barca, Fabrizio. 1994. *Imprese in cerca di padrone. Proprietà e controllo nel capitalismo italiano*. Rome-Bari: Laterza.
Barca, Fabrizio, Magda Bianco, Luigi Cannari, Riccardo Cesari, Carlo Gola, Giuseppe Manitta, Giorgio Salvo, and Luigi F. Signorini. 1994. *Assetti proprietari e mercato delle imprese. Vol. I. Proprietà, modelli di controllo e riallocazione nelle imprese industriali*. Bologna: Il Mulino.
Barca, Fabrizio, and Sandro Trento. 1997. "State Ownership and the Evolution of Italian Corporate Governance." *Industrial and Corporate Change* 6: 533–559.
Bianchi, Patrizio. 2002. *La rincorsa frenata. L'industria italiana dall'unità nazionale all'unificazione europea*. Bologna: Il Mulino.
Bonelli, Franco. 1978. "Il capitalismo italiano: linee generali di interpretazione." In *Annali della storia d'Italia. Dal feudalesimo al capitalismo*, edited by Ruggiero Romano and Corrado Vivanti, 1195–1255. Turin: Einaudi.
Bresnahan, Timothy F., and Manuel Trajtenberg. 1995. "General purpose technologies: Engines of growth?" *Journal of Econometrics* 65: 83–108.
Bruno, Giovanni, and Luciano Segreto. 1996. "Finanza e industria in Italia (1963–1995)." In *Storia dell'Italia repubblicana, Vol. 3: L'Italia nella crisi mondiale, t. 1: Economia e società*, edited by Francesco Barbagallo, 497–694. Turin, Italy: Einaudi.
Carnevali, Francesca. 2000. "State Enterprise and Italy's 'Economic Miracle': The Ente Nazionale Idrocarburi, 1945–1962." *Enterprise & Society* 1: 249–278.
Chiesi, Antonio M. 1985. "Property, Capital and Network Structure in Italy." In *Networks of Corporate Power*, edited by Frans N. Stokman, Rolf Ziegler, and John Scott, 199–214. Cambridge: Polity.
Colli, Andrea. 2002. "'Pocket Multinationals': Some Reflections on 'New' Actors in Italian Industrial Capitalism." In *Transnational Companies. 19th-20th Centuries*, edited by Hubert Bonin, Christophe Bouneau, Ludovic Cailluet, Alexandre Fernandez, and Silvia Marzagalli, 155–178. Paris: PLAGE.
Colli, Andrea, Alberto Rinaldi, and Michelangelo Vasta. Forthcoming. "The Only Way to Grow? Italian Business Groups in Historical Perspective." *Business History*.
Confalonieri, Antonio. 1992. *Banche miste e grande industria in Italia 1914–1933, vol. 1: Introduzione. L'esperienza della Banca Commerciale e del Credito Italiano*. Milan: Banca Commerciale Italiana.
Confalonieri, Antonio. 1997. *Banche miste e grande industria in Italia 1914–1933, vol. 2: I rapporti banca-industria*. Milan: Banca Commerciale Italiana.
David, Thomas, Gerhard Schnyder, and Gerarda Westerhuis. 2011. "Corporate Networks in Small Open Economies: The Case of Switzerland and the Netherlands (1910–2010)." Paper presented at the 15th Annual Conference of the European Business History Association, Athens, August 24–26.
Davis, Gerald F., and Mark S. Mizruchi. 1999. "The Money Center Cannot Hold: Commercial Banks in the U.S. System of Corporate Governance." *Administrative Science Quarterly* 44: 215–239.
De Nooy, Wouter, Andrej Mrvar, and Vladimir Batagelj. 2006. *Explanatory Social Network Analysis with Pajek*. New York: Cambridge University Press.

Deeg, Richard E. 2005. "Change from Within: German and Italian Finance in the 1990s." In *Beyond Continuity: Institutional Change in Advanced Political Economies*, edited by Wilhelm Streeck and Kathleen Thelen, 169–202. Oxford-New York: Oxford University Press.

Dosi, Giovanni. 1982. "Technological Paradigms and Technological Trajectories: a suggested interpretation of the determinants of technological change." *Research Policy* 11: 147–162.

Dosi, Giovanni, and Richard Nelson. 2010. "Technical Change and Industrial Dynamics as Evolutionary Processes." In *Handbook of the Economics of Innovation*, vol. 1, edited by Bronwyn H. Hall and Nathan Rosenberg, 51–127. Amsterdam: Elsevier.

Freeman, Chris, and Francisco Louçã. 2001. *As Time Goes by: From the Industrial Revolution to the Information Revolution*. Oxford: Oxford University Press.

Gerschenkron, Alexander. 1962. *Economic Backwardness in Historical Perspective: A Book of Essays*. Boston, MA: Harvard University Press.

Giannetti, Renato, and Michelangelo Vasta, eds. 2006. *Evolution of Italian Enterprises in the 20th Century*. Heidelberg-New York: Physica Verlag.

Grossman, Sanford, J., and Oliver Hart. 1986. "The Costs and Benefits of Ownership: A Theory of Vertical and Lateral Integration." *The Journal of Political Economy* 94: 691–719.

Hall, Peter A., and David Soskice. 2001. "An Introduction to Varieties of Capitalism." In *Varieties of Capitalism. The Institutional Foundations of Comparative Advantage*, edited by Peter A. Hall and David Soskice, 1–68. Oxford: Oxford University Press.

Hart, Oliver. 1989. "An Economist's Perspective on the Theory of the Firm." *Columbia Law Review* 89: 1757–1774.

Hart, Oliver, and John Moore. 1990. "Property Rights and the Nature of the Firm." *Journal of Political Economy* 98: 1119–1158.

Höpner, Martin, and Lothar Krempel. 2002. "The Politics of the German Company Network." *Competition and Change* 8: 339–356.

Jones, Geoffrey, Marco H.D. van Leeuwen, and Steve Broadberry. 2013. "The Future of Economic, Business and Social History." *Scandinavian Economic History Review* 60: 225–253.

La Francesca, Salvatore. 2004. *Storia del sistema bancario italiano*. Bologna: Il Mulino.

La Porta, Rafael, Florencio Lopez-de-Silanes, Andrei Shleifer, and Robert W. Vishny. 1999. "Corporate Ownership around the World." *The Journal of Finance* 54: 471–517.

Mori, Giorgio, 1977. "Le guerre parallele. L'industria elettrica in Italia nel periodo della grande guerra." In *Il capitalismo industriale in Italia. Processo di industrializzazione e storia d'Italia*, edited by Gorgio Mori, 141–215. Rome: Editori Riuniti.

Nelson, Richard R. 1994. "The Co-evolution of Technology, Industrial Structure, and Supporting Institutions." *Industrial and Corporate Change* 3: 47–62.

Pagano, Ugo, and Sandro Trento. 2003. "Continuity and Change in Italian Corporate Governance. The Institutional Stability of One Variety of Capitalism." In *The Italian Economy at the Dawn of the XXI Century*, edited by Massimo Di Matteo and Paolo Piacentini, 177–211. Aldershot-Burlington, VT: Ashgate.

Piore, Michael J., and Charles F. Sabel. 1984. *The Second Industrial Divide. Possibilities for Prosperity*. New York: Basic Books.

Posner, Michael J., and Stuart J. Woolf. 1967. *Italian Public Enterprise*. London: Duckworth.

Rangone, Marco, and Stefano Solari. 2012. "From Southern-European model to nowhere: the evolution of Italian capitalism, 1976–2011." *Journal of European Public Policy* 19: 1188–1206.

R&S-Mediobanca. 2000. *The Privatisations in Italy since 1992*. Milan: Mediobanca.
Rinaldi, Alberto, and Michelangelo Vasta. 2005. "The Structure of Italian Capitalism, 1952–72: New Evidence Using the Interlocking Directorates Technique." *Financial History Review* 12: 173–198.
Rinaldi, Alberto, and Michelangelo Vasta. 2012. "The Italian Corporate Network After the 'Golden Age' (1972–1983): From Centrality to Marginalization of State-Owned Enterprises." *Enterprise & Society* 13: 378–413.
Schmidt, Vivien A. 2002. *The Futures of European Capitalism*. Oxford: Oxford University Press.
Schnyder, Gerhard, Martin Lüpold, André Mach, and Thomas David. 2005. "The Rise and Decline of the Swiss Company Network during the 20th Century." *Travaux de Science Politique, Nouvelle Série*, no. 22. Université de Lausanne, Institut d'études politiques et internationals.
Scott, John. 1985. "Theoretical Framework and Research Design." In *Networks of Corporate Power*, edited by Frans N. Stokman, Rolf Ziegler, and John Scott, 1–19. Cambridge: Polity.
Sereni, Emilio. 1966. *Capitalismo e mercato nazionale*. Rome: Editori Riuniti.
Toninelli, Pier Angelo. 2004. "Between State and Market. The Parabola of Italian Public Enterprise in the 20th Century." *Entreprises et histoire* 37: 53–74.
Toninelli, Pier Angelo, and Michelangelo Vasta. 2010. "State-owned Enterprises (1936–1983)." In *Forms of Enterprises in 20th Century Italy. Boundaries, Structures and Policies*, edited by Andrea Colli and Michelangelo Vasta, 52–86. Cheltenham-Northampton, MA: Edward Elgar.
Toniolo, Gianni. 1980. *L'economia dell'Italia fascista*. Bari: Laterza.
Windolf, Paul. 2010. "Germany, France and the US: a Statistical Network Analysis (1900–1938)." Paper presented at the International Workshop "Corporate Networks in Europe during the 20th Century," Utrecht, November 12–13.
Zamagni, Vera. 1993. *The Economic History of Italy 1860–1990. Recovery after Decline*. Oxford: Clarendon Press.

Part IV
"Peripheral" Europe

10 Business Coalitions and Segmentation
Dynamics of the Portuguese Corporate Network

Álvaro Ferreira da Silva and Pedro Neves

1. INTRODUCTION

Using data from a century of Portuguese capitalism since 1913, this chapter investigates the configuration of corporate networks in Portugal, identifying patterns in its evolution and contributing to a comparative analysis. There are three main questions: How has the long-term evolution of the Portuguese corporate networks been shaped? Which phases can be distinguished? Which factors explain the identifiable changes and continuities? Corporate networks are analyzed using interlocking directorates.

Like so many social phenomena, there is no single reason for having the same person serving on two different boards. For this reason, explanations for interlocking directorates are not without controversy. Management control, communication devices, access to resources, restricting competition through inside information and collusion, reputational gains for individuals or firms, career advancement for directors sitting on different boards or mechanisms of class cohesion; all constitute plausible reasons for the generation of interlocking directorates (Koenig, Gogel, and Sonquist 1979; Mizruchi 1996; Scott 1991).

Interlocking directorates may constitute representations of underlying and structural realities that identify various modalities of capitalism (Maclean, Harvey, and Press 2006; Windolf 2002). Taxonomies of different types of market economies not only provide systemic comparisons between economic institutions, but innovation and education structures, as well. The structural analysis of interlocking directorates can add another dimension to the comparative literature on varieties of capitalism, bringing firms back into the comparative study of business systems (Hall and Soskice 2001; Morgan 2007).

Further, Maclean et al. (2006) argue that the configuration assumed by corporate networks result from changes in governance regimes. These are defined holistically, including the legal framework, governance practices, the nature of the business system, the resulting relationships among firms, and the dominant values and beliefs that structure governance codes and practices. The holistic perspective proposed by Maclean et al. can be further expanded to include the political, social and economic context that supports continuities and changes in corporate networks.

The historical perspective is particularly well-suited to provide a holistic understanding of the interaction between governance regimes and corporate networks because it highlights changes and continuities. Indeed, while the values that support governance rules are particularly resilient and long lasting, a historical perspective can also be seen to increase understanding of the more transient legal frameworks and business systems.

The Portuguese case has not yet been the subject of such historical studies, although van Veen and Kratzer (2011) carried out a comparative analysis of interlocking directorates across 15 European countries in 2005, using for Portugal the 20 companies included in the Portuguese stock exchange index. The study of the Portuguese case not only 'fills in' a knowledge gap, it also explains how corporate networks change under different governance regimes. Throughout the twentieth century, several political regimes and institutional changes affected the business structure in Portugal, making the country an interesting case study to further analyze how nationalizations, privatizations, state-led or market-driven economies and various regulatory regimes affected the business network. These changes occurred in periods characterized by different economic and social conditions, adding a further factor to the explanation of changes in governance regimes. Portugal is a country that cannot be easily classified in the different models used to create taxonomies of market economies (Hall and Soskice 2001, 21; Hall and Gingerich 2004, 17). Therefore, studying corporate networks in Portugal might help overcome poorly specified business systems and market institutions.

This study uses network analysis to trace the evolution of the Portuguese corporate network, making use of data on the composition of the boards of the 125 largest firms (by assets) in several benchmark years.[1] These years reflect the different contexts faced by business firms over roughly a hundred years—1913 to 2010. The first year—1913—comes at the end of the 'long nineteenth century', which was characterized by institutional transformation, but slow economic growth and weak industrialization. The second benchmark year—1925—marks the end of the buoyant first half of the 1920s, when several industrial sectors reaped the benefits of tariff protection. The next—1937—captures the impact on the top of the business structure of the domestic monetary and fiscal stabilization policies of the late 1920s, which was followed by the Great Depression. By 1957, another benchmark year, Portugal was entering a period during which modern economic growth emerged following two decades of a corporatist environment. The year 1973 represents the summit of Portuguese economic growth, and we analyze the corporate network just before the 1974 revolution and the subsequent institutional shock suffered by the business structure because of the nationalizations of 1975. A snapshot of the corporate network after the impact of nationalizations is provided in 1983. The next benchmark year, 1997, captures the corporate network during the privatization process and 10 years after the entry into the European Economic Community. Finally, in the last year—2010—we look at Portugal's current corporate structure.

Throughout the whole period, the Portuguese corporate network shows an extraordinarily low level of density and cohesion, much lower than most of the other countries studied in this book. The low network density seems to be the result of weak, underdeveloped capitalism, rather than an unambiguous sign of a liberal market economy in which loose corporate networks are the consequence of strong regulation and developed financial markets. Companies occupying a central place within the network present very high volatility, signaling that low structural integration hides greater diversity over the long term. In fact, the network evolution is rather complex and results from the impact of several major economic and institutional changes that shape the governance regime and change the dynamics of the corporate network over time. Before examining the reasons for this evolution, we analyze the structure of the network, identifying its main drivers.

2. THE PORTUGUESE CORPORATE NETWORK: AN OVERVIEW

The largest Portuguese firms are small in international terms; few are large enough to qualify among the top 125 firms of the most developed countries. The largest Portuguese manufacturing firm in 1913 would rank 88th in the British list of largest firms and 42nd in the French one, for example. In 2010, Portugal had no firm large enough to be ranked in the Fortune Global 500. This perhaps is not surprising within a small, peripheral and relatively closed European economy. There were also large differences in size among the firms included in the sample for each year. For instance, in both 1913 and 2010, the ratio between the average assets of the top five non-financial firms and of the five lowest ones is almost 100:1, meaning that the 100 largest Portuguese firms had very different scales.

The average rate of turnover for firms in the sample is 50% in non-financial sectors, increasing over the period and reaching the highest levels at the end of the twentieth century (Table 10.1). This rate of turnover reflects the rise of new sectors that resulted in the disappearance of firms belonging to the old sectors, as well as revealing sectoral restructuring through mergers and acquisitions. Financial firms show lower turnovers but higher volatility, concentrated in the three most important periods of sectoral restructuring in banking: in the early 1920s, which was followed by 50 years of consistent low rates of turnover; after the 1975 nationalizations, reflected in the statistics for 1983; and at the turn of the century, when mergers and acquisitions from either Portuguese or foreign firms redesigned the composition of the banking sector.

194 *Álvaro Ferreira da Silva and Pedro Neves*

Table 10.1 Portuguese Big Business—Network Indicators

	1913	1925	1937	1957	1973	1983	1997	2010
Number of non-financial firms	100	100	100	100	100	100	100	100
Rate of turnover (%)	–	47.0	43.0	55.0	59.0	52.0	62.0	47.0
Total number of seats	436	581	487	484	596	478	643	816
Mean number of seats per firm	4.4	5.8	4.9	4.8	6.0	4.8	6.4	8.2
Number of financial firms	25	25	25	25	25	25	25	25
Rate of turnover (%)	–	44.0	28.0	16.0	24.0	44.0	24.0	60.0
Total number of seats	100	115	119	149	177	127	253	269
Mean number of seats per firm	4.0	4.6	4.8	6.0	7.1	5.1	10.1	10.8
Total number of firms	125	125	125	125	125	125	125	125
Mean number of seats per firm	4.3	5.6	4.8	5.1	6.2	4.8	7.2	8.7
Number of cliques	21	27	17	15	13	2	14	30
Number of central companies	18	26	15	13	15	0	11	17
Central companies average degree	7.4	10.7	8.3	5.9	6.1	–	7.4	7.7
Nº companies also central in previous year	–	7	10	2	5	–	0	5

Note: See also Appendix I for other network indicators.

The distribution of firms by sectors changed significantly over the period in question. Colonial firms occupied top positions in the early twentieth century, representing approximately 30% of the non-financial firms. Their number declined after the 1950s and disappeared altogether with the decolonization of 1975. The manufacturing sector maintained its importance until 1983 (around 45% of the non-financial firms, peaking at 53% in 1983). Its rate of turnover was greater if different manufacturing branches are taken into account, from a dominance of textiles in 1913, becoming a more diversified sector after the 1950s. The dominance of the manufacturing sector declined in the last two decades of the study, the Portuguese economy becoming increasingly tertiary. This trend explains the rise of real estate and construction, trade and IT firms.

Family firms dominated at the top of the business structure. The Portuguese stock market remained small and had little impact on corporate finance; the proportion of the largest 125 firms listed on the stock exchange never exceeded 50%. Further, families controlled many of the listed companies (La Porta, Lopez-de-Silanes, and Shleifer 1999). State-owned firms appeared after the 1930s, but their presence was insignificant until the 1975 nationalizations. Unlike corporatist experiences in other European economies during the interwar period, the Portuguese *Estado Novo* did not embark on a massive nationalization program in the aftermath of the Great Depression (Rosas

1986). Indeed, the state already owned a savings bank, and two other banking firms—*Banco Nacional Ultramarino* (BNU) and *Banco de Angola*—were added to the state portfolio in the early 1930s. It is perhaps not by chance that these banks were operating in the colonies, the part of the Portuguese economy hardest hit by the Great Depression. After being almost absent in 1937, by 1957, the state had become a controlling shareholder in 10% of the 125 largest firms. By 1973, this presence had increased to 15% of these firms, through different financial vehicles (the treasury, its banking arms, the corporatist institutions and the social welfare agencies). These companies operated mostly in energy (electricity or oil), transportation and the chemical sector. The 1975 nationalizations increased the number of state-owned firms within the top 125, representing more than 57% by 1983, including every financial firm. The presence of the state-owned firms decreased during the 1990s and 2000s, due to the privatization program. By 2010, these firms had a lower but still visible presence, comprising 15% of the 125 firms.

The number of directorship positions available in the top 125 firms doubled during the period in question. The average number of directors per board increased from 4.3 to 8.7, revealing a steady increase over time, with the exception of 1983—in other words, just after the nationalizations. No matter the period, this is a low board dimension in comparative terms, which reflects the relative size of big business in Portugal. Nevertheless, it should be recognized that this average covers very diverse realities. For instance, 20 directors sat on the board of the largest railway company in 1913, a time when two-thirds of the firms had a board with three or less. In the early twentieth century, the average size of a board was similar between financial and non-financial companies, though slightly larger among the latter. From the mid-twentieth century onwards, the size of financial firms' boards increased markedly. By 2010, the average number of directors had reached eleven in these firms and eight in non-financial companies.

The vast majority of these directors sat on the board of just one company, which explains why the Portuguese corporate network had a very low integration level. The density never exceeds 2.6% over the period, well below the level displayed by other countries during most of the twentieth century (see Appendix I). The proportion of firms that had at least one connection was only 68% in 1925, more usually being around 60%, while the levels for other countries are above 90%. Excluding the number of marginal firms (with one or two ties) reduces the proportion of interconnected firms to an even lower number. The non-marginal firms include only 20–25% of the total number of firms, with the exception of 1925 and 2010, when they reached slightly more than 30%. The main component never concentrates more than 55% of the sample, even though it is not uncommon to find countries where the main component clusters more than 75% of the companies. Every network statistic reveals low integration as a structural characteristic of the Portuguese corporate network.

This structural low integration and cohesion seems to be the consequence of the size and level of development of the Portuguese economy. A small country of emerging capitalism in the early twentieth century, it has maintained a business structure based on a vast number of small and micro enterprises, while relying on a very tiny group of large enterprises. Such a business structure discourages interlocking directorates because a large proportion of the firms at the top of the business structure are not large enough to favor interlocking. Having one person on the board of more than one firm may derive from underlying capital ties or access to resources, or is perhaps a means to gain advantages for that person's reputation or to promote information flows. Whatever the reason, many of the largest 125 Portuguese firms did not have enough reach to favor interlocking directorates. Other small countries, where big business had a larger share, have a higher probability of developing denser networks. Thus, differences in network integration may reveal not only distinctive governance regimes, but also different levels of corporate development—an issue not emphasized in the existing literature.

An analysis of the companies capable of mobilizing a greater number of ties reveals other network dynamics. The number and average degree of these central companies within the network remain very low over the period in question. Volatility is the rule, not the exception, with no company lasting for the entire period. Some companies—mostly related to colonial businesses—were able to survive as central companies until 1937. But the firms that overcame the first two institutional breaks that affected the network—the 1930s (corporatism) and the mid-1970s (nationalizations)—are very rare. After 1937, only three firms maintained their previous role as central network actors: *Banco Burnay* (BB), CRGE (electricity production and distribution) and *Companhia União Fabril* (CUF). After the 1975 nationalizations, the number of firms that maintained their position as top central actors shrunk even further. Within the central firms' group, only BES (a bank) and EDP (electricity production and distribution) could trace their origins to 1957.

This volatility suggests that the structural low integration hides a more complex evolution. The network statistics and sociograms allow the identification of four phases in the evolution of the Portuguese corporate network: the creation of the corporate network until the late 1920s, the segmentation of the network (early 1930s to mid-1970s), the disappearance of the corporate network after 1975 nationalizations and the re-emergence of the network since the mid-1990s. The following sections will trace this evolution, explaining the reasons for these different trends as it unfolds.

3. THE EMERGENCE OF THE CORPORATE NETWORK

Nineteenth-century liberalism introduced a new institutional framework based on modern property rights and liberal market institutions, which still characterized the economic and business environment in the early twentieth century. The new republican regime established in 1910 did not significantly change this institutional framework.

The setting up of large firms in transportation, manufacturing, utilities and colonial exploitation resulted in the emergence of the corporate network in the late nineteenth century. During the second half of the nineteenth century, the construction of the national railway system, as well as the provision of modern energy networks to major cities, led to the creation of several companies with elevated capital requirements. Although the Portuguese manufacturing sector did not show great signs of modernization, in some of its more capital-intensive branches—such as tobacco, flour, chemicals and glass—a process of concentration occurred at the turn of the century resulting in an increased scale of operation and greater financing needs. Since the late nineteenth century, some Portuguese banks—such as BNU, BB, *José Henriques Totta* (JHT) and *Fonsecas, Santos & Viana* (FSV)—invested in railways, utilities and manufacturing. This period was also characterized by the investment rush to the African colonies. The colonial firms were engaged in a wide range of activities, from mining and farming to transportation and trade. These firms also had close links to some of the most important banking houses, as well as to manufacturing and transport companies.

The Portuguese corporate network reached maximum integration in the 1920s; 1925 represents a peak in several network indicators (density, average degree, number of central companies, interlockers and big linkers as a percentage of directors). The larger density attained in 1925 has an equivalent in the number of central firms and their average degree (see Table 10.1 and Appendix I).

In the early twentieth century, colonial companies dominated the group of central firms. The greater cohesion and integration that can be seen in the corporate network in the early twentieth century resulted from the multiple and diversified links that colonial firms had with companies from different industries.

The central position occupied by colonial companies had an impact on the shape of the overall network. The network configuration for 1925 exemplifies this dense interlocking and the role performed by the central companies (Figure 10.1). Denser and more complex, the largest group of interconnected firms within the network was able to capture about 50% of the business firms in the sample. Colonial firms accounted for most of this main component, with five out of the seven largest central firms in 1925 (with degree 15 or higher). The apparent exceptions—BNU and *Companhia dos Tabacos de Portugal* (CTP)—in fact, also had privileged relations with the colonies. The first was a bank with a monopoly in banknote issuing in the colonies. Together, with another bank (and central company—the BB) and with the involvement of foreign investors, BNU created a cluster of colonial ventures that mainly involved mining and agricultural production. The other top central firm was CTP (tobacco manufacturing), using colonial raw products and where several of the former business interests also converged. Tobacco manufacturing was an appealing business, under state concession and intimately linked to state finance (Mata 2010; Mónica 1992).

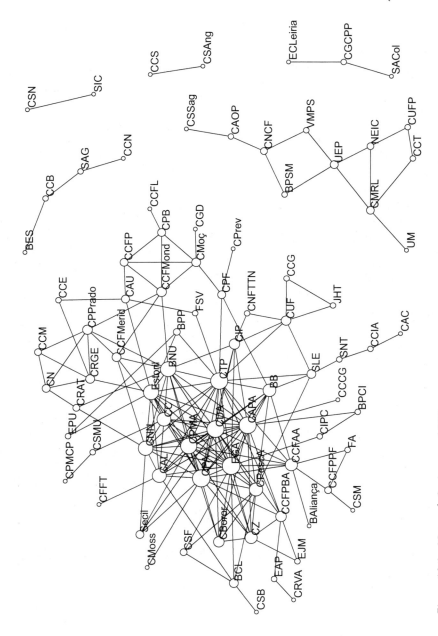

Figure 10.1 Network Sociogram, 1925

These seven companies can be seen to be responsible for the density of the network, concentrating about 35% of all ties in the main component. All these firms were interconnected, constituting a typical case of a clique in network analysis. Besides this large clique, the dense configuration of the network arose from the intersection of multiple clusters and cliques. The intersection was enabled by the preeminent position retained by some top companies, operating in colonial, tobacco and transport. They established radial connections that centered on them—connections that linked otherwise isolated cliques and clusters. A federative rationality prevailed in the group of top firms that head these densely interconnected clusters. Colonial ventures, tobacco and transport mobilized domestic and foreign entrepreneurs, resulting in the merger of different financial interests and depending on leveraged political and administrative influence.

The aggregative function associated with the tobacco business illustrates this logic. The tobacco company (CTP) integrated the 'colonial' cluster described above through several interlocked boards and centralized the largest number of ties. Aside from BNU, two further banks were actively involved in this business and were represented on CTP's board. Burnay was a family bank, with several other interests in the colonies, as well as in mainland activities (railways, glass and chemical manufacturing sectors, for example). It superimposed its network ties on those formed around the tobacco firm. The same happened with another leading family bank, FSV.

Identical integrative and federative logic, articulating intra-cluster and inter-cluster ties, could also be applied to the railway companies. It is this pervasiveness of financial interests around the colonial, transportation and tobacco businesses that gave rise to a network configuration with multiple overlapping clusters and dense interlocking.

4. THE SEGMENTATION OF THE NETWORK: ECONOMY, INSTITUTIONAL CHANGE AND THE RISE OF BUSINESS GROUPS

After the density apex in the 1920s, the cohesion of the network gradually decreased until the mid-1970s. The number of ties in 1973 was about half of the 1925 level, the density falling from 2.55 to 1.32 and the average degree from 3.17 to 1.62. The number of central companies and 'big linkers' also decreased after 1925; every statistic shows a decreasing trend in the cohesion of the network.

The analysis of components further highlights the segmentation of the network. In 1957 and 1973, the network was rather different from how it appeared in the initial period. The number of components splitting the network rose between 1925 and 1973. The second difference is the concentration of firms in the main component. In 1913 and 1925, this concentration accounted for more than 50% of the firms, but later attracted fewer. In 1973, the main component's capacity of attraction reached the lowest level for the entire period, excluding the abnormal case after the nationalizations in 1975. In this evolution, the 1937 benchmark year seems closer to the characteristics displayed in the early twentieth century, constituting a transitional moment to the network, crystallized during the heyday of the *Estado Novo* period.

The Great Depression and several institutional changes explain this segmentation of the corporate network. The relatively low integration of the Portuguese economy with world trade and capital flows mitigated the impact of the Great Depression (Madureira 1998; Reis 1995; Rosas 1986). In contrast, the colonies suffered greatly from the effects of the Depression because of the fall in global demand for tropical and semi-tropical goods. As a consequence, the central role of colonial firms in articulating the network almost disappeared by 1957 and vanished by 1973. Once again, 1937 appears to be a moment of transition.

The impact of the Great Depression also increased state intervention and led to major institutional changes. In Portugal, unlike other countries, state intervention did not lead to the emergence of a large public sector (Toninelli 2000). There was a formal defense of the market economy, imposing constitutional limits on the creation of state-owned enterprises. However, it was believed that a liberal economy could be a source of value destruction, rather than a driver of efficiency and increased productivity. The establishment of a corporatist economy sought to square the circle, seeking an ideal harmony between employers and employees or between conflicting business interests (Confraria 2005; Garrido 2005).

After the 1930s, the corporatist institutional framework created mechanisms and administrative bodies intended to regulate and contain competition. In several economic sectors, it established cartelized structures, organizing production, distribution and procurement. Price controls and administrative profit margins were also employed to regulate the market (Lucena 1976; Madureira 2002). The creation of new firms, the expansion of existing ones, and mergers and acquisitions needed to be licensed by the administrative authorities, a new legal framework that became known as 'industrial conditioning' (Brito 1989; Confraria 1992).

The new regime (*Estado Novo*) pursued a more active developmental policy, believing that greater public voluntarism would innovate and diversify the industrial structure, replace imports of basic or manufactured industrial goods and promote economic growth. This new developmental role principally employed indirect means as a way of promoting import-substitution projects: namely, protectionism, subsidies, exclusivity clauses during the initial phase and the use of industrial conditioning. The state supported some private ventures in a more tangible way, by becoming a shareholder in firms created in what were considered strategic sectors (oil, paper pulp, energy, basic metals) or using *Caixa Geral de Depósitos* and

Banco de Fomento Nacional (public banks) to award credit under favorable conditions.

The banking sector faced significant changes in its regulatory framework. An outbreak of speculative activity in the financial sector characterized the early 1920s, leading to the 1925 banking law (Amaral, 2013). The main objective of the new law was to stipulate a set of prudent rules, defining high capital requirements and cash reserves, limiting long-term credit possibilities and making the creation or merging of banks dependent on government authorization. The liquidity difficulties suffered in the late 1920s by some banks that were more closely involved in investment banking (BNU and JHT) led to further limitations in banking activity. In the aftermath of the Great Depression, a new law (passed in 1935) sought to curtail excessive exposition of credit institutions to long-term credit and investment by limiting the acquisition of securities by banks. It followed similar legislation that strictly regulated the banking industry worldwide, but without assuming more drastic measures, such as the separation of commercial and investment banking.

To summarize, the Great Depression and the transformation of the institutional framework created a major discontinuity, which directly affected the structure and configuration of the network. The economic crisis disrupted the fortune of colonial businesses, ending their central place within the network. Regulatory changes discouraged banks from investing in industry, reducing their ability to nurture interlocking ties. The new corporatist institutions created a new environment for business activities in which industrial conditioning limited the entry of firms in the various industrial markets.

The new institutional framework favored the development of family-owned business groups, clustering legally independent firms operating in diversified, but usually unrelated, sectors. These business groups were mostly hierarchical in nature, as defined by Colpan and Hikino (2010). Some had their roots in the first post-war period, when the inflationary surge allowed the rapid expansion of some business ventures. However, it was after World War II that these groups became more important, which coincided with the golden age of Portuguese economic growth. State intervention in the economy might have supported the development and economic resiliency of those groups. Industrial policy was used to signal investment pathways to the private initiative, but also gave a discretionary role to the state in the promotion of certain business ventures. The state's involvement, directly or indirectly, in the promotion of certain projects, while limiting the entry of foreign capital, provided Portuguese firms with a brokering role for accessing domestic and overseas markets.

The development of these groups might imply a structure of collusion within the corporate network. The evidence presented here does not confirm this view, however, whatever the statistics or analytical approach taken. The emergence of business groups and their development during the 1950s and 1960s did not create a 'thicker' network, more integrative among the firms at the top of the business structure. On the contrary, network integration and cohesion decreased, the clusters of interconnected firms became more exclusive, more entrenched and more fragmented.

In 1957 and 1973, the network configuration emphasized the segregation between different clusters that favored linear and one-to-one ties, in contrast with the overlapping and dense nature of the early-century network. The configuration in 1973 exemplified this trend (Figure 10.2), exacerbating characteristics already visible in 1957: more segmented, with a lower density of ties and weaker interconnection between the different clusters. The cluster structured around the CUF group illustrates the new characteristics of the network. In 1957, ten companies belonged to the group—eight firms in manufacturing, banking, insurance and maritime transport, and two colonial firms that are still surviving as central companies. The ties polarized by these firms were mostly intra-group connections, cementing the group's cluster, rarely expanding to other non-affiliate firms. This business group continued to dominate the central companies in 1973, still maintaining its inward-oriented structure. In 1973, 80% of the ties gathered by the firms belonging to the group were intra-group ties.

Other smaller business groups reveal identical or even more exacerbated behavior than CUF, as was the case of the *Champalimaud Group*. BPSM was its financial arm, which clustered insurance companies (CSM and CSConf), metal manufacturing (*Cometna*) and cement (ECL). The *Champalimaud Group* was completely separate from the main component, creating a secondary component centered on the bank.

The firms connecting small clusters or cliques into a larger component were decisive for the structure of the network. In the early twentieth century, most of the companies that had a brokering position were the same firms (and sectors) that had a central position in the network. Colonial and transport companies excelled in this dual role. By 1957 and 1973, this dual role almost disappears, revealing a smaller economic role held by the colonial and transport firms after the Great Depression. In 1957, electricity companies also connected different clusters, complementing their role as central companies with a mediating role. For example, the largest electricity company (CNE) performed a central role, but also mediated ties to adjacent companies and clusters. The creation of a network of electricity production and distribution became one main economic policy objective, mostly after the 1940s (Madureira 2007). These business ventures, based on public-private partnerships, were an inherent part of this process.

In 1973, electricity firms were replaced as network brokers by firms involved in the oil business; refiners, processors or distributors (*Petrosul, Sonap, Sonarep* and *Sacor*). These firms mobilized different business interests that were placed outside the inward-oriented investment that was typical of business groups (Ribeiro, Fernandes, and Ramos 1987). This was the reason for their linking of different clusters. The intermediary position of

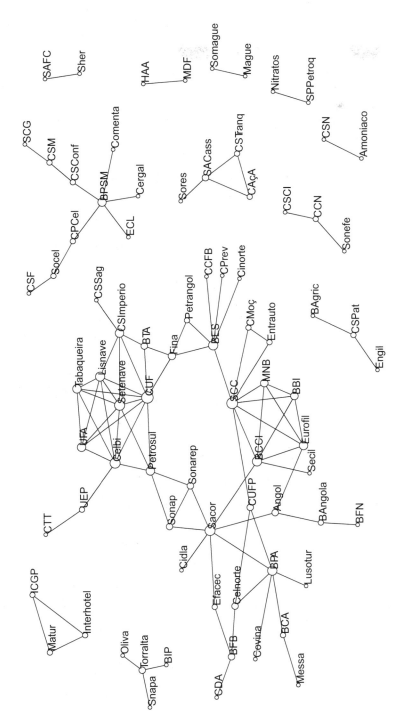

Figure 10.2 Network Sociogram, 1973

the oil segment in the 1973 network shows this very clearly (Figure 10.2). It linked the CUF group (in a joint-venture with *Sonap* to create *Petrosul*) to *Sacor*, which, in turn, radiated ties to the clusters formed by the banks BPA and BBI/BCCI, heading two other business groups. Another oil firm (*Fina*) plays a similar role, linking the CUF group to the BES group.

Even in a period characterized by network segmentation, some sectors acted as brokers and distilled a federative logic. The aggregative, federative role played by colonial and transport companies in the early part of the century was replaced by the energy sector after the 1950s. Electricity and oil became federations of different business interests, involving several groups and entrepreneurs. The state supported this federative logic, sometimes actively through direct participation as a shareholder, but always through its administrative (e.g., concessions) and regulatory action (Ribeiro et al. 1987).

In the *Estado Novo* period, a stance of state intervention coexisted with the emergence of important business groups. These new forms of business organization segmented the corporate network, rather than making it denser. On the contrary, the companies taking an intermediary role, which are critical to the network interconnection, were companies outside the groups' boundaries, in which the state was often a shareholder.

The corporate network became less dense and more segmented when state-led cartelization and other corporatist devices shaped the business system, providing more formal means of coordination between firms and across markets. In other countries, cartels matched more integrated corporate networks (Windolf, this volume), but this matching did not occur in Portugal during the *Estado Novo* period. Corporatist institutions tried to rule competition and promote cooperation between business interests, as well as between businessmen and workers. They constituted an alternative mechanism of business coordination toward corporate networks, explaining why the density decreased even below the already lower levels of network integration existing until the 1930s.

5. THE 1975 NATIONALIZATIONS AND THE DISSOLUTION OF THE NETWORK

The dissolution of the network resulted from a clearly-defined institutional change. The 1974 revolution ended the *Estado Novo* regime and opened a tumultuous process of democratization. Unlike past political transformations, this revolution brought about profound changes in the business environment. First, the process of decolonization, with the confiscation of property and assets (Ferreira 2002), ended the presence of colonial companies at the top of the business structure. Second, the withdrawal of previous restrictions on the exercise of trade union activity, together with the fragility of the first democratic governments, unleashed a wave of industrial and political turmoil. The increase in labor costs and the adoption of legal measures limiting labor redundancies, as well as the rise of political and social instability, made the country less business-friendly. Third, the *Estado Novo*'s corporatist institutions were abolished or integrated into the post-revolutionary mechanisms of economic coordination and intervention.

However, the most persistent and profound transformation of the business environment occurred after March 1975, when the entire financial sector was nationalized. As banks, insurance companies and investment funds had a substantial presence in the capital of other firms, this entailed the indirect nationalization of about 2,000 companies (Pintado and Mendonça 1989). Between April and August 1975, other large companies were nationalized, covering the basic economic sectors of energy, steel, transportation, media, shipbuilding and repair, cement, paper pulp, chemicals and petrochemicals. The nationalizations effectively incapacitated the business groups and changed the ownership and control of the largest Portuguese companies overnight. By 1983, over 50% of the top 125 Portuguese firms were state-owned enterprises.

The accommodation of this large state-owned business sector determined the creation of a holding that was responsible for running the large number of public firms. Simultaneously, multiple mergers between companies in the same industry sought to rationalize horizontal and vertical linkages. The average size of the boards fell, becoming much more executive-oriented and rarely including non-executive directors. As many of these non-executive directors formerly constituted 'big linkers' and brokers, the more executive-oriented boards in state-owned enterprises diminished the possibility of interlocking. After the 1975 nationalization of the business groups, the previous interlocking ties based on ownership disappeared. State ownership did not tend toward interlocking. In fact, the policy regarding the appointment of directors to state-owned firms discouraged the accumulation of seats on the boards of different firms, favoring an extensive distribution of directorships by the clientele of the parties in government. Any coordination or information flow therefore resided in the ministries directing the state-owned enterprises, which effectively prevented interlocking ties from acting as channels of information between different firms.

After the vast increase of state ownership, interlocking ties between private and public firms were rare, presenting a marked contrast with the situation in France (Maclean et al. 2006) and Italy (Rinaldi and Vasta 2005). There are two reasons for this disparity. The nationalization of the largest firms incapacitated the Portuguese business structure and removed the most likely private candidates to house 'big linkers'. Second, a dozen years after nationalization, the state-owned sector started to be dismantled. The time in which private-public interlocking could be crystallized was brief. At the same time that new forms of private big business started to emerge—in the late 1980s—the state-owned sector approached its rapid decline.

Thus, nationalizations led to the destruction of the previously established corporate network. The analysis of the interlocking directorates network in 1983 faces a virtually nonexistent object. There were a very small number of interconnected companies, together with a lack of any important component in the network. Network statistics, which were structurally low for the other benchmark years, reached unthinkably low figures in 1983.

6. THE RECONSTRUCTION OF THE NETWORK, 1990–2010

The re-emergence of the corporate network in the mid-1990s makes the benchmark years of 1997 and 2010 the reversal of the 1974–1975 institutional shock. The corporate network re-emerged in the mid-1990s. In 2010, a remarkable cohesion and interconnection was revealed that was closer to the levels that existed during the early twentieth century, rather than during the period immediately before the 1975 nationalizations. The network density and average degree were comparatively high, just below those of 1925. The corporate network became more concentrated, too. The capacity of attraction displayed by the main component increased in 2010, surpassing the levels of 1913 and 1925. By 2010, more than 50% of the firms were integrated in the main component, leaving a few to a very small secondary component. The number of cliques in 2010 was closer to the level in 1925, and far beyond that of 1957 or 1973.

The re-emergence of the corporate network can be associated with several institutional changes, such as the privatization process, economic liberalization and European integration. In 1997, the corporate network was at an intermediate stage, when some of these forces were still in motion; by 2010, this process was completed. Those institutional changes started in the 1980s and launched the process that led to the new network configuration. After the nationalizations, the finance and basic sectors remained closed to private initiative for a further decade. The 1982 constitutional revision and the 1983 law for the delimitation of economic sectors both allowed private investment in previously closed business activities, namely banking and insurance. Portugal's entry to the European Economic Community in 1985 led to further changes in the institutional framework that reduced state intervention in the economy. In 1989, a process of privatization of public enterprises started and the proportion of state-owned enterprises decreased from 24% to 8% of the public sector gross value added on GDP (Viegas 1996; Pereira 2011).

Privatizations were carried out over the next two decades. The financial sector was privatized first, and by the mid-1990s, with the exception of CGD, all other banks were private. The financial sector also underwent a process of consolidation, with a wave of mergers and the entry of foreign players. The privatization of the principal non-financial companies began in the mid-1990s. In 1997, some of the these companies (oil, electricity, telecommunications, transportation, paper pulp) were still controlled by the state, but by 2010, state ownership remained in only rail, air and urban transport, water supply and electricity. The state still maintained 'golden shares' in a few of the largest companies that were already privatized (telecommunications and electricity production and distribution), which gave it special control privileges.

The banking sector plays a key role in the new network configuration (Figure 10.3). The four largest Portuguese banks are among the main central firms, ensuring some interlocks with subsidiaries, but mostly with other companies. The case of BPI can be used as an example. Two of the companies with which it has interlocks are subsidiaries of BPI (insurance, BPI V, and investment banking, BPI I). The other 10 interlocks centered on BPI show the federative logic behind the capital structure of the bank, gathering together a number of business firms, especially in Northern Portugal, which are present on the bank's board. The same logic can also be applied to another leading commercial bank, BCP.

Two other banks, BES and CGD, show some differences from this basic model. Their interlocking ties typically represent their stock participation in other companies. For CGD, interlocking directorates have yet another purpose. As it is a state bank, its presence in some of the leading Portuguese firms is closely related to policy. It serves to maintain some state influence over the largest firms (*EDP, EDP Renováveis* and *PT*) in which, until very recently, the state maintained some direct or indirect shareholdings, but are now privately controlled.

Besides banks, other firms operating in utilities, media, trade and other services showed a leading central position in the 2010 corporate network. In some of these firms, the state continues to have shareholding control (*Águas de Portugal*, AdP water supply), whereas in others, it had 'golden shares' (*EDP* and *PT*).

In 2010, the business groups did not show the same level of importance that they attained during the corporatist period. None equaled the size and diversification of the CUF group in the 1970s. Its successor, the Mello group, clustered only five firms and lacked the diversification characterizing its ancestor. A new group (*Sonae*) revealed more diversification, being active in manufacturing, mass retailing, tourism, real estate, media, telecommunications and IT. Both of these business groups were, however, not within the leading central companies, failing to contribute in any important way to the cohesion of the corporate network, unlike the firms mentioned in the previous paragraphs. In this sense, they would be closer to the segmentation logic that characterized the *Estado Novo* groups.

By contrast, the leading banks, media companies and services, energy and telecommunications utilities were more easily associated with the mobilization of business interests, reflecting the federative logic behind

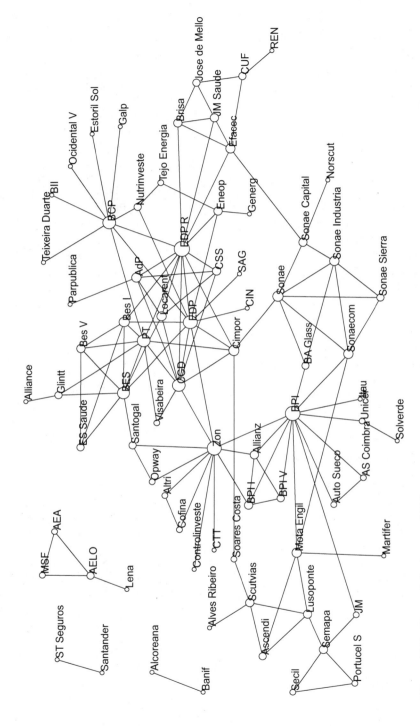

Figure 10.3 Network Sociogram, 2010

multiple interlocking relationships. Ultimately, they played a role similar to that played by the utilities in 1957, the oil sector in 1973, and the colonial enterprises in the first third of the twentieth century, creating a 'constellation of interests' (Scott 1979).

7. CONCLUSION

Two distinct principles ruled the organization of the network over the 100 years we analyzed. In the early twentieth century, or at the turn of the century, a federative principle dominated in which investments in more capital-intensive or political-dependent business ventures mobilized a vast coalition of business interests. Colonial businesses, transport infrastructure, energy and media and communications drove this federative logic. Banks contributed to network cohesion, assuming a double role, either as big linkers or brokers between different clusters of firms. This double role came about as a result of their participation in those business ventures animated by a federative rationality (transport, colonies, energy, media and communications), as well as their own place as coalitions of different business interests.

The network configuration during the *Estado Novo* was based on more exclusive ties within business groups—a conclusion consistent with findings from another study (Silva, Amaral, and Neves 2012). The reconstruction of these groups' capital ties emphasizes that they were inward-oriented organizations, segregating affiliate firms from more inclusive partnerships with firms outside the groups. This behavior contributed to the fragmentation of the network; business groups segmented and hierarchized the corporate network instead of making it denser and more cohesive. Corporatist institutions also led to the lowering of network density: their institutionalized and state-driven framework constituted a 'hard' coordination device that dispensed with the 'softer' interlocking ties.

The position of banks within this more segmented network changed. They lost their earlier position as big brokers that contributed to the cohesion and density of the network. Some of those functioning as heads of business groups still drew together affiliate firms within self-contained clusters. Others became financial arms of business groups, losing their roles as either central companies or brokers. The re-emergence of the corporate network in the late twentieth century restored this double role of the banking sector.

The 1975 nationalizations dismantled the existing network and resulted in a configuration in which isolated or marginal firms entirely dominated. State control of the largest Portuguese firms replaced the previous interlocking directorates, however feeble, with state coordination through public holding. The lack of interlocking directorates between state-owned firms, or with private ones, contrasts with the Italian case. In Italy, state-ownership had been stable since the early 1930s, when a large part of the top companies were nationalized. In Portugal, however, a very large state-owned sector survived for only two decades.

As the twentieth century turned to the twenty-first, density increased. This upward trend did not bring the network cohesion back to the low level that existed before nationalization, but to the relatively high levels of the early twentieth century. This was a divergence from what was happening in other European countries in the late twentieth century, where the trend to lower network densities accelerated. The return of a business system where a 'constellation of interests' dominated the largest Portuguese firms explains the rise in network integration. The same federative logic that existed in the early twentieth century can be seen to increase interlocking one century later. Another reason is the more mature business system in 2010, in which big business occupied a larger share of the top firms, increasing the likelihood of interlocking at a time when it decreased across the rest of Europe.

In fact, Portugal's very low density levels are a long-term characteristic. This cannot be attributed to the structural dominance of market-driven institutions that are typical of the liberal market economies (Hall and Soskice 2001). In the Portuguese case, the structural low density has mostly indicated a business system where small and micro firms have dominated. Using the metaphor that Langlois (2013) proposed, small and flat-hierarchical firms would be the "natural state" of the Marshallian forest. In such a business system, the likelihood of interlocking is small, as big business is thin, even among the top 125 firms.

This conclusion re-aligns the relationship between the varieties of capitalism and the density of corporate network. Previous studies have been mostly concerned with mature economies, in which denser networks are a consequence of more coordinated forms of capitalism and lower network density involves liberal market economies. Economic backwardness may generate similar conditions for corporate networks where low density dominates. Under such circumstances, business systems would fail to spin off large and dense interlocking ties.

NOTE

1. A detailed description of the data, sources and methodology is presented on the website (see http://www.cgeh.nl/power-corporate-networks-comparative-and-historical-perspective).

REFERENCES

Amaral, Luciano. 2013. "Imperfect but True Competition: Innovation and Profitability in Portuguese Banking during the Golden Age (1950–1973)." *Financial History Review* 20 (3) 305–333.
Brito, José M. B. 1989. *A Industrialização Portuguesa no Pós-Guerra (1948–1965)*. Lisbon: Publicações D. Quixote.

Colpan, Asli M., and Takashi Hikino. 2010. "Foundations of Business Groups: Towards an Integrated Framework." In *Oxford Handbook of Business Groups*, edited by Asli M. Colpan, Takashi Hikino, and James R. Lincoln, 15–66. Oxford: Oxford University Press.
Confraria, João. 1992. *Condicionamento Industrial: Uma Análise Económica*. Lisbon: Direcção-Geral da Indústria.
Confraria, João. 2005. "Política económica." In *História económica de Portugal, Vol. III—O século XX*, edited by Pedro Lains and Álvaro F. Silva, 397–421. Lisbon: Imprensa de Ciências Sociais.
Ferreira, Manuel E. 2002. "Nacionalização e confisco do capital português na indústria transformadora de Angola (1975–1990)." *Análise Social* 37 (162): 47–90.
Garrido, Álvaro. 2005. "Conjunturas políticas e economia." In *História económica de Portugal, Vol. III—O século XX*, edited by Pedro Lains and Álvaro F. Silva, 451–473. Lisbon: Imprensa de Ciências Sociais.
Hall, Peter A., and Daniel W. Gingerich. 2004. *Varieties of Capitalism and Institutional Complementarities in the Macroeconomy: An Empirical Analysis*. Max Planck Institute for the Study of Societies Discussion Paper 04/5.
Hall, Peter A., and David Soskice, eds. 2001. *Varieties of Capitalism. The Institutional Foundations of Competitive Advantage*. Oxford: Oxford University Press.
Koenig, Thomas, Robert Gogel, and John Sonquist. 1979. "Models of the Significance of Interlocking Corporate Directorates." *American Journal of Economics and Sociology* 38: 173–186.
Langlois, Richard N. 2013. "Business Groups and the Natural State." *Journal of Economic Behavior & Organization* 88: 14–26.
La Porta, Rafael, Florencio Lopez-de-Silanes, and Andrei Shleifer. 1999. "Corporate Ownership around the World." *Journal of Finance* 54 (2): 471–517.
Lucena, Manuel. 1976. *A Evolução do Sistema Corporativo Português*. Lisbon: Perspectivas e Realidades.
Maclean, Mairi, Charles Harvey, and Jon Press. 2006. *Business Elites and Corporate Governance in France and UK*. London: Palgrave Macmillan.
Madureira, Nuno L. 1998. "O Estado, o patronato e a indústria portuguesa (1922–1957)." *Análise Social* 33 (4): 777–822.
Madureira, Nuno L. 2002. *A economia dos interesses. Portugal entre as guerras*. Lisbon: Livros Horizonte.
Madureira, Nuno L. 2007. "Enterprises, Incentives and Networks: The Formative Years of the Electrical Network in Portugal, 1920–1947." *Business History* 49 (5): 625–645.
Mata, Eugénia. 2010. "Portuguese Public Debt and Financial Business before WWI." *Business and Economic Horizons* 3 (3): 10–27.
Mizruchi, Mark S. 1996. "What Do Interlocks Do? An Analysis, Critique, and Assessment of Research on Interlocking Directorates." *Annual Review of Sociology* 22: 271–298.
Mónica, Maria F. 1992. "Negócios e política: os tabacos (1800–1890)." *Análise Social* 27 (116–117): 461–479.
Morgan, Glenn. 2007. "National Business Systems Research: Progress and Prospects." *Scandinavian Journal of Management* 23: 127–145.
Pereira, Álvaro S. 2011. *Portugal na hora da verdade*. Lisbon: Gradiva.
Pintado, Miguel R., and Álvaro Mendonça. 1989. *Os novos grupos económicos*. Lisbon: Texto Editora.
Reis, Jaime. 1995. "Portuguese Banking in the Inter-war Period." In *Banking, currency, and finance in Europe between the wars*, edited by Charles Feinstein. Oxford: Clarendon Press.
Ribeiro, José F., Lino G. Fernandes, and Maria M. C. Ramos. 1987. "Grande indústria, banca e grupos financeiros, 1953–1973." *Análise Social* 23 (99): 945–1018.

Rinaldi, Alberto, and Michaelangelo Vasta. 2005. "The Structure of Italian Capitalism, 1952–1972: New Evidence Using the Interlocking Directorates Technique." *Financial History Review* 12 (2): 173-198.
Rosas, Fernando. 1986. *O Estado Novo nos Anos Trinta, Elementos para o Estudo da Natureza Económica e Social do Salazarismo (1928–1938)*. Lisbon: Editorial Estampa.
Scott, John. 1979. *Corporations, Classes and Capitalism*. London: Hutchinson.
Scott, John. 1991. "Networks of Corporate Power: A Comparative Assessment." *Annual Review of Sociology* 17: 181–203.
Silva, Álvaro F., Luciano Amaral, and Pedro Neves. 2012. "Business Groups in Portugal in the Estado Novo Period (1930–1974): Strategy and Structure." Paper presented at the Sixteenth World Economic History Congress, Stellenbosch, July 9–13.
Toninelli, Pier A., ed. 2000. *The Rise and Fall of State-Owned Enterprise in the Western World*. Cambridge: Cambridge University Press.
Viegas, José M. L. 1996. *Nacionalizações e privatizações. Elites e cultura política na história recente de Portugal*. Oeiras: Celta Editora.
van Veen, Kees, and Jan Kratzer. 2011. "National and International Interlocking Directorates within Europe: Corporate Networks within and among Fifteen European Countries." *Economy and Society* 40 (1): 1–25.
Windolf, Paul. 2002. *Corporate Networks in Europe and the United States*. New York: Oxford University Press.

11 Bulgarian Business Elite, 1900s–2000s

Martin Ivanov and Georgi Ganev

1. INTRODUCTION

New institutional economics brought a growing consensus on the crucial importance of institutions and transaction costs as a prerequisite for economic growth. As early as the 1960s, Gerschenkron (1962) forcefully insisted that financial institutions (mixed banking and interlocking directorates) were among the key elements that facilitated "the most impressive catch-up in the 19th century" (that of Germany). More recently, Fukuyama (1995) found that trust, propensity for spontaneous sociability, and intermediary institutions between the state and the households (business associations and interlocks, among others) can explain why some countries are able to embark on a sustainable growth path.

Drawing on the works of Hilferding and Lenin in the 1970s and 1980s, business historians rushed into quantitative studies of interlocking directorates in various 'core' countries of Western Europe and North America. Because of data limitations, however, the role of networks in the 'periphery' has not yet been properly explored. This chapter takes this unconventional perspective and uses it to try to shed more light on the effects of interlocking institutions on economic modernization in Southeast Europe.

Until the 1960s, Bulgaria was the epitome of a peasant nation. Before World War II, more than 75% of the population were still on the land. It is still a matter of debate whether Bulgaria and its Balkan neighbors were locked in a downward growth spiral until the 1920s (Palairet 1997) or achieved only a slow growth, unaccompanied by any significant change (Ivanov 2012). Institutional explanations are often proposed for this 'growth without development'. In his chapter on Bulgaria, Gerschenkron (1962) famously blamed the banks and the state for what he called 'failed modernization'. In addition, Lampe (1986) and Lampe and Jackson (1982) insist on institutional rigidities (large bureaucracy, corruption and ill-functioning legal system) as the cause of sluggish economic performance. All of these hypotheses are presented in the form of qualitative narratives, which creates two problems. First, they are not necessarily mutually exclusive, and second, they are not formulated in a way that allows for rigorous hypothesis testing.

The interlocking networks perspective offers a unique chance to take a more rigorous and quantitative look at many of those propositions in a historical context. They could be a good indicator of trust and aptitude for creation of intermediate structures of sociability (Fukuyama 1995). If, for example, it was the institutional settings that caused the 'failed modernization' in the European 'periphery', then we would expect to see low business interconnectedness (low trust, few intermediary structures) and an absence of German-type *Kreditbanken.*

Surprisingly, however, big business achieved comparatively high integration during the First Bulgarian Capitalism (1878–1947). Initially, high levels of network density (3.7% in 1911) continued to increase (4.6% in 1929) until the end of 1930s, when it reached 4.9%. World War II and the communist takeover that followed reversed that growth trend and, by 1946, density dropped to 4.0%. With the nationalization that was declared in 1947, voluntary business connectedness was transformed into obligatory political connectivity. From that point on, company management was fully appointed by the communist party, wiping out any interlocks that existed prior to nationalization.

The communist takeover was accompanied by a wave of violence. Different estimates put the number of the victims in the immediate aftermath of the coup at between 20 and 50 thousand. Many of them belonged to the pre-World War II business elite. Others of the business elite emigrated or were sent to concentration camps. In 1946, private business property continued to exist and this allows for an assessment of a network. However, in December 1947, all Bulgarian industry was nationalized, followed by all of Bulgaria's agriculture in the first half of the 1950s. After this, private business property did not exist in any legal form until after 1989. Thus, 1947 marks a sharp discontinuity in the personal and structural composition of production-related networks in Bulgaria. Almost none of the managers of the state-owned enterprises of the socialist era came from the pre-communist business elite. Structurally, horizontal links between enterprises were no longer important and emphasis shifted toward vertical linkages, especially linkages between managers of companies and party officials.

These linkages were usually formed at the local level, with local party officials often trying to boost their party careers by securing the construction of large enterprises in their regions. They promoted their economic importance to 'petition' the higher layers of the party hierarchy, more often than not dragging their comrade enterprise managers and directors up the enterprise management structure with them. Formal studies assessing these linkages in Bulgaria are rare. For obvious reasons, the autobiographical literature does not stress this networking aspect of the socialist era. However, the authors have received confirmation of its existence through conversations with economists and economic historians of the socialist period.[1]

While close links probably existed between enterprises and the Communist Party, links between enterprises themselves were strictly mediated and controlled by the central plan: a complex, iterative and multidimensional coordinating process. In all probability this process involved equally complex networking activities with each stakeholder striving to strategically position him or herself. However, no formal study of this important strategic mode of interaction—blending power, ideology, party organization and business considerations—has been carried out for Bulgaria. As in many other countries, after some successes in terms of capital accumulation, industrialization and increased production, eventually, central planning proved to be a failure in Bulgaria. This failure was clearly felt by the 1980s, which were marked by a series of impotent attempts at reforming the Bulgarian socialist economy (Ivanov 2007). From the perspective of business networking, the most important of these reforms were those from July 1987. Individual factories of the same production line were merged into larger 'economic associations'. This brought about a broad and deep overhaul of the way the management of the economy was organized and involved a significant change in different linkages.

Only two years later, the centrally planned, socialist economy disintegrated and the process of slow creation of a market economy began. This process entailed a qualitatively different mode of selection of entrepreneurs, managers and business elite. Thus, the years 1987–1990 represent another sharp discontinuity in the Bulgarian history of business networking.

Both sharp discontinuities—1944–1947 and 1987–1990—had a serious impact on business, and when the market economy reemerged after 1989, previous levels of integration were never again achieved. Both in 1994 and 2005, the connectivity was so low (0.3%) that formal statistical analysis is meaningless.

Since the phenomenon of interlocking appears to be almost non-existent for the period of post-communist transition in Bulgaria, the major thrust of the analysis here concentrates on the period of the First Bulgarian Capitalism. It is followed by a section of the main characteristics of the post-communist period, with the caveat already noted that the realities in that period do not permit any formal analysis.

2. METHODOLOGY AND SOURCES

To be able to make comparisons with other countries, we selected six benchmark years: 1911–1915, 1929, 1939, 1946, 1994 and 2005. Although 1911 was chosen as the earliest possible year for which company data could be collected, the lack of 100 non-financials in that year led to an extension of the duration of the first benchmark 'year', so that the data are an average for 1911–1915. The benchmark 1929 was the year before the Great Depression, while 1939 was the last peaceful year for Bulgaria before World War II, and 1946 was the year before total nationalization of industrial enterprises and banks. After the beginning of Bulgaria's transition to a market economy in 1989, it took several years to establish new banking and company laws, while in 1996, the country plunged into a deep financial and economic crisis, making 1994 probably the best year of this sub-period. Finally, 2005 was the last year for which data was available at the time of the research.

No formal centralized records of Bulgarian businesses existed before the late-1990s, so various sources for identifying companies that would meet the requirements of the sampling procedure were used. For the period before 1947, this was achieved by utilizing the practice of most firms of publishing their balance sheets in *Durzhaven Vestnik* (State Gazette). This source provided an almost complete set of balance sheets and allowed rating of the companies on the basis of their assets.

Data were far less accessible for the years immediately after 1989. Joint-stock companies are legally required to publish their balance sheets, but it is up to them how and where these are published. As a result, most of the data appeared in obscure regional newspapers or on websites. So it became necessary to consult many publications, including those by the Ministry of Finance, Financial Supervision Commission, National Statistical Institute (NSI) and Bulgarian National Bank.

Before 1947, Bulgaria fell within the so-called 'German boards system' with well distinguished managerial (MB) and supervisory boards (SB) (Stokman, Ziegler, and Scott 1986). In addition, some big companies could elect an executive (also called administrative) board from MB members to assist executive-directors in their daily work. It was common to have outsiders appointed as executive-directors. The law required all changes in MB and advisory council (AC), as well as in management (executive-directors), to be registered with the court. In practice, however, only few of the consulted company dossiers contained information on executives. For that reason the vast majority of those listed in the pre-1947 database are MB and AC members.

The lengthy process of data mining included visits to 23 of the 27 regional archives, where company files, credit dossiers and commercial registers were consulted. After browsing these and carefully selecting members of the business elite, 2,937 individual names of businessmen sitting on the boards of the top 125 companies before 1947 were identified. For the post-1989 period, the collection of directors' names in top 125 companies was significantly easier because of the existence of the DAXI database. Utilizing this resource, we were able to select 1,388 relevant entries of 1,291 individuals sitting in the MB of the 125 largest Bulgarian businesses.

In the final stage of the data collection, we attempted to amass additional information at both personal and firm level. For the pre-1947 period, an additional data set with the names of members of independent professions, politicians, MB members of various non-governmental organizations (NGOs), learned societies and professional associations, as well as directors of the state-owned Bulgarian National Bank and Bulgarian Agricultural and Co-operative Bank, was collected. This additional data set comprised 14,694 entries with over 10,000 individuals: members of Bulgarian political, cultural and economic elite. To reconstruct the biographies of selected directors during the transition period (1989–2005), we consulted various sources, such as encyclopedias and the Internet.

3. FIRST BULGARIAN CAPITALISM, 1911–1915 AND 1946

Personalities

Affiliation to the (business) elite of one or another person is always subjective. We decided to 'draw a line' that restricts elite membership to participation in five or more top 125 companies for the entire period of 1911 to 1946. Even though still subjective, this criterion appears to produce a sufficiently representative list of big business prior to World War II. All of the 'usual suspects' are included: the Burovs are presented by four of their members; the Gubidelnikovs, by three; the Geshovs, by two, and so on.

Of the 137 names in this elite club as defined previously, 25 (18%) were politicians (ministers, or MPs). Another 39 were members of various professional associations, while 19% were connected with NGOs. It is unsurprising that the 'inner circle' (Useem 1984) included five financial ministers and twelve directors of the Bulgarian National Bank, as well as the Bulgarian Agricultural and Co-operative Banks.

Managers and top administrators deserve special attention. Their significant presence in the big business sample is particularly interesting since it marks the beginning of managerialism, which was thought to be characteristic of only the most developed economies. The managers (over 20% of the 'inner circle') were indeed large banks' CEOs, but also there are middle-level administrators, accountants, legal advisors and branch or department managers.

Taking a wider perspective than simply the 'core' (137 individuals) and moving to the whole sample (2,937 businessmen) allows us to study another facet of pre-1946 business elite. Over time, the level of the qualifications of the elite grew considerably: the group of specialists with scientific titles and ranks more than doubled. Foreigners and minority members had a significant presence in the big business, occupying almost a third of the management positions. After the Great Depression, their share started to diminish. Under the communist regime, however, minorities and foreigners almost vanish from the sample.

Our data provide an interesting overview of the family connections within the business elite: 'blood ties' bind at least one-tenth of the large sample. Indeed, this figure may underestimate the phenomenon, as we were unable to recover a complete record of family relations among members of Bulgarian big business.

Fiercely criticized by contemporaries (e.g., Zahary Stoyanov, 1885), the so-called 'brothers-in-law syndrome'[2] had a rational explanation. In a low-trust, low-predictability society, 'partial networks' (Scott and Griff 1984) created an archipelago of stability within which doing business was safer and cheaper. Morally and ethically based, the kin-econ group (networks based on kinship and economic ties) (Zeitlin and Ratcliff 1975) significantly reduced risks of disloyal behavior and fraud. In the absence of a functioning legal system and state regulation, the easiest way to reducing transaction costs was by connecting a market institution (the firm) with a non-market structure (the family), based on moral and mutual aid. In the West, religious (notably, Quakers) or minority groups (Huguenots, Jews) took on this stabilizing role. However, because of the marginal presence of such groups in Bulgarian society, the family was a successful substitute. In the East, 'blood relations' constituted a special type of social capital, one that could be mobilized to compensate for the poor state regulations. To some extent this is still the case.

Data limitations prevented us from undertaking a full comparison between the Bulgarian political and business elite. Big business is defined as a selection of those who own large companies, and these have been analyzed using four benchmark years: 1912, 1929, 1939 and 1945. For politicians, however, it is possible to reconstruct the full time series; i.e., the whole period of 1878–1947. Although we recognize the methodological discrepancy, the similarity between the two groups is astonishing.

Seven out of ten businessmen appear only once in the sample, compared to six out of ten politicians. As is apparent in Table 11.1, the similarity between big business and the political elite holds not only for those businessmen and politicians who appear only once in the sample, but also for those who appear from two times to those who appear twenty times. Indeed, the similarity can be seen to hold even for those who appear more than 20 times in the sample. However, if we focus again on the 'inner circle' (those sitting on five or more company boards) and exclude foreign citizens, we find a surprisingly small overlap between both groups. Only about 20% of the business elite are involved in politics. Neither of the two groups exerted special dominance, and the contacts between politics and economics seem sporadic. Speculation on possible reasons for this comes later in the chapter.

Companies

Shifting from people to companies, we are able to describe the 'working places' of big Bulgarian businessmen. The sample before 1947 consists of 376 firms, 69 of them financial and 307 non-financial. For 35 of them, no data about board members was found—these were excluded from the sample. They were substituted with the next 35 companies for which the relevant information was available. Because the data was available for these companies at the corporate level, rather than the personal level, we

Table 11.1 Cluster Fragmentation of the Business Elite, 1911–1946

	1911/5	1929	1939	1946
Clusters	5	7	8	6
1. Cluster Properties				
Average number of members	9.2	8.0	8.8	8.2
Number of members in the largest cluster	13	16	18	13
Average number of connections	9.0	9.8	9.9	7.9
Integration coefficient*	1.0	1.2	1.1	1.0
2. Cluster Types				
Financial	4	5	**5 + 2	4
Geographic	0	0	0	0
Suppler-client	0	0	0	0
Foreign company	1	0	0	0
Managerial	0	1	2	1
Falling outside the 'inner circle'	0	2	1	1

Source: Ivanov and Ganev 2009.

Notes:
* Integration coefficient returns the ratio between the average number of connections in the cluster and the number of its members.
** Five (5) of the clusters are totally controlled by a financial corporation and in the other two (2), the control is shared by a financial and non-financial company.

included them for all analyses at the corporate level. We felt that, even without data about management, those companies were still members of the big business group. For this reason, the number of firms analyzed in this section is as follows: 133 in 1911–1915, 141 in 1929, 149 in 1939 and 138 in 1946.

Company continuity was relatively weak. More than two-thirds of all corporations appeared only once in the four benchmark years, while another 20% qualified in the elite group twice. It is particularly interesting to focus on the firms that are present in all benchmark years (1911–1915, 1929, 1939 and 1946). Half of those twelve companies were in the financial sector, while the other six were producers of cement, electricity, beer, paper, vegetable oil and tobacco. Only two of them exploited relatively 'high' technologies: United Tobacco Factories and *Grantion*, both of which were the largest Bulgarian firms before and after World War I. All of the remaining corporations operated in low-tech, low-capital segments (vegetable oil, beer) or in first-generation sectors (textile, paper and pulp). Industries that formed the backbone of most advanced economies—such as engineering, chemicals, pharmaceuticals, automobile and aircraft construction—were simply not present in Bulgaria.

Before World War I, big Bulgarian business existed predominantly in the countryside. In 1911–1915, only 39% of all top 125 firms were created in the capital city. Economically, the most dynamic competitors to Sofia were the cities of Ruse (15% share in 1911–1915), Varna and Plovdiv. In the 1920s, and especially in the 1930s, geographic decentralization weakened, and the capital city almost completely dominated the profile of large Bulgarian business. Spatial coverage, however, was astonishingly stable, only varying from 22 to 25 cities/towns. Among the preferred foreign cities were big sea ports like Amsterdam, Rotterdam, New York, Manchester and Trieste, or the capitals of Bulgaria's main trading partners: Berlin, London, Paris and Bucharest.

The data reveal the high level of sectoral rigidity of large business during the four decades under review. Bulgarian entrepreneurs seemed unable to develop second-generation industries. Low-tech, low-capital branches dominate the profile of the sample. Individual trajectories of the chemical and electricity producing industries only confirm that picture. During the interwar years, their share in the selected companies in our big business sample hardly progressed, as compared with the period before World War I. Textile seems to be the only 'success story'. The 1920s and 1930s were particularly good for Bulgarian textile industry, representing a period when it attracted a growing number of foreign—mainly Italian and German—investments.

Inner groupings within big business traditionally attract research interest and trigger heated debates. Various quantitative measures are usually applied in the literature to detect power hubs within the business network (e.g., Mizruchi 1982). In their pioneering study of the so-called 'monopolistic capitalism', however, Natan and Berov (1958) base their analysis of large Bulgarian companies on more qualitative information. Having constructed a large database at the company level, we were able to bypass many of the problems encountered by Natan and Berov and apply quantitative measures to distinguish different clusters. It is a common wisdom in the literature to define 'social cliques' as a "small group within the social network in which members are closer and more tightly connected than other members of the network" (Degenne and Forse 1999, 79).

In a case study of the cluster around *Bulgarska Tugrovska Banka* (BTB) (Ivanov 2010), however, it became apparent that the standard definition (a segment of the network where all members are closely connected with one another) cannot be directly applied to the pre-1947 Bulgarian economy. For this reason, we applied instead the Seidman and Foster (1978) methodology that is based on k-plexes. Drawing again on the BTB case study, we determined n to be 5 and k -1. Using *UCINET 6* software, we searched for any 'social cliques' that consisted of at least five members, who were connected either with all other members or with all other members but one. Using this method, we discovered 17 'social cliques' in 1911–1915, 22 in 1929, 20 in 1939 and 17 in 1946. It is usual for the k-plex methodology to yield such fragmentation of the network. So, following Sonquist and Koenig (1976) as a second step, we attempted to group many of the

Table 11.2 Business Network Density (in %)

	1900s	1920s	1930s	1940s
Bulgaria	3.70 (1911)	4.60 (1929)	4.90 (1939)	4.00 (1945)
Sweden	2.70 (1903)	5.60 (1924)	5.00 (1939)	n/a
United Kingdom	1.30 (1904)	n/a	1.90 (1938)	n/a
United States	7.20 (1912)	7.60 (1919)	5.60 (1935)	n/a

Source: Bulgaria—authors' calculations; Sweden—personal communication with Jan Ottosson; UK—Scott and Griff (1984, 40); US—Mizruchi (1982, 105).

smaller 'social cliques' into larger clusters: all groups where at least one-third of their members overlapped were joined.

Two important findings stand out from Table 11.1. The first is the stability of the internal fragmentation within the elite. Measured both by the average number of members and by the connections between them, Bulgarian business 'cliques' seem to be rigid formations with a stable integration coefficient. Second, most, if not all, groups were clustered around a financial institution.

If we disaggregate the picture in Table 11.1, several important trends appear. On the eve of World War I, the business elite was distributed among five distinct 'cores'. Two decades later, boundaries between different 'factions' become increasingly blurred. The growing number of 'cliques' in 1929 and 1939 could be attributed not only to the entry of new players—the Italian bank, *Commerciale,* the German group of *Granitoid* and the Credit Bank, for example—but also to the creation of intermediate sub-structures, which reconciled contradictions among the former separate cores of the elite. By 1946, half of all clusters were actually connecting links between the traditional 'factions' of the big business.

Elite consolidation and the wiping out of former boundaries through a dense network of cross-investments had important social significance. Corporate alliances came about as a response to the growing public hostility toward big business. The end of industrial protectionism in the early 1930s, the growing influence of anti-capitalist parties—on the left and right—after World War I and the emergence of a serious competitor in the face of the co-operative movement (Avramov 2007) all contributed to the unification of the elite. It was not just the clusters that tended to consolidate—all big companies showed a persistent, high propensity to co-operation, as well.

Bulgarian businessmen were certainly not less inclined to network and co-operate than their UK or Swedish colleagues, and displayed these characteristics in the same order of magnitude as the US (see Table 11.2). While there are certainly different methodologies used in the different studies, it is unlikely that this fact changes the picture qualitatively. The Bulgarian level of network density is comparable to that in the US and Sweden, and significantly exceeds the cohesion of British big business.

Over time, a growing number of firms were integrated into the big business network. The share of the companies that were not connected to any other of the top 125 corporations drops from 24% in 1911–1915 to just 14% in 1946. In other words, almost 90% of all large companies had some links with other members of the elite. This increasing connectivity is even more striking when compared with other European countries. A fifth of British big businesses were unintegrated, and this reluctance to integrate appears to be a stable phenomenon in the UK. As Scott and Griff (1984) report, the share of companies that were not connected to any other firm in the UK sample was surprisingly constant between 1904 (21%) and 1938 (20%).

The interlocked position ratio (IPR), proposed by Mizruchi (1982), also confirms the rising homogeneity of the Bulgarian business elite. IPR measures the ratio between total number of directors in the sample and the number of all established connections among them. Since 1910, Bulgarian business IPR was twice as large as that of the US. Moreover, by the 1930s, Bulgarian IPR reached 92.7, while American big business only managed 32.3.

What stands out is the high level of consolidation among the Bulgarian business elite. This quantitative evidence is reinforced by the qualitative narrative. Perhaps most compelling is the reaction to the growing political threats from the left and populist movements in the early 1920s. As a result of World War I, the Agrarian Union won the 1919 elections decisively, while the Bulgarian communists formed the second largest faction in the National Assembly. Controversial Agrarian legislation—land reform, limited nationalization of urban property, increased taxation on joint stock companies and significant tax cuts for co-operatives, for example—constituted vivid political threats to big business. Putting its faith in the support of the para-military Orange Guard, the Agrarian Union 'broke the neck' of the opposition. The leaders of 'bourgeois' parties were imprisoned or beaten by raging Orange Guard squads, and opposition rallies were disbanded.

With all opportunities for political opposition to the Agrarian regime shut down, large corporations opted for consolidation. By the end of 1921, key figures of the 'inner circle' had initiated a new political formation: *Naroden Sgovor* (People's Accord). It was designed to unite politicians from different parties. With the same purpose, 'to unite and organize' all anti-Agrarian forces, the *Stopansko Razvitie* company was also created, while its official aim was to finance the *Naroden Sgovor* newspaper (Gerogiev 1989). Its importance, however, vastly exceeded that of a funding body for the opposition. The urgency of the situation required extraordinary measures, and it resulted in the Bulgarian 'inner circle' formally revealing its informal power to the public for the first time. Institutionalization of *Stopansko Razvitie*, where the board comprised many of the most important business leaders, was nothing less than a declaration of war on the Agrarian regime.

Table 11.3 Assets of the Largest Bulgarian Companies, 1911–1946, as % of GDP

	1911/15	1929	1939	1946
Top 125 companies	39.38	36.49	41.69	42.50
Top 50 companies	25.95	33.56	37.57	39.57
Top 10 companies	17.29	23.64	27.47	33.41

Source: See text

In addition, this corporate project also functioned as a positive test for the high level of integration among the elite and its readiness for collaboration. Through the *Stopansko Razvitie* company, Bulgarian big business took the lead in organizing its 'class' resources to attempt to neutralize the government's business-unfriendly agenda. The result of this open political activism by the large corporations was the creation of a new trans-party group, which, in 1923, succeeded in deposing the Agrarian regime, with the help of the military (Petrova 1988). As can be seen in Table 11.3, the 'inner circle' was well prepared to take on leadership.

In 1911–1915, the core of the 'inner circle' (the top 10 companies) controlled about one-eighth of total gross domestic product (GDP). Two decades later, its assets had increased to 33% of GDP. Furthermore, the top 50 companies achieved almost full control of all assets of big business. It was precisely this gain in resources that compensated the low (20%) overlap between political and business elite mentioned above. In possession of a disproportionate share of the national wealth, big business apparently felt no need to take manual control of politics by placing agents in either political parties or state administration.

4. THE BULGARIAN PARADOX

The high coherence of Bulgarian business elite and the wide spread of interlocking practices in a low-trust society demands an explanation. Different accounts have been proposed in the literature. According to some, these subgroups were specially tailored to ease access to various resources (e.g., financial interlocking, supplier-client interlocking). Others insist on a regional or political motivation for the creation of business 'cliques'. A third strand of thought highlights the exploitation and control of big business over small and weak companies.[3] We also explored the following: whether interlocking increased effectiveness (and profits), whether capital-intensive subsectors (heavy industry) were more prone to interlocking and whether the more established or younger companies were more prone to interlocking.

Several dependent variables were tested for measuring various forms of company centrality, including centrality degree, centrality power and

Table 11.4 Explanatory Variables for Interlocking

	Centrality degree	Centrality power	Betweenness
Size (per million levs)	0.004 (0.42)	0.001 (0.86)	0.141 (0.03)
Age (years)	0.128 (0.01)	−0.010 (0.83)	1.670 (0.01)
ROE	−0.005 (0.47)	−0.002 (0.77)	−0.003 (0.98)
ROA	2.541 (0.59)	−7.882 (0.10)	93.90 (0.18)
Sofia	3.658 (0.00)	0.295 (0.75)	63.88 (0.00)
Banks	5.119 (0.00)	−0.164 (0.88)	65.21 (0.00)
Heavy industry	1.561 (0.13)	−1.407 (0.17)	15.92 (0.29)

Source: See text

Note: P-values in brackets

'betweenness'. For independent variables, the following indicators were used: size measured by equity; age in years since establishment; ROE and ROA (both in %). Additional dummy variables were added for Sofia, for banks and for the heavy industry branch. (See Table 11.4.)

The regression analysis, with all probable explanations suggested in the literature, proved negative. Neither financial interlocking, nor regional/geographic interlocking nor profitability could completely explain the high density levels of Bulgarian business network. The answer, however, may come from somewhere unexpected. Compelled to operate in a low-trust society, ravaged by corruption and inefficient administration, perhaps Bulgarian entrepreneurs sought 'domestication' of business environment through interlocks, rather than improvement in efficiency and profitability. By entering into strategic coalitions with other companies, large corporations attempted to secure their survival (and longevity). This is not to say, indeed, that everywhere in Europe interlocking was undertaken to compensate for deficiencies of the legal system (for opposite examples, compare the situation in Switzerland and the Netherlands). In the 'periphery', however, we have strong reasons to believe that high coherence was perceived as a tool for improving the business environment.

This corroborates Ivanov's (2010) case study of *Bulgarska Tugrovska Banka*, established in 1895. For many decades, it was one of the most prominent universal banking institutions in Bulgaria. In the financial services sector, a hostile, low-trust business environment was exacerbated by the fundamental discrepancy between short-term (even sight) liabilities and the long-term structure of assets. Most of the savings in a non-market agrarian economy, based on smallholding, were non-monetary in nature—food surpluses, for example—and rarely entered the banking system. When banks were geographically far away (in towns) or untrustworthy, cash savings were either hoarded 'under the mattress' or came as sight deposits, at best. On the other side of the equation was the bank credit portfolio, which was flooded with long-term claims (on current account or quasi-short-term discount bills that were often renewed at maturity). To make the business of banking even more hazardous, there was no safety net. Prior to World War I, the central bank had no legal responsibility to provide additional liquidity as a lender of last resort.

At first, *Bulgarska Turgovska* tried to balance this fundamental discrepancy by maintaining an extremely high capital adequacy of greater than 30%, when 18% was the norm advocated by George Rae (1885). Their capital to credit ratio was over 50% and, at times, even reached 80%. Just like the early American banks (Lamoreaux 1994; Wang 2008), in an effort to minimize information asymmetries, *Bulgarska Turgovska* invested most of its funds in large internal credit. This was a lucrative business when the economy was growing in the early 1890s. Several bad harvests at the turn of the century, however, put an abrupt end to the success of this model. Two of BTB's key shareholders and debtors declared bankruptcy in 1899 and 1902, which almost sank the bank. *Bulgarska Turgovska* managed to survive due only to its high capital ratio and the small amount of deposits attracted in the previous boom years.

It took almost a decade to clean the balance sheet of the burden of toxic credit. Meanwhile, large German, Austrian and French banks entered the market, dramatically changing the Bulgarian banking landscape. In order to preserve its leading position in the financial sector, this flagship of Bulgarian business had to abandon its previous strategy of overcapitalization and opt for a more outward model. Inherent risks of credit expansion were addressed by new, more rigid, procedures of approving credit applications and through membership of a series of social and economic networks.

After 1905, *Bulgarska Turgovska* initiated or entered several networks, a tactic that soon proved very successful. The geographic expansion of regional branches, the interlocking of the 'kin-econ' (intermarriages), and the political (the conservative Popular party) networks with industry had an important impact on future bank development. It is these investments in *social* capital that enabled BTB to overcome the 1899–1902 crisis, to effectively compete with foreign banks after 1907 and to become the largest Bulgarian company in 1912 with over 50 million levs in assets. The dense network of social and economic interlocks provided *Bulgarska Turgovska* with a high-trust, low-risk hinterland, which was far more diversified than the once-practiced insider lending to board members.

This coalition of industrial and financial companies had the potential to tackle many of the fundamental deficits of the Bulgarian financial sector. Through tighter monitoring and routine contacts, *Bulgarska Turgovska* could collateralize credit to interlocked enterprises and secure better information. In addition, special relations with key clients could increase maturity of their deposits held with BTB, thus reducing the overall temporal discrepancy between assets and liabilities. Last, but not least, surrounded by large, lucrative companies, if it found itself in trouble, *Bulgarska Turgovska* was in a position to draw liquidity from 'family member' corporations, substituting them for the missing lender of last resort.

If it was the case in Germany that *Kreditbanken* were able to hasten the industrialization effort (still much debated in the literature, cf. Fohlin 2007; Battilossi 2009), in the 'periphery', universal banking institutions were completely different both in profile and in their tasks. In Central Europe, it is likely that mixed banking served as an instrument to break down 'road blocks' to industrialization and to channel capital into manufacturing. In the south and southeastern fringes of the continent, however, mixed banking should be seen more as a compensatory mechanism for severe deficits in the business environment (low-trust) and fundamental problems of the financial sector (fundamental discrepancy between assets and liabilities). It is no wonder that in the Eastern European 'periphery', purely from a developmental perspective, universal banks had minimal impact on economic growth. Here, their task was not to destroy, but to compensate for social and economic rigidities, thus perpetuating the existing ineffective institutions.

5. NO INTERLOCKING: 1989–2005

The methodology used in this study, based on social networking analysis techniques, does not allow for an analysis of any year during the communist period in Bulgaria. As already mentioned, the reasons for this are twofold. First, all managerial appointments were made through party decision, so all companies were connected through the communist party. Second, the managerial structure stressed the person of the executive director; the members of what could be conditionally seen as a managerial board were involved in principle with only one enterprise and, if interlocked directorships were to be found at all, the same person being involved in directorships in different enterprises was a rare exception. Enterprises were interlocked not through people but through the communist party, line ministries and, especially, through the central plan. None of these type of linkages can be captured through social network analysis methods. It is not that no network analysis of the communist period is possible; on the contrary, it may be of considerable value, but it cannot possibly be performed using the instruments of the methodology used in the present study.

Initially, we wanted to include 1989 as a benchmark year. It was the final year of the communist rule and a period when the regime experimented with moderate economic reforms. A special Decree 56 was adopted and tailored to transform the state-owned factories into joint-stock companies. The fall of the Berlin Wall prevented the reform from being implemented fully, but following the decree, in the months before November 1989, several hundred firms were re-registered.

It had been our hope that this new registration would provide the necessary information. However, on closer inspection, it became apparent that only small factories had been re-registered following Decree 56. The majority of big socialist enterprises, like the nuclear power plant at Kozloduy, the *Neftochim* oil refinery or the *Kremikovtsy* steel plant, were all excluded from the reform. It was therefore regrettable that, due to those data limitations, 1989 could not feature as a benchmark year.

Personalities

As mentioned earlier in the description of the data collection, the year 1989 created significant problems for the collection of the data in the format required by the methodology used here. However, the list of available managers of companies, which were transformed into joint-stock firms in 1989 under Decree 56, allows for an expansive interpretation of who is a member of the business elite at this time. In this case, such an expansive interpretation might be misleading if the data indicate many names that appear in both 1989 and in later lists of business elite members. But since this is not the case in Bulgaria, the use of this expansive list of 1989 is still quite interesting. All in all, there are 1,847 names among the managers and directors of the largest (for 1989—all listed) companies. As Table 11.5 shows, the proportion of multiple participations is extremely low.

With less than half of one percent of the sample having three connections, and none with more than three for the whole period, it is impossible to talk about a 'core' group of interlockers.

Companies

The fact that there are only two data points in our study for the post-communist period in Bulgaria, which are made under the adopted methodology, means that there is insufficient longevity to make informative inferences about the continuous presence of some companies among the top 125 in the country's economy during this period. However, because we observe that in the relatively short period between 1994 and 2005, 85 companies—or 68% of the sample of big firms—were replaced by others reflects a distinct lack of continuity. This is not difficult to justify. Within the decade framed by the two observation points, Bulgaria's economy underwent two severe structural shocks: the financial and deep economic crisis of 1996–1997, followed by a massive wave of privatization.

Table 11.5 Bulgarian Big Business Elite, 1989–2005

Number of times person appears in the sample	Business Elite People	Share, %
1	1739	94.1
2	101	5.5
3	7	0.4

Source: See text

Table 11.6 Levels of Business Connectivity in Bulgaria, 1994 and 2005, in %

Number of connections	Bulgaria 1994	Bulgaria 2005
0	72.8	67.2
1	18.4	25.6
2	8.0	6.4
3	0.8	0.0

Source: See text

In the period after 1989, there were very low levels of business connectivity in Bulgaria among the top 125 firms. Less than a quarter of the companies had even one connection; all the rest had one or two, and only one company (*Biochim Bank*) had three connections in 1994, from a list of 210 different companies that comprised the top 125 companies between the two benchmark years. (See Table 11.6.)

In line with the observed extremely low connectivity among the top 125 firms in Bulgaria in the post-communist period, all measures describing the group, such as density, centrality and 'betweenness', are extremely small and indicate the *de facto* lack of a social network. For example, in both 1994 and 2005, the density of the connections between the top Bulgarian firms is 0.3%, and the average degree is 0.2. If a valued, rather than binary, matrix is used to reflect the likelihood of connection of firms through more than one person, and the appropriate maximum theoretical number of links accommodating the number of seats in the governing bodies of the firms is used, the densities in both years are even lower at 0.1%.

Under these conditions, a formal analysis of clusters or of factors determining cliques, or central players and their role in the economy or on specific sectors, becomes statistically meaningless. Only several clear tendencies can be outlined. First, in both 1994 and 2005, a leading connecting factor is whether a company belonged to a certain branch of industry. Second, foreign ownership through privatization had become a major connecting factor, including a significant increase in the number of foreign citizens becoming interlockers. Third, between the two benchmark years, the role of banks as connecting factors had decreased.

6. SOME INTERPRETATIONS OF THE POST-COMMUNIST RESULTS

These results can serve only as a very limited basis for comparing Bulgarian post-communist realities with other post-communist nations, especially the well-studied case of Hungary, as investigated by Stark and Vedres

(2006, 2012). In their research, they use a rich sample of almost 1,700 firms continuously from 1987 to 2001 in order to study the dynamics of business networking from various perspectives: strategies toward uncertainty, foreign capital involvement and political party affiliations, for example. They show that "between 1987 and 2001 networked property grew, stabilized and involved a growing proportion of foreign capital" (Stark and Vedres 2006, 1367) and that, during the same period, "director interlocks depend[ed], to a significant extent, on political affiliations" (Stark and Vedres 2012, 700).

The Hungarian dataset is much richer than the available set for Bulgaria by significant orders of magnitude in both number of firms and years of observation. However, despite the very limited comparability, one definite similarity and one possible difference can be observed. The similarity is the obvious increase between 1994 and 2005 in Bulgaria of the role of foreign-owned networked firms, mostly due to banking and industrial privatization (Ivanov and Ganev 2009, 79). The possible difference is in the political linkages of networked firms. In Hungary, Stark and Vedres (2006; 2012) show that political affiliations with a specific party were significant; in Bulgaria, a different model of links between businesses that relied on political connections and politics seemed to emerge. In both Bulgaria and Hungary, firms felt compelled to manage political risks through having specific connections to political parties. As the studies conducted by the Center for the Study of Democracy (CSD Hidden Economy; CSD SOCTA 2012) indicate, the way in which both the hidden and criminal, as well as the larger and legitimate businesses, control the surrounding political uncertainty is by developing connections with all political parties, rather than with a specific one (in a sense, buying insurance). This strategy limited their opportunities to times when 'their' party was in power, but also limited the threats in times when 'other' parties were in power.

The lack of a social network among the top Bulgarian firms in the post-communist period is an interesting phenomenon; its explanation may provide valuable knowledge about the state of the Bulgarian economy. Given the paucity of available network data, however, such an explanation cannot be arrived at using the tools on which the analysis presented here is based. At present, these tools give only one certain inference: the two periods of Bulgarian capitalism (pre-World War II and post-1989) were radically different in terms of how business elites were formed and interacted.

At this point, without any formal checking of hypotheses, only theoretically possible explanations for the missing Bulgarian elite business network of the post-communist transition can be offered.

The first group of such hypotheses are based on the assumption that people and companies have rational reasons not to connect. Connectivity is costly, and if the costs exceed the benefits, it may not happen. Strategies to achieve access to, and control over, scarce resources in ways that are an alternative to (direct) business connectivity may be more attractive—such as relations with a foreign or governmental owner or maintenance of achieved or inherited monopoly positions. Time may also be an important factor for this group of hypotheses. With connectivity costs being incurred more in the short run, and benefits in the long run, a viable network might be slow to emerge—perhaps 15 years, since 1989 is too short a period. There might even be legal impediments to the quick emergence of business connections among the top firms in the country.

The second group of possible hypotheses that could explain the lack of an elite business network in Bulgaria after 1989 relates to the focus of the methodology. It looks at only the largest enterprises, and assumes that the members of the elite directly participated in their governing bodies. In a post-communist context, for various reasons, both assumptions may be problematic. Firms may be connected not directly, but through common participation in other firms that are smaller in size, but perhaps not in influence. Directors of big companies may simply be representatives of the truly influential elite connected not through sharing board seats, but through alternative social networks, like clubs, biographical personal connections or connections clustered around political entities. This is especially possible when business connections are deliberately hidden. If a member of the business elite is associated with the grey or black economy, for example, there is a strong incentive to hide. Or perhaps they do not wish to attract attention to corrupt practices. Attempts to circumvent anti-trust legal provisions would also provide incentive to keep linkages hidden.

7. SUMMARY OF THE MAIN RESULTS

The study presented here performs a social network analysis of the largest Bulgarian firms in six different benchmarks years in the twentieth century: four from the first half of the century, reflecting the period of the First Bulgarian Capitalism, and two marking the transition from centrally planned to market economy.

The results from the two periods are very different. Prior to 1947, the network connectivity among Bulgarian elite businesses was at levels comparable to the then-developed economies. The presence of a large number of personalities with multiple participations—with specific characteristics and biographies—also confirms a clear emergence of managerialism. There are also clearly identifiable important subgroups of companies. The level of 'intermingling' of the business and political elites was relatively low. The statistical analysis lends some support to the inference that interlocking served as a compensatory mechanism for existing deficiencies and rigidities in the business environment.

In stark contrast, the methodology employed detects no elite business social networks in the post-communist period; groupings among the largest companies are rare and small. In fact, connectivity is so low that formal statistical analysis is impossible or meaningless. There are various possible reasons for the lack of detection of a network among the largest Bulgarian companies after 1989 under the methodology of this study, the hypothesizing and testing of which might be usefully pursued in future research.

NOTES

1. Specific questions about such linkages were asked in the fall of 2012 during conversations with Roumen Avramov, Professor Ivan Angelov and Lubomir Christoff. They were able to recall careers of managers and directors closely related to party careers.
2. The term was coined after the big Gubidelnikov family, which was both politically and economically active. Through intermarriages, the Gubidelnikovs managed to become allied with many other prominent business families. As a result, they were brothers-in-law with many key figures of the elite.
3. For an extensive review of the literature, see Mizruchi (1982), Sweezy (1953) and Pennings (1980).

REFERENCES

Avramov, Rumen. 2007. *Communal Capitalism, Vol. 1–3*. Sofia: FBNK & CLS.
Battilossi, Stefano 2009. "Did Governance Fail Universal Banks? Moral Hazard, Risk Taking, and Banking Crisis in Interwar Italy." *Economic History Review* 62: 101–134.
CSD Hidden Economy, Center for the Study of Democracy. 2002–2012. "The Hidden Economy in Bulgaria" series of reports and briefs. Retrieved June 10, 2014. http://www.csd.bg/?id=118
CSD SOCTA, Center for the Study of Democracy. 2012. "Serious and Organized Crime Threat Assessment." Retrieved June 10, 2014. http://www.csd.bg/fileSrc.php?id=20796
Degenne, Alain, and Michel Forse. 1999. *Introducing Social Networks*. London: Sage Publications.
Fohlin, Caroline. 2007. *Financial System Design and Industrial Development: International Patterns in Historical Perspective*. Cambridge: Cambridge University Press.
Fukuyama, Francis. 1995. *Trust: The Social Virtues and Creation of Prosperity*. New York: Free Press.
Gerogiev, V. 1989. *People's Accord 1921–1923*. Sofia: Sofia University Press.
Gerschenkron, Alexander. 1962. *Economic Backwardness in Historical Perspective: A Book of Essays*. Cambridge, MA: Belknap Press.
Ivanov, Martin. 2007. *Reformism without Reforms: The Political Economy of Bulgarian Communism, 1963–1989*. Sofia: Ciela.
Ivanov, Martin. 2010. *Network Capitalism: Bulgarian Commercial Bank and Its Related Companies, 1890–1914*. Sofia: Gutenberg.
Ivanov, Martin. 2012. *The Gross Domestic Product of Bulgaria, 1870–1945*. Sofia: Ciela.
Ivanov, Martin, and Georgi Ganev. 2009. *Bulgarian Business Elite, 1912–1947, 1989–2005*. Sofia: East-West.
Lamoreaux, Naomi. 1994. *Insider Lending: Banks, Personal Connections, and Economic Development in Industrial New England*. Cambridge: Cambridge University Press.

Lampe, John R. 1986. *The Bulgarian Economy in the Twentieth Century.* London: Croom Helm.
Lampe, John R., and Marvin R. Jackson. 1982. *Balkan Economic History, 1550–1950. From Imperial Border Lands to Developing Nations.* Bloomington: Indiana University Press.
Mizruchi, Mark. 1982. *The American Corporate Network, 1904–1974.* Beverly Hills and London: Sage Publications.
Natan, J., and L. Berov. 1958. *The Monopoly Capitalism in Bulgaria.* Sofia: Nauka i izkustvo.
Palairet, Michael. 1997. *The Balkan Economies ca. 1800–1914: Evolution without Development.* Cambridge: Cambridge University Press.
Pennings, Johannes. 1980. *Interlocking Directorates.* San Francisco, Washington and London: Jossey-Bass Publishers.
Petrova, Dimitrina. 1988. *Government of Bulgarian Agrarian National Union.* Sofia: Nauka i izkustvo.
Rae, George. 1885. *The Country Banker: His Clients, Cares, and Work. From an Experience of Forty Years.* London: J. Murray.
Scott, John, and Catherine Griff. 1984. *Directors and Industry: The British Corporate Network 1904–1976.* Cambridge: Polity Press.
Seidman, Stephen B., and Brian L. Foster. 1978. "A Graph-Theoretic Generalization of the Clique Concept." *Journal of Mathematical Sociology* 6: 18–31.
Sonquist, John, and Thomas Koenig. 1976. "Examining Corporate Interconnections through Interlocking Directorates." In *Power and Control: Social Structures and their Transformation,* edited by Tom R. Burns and Walter Buckley, 53–83. London: Sage Publications.
Stark, David, and Balazs Vedres. 2006. "Social Times of Network Spaces: Network Sequences and Foreign Investment in Hungary." *American Journal of Sociology* 111: 1367–1411.
Stark, David, and Balazs Vedres. 2012. "Political Holes in the Economy. The Business Network of Partisan Firms in Hungary." *American Sociological Review* 77 (5): 700–722.
Stokman, Frans N., Rolf Ziegler, and John Scott, eds. 1985. *Networks of Corporate Power. A Comparative Analysis of Ten Countries.* Cambridge: Polity Press.
Sweezy, Paul. 1953. "Interest Groups in American Economy." In *The Present as History,* edited by Paul Sweezy, 7–21. New York: Monthly Review Press.
Useem, Michael. 1984. *The Inner Circle. Large Corporations and the Rise of Business Political Activity in the U.S. and the U.K.* New York and Oxford: Oxford University Press.
Wang, Ta-Chen. 2008. "Banks, Credit Markets, and Early American Development: A Case Study of Entry and Competition." *Journal of Economic History* 68 (2): 438–461.
Zeitlin, Maurice, and Richard E. Ratcliff. 1975. "Research Methods for the Analysis of the Internal Structure of Dominant Classes: The Case of Landlords and Capitalists in Chile." *Latin American Research Review* 1 (3): 5–61.

12 "From Dense to Loose?"—Corporate Networks and Interlocks in Finnish Business in the Twentieth Century

Susanna Fellman, Kari-Matti Piilahti and Valtteri Härmälä[1]

1. INTRODUCTION

In an international study from the 1970s, it was argued that Finland had a significantly high rate of interlocking directorships (Heiskanen and Johanson 1986, 171). Now, in the 2010s, Finland seems to have quite dense corporate networks, although countries like Germany and France score higher (see van Veen and Kratzer 2011). Heiskanen and Johanson (1986) concluded that this phenomenon is the result of two factors. First, the Finnish system allows two company boards, both an outside board of directors (*styrelse, hallitus*) and a so-called supervisory board (*förvaltningsråd, hallintoneuvosto*). As a result, there are increased chances of 'collecting' a large number of positions of trust in Finnish business, and so many opportunities for interlocks. Second, the economic environment during the post-war period, and in particular in the 1970s and 1980s, supported the phenomenon of dense networks. Cross-ownership and the significance of a bank-centered financial system made for numerous interlocks, especially between banks and industry. Owners and managers of banks and insurance companies sat on the boards of industry, while the industrial managers were members of the boards of financial companies. The large number of co-operatives and state companies also reinforced the numerous interlocks. These companies, as a rule, had a supervisory board, in addition to the executive group and the board. Finally, the importance of the bilateral trade with the Soviet Union after World War II, in which the trade agreements were agreed at the highest political level, strengthened the corporate networks and the connections between politicians, civil servants and large-scale corporations.

However, it is also the case that corporate networks were dense in Finland in both the late nineteenth and early twentieth centuries. This phenomenon might have come about because of other factors—the importance of family ownership and smallness of the country, for example. In Finnish business, 'everybody knew each other'. Moreover, some specific institutional features probably also strengthened the density of the networks. Finland is a bilingual country (Finnish and Swedish) and this language division affected business life and corporate networks. This probably made the networks even denser and also somewhat polarized.

In spite of the 'common knowledge' that Finnish business networks have been close and dense, there are no systematic studies of this phenomenon and its development. Apart from the article from the 1970s, only scattered studies from specific industries and/or time periods exist; all other arguments presented in both public debate and in scholarly literature have been based solely on anecdotal evidence.

In this chapter, we will examine how the structure of the corporate network in Finnish big business has changed over the course of the twentieth century, both from the perspective of the company and of individual directors. We will look at the centrality of the companies in the network and to what extent the companies were connected through interlocking directorships. We will also investigate whether there were so-called *big linkers* in Finnish business, who these big linkers were and why they gained these multiple positions. This will be carried out by means of a unique dataset on the largest Finnish companies (see data following). This material will be analyzed using formal network analysis. Apart from new and systematic knowledge of the inter-corporate relations in Finnish big business over the long term, this investigation will reveal transformations in the power structures in Finnish business.

A principal focus of this paper is on the role of interlocks between banking and industry. This is an important question resulting from the bank-centered financial system apparent until the 1980s. Moreover, the 'dominant narrative' in Finnish business history has been framed in terms of some key banks controlling manufacturing companies. An additional focus is the effect of the language division in Finnish business, which was especially important before World War II. We will also briefly discuss the role of state companies and co-operatives in an attempt to achieve an overview of Finnish networks.

These issues will be analyzed within a wider economic and institutional context. We believe that the institutional environment is significant in providing explanations for transformations in corporate networks and patterns of interlocks. Scholars have emphasized that the pattern of interlocking directorships is embedded in the national business system (cf. Cárdenas 2012; Windolf 2002; also Schnyder and Wilson, this volume). Although we will not adopt a strict 'varieties of capitalism' framework, as, for example, Cárdenas (2012) has, we will discuss our questions in the context of specific turning points and structural changes in the Finnish business environment.

Our analysis then will show that Finnish corporate networks in big business were indeed dense, especially bank-industry networks in the post-World War II period up to the 1980s. Big linkers also existed throughout this period. We will also show that the density of the networks decreased over time. A particularly interesting break occurred in the 1980s and early

1990s, after which bank-industry networks also loosened. This period brought about a fundamental rupture in the Finnish economic and institutional model (see Fellman 2008), and the development in the pattern of the networks can clearly be linked to this development.

We will also argue that Finnish corporate networks were not as tight as perhaps has been previously assumed. A very dense 'core' network consisting of big banks, insurance companies and big business in the manufacturing industry (often within the key export sector) existed, but outside of this network, we can find ample examples of companies that are not tied to any other companies in the network. Therefore, we will argue that the Finnish corporate network was more fragmented than the 'dominant narrative' would indicate.

Finally, we will draw attention to an interesting feature of the bank-industry networks: language division. It is no surprise that the networks were close; this is a common phenomenon in many parts of the world, but in the Finnish bank-industry networks, language worked as a dividing factor. The language division between the Swedish-speaking and the Finnish-speaking population made the industry-bank networks develop in two spheres: one around the 'Swedish-language' banks and one around a 'Finnish-language' bank. We considered this to be a quite unique characteristic. Further, these two spheres continued to exist after the language as a dividing factor in Finnish business had lost most of its significance.

2. THE DATABASE AND METHODOLOGY

We collected information on the CEOs and boards of directors of 100 of the largest companies in Finland for specific benchmark years: namely, 1912, 1927, 1938, 1974, 1984, 1994 and 2004. Contrary to the study by Heiskanen and Johanson, mentioned previously, we only included the boards of directors, but not the (non-compulsory) supervisory boards (*hallintoneuvosto/förvaltningsråd*). Supervisory boards were common in state companies and co-operatives in the post-war period until the 1980s. Many privately owned firms also had supervisory boards at that time. Today, however, most Finnish companies opt for the one-tier model.

Although many Finnish companies had a two-tiered system that gave individuals the opportunity to 'hoard' positions, the size of the boards of directors has been fairly small when taken in an international context. The average size of the boards (plus the CEO, irrespective of whether he/she is a member of the board) increased only slightly over time (see Table 12.1). The small relative size of Finnish boards of directors is supported by a recent international study (Heemskerk 2011, 447).

In fact, there was a minor decrease in board size recently. One possible reason for this is that the share of co-operatives and state companies in our dataset decreased; these companies commonly have larger boards. However, there was also a general trend toward 'slimming down' the boards. The view that smaller boards were more efficient gained ground, especially among the business elite, in the 1990s (Lainema 2006, 46–47). At that time, this was supported by research (Yermack 1996; Jensen 1993).[2]

As mentioned earlier, for every benchmark year, we selected 100 companies from the manufacturing industry, financial industry, trade and services and the utilities. We collected information about managing directors/CEOs and boards of directors for these companies.[3] The data for the period before World War II were collected from archival material in the National Board of Patents and Registration and several printed publications (Hjerppe 1979; *Banker och Aktiebolag i Finland*). After World War II, the sample was based on the list of biggest firms in Finland that is published yearly in the economic weekly magazine, *Talouselämä*, which has collected and published lists of the biggest companies in Finland since the early 1970s. The information on board members and CEOs was collected from a variety of printed and primary sources. Unfortunately, in the benchmark years 1974, 1984 and 1994, some companies had been omitted because of missing information. This variation in sample size has, of course, been taken into consideration when carrying out calculations.

Although the total sample for every benchmark year is small, increasing the sample size would result in much smaller business being 'captured' and erroneously labeled 'big business' when, in fact, they are too small to fit the category. Due to the small size of the economy and the late industrialization, Finnish firms were small, at least from an international perspective, until the late twentieth century. It is only in 1994 and 2004 that all the companies in the dataset can be labeled 'big business' from an international perspective. The total dataset consisted of 329 firms. Interestingly, the change in the firm sample was significant: of those included in 1912, only 10 could be found in the last benchmark years.

We divided our analysis into three periods: the period before World War II, the post-war period up to the 1980s and the 1990s onwards. The early twentieth century was marked by industrial breakthrough and modernization, representing quite a liberal economic model. World War II is, on the other hand, often considered as a break in the Finnish model of capitalism—a transition, moving toward a period of regulation and significant state interference (see Fellman 2008). When studying interlocks in big business, World War II does not seem to represent a big divide, however—the 'big break' occurred in the 1990s.

We also look at 'big linkers'. A big linker can be measured by looking either at how many people an individual meets, or by studying how many positions of trust he or she has. For the first criteria, the assumption is that the individual receives a significant amount of information by meeting many people. For the second, information about a person's power and influence is considered to be given by how many positions of trust they hold, (e.g., Heemskerk 2011; Mizruchi 1983). Both measures have their limitations, but especially the degree—the number of people with whom one person connects—depends significantly on the size of the boards. For this reason, we focus primarily on the number of positions a person holds.

The data from each of the seven sample years were first coded into Pajek (software for network analysis) as a 2-mode network consisting of companies and their board members (De Nooy and Batagelj 2011). The 2-mode network was then transformed into two 1-mode networks, one for the companies and the other for the members of the board. In the 1-mode networks, the businesses are connected to each other by common board members, whereas the directors are connected by having a seat on a board or being a CEO in a specific company.

3. DEVELOPMENT OF CORPORATE NETWORKS IN FINLAND: 'THE BIG PICTURE'

In the case of the network of companies, the average degree and density measures suggest that the density decreases over the time period in question. The first sample year has the highest average degree and density measures (see Table 12.1). These measures show a somewhat steady decline in centralization, which suggests a diminishing density and a transition to a less centralized network structure over time.

The first benchmark year also has the smallest amount of outliers, i.e., companies that are not connected to any other company in the network. The number of outliers in 1912 was only 14, whereas by 2004, this number had risen to 36.

The number of companies in 2-slice—in other words, companies connected to another company with at least two board members—diminishes over time. In 1912, almost one-half of the companies in the network shared at least two board members with another company, whereas in 2004, only 17% of the companies were left in the 2-slice. The diminishing centrality

Table 12.1 Some Basic Figures about the Network of Companies

Year	N	Density (no loops allowed)	Average degree	Average board size	Number of outliers	Companies in 2-slice
1912	100	0,0436	4,32	5,51	14	47
1927	100	0,0329	3,26	6,07	31	28
1938	100	0,0382	3,78	6,65	23	41
1974	88	0,0405	3,52	7,06	23	36
1984	86	0,0391	3,33	7,30	22	33
1994	87	0,0334	2,87	6,82	27	15
2004	100	0,0298	2,96	7,02	36	17

Source: Database on Finnish CEOs and board members.

scores and weakening interlocks between companies tell the story of a development in which the Finnish company networks became less centralized over the course of the last century. Companies had less direct contacts with each other through the members of the boards, especially in 1994 and 2004, than they had before this time. In addition, the strength of the contacts between companies weakened dramatically over time. In this sense, the big change seems to have occurred during the 1990s.

4. CORPORATE NETWORKS IN THE FIRST DECADES OF THE TWENTIETH CENTURY

In the middle of the nineteenth century, the core of Finnish business life consisted of iron mills and wealthy trading houses founded and managed by families with Swedish or German as their mother tongue. Many of the new and developing industrial companies were also founded by members of these trading houses. Finnish industry is usually said to have 'taken-off' in the latter part of the nineteenth century; a continuous economic boom from the 1890s to the start of World War I favored business life. During the last decades of the nineteenth and first decades of the twentieth century, there were numerous changes in Finnish business life that left a mark on corporate structure. These transformations were manifestations of economic liberalism, which defined Finnish economic policy from the 1850s onwards.

From the last quarter of the nineteenth century onwards, the most important branch of industry was wood processing. The significance of metal and textile companies grew in the 1930s, however. Particularly common in commerce, the co-operative movement gained ground at the turn of the nineteenth and twentieth century, and new co-operative societies became powerful in wholesale and retail trade (Hjerppe 1979, 174–175). Co-operatives also existed in the financial industry; the central co-operative bank was founded in 1903.

Liberalism remained an economic guideline until World War I, when it came to an end due to export difficulties. The effect of the legislation remained quite limited, however, and after World War I, the economic policy of Finland can be best described as a form of 'qualified liberalism' (Rasila 1982). Regulation of entrepreneurship was accepted, to some extent, and state companies emerged. In 1918, the majority of capital stock of three companies was transferred to the ownership of the state and, by the mid-1930s, the state had reached quite an influential position in Finnish business life—four of the 30 biggest industrial enterprises (*Enso-Gutzeit, Tornator, Veitsiluoto* and *Oulu*) were state-dominated, for example. In fact, the state interfered little in the economy, but nevertheless, companies and industrial organizations were in close co-operation with ministries, and their opinions were taken into consideration in policy making (Ahvenainen and Vartiainen 1982, 178–183).

Language as a Dividing Factor in Business

Foreign ownership and foreign managers were rather scarce in Finnish business in the period between 1900 and 1940. The share of foreigners diminished over this period, especially during and after World War I. Take, as an example, the biggest industrial company in the interwar period, *Enso-Gutzeit*. Enso-Gutzeit was formed in 1918, after a massive trade of stocks between its Norwegian owners and the state. The few foreign-born CEOs that we already see in the cohorts were well established in Finnish society, but in order to minimize the influence of foreign capital, at least half of board members were to be Finnish citizens, according to the Company Act of 1864 (see Hjerppe 2004). This principle remained basically in force until the late twentieth century.

A focal feature of the structure of the Finnish corporate network before World War II was language and culture. In the last decades of the nineteenth century, the language polarity between the Finnish-speaking majority and Swedish-speaking minority sharpened in society in general and this was reflected in business. The Swedish-speakers had hitherto nearly monopolized business, as many of the leading business families were Swedish-speaking Finns. The wealthiest merchants operating in the export and wholesale trade were still mainly Swedish-speaking families. However, at the turn of the century, companies owned by Finnish speakers ('Fennoman businesses') emerged and trade, especially, became a battleground for the two language groups.

The antagonism between the language groups was not so visible in industry, probably due to the heavy dominance of the Swedish-speakers, but in the 1910s, Finnish-speakers had succeeded in gaining ground in the saw mill industry. In addition, the state companies and co-operative firms provided increasingly new and important career pathways for Finnish-speakers. In trade, they already dominated by the 1930s, while the grip of Swedish-speakers was at its tightest in transport and industry. In 1927, a Finnish-speaking director led 26 of the 100 enterprises examined; by 1938, this number had risen to 34. Yet, the management was solely in the hands of Swedish-speakers in 15 companies.[4] The notable rise in the number of Finnish-speaking directors just after World War I can be explained partly by the emergence of the state-dominated companies and the focal role of the co-operative movement.

This language divide was especially noticeable in the financial industry. In 1889, *Kansallis-Osake-Pankki* (KOP) was founded to improve the acquisition of capital for Finnish-speaking entrepreneurs (Paavilainen 2005; Blomstedt 1988). The other main commercial bank, *Nordiska Föreningsbanken–Pohjoismaiden Yhdyspankki* (PYP, later *Föreningsbanken i Finland–Suomen Yhdyspankki*, SYP), financed mainly companies dominated by Swedish-speakers. The distinction between language groups can also be seen in the composition of the directors of these banks: the members of the corporate management of PYP were Swedish-speaking and in KOP, they were Finnish-speaking.

The banks' close connection with industry is an international phenomenon and, therefore, not surprising; it is part of their strategy to manage and control their activities. It is a concept of a stable customer relationship that has been typical in banking (see Engwall and Johanson 1990). Neither is the existence of bank spheres uncommon. Significant interlocks between banks and industry can thus be found in many other countries (e.g., Mizruchi 1983; Fohlin 1997; Vasta and Baccini 1997; Ottosson 1993). Language as a basis for networks is probably uncommon, whereas the role of ethno religious background—Jewish families in banking, for example—has been previously identified as a basis for networking (Gutwein 1994; Mosse 1989; Windolf 2011).

Centrality of the Companies Before World War II

One notable feature, observed from Table 12.1, is that the network was at its most dense in 1912. This is interesting in comparison to the other countries included in this book. In the first decades of the twentieth century, the big Finnish industrial companies were situated at the core of the networks based on interlocks (see Figure 12.1). In each cohort, there were seven industrial firms among the ten most interlocked companies, based on degree. Two firms remained among the most interlocked during this period: namely, *Tampella* and PYP. Although not the biggest industrial company of Finland, *Tampella* was clearly the most interlocked in the 1910s and 1920s.

However, the dominance of manufacturing industry and banks among the top interlockers weakened slightly during the first decades of the twentieth century, and the most connected firms became more heterogeneous with respect to branch. Also, the degree of centrality among the top interlocking firms decreased, with respect to the whole cohort of large companies studied here.

Prior to World War II, companies outside the tight network operated mostly in commerce. This might be partly caused by the greater emphasis on locality in the field of commerce. Many of the firms in wholesale business were quite new and thus not yet integrated into the network. Therefore, the high density in 1912 might also be the result of the narrowness of Finnish business life, it having few big companies. In the 1920s and 1930s, 'new blood' flowed into Finnish business, especially in commerce and trade, which expanded rapidly.

The language division also influenced the dense interlocks; interlocks seem to have been less common among Finnish-speaking companies. Finnish-speaking entrepreneurs were more common in the smaller and more regional companies in trade, while Swedish-speakers were to be found in big industrial companies, so they had been well connected for a long time through

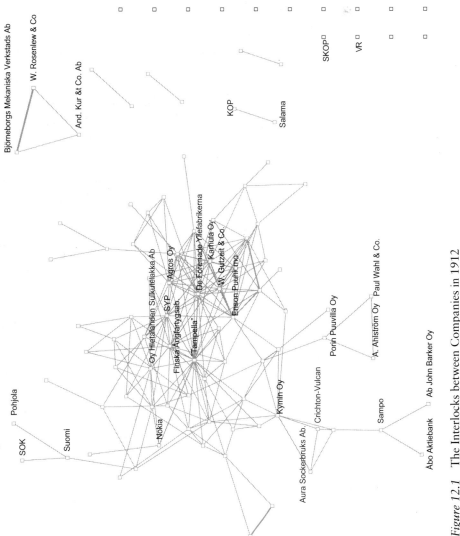

Figure 12.1 The Interlocks between Companies in 1912
Source: Database on Finnish CEOs and board members

business, family and other kinship relations. Moreover, as a small minority and feeling increasingly threatened in the 1930s, the preservation of a small and dense network was perhaps a more active strategy among Swedish-speakers.

The industry-bank relationship grew during the interwar period. The first commercial banks' original aims did not include becoming active in the management of manufacturing companies through board membership (see Fellman 2008). This became more common in the interwar period, however, partly as a result of a more active strategy of the banks, and partly as an unintended consequence of manufacturing companies running into financial difficulties. Both of the leading commercial banks, PYP and KOP, were important for the financing of manufacturing companies during this period.

This development can also be identified by an increase in multiple interlocks between directors in finance and industry. For instance, in 1927, PYP had four board members with multiple interlocking directorships to industry but only one of them had more than three links to industrial companies. In 1938, the equivalent numbers were six and three, respectively.

Interlocks of Corporate Managers Before World War II

The share of people with multiple executive directorships was also fairly high in the first decades of the twentieth century: 22% in 1912, 17% in 1927 and 22% in the 1930s. However, only 3–5% had more than three directorships, and to hold five or more positions was extremely rare. The emergence of the co-operative firms, state-owned companies and the growing significance of the local banks are the most likely reasons for the drop in multiple executive directorships in 1927. It was because of these reasons that many people with no previous connections to other firms were elected to the boards of new companies.

As mentioned earlier, the interlocks between banks and industry were already quite numerous in the 1910s. This is also visible at the level of individual managers. One of the principal figures of the corporate networks in this period was Johan Osvald Wasastjerna. In 1912, with a degree of 53, he held membership in 10 boards and was director of the *Pohjoismaiden Yhdys-Pankki* (PYP). In the 1910s and 1920s, he sat on the boards of various industrial companies (*W. Gutzeit & Co Oy, Yhdistyneet Villatehtaat Oy, Enson puuhiomo*) and trading enterprises (*Agros*). These simultaneous board memberships represent an 'all-time high' in the dataset. In 1938, the most connected person was Yrjö Pulkkinen, an ombudsman of the Central Chamber of Commerce, a former bank manager and minister, with the degree of 35 and membership of six boards. Pulkkinen can also be seen as a typical businessman-politician, which was common at this time period; he served as Minister of Finance (Conservatives) in the mid-1920s and remained active in politics until the end of the decade. The direct participation of businessmen in state politics diminished, however, toward the end of the 1920s, while indirect lobbying became more common.

In spite of the relative growth of the state in company ownership during the interwar period, it seems that the direct effect of the state on business life remained quite limited. Interestingly, however, the most important channel of influence that the people operating in state-dominated enterprises had to the private sector was through numerous interlocks.

However, positions of leadership in big business that stretched over several decades were quite rare. There were just five managing directors who remained CEO in the same company during the whole period. Multiple CEOs were also exceptional: there were only three people who held the CEO position simultaneously in two firms (or more).[5] Nevertheless, to have several positions of trust, i.e., several board memberships, was common, including the aforementioned Wasastjerna and Pulkkinen. Among those with multiple directorships, it was also common to hold positions in two lines of business. The most common combinations were industry and trade or industry and banks. The structure of these multiple positions did not change significantly during the period. In each cohort, there were only two or three people contributing to three lines of business. These 'three-traders' cannot be typecast; while all of them operated in industry, their other links varied.[6] The connections to the banks and commerce were slightly more common than to the other branches, again highlighting the importance of bank-industry networks.

On the other hand, during this period, some significant and well-connected managers, like Gösta Serlachius (CEO of *G.A.Serlachius Ab* between 1913 and 1942) were not to be found among the big linkers. Serlachius had significant positions of trust in which he exercised extensive power and influence at the highest political level, but these positions were in organizations, like the Confederation of Employers and the Finnish Paper Mill Association, and not business, and are thus not visible in our database.

5. Tightening Bank Spheres after World War II

After World War II, Finland had a fairly regulated economy with strong corporatist features. The state's active interference in the economy had grown during and after the war, and the post-war period was marked by top-down policies (for a lengthy discussion, see Fellman 2008). The regulation of the financial markets was especially strict during this period. The aim was to keep interest rates artificially low—making the real interest rate negative—in order to stimulate investment in fixed capital and, ultimately, promote economic growth. Moreover, the institutional and political environment, as well as global economic trends, supported stronger state interference in the economy.

The number of state companies grew and they became more closely tied to state bureaucracy (see Kuisma 2008). One reason for this was the growing Soviet trade, in which trade agreements were conducted at the highest political level. It is worth noting, however, that this trade was also crucial for many private companies. The long-time president, Urho Kekkonen (president 1956–1982), took an active role both in governing this trade and in the state companies, thus strengthening the ties between privately-owned big business, state companies and the political elite.

As already discussed, the issue of language had, in the late nineteenth and early twentieth century, been significant in the banking industry, in particular. The networks between banks and industry had polarized into one sphere around the 'Swedish-language' SYP and another around the 'Finnish-language' KOP (see also Figure 12.2). The tensions between the two language groups diminished after the war, but the division based on language continued in the Finnish banking sector.

The role of the banks as financiers also grew in the post-war decades, partly due to the strict financial regulation of this period. The low interest rate made loan financing expand at the expense of the stock market, but bank ownership in manufacturing had also increased. This deepened the already close connections between banks and industry, and the direct influence of banks in manufacturing industry was extensive. Companies came to rely heavily on their 'house banks' at the same time as the two big banks guarded their interests in specific companies, which they considered as 'belonging to their realm'.

New legislation in the early 1950s limited the direct ownership of banks in industry, trade and transport companies to a maximum of 20%, in order to avoid excessive influence, but this did not alter the situation to a considerable extent. The overall dispersion of ownership of big business enabled banks to exercise significant influence with only a small minority stake. Further, the banks often strengthened their influence in a specific company through other companies. For example, in 1991, the companies belonging to the 'SYP sphere' (or 'realm') together controlled as much as 30% of the shares in *Nokia Oy* (Häikiö 2002 II, 298). As a result, the big commercial banks, in close collaboration with loyal companies, could often control a much higher percentage of the shares than that of their direct ownership.

In Figure 12.2, we concentrate solely on the two big banks and their spheres in 1984. From this figure, it can be observed that the network around KOP is extremely tight. This supports the idea of the KOP and its connections to the 'Fennoman' big business, consisting of manufacturing companies like *Kajaani, Rauma-Repola* and *Yhtyneet Paperitehtaat,* and some state companies like *Veitsiluoto,* as well as the Fennoman insurance company, *Pohjola*. The key figure was the CEO of KOP Jaakko Lassila. He was the biggest interlocker in the post-war period and a legendary figure in Finnish banking history. Even though he was famous for his large influence through his interlocks, the basis for the network around KOP had been laid throughout the twentieth century. From Figure 12.2, the sphere around SYP seems weaker than that of KOP—it appears that it had already started to loosen.

Interestingly, one company was linked to both banks: namely, *Nokia* (Figure 12.2). This could be seen as an anomaly in Finnish business history. Although manufacturing companies as a rule belonged either to the SYP or KOP sphere, both banks were shareholders in *Nokia*. This phenomenon, which continued until the early 1990s, was a result of the emergence of the 'modern' *Nokia* in 1967 through a merger of three separate companies. As two of these companies belonged to the SYP sphere and one to the KOP sphere, both banks (and their spheres) gained ownership in the company (Häikiö 2002 II, 105). This 'terror balance' led, however, to both external and internal tensions and lasted until the early 1990s, when KOP sold their shares. When KOP decided to sell out, the 'SYP sphere' had strengthened its controlling position to 30% of the shares, while the group around KOP controlled somewhat less at 24% (Häikiö 2002 II, 298).

Also, in the post-war period, key people in Finnish business held many positions of trust. In both 1974 and 1984, 28 directors held three or more positions. The key interlockers were bankers and important industrialists, not uncommonly in family firms, although salaried managers in state companies

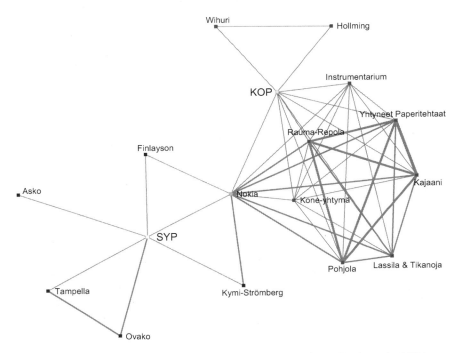

Figure 12.2 The Pattern of the 'Bank Spheres' in Finnish Big Business in 1984
Source: Database on Finnish CEOs and board of directors

also appear among the group of big linkers. In 1974, the biggest linker, measured by number of board positions (seven directorships), was Jacob von Julin Jr. At the time, he was chairman of the board and significant owner of Fiskars, and descendant of a legendary business family. Among other big linkers, we can find the CEO of SYP, Mika Tiivola, and Göran Ehrnrooth, former CEO of SYP (1950–1970). The Ehrnrooth family members have, for several generations, been significant in Finnish business, coming close to a 'dynasty', although not as influential as the Wallenberg family in Sweden. Göran Ehrnrooth's influence in Finnish big manufacturing was strengthened by his marriage to Louise von Julin, sister of the aforementioned Jacob von Julin.

In 1984, we find the biggest linker in the post-war period, the head of KOP Jaakko Lassila, who enjoyed nine positions of trust in big business. The Ehrnrooth family was, however, still at the core of the network. As the son of Göran Ehrnrooth, Göran J. Ehrnrooth had as many as six directorships in that year.

6. ECONOMIC CRISES AND REGIME SHIFTS: TRANSFORMING INTERLOCKS SINCE THE 1990s

Big changes in the Finnish model of capitalism occurred in the 1980s and 1990s. Finland went from being very coordinated to a much more liberal market economy in a short period of time. The most profound transformation—which also had significant effects on the big banks and their role in Finnish business—occurred in the financial market. The Finnish economy had gradually liberalized since the 1960s, when the country became an associated member in the European Free Trade Association (1961), but the strict regulation of the financial markets and capital flows remained in force until the early 1980s, after which a swift liberalization of the financial markets began. This led to a partly uncontrollable development, with overheating, credit expansion and 'bubbles' in housing and stock prices. The 'bubble' suddenly burst in the beginning of the 1990s. Simultaneously, the Soviet trade crashed with the breakup of the Soviet Union and, as some industries had relied heavily on this trade, there was a wave of bankruptcies. This, in combination with an overvalued currency (Finnish *markka*) and a looming recession in Western markets, plunged the Finnish economy into a deep crisis. The wave of bankruptcies and sharply rising unemployment, followed by a rapid fall in the stock market and housing prices, also led to a severe banking crisis. This development severely weakened the banks and the whole banking industry was plunged into turmoil. Among other things, the old 'archenemies', SYP and KOP, were merged into the *Merita Bank* (which, today, is part of the Nordic banking group *Nordea*).[7]

After a large devaluation of the *markka* in 1991, and finally letting it freely float in 1992, the road to recovery started. The last regulations concerning foreign capital flows and foreign direct investments were removed in 1993, and Finland joined the EU in 1995. There was rapid growth in new industries, most notably the ICT sector with the expansion in mobile phone production in *Nokia*. Finland entered a period of favorable growth and the inflow of foreign capital grew swiftly.

As a consequence of this turmoil, the bank's role in the Finnish economy changed profoundly, especially as financier in industry. With the opening of the border for capital, the heavy reliance on domestic bank financing disappeared and Finland went swiftly from a bank-centered to a market-based financial system. Moreover, with the banks' own strategies transformed, *Nordea*, for example—which included the remains of the SYP and KOP—turned its focus toward international markets. At the same time, investment banking and private equity firms emerged on the Finnish 'financial map'.

From Table 12.1 and Figure 12.3, we can see the growing fragmentation and loosening of the network at the beginning of the twenty-first century. The key figures show decreasing density and that the number of outliers, i.e., companies not linked to any other in the network, is rising. This supports the picture of decreasing density and increasing fragmentation. Figure 12.3 also shows that in 2004, the banks appear to have been replaced by insurance companies. Further, at the level of the individual, there is a loosening of the network. The share of people with multiple executive directorships was between 16% and 17% in the post-war decades, but had shrunk to 14%

Figure 12.3 Corporate Networks in Finland in 2004
Source: Database on Finnish CEOs and board of directors

248 *Susanna Fellman et al.*

in 2004. In 1974, 6% of all people with multiple directorships had at least three, but this decreased over the period and was 4% in 2004. Five or more positions were rare, as they were in earlier decades.

This increasing fragmentation and decreasing degrees of interlocks was connected to the significant transformations of Finnish business. It is safe to conclude that the growth in foreign ownership and the decreasing role of banks in industry were particularly important; some of the outliers were foreign companies. Thus, the hypothesis that a liberal market economy is characterized by lower degrees of interlocking directorship and a lower density in the business networks (Cárdenas 2012) does seem to be valid for the Finnish case. This development was also part of a broader international phenomenon: the 1980s and 1990s formed a 'break' in many other countries, as can be seen from several of the articles in this volume (see Schifeling and Mizruchi; Schnyder and Wilson; Ginalski, David, and Mach, this volume). Globalization and the increasing amount of trans- and multi-national companies made national networks lose importance.

However, multiple interlocks still existed in 1994 and 2004. The biggest and most significant industrial firms were often connected through multiple interlocks—*Nokia* with *UPM-Kymmene* and *Wärtsilä* with *Fiskars*, for example. The insurance companies had also now become something like spiders in the tightest nets. To illustrate this point, the biggest linkers in 1994 were the two CEOs of insurance companies: Jouko K. Leskinen (*Sampo Group*) and Yrjö Niskanen (*Pohjola Group*), although both held 'only' five positions. Figure 12.3 shows that also in 2004, several companies within the financial industry were connected through multiple interlocks, such as *Sampo* and *Varma*, and *Pohjola* and *Ilmarinen*. Some of these links originated in the strong prevalence of mutuality in insurance. The financial industry has reorganized since then, however, and several companies have merged.

In 2004, the really big linker was Georg Ehrnrooth, who held as many as six board positions. He was former CEO of Metra Oyj (now under the name Wärtsilä Oyj), but in 2004, he held only board positions. He was also well linked internationally (van Veen and Kratzer 2011). It is more usual, however, for Finnish companies to be weakly linked to companies from other countries (Heemskerk 2011; van Veen and Kratzer 2011). However, it can be assumed to grow in the future, due to, for instance, international cross-border mergers.

7. THE 'OUTLIERS'

One of the most interesting results was that throughout the whole period of investigation, there was a considerable amount of outliers—companies not connected to any other company in the dataset. This can be explained in part by the sample. For example, until the 1980s, there were corporations that were not particularly large and were regional in character, with little contact with the core of big business. Some of these companies might have been linked to other firms not included in the data. As the number was quite big and this phenomenon continued over the years, it can be interpreted as evidence of somewhat larger fragmentation in Finnish big business than previously assumed. Finnish business historiography has more usually dealt solely with the corporations surrounding the two big banks. This has then been taken as proof of the dense networks and smallness of the 'inner circles' in Finnish business. Firms outside the core industries—meaning, primarily, the big commercial banks, the main insurance companies and large firms in the export industry—have traditionally been somewhat overlooked. The apparent fascination with relations between bank and (export) industry has overshadowed the structures of the often domestically oriented and more regionally connected firms.

Before World War II, the outliers were mostly regionally based and often fairly young enterprises, especially in the field of commerce and services. Among these companies, the big co-operative firms should be mentioned, such as *SOK* (founded in 1903), *Hankkija* (founded in 1905) and *OTK* (founded in 1917), which had few connections to other significant companies. In 1912, an interesting triad is found linking the family firm *W. Rosenlew & Co Ab* to *Björneborgs Mekaniska Verkstad* (BMV) and *Kurt And. & Co*. The companies in this triad were situated in a small industrial town, Pori. The majority of the shares in BMV and *Kurt And.* were owned by Rosenlew and later merged with the mother company.

Also in the post World War II era, many of the outliers were firms tied to their own regional network, like the *Rederiet Sally Ab,* which was situated on the Åland Islands. We can also find some family firms (*Oy Huber* in 1984, *Oy Kyro Ab* in 1974) with their own family and kinship networks, co-operatives like the *Hankkija, Elanto* and *OTK* forming a triad in 1974, or the producer co-operatives *Keskusosuuskunta Liha OK* in 1984, which had extensive local networks with their producers, but were not linked to the close elite network. However, some of these bigger co-operatives were probably linked to the dense network of banks and big industrial companies through their supervisory boards (*förvaltningsråd),* members of which were often representatives of the political and economic elite.

Notably, the outliers in 2004 showed a new form consisting, at least to some extent, of other firms than had previously been the case. As expected, we can find several foreign-owned firms and subsidiaries to multinationals among the outliers, while family firms had more or less disappeared by this time, Hartwall being the only exception.

8. CONCLUSION

We previously noted that the interlocks between banks and insurance and core companies in the export sector have been numerous. The Finnish network was at its densest in 1912, but remained close until the 1980s, when it quickly loosened. It was also easy to discern corporate spheres 'rotating' around the two banks.

Big linkers did, indeed, exist throughout the time period and the names that emerged were well-known figures in Finnish industrial history, as a rule; 'a few good men' controlled a large part of Finnish business for a long time. Who these linkers were changed over time, however. According to Mizruchi, in the US between the 1910s and 1970s, there was an 'institutionalization of the inter-corporate relations' (Mizruchi 1983). In Finland, as well, the big linkers in the network increasingly represent some key institutions.[8] Nevertheless, there were also 'big linkers' who represented the same types of circles, especially family businesses, and who continued to be influential during the whole period in question.

The network loosened and fragmented in the 1990s and early 2000s. The decreasing role of banks and the growing role of foreign ownership and foreign companies in the Finnish economy, in conjunction with the transition from a coordinated to a more liberal market economy, affected this development. We can also observe a trans-nationalization of the networks; in 2004, a growing number of foreigners are found on the boards in our dataset. In fact, it has been argued that the increasingly globalized business in the 2000s had made the study of only domestic links a fairly limited—even outdated—approach (see Heemskerk 2011). An overwhelming majority in the network were, however, still native Finns in the early twenty-first century.

Our study thus supports the 'common knowledge' about the Finnish dense networks within key industries. This is not surprising; small countries usually have dense networks. In the Finnish case—as in the other Nordic countries—significant block holders have existed and still do today.

However, when our analysis is extended beyond this tight group of firms, which are usually studied in Finnish business history, the picture becomes more varied. First, throughout the period, there were a large number of outliers. Obviously, this may be due to the limitation of the dataset, but it is safe to say that the very tight network on which the literature usually focuses has formed a very special group. Second, the big linkers were, after all, few in number. Most of the individuals in the dataset had less than three board positions—even in big business.

Further, it is not necessarily clear that holding many board positions brings with it a lot of power. Sometimes, a smaller number of positions provide a better platform for power; it might be more important to sit on the board of a specific key company than on the boards of many companies. In addition, the positions of chairman of the board, which have not been separated in this analysis, can be considered as more influential than simply membership of a board. The biggest linkers in the data often had several positions as chairman of the board. Some influential people, with many and important connections to other types of organizations in the Finnish economy, will not be visible as 'big linkers' from this data. Gösta Serlachius exercising power in influential organizations was mentioned above, but this is also the case with regard to notable Finnish managers linking with, for example, big multinationals, like Jorma Ollila, who, since 2006, has been chairman of the board of Shell.[9] He could certainly be considered a big and powerful 'linker', despite having only two positions significant for this study.

What are the consequences of this? Why is the study of networks and interlocks at all significant? A tight network is usually seen as leading to close ideological and political cohesion within the business community (Mizruchi 1992; Burris 2005). Indeed, such a strong political and ideological cohesion has been typical for the Finnish business elite. As there are still some significant big linkers, we can assume that the control function that the networks commonly play is still present, contrary to what Schnyder and Wilson in this volume discuss with regard to the UK. According to them, the British business elite have moved away from direct control toward what they term 'more diffuse class cohesion'. The networks and interlocks are still important, but not for strategic use to control other companies as much as for information flows and for the diffuse of social values and norms. Indeed, in Finland, direct control still seems to be important. Latterly, a new phenomenon has arisen in Finland: the so-called 'board professionals', whose main 'job' is only to sit on various boards. This phenomenon indicates the (assumed) significant influence that (multiple) board membership has.

It is obviously important to reach beyond the level of anecdotal evidence—which was our first aim here. But these results also open up possibilities for further research. As mentioned, the tightness of the network is usually seen as leading to ideological and political cohesion within the business community, and this has often been considered typical for the Finnish business elite. But what role did the close and dense network play in the formation of such cohesion? This is not dwelled on here. How were these connections exploited? What kind of information was transmitted through these channels? Moreover, as dense networks, multiple interlocks and shared board positions provide opportunities for power and influence, this study raises the question of how power structures in big business have been transformed because of transforming 'core groups' in Finnish business. These questions remain for further study.

NOTES

1. We wish to thank Jenny Heikka and Isabella Holm for their research assistance.
2. Although smaller boards might be more efficient, later research has questioned the idea of an optimal board size. Companies are different, and, thus, they need boards of different types and sizes (see Beiner et al. 2004). Interestingly, both Yermack and Jensen suggested seven or eight people as some kind of 'optimal' board size, i.e., close to the average size of Finnish boards in big business.
3. According to Finnish company law, the managing director/CEO could, but did not have to be, a member of the board. In a majority of the companies studied here, he has also been so.

4. The classification of language is occasionally difficult. Some managers were bilingual and some changed language over their life (see also Fellman 2000, 60–62).
5. People holding multiple CEO positions were Lauri Forsblom (a technical director of *Osakeyhtiö Abborfors Aktiebolag* and CEO of *Etelä-Suomen Voimaosakeyhtiö*), V. A. Kotilainen (CEO of mainly state-owned firms *Enso-Gutzeit* and *Tornator*) and Hugo Vasarla (CEO of the co-operative SOK and its industrial enterprises).
6. One of the three traders was Karl Stockmann (1865–1938), the owner of the Stockmann department store, who in the 1930s, sat on the directorates of an industrial firm (*Tampella*) and an electricity company (*Etelä-Suomen Voimaosakeyhtiö*).
7. An old saying about the two rival banks was that "hell will freeze before KOP and SYP will merge".
8. Susanna Fellman (2000, 190) has, in a previous work, labeled the post-World War II networks forming the 'internal labor markets' from which top managers were recruited as 'bureaucratic networks'; i.e., these networks were based on personal relations, but the basis for these relations originated in the organization that these key individuals represented.
9. Thus, he would not be found in this position in 2004 data.

REFERENCES

Ahvenainen, Jorma, and Henry J. Vartiainen. 1982. "Itsenäisen Suomen talouspolitiikka." In *Suomen taloushistoria 2. Teollistuva Suomi*, edited by Jorma Ahvenainen, Erkki Pihkala, and Viljo Rasila, 175–191. Helsinki: Tammi.

Beiner, Stephen, Wolfgang Drobertz, Frank Schmid, and Heinz Zimmermann. 2004. "Is Board Size an Independent Corporate Governance Mechanism." *Kyklos* 57 (3): 327–356.

Blomstedt, Yrjö. 1988. *Kansallis-Osake-Pankin historia I 1889–1939*. Helsinki: Kansallis-Osake-Pankki.

Burris, Val. 2005. "Interlocking Directorates and Political Cohesion among Corporate Elites." *American Journal of Sociology* 110 (1): 249–283.

Cárdenas, Julián. 2012. "Varieties of Corporate Networks: Network Analysis and fsQCA." *International Journal of Comparative Sociology* 53 (4): 298–323.

De Nooy, Wouter A., and V. Mrvarand Batagelj. 2011. *Exploratory Social Network Analysis with Pajek: Revised and Expanded*. Structural Analysis in the Social Sciences 34. New York: Cambridge University Press.

Engwall, Lars, and Jan Johanson. 1990. "Banks in Industrial Networks." *Scandinavian Journal of Management* 6 (3): 231–244.

Fellman, Susanna. 2000. *Uppkomsten av en direktörsprofession. Industriledarnas utbildning och karriär i Finland 1900–1975*. Helsingfors: Finska Vetenskaps-societen.

Fellman, Susanna. 2008. "Growth and Investment: Finnish Capitalism, 1850–2005." In *Creating Nordic Capitalism—The Business History of a Competitive Periphery*, edited by Susanna Fellman, Martin Iversen, Hans Sjögren, and Lars Thue, 139–217. Basingstoke: Palgrave-Macmillan.

Fohlin, Christina. 1997. "Universal Banking Networks in Pre-War Germany: New Evidence from Company Financial Data." *Research in Economics* 51 (2): 201–225.

Gutwein, David. 1994. "Jewish Financiers and Industry, 1890–1914: England and Germany." *Jewish History* 5 (2): 23–45.

Häikiö, Martti. 2002. *Nokia Oy:n historia I–III*. Helsinki: Nokia Oyj.
Heemskerk, Eelke. 2011. "The Social Field of the European Corporate Elite: a Network Analysis of Interlocking Directorates among Europe's Largest Corporate Boards." *Global Networks* 11 (4): 440–460.
Heiskanen, Ilkka, and Erkki Johanson. 1986. "Finnish Interlocking Directorships: Institutional Groups and Their Evolving Integration." In *Networks of Corporate Power. A Comparative Analysis of Ten Countries*, edited by Frans N. Stokman, Rolf Ziegler, and John Scott, 166–183. Polity Press.
Hjerppe, Riitta. 1979. *Suurimmat yritykset Suomen teollisuudessa 1844–1975*. Bidrag till kännedom av Finlands natur och folk 123. Helsinki: Finska Vetenskaps-Societeten.
Hjerppe, Riitta. 2004. "Monikansallisten yritysten tulo Suomeen ennen toista maailmansotaa." *Kansantaloudellinen aikakauskirja* 100 (3): 216–238.
Jensen, Michael C. 1993. "The Modern Industrial Revolution, Exit, and the Failure of Internal Control Systems." *The Journal of Finance* 48 (3): 831–888.
Kuisma, Markku. 2008. *Metsäteollisuuden maa. Suomi, metsät ja kansainvälinen järjestelmä 1620–1920*. Helsinki: Suomalaisen Kirjallisuuden Seura.
Lainema, Matti. 2006. *Strateginen hallitus*. Helsinki: Boardman.
Mizruchi, Mark. 1983. "Relations among Large American Corporations, 1904–1974." *Social Science History* 7 (2): 165–182.
Mizruchi, Mark. 1992. *The Structure of Corporate Political Action*. Cambridge, MA: Harvard University Press.
Mosse, Werner E. 1989. *The German-Jewish Economic Elite, 1820–1935. A Socio-Cultural Profile*. Oxford: Clarendon Press.
Ottosson, Jan. 1993. *Stabilitet och förändring i personliga nätverk. Gemensamma styrelseledamöter i bank och näringsliv 1903–1939*. Ekonomisk-historiska institutionen: Uppsala universitet.
Paavilainen, Marko. 2005. *Kun pääomilla oli mieli ja kieli. Suomalaiskansallinen kielinationalismi ja uusi kauppiaskunta maakaupan vapauttamisesta 1920-luvun alkuun*. Jyväskylä: Bibliotheca Historica 96.
Rasila, Viljo. 1982. "Liberalismin aika." In *Suomen taloushistoria 2. Teollistuva Suomi*, edited by Jorma Ahvenainen, Erkki Pihkala, and Viljo Rasila, 13–26. Helsinki: Tammi.
Vasta, Michelangelo, and Alberto Baccini. 1997. "Banks and Industry in Italy, 1911–36: New Evidence Using the Interlocking Directorates Technique." *Financial History Review* 4 (2): 139—159.
Van Veen, Kees, and Jan Kratzer. 2011. "National and International Interlocking Directorates within Europe: Corporate Networks within and among Fifteen European Countries." *Economy and Society* 40 (1): 1–25.
Windolf, Paul. 2002. *Corporate Networks in Europe and the United States*. New York: Oxford University Press.
Windolf, Paul. 2011. "The German-Jewish Economic Elite (1900 to 1930)." *Zeitschrift für Unternehmensgeschichte*, 56 (2): 135–162.
Yermack, David. 1996. "Higher Market Valuation of Companies with a Small Board of Directors." *Journal of Financial Economics* 40 (2): 185–211.

Part V
Developed Economies in Asia and Latin America

13 Longitudinal Study of Interlocking Directorates in Argentina and Foreign Firms' Integration into Local Capitalism, 1923–2000[1]

Andrea Lluch and Erica Salvaj

1. INTRODUCTION

Interlocking directorates can play important roles for the organization and performance of business, as well as for the structuring of economic power (Mizruchi 1996). We are particularly interested in the historical embeddedness of board interlocks and transformations in their significance and structure over time. This chapter focuses on the factors that fueled changes and shifts in Argentine board interlocks throughout the twentieth century. Argentina offers an interesting context because its troubled economic performance has been a puzzling case in literature concerning development economics. Its capitalist system has undergone multiple transformations over the years. Despite its ranking as a comparatively rich country in the early twentieth century, it steadily drifted farther from industrial economies, until the collapse of the economy in 2001.

This chapter shows that the corporate networks built by Argentina's largest firms never achieved a very cohesive structure, and that by the middle of the twentieth century, they progressively lost any cohesiveness they might have had. During the period 1923–2000, board ties evolved into highly fragmented, uncoordinated networks, but until the end of World War II, Argentina's board interlock networks were relatively stable and cohesive. The year 1954 might be viewed as a transitional period in which interlocking directorates experienced a contrasting tale of two sub-networks: a stable core that became slightly more agglomerated and an external periphery with weak connectivity and of smaller size. Structural changes in the late 1950s brought about deep changes in the corporate world, prompting a complete turnaround of the network core. By the year 2000, following another structural change, its main component disappeared and the corporate board network crumbled away.

This historical path, from integration in the 1930s to a lack of cohesion in the 2000s, was driven mainly by changes in the economic structure of local capitalism. Another driving factor was the number and profiles of directors with multiple board appointments, as well as the dynamics operating within the inner circle of corporate leaders, all of which can be seen as part of an endogenous social deconstruction process (Chu 2012).

Because the different paradigms that oriented Argentina development patterns[2] transformed the nature of inter-firm relations, we propose that they also altered the meaning of interlocking directorates. In this long-term process of social deconstruction, external shocks were as important as endogenous forces. These findings are consistent with the theory that suggests that the overall structure of interlocked networks depends on institutional and economic changes (Kogut 2012; Lluch and Salvaj 2012; Windolf 2002).

In the first half of the twentieth century, interlock ties served to lower information and transaction costs, reduce risk, increase coordination and gain privileged access to markets, in line with the resource dependence theory (Pfeffer and Salancik 1978). The political and institutional turmoil that followed 1950, together with the decoupling of multi-board memberships from the elite controlling ownership, transformed the meaning of interlocking directorates and reduced their usefulness over time.

The changing nature of interlocking directorates also reflects influential interactions between local business interests and multinational enterprises (MNEs)—a classic topic in the debate of the economic development of Latin America. Our findings, from a corporate network perspective, provide new insights for the study of alliances among MNEs, local capital and public policy makers in developing economies. This, in turn, helps to illuminate a key factor in explaining structural economic changes (Chang and Evans 2005; Maxfield and Schneider 1997; Stark and Vedres 2006).

Argentina´s natural resource-based production and export-led economy created highly interactive and strongly resilient business alliances between local and foreign capital that, as a part of a defensive strategy, persisted after the Great Depression (Nollert 2005). In fact, these enduring alliances showed more continuity than is generally recognized in previous literature on the subject. They almost disappeared, however, during the late 1950s and 1960s, when MNEs became central actors in the second phase of the state-led industrialization, in which manufacturing expanded into heavy intermediates (steel and petrochemicals), consumer durables and some capital goods (Ocampo and Ros 2011). In the 1980s, a more troubled environment created pressures for change. State policies prioritized the largest local business interests and MNEs were displaced, taking secondary roles in the network. An era of market reforms began in the 1990s that returned MNEs back to the center of the economy; as the result, the corporate network was completely different from the earlier one and was now highly fragmented.

2. LONG-TERM EVOLUTION OF THE CORPORATE NETWORK

Based on our dataset, we identify five evolutionary phases in the network. We collected information about the 100 largest non-financial corporations, ranked according to their share capital in four benchmark years—1923,

Argentina and Foreign Firms' Integration 259

1937, 1944 and 1954—and according to their annual sales in three further benchmark years: 1970, 1990 and 2000. The final sample included 100 non-financial firms for all benchmark years, with the exception of 1970 and 1990. In 1970, the sample included 95 firms, and 102 in 1990. We also included the 25 biggest banks in each year, with the exception of 1970, in which we sampled 28. The banks were selected principally on the basis of total deposits. Appendix I (included at the end of the book) and the file "Data and Methods" on the website describe our sources, methodology and dataset in greater detail and provide more information about the network measures (see http://www.cgeh.nl/power-corporate-networks-comparative-and-historical-perspective).

It was in the last stage of primary-export capitalism—the 1920s—that the main network component began to emerge. The main component increased in size after 1923, sparking a stage of consolidation and resilience between 1937 and 1954. This can be seen to coincide with the first phase of horizontal industrialization policies and enhanced state intervention that took place between 1930 and the mid-1950s. The main network remained very stable during this phase. It included more than 60% of all firms and reached its highest value (66%) in 1954. After 1954, the number of firms in the main component steadily decreased, leading to a complete shift in the core of the network. A new, more fragmented network emerged, and by 1990, the number of isolated and marginal firms peaked at 82%. In the last period—the 2000s—the main network component had collapsed into many small cliques containing six firms or less, as well as multiple isolated companies. Figures 13.1 and 13.2 capture the trend of disintegration. Figure 13.1 reveals how the main component's size decreases, while the number of isolated companies increases. Figure 13.2 shows the evolution of the number of links among companies, with the same trend of fragmentation and disintegration.

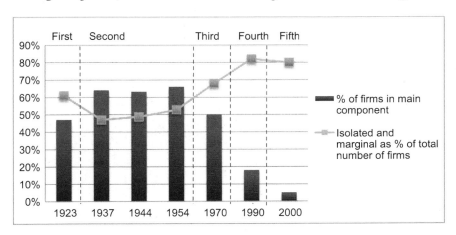

Figure 13.1 Evolution of Percentages of Firms in Main Component vs. Isolated and Marginal Firms

In the following sections, we describe the results of this study of interlocking directorates across five phases.

Toward Consolidation of the Corporate Network: The Last Stage of the Primary-Export Phase

Until 1914, Argentina's open economy remained fully integrated with international markets, both as a producer of 'staple' goods and as a major destination for foreign investment. The first global economy entailed massive investment by Western firms in the developing world. Argentine economic growth was supported by a significant inflow of foreign capital; by 1900, it had attracted more foreign capital than any other Latin American nation. In line with the predominant, open, primary-export development strategy, most European companies focused on financial operations (banking, insurance, mortgages), railways, utilities, cattle farming, forestry or real estate.[3]

However, the ranking of the largest companies in 1923 built up for this study does not include all foreign companies[4] (mainly in utilities and transportation), despite their importance, because many of them did not have boards in Argentina. Therefore, domestic companies accounted for 77% of all firms shown in the 1923 corporate network. Of course, not having a domestic board does not necessarily mean that MNEs were isolated. For example, 14 of the 35 largest MNEs without a board in Argentina had links to other firms because their general managers or legal representatives (mainly of Belgian, English or Dutch origin) sat on the boards of other companies.

In the prevailing, primary export-led growth process, shared directorships or interlocking directorates between local firms and foreign capital do not seem particularly relevant. By this time—the 1920s—Argentina's industrial structure had developed a dual configuration with some sectors—railways, meat packing and utilities, for example—dominated by foreign companies and others, such as cigarettes, wine, glass and shoe manufacturing and leather processing, controlled by large, domestic companies (Barbero and Rocchi 2003). This duality (or low interdependence) kept the sectors separate, without any need to create the interorganizational links suggested by the resource dependence model (Boyd 1990; Pfeffer and Salancik 1978). In fact, market duality combined with the effects of the increased numbers of industrial stand-alone and family-owned firms, can explain the significant proportion of isolated firms (61%), few links among companies (263) and the low average degree (2.7), or average number, of ties per board. Another key metric of corporate network cohesion is density, capturing the idea that more ties between firms produce a tighter, more cohesive structure. In 1923, just 9.1% of all possible ties were present within the main network component (see Appendix I and Figure 13.2).

A core network began to emerge due to the crucial role of local and diversified business groups (DBGs[5]). Degree and eigenvector centrality measures highlight the crucial role of these actors in the corporate network.

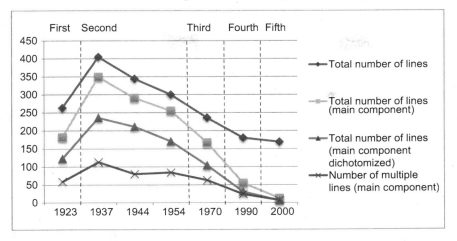

Figure 13.2 Evolution of Number of Lines, 1923–2000

While previous studies have identified DBGs as typical of Argentina's capitalism since the beginning of the century (Barbero 2011), our study highlights that DBGs also served as connectors. These business groups networked mainly with European companies and business people, sharing family and friendship ties, as well as close business relationships. The vast majority of DBGs were built by immigrants or Argentine entrepreneurs whose families were of foreign origin, maintaining strong ties with their ancestors' communities. This illustrates the significant role played by immigration and international business networks in the creation of Argentina's corporate networks in the early twentieth century. For example, the largest business group at this time, the Tornquist, while based in Buenos Aires, conducted much of its business with Belgian investors, mostly from Antwerp, as well as other European companies (Gilbert 2001). This group owned seven firms of the top ten in the eigenvector-based ranking, indicating the intensive use of interlocking directorates as a control mechanism.

The betweenness centrality measures reveal the prominence of a second local business group, the Roberts.[6] Unlike Tornquist, it structured investments with minority stakes in several companies. Both groups, however, share a common feature: they served as brokers between local and foreign investors and merchant banks in Argentina's corporate network, such as J. P. Morgan, Rothschild and Baring Brothers.

These two local business groups had diversified profiles, but both had financial business at their core. With their strong international connections, they were key in establishing bridges between the financial markets of Latin America and those of Europe that began in the 1880s (Quennouëlle-Corre and Cassis 2011). By 1923, the owners and managers of these business groups were also participating in the boards of several financial institutions and, as a result, *Banco de Buenos Aires, Banco Italiano y Río de la Plata and Banco Uruguayo* had brokerage roles ranking among the top 10 firms in terms of betweenness centrality. Despite this, commercial banks in Argentina did not play such a significant role in connecting industrial firms in the corporate network, as was the case in many other countries (Davis and Mizruchi 1999). This could be because of the role of private-financial intermediaries and because state-owned banks rarely funded industrial ventures before 1944, when the first national industrial credit bank was established.

We can see that, in 1923, market duality, together with the elevated number of industrial stand-alone and family-owned firms, shaped a rather dispersed network. The MNEs were not yet fully integrated into the interlocking directorates because several had not established subsidiaries in the country (and did not have board or shareholder meetings in the country). Local business groups with diversified profiles, but also a core in the financial industry, represented the center of the corporate network. Most central directors were finance capitalists, members of traditional Argentine families and managers recruited in Europe.

3. CONSOLIDATION AND RESILIENCE OF ARGENTINA'S CORPORATE NETWORK DURING THE "HORIZONTAL" ISI PHASE, 1937–1954

A period of internal and significant adjustment followed the Great Depression. Like all countries involved in the world market, Argentina was deeply affected by both the Depression and World War II. In the increasingly complex global setting, the economy became more closed than in preceding decades. Economic growth rates slowed and manufacturing became the most dynamic productive sector. The collapse of the primary export-led growth process led to the emergence of a new development strategy combining industrialization and increased state intervention. Starting in 1930 both overall economic conditions and state policies (exchange controls, tariff raises) then led to the substitution of local manufacturing of light consumer goods for imports (i.e., the so-called horizontal Import Substitution Industrialization [ISI] stage).

External shocks consolidated the network's core. The number of marginal and isolated firms decreased between 1923 and 1937 as Argentina's corporate networks grew more integrative. The main component increased in size; in both 1937 and 1944, it displayed a relatively stable cohesion characterized by short path lengths between companies (average distance decreased, compared with 1923, to 2.8 in 1937 and 3.15 in 1944) and an 'inner circle' of well-connected directors. The main component density stood at 13% in 1937 and 11% in 1944 (see Appendix I).

These years seem to have marked a turning point for the MNEs' traditional operating schemes and organizational structure, one that had a direct impact on Argentina's corporate network. The new paradigm of economic development (associated with a more active role of the state and the promotion of industrial activities) generated modifications in the MNEs' organizational strategies. In the 1930s, several railway and utility firms established local boards, which resulted in MNEs taking a more important role in the corporate network. This finding is consistent with Lanciotti and Lluch's (2009) recognition of a significant shift in the organizational schemes of foreign companies incorporated in Argentina in the 1930s.

In a context of declining profitability, increasing regulations and intense contract negotiations,[7] many foreign companies not only transformed into Argentine corporations, but also built local boards that included well-connected members of Argentina's traditional elite. This period thus reveals a high share of 'traditional' foreign companies in Argentina's corporate network (e.g., utilities and railroads) directly associated with the previous type of open, primary-export development pattern.[8] We argue that these new boards helped forge/shape reciprocal ties between foreign and local capital. Interlocks signified a sort of 'coalition', aimed at facilitating a protective and collaborative strategy in order to overcome the challenges set by increased regulation and protectionism.

Three measures capture this defensive strategy: average degree, network density and multiple directors. The average degree reveals company dynamism when interacting with others. When all firms have a higher average degree, the network grows denser. The increasing density of the Argentine corporate network in 1937 (13%) is consistent with the growth of the average degree (10.3). Interlockers and big linkers, the 'glue' holding the network together, peaked in 1937 at 18.6%.

The outbreak of World War II strengthened this 'defensive strategy'. A network analysis of 1944 confirms the presence of electricity firms at the core, with railway companies emerging among the members most central to the network (see the Excel file for their betweenness, degree and eigenvector centrality on the website). The latter firms networked more actively, at a time characterized by a profitability crisis and their impending sale to the government. Thus, in 1944, the networking strategies of conflicting sectors stricken by a financial crisis reinforced the network's core.

Considering firms' centrality and directors' profiles, we can confirm the prominence of long-established local groups or members of the so-called 'traditional elite', who connected foreign companies to the local corporate network. From the foreign investors' perspective, the selection of specific types of directors seems to have followed strategic choices. Big linkers (around 6% in 1937 and 1944), such as Roberts, Meynell, Mayer, Sánchez Elía and O'Farrell, helped guarantee the reliability of local ventures in which they were involved. The elite members' personal reputations, as well as their contacts across social and political circles, mitigated the uncertainty involved in doing business in a more complex environment. In 1944, several directors occupied some of the most central government positions; political connections seemed to have grown even more important in 1944 than in 1937.

During the 1930s and 1940s, growing state intervention reshaped the network's core but did not substantially alter the integrative structure of interlocking directorates. Rather, in this historical stage, most interlocking directorates provided a network of communication and coordination for the business community as a means of reducing risk and uncertainty in a changing world. Enduring relationships resulted from actors' strategies to respond to the impact of institutional changes by attempting to preserve the substance of these ties.

A transitional moment between resilience and change occurred in 1954. An analysis of the 1954 network sheds some light on the impact of the Perón government (1945–1955) on Argentina's corporate structure. During this period, a domestic market-oriented economic policy sought to redistribute income in favor of workers and promote industrialization. For that, Perón's government used wartime reserves to pay off overseas debt, nationalize foreign-owned enterprises and subsidize industry and consumer spending (Brennan 2007). Industrial growth had been significant during the war in both the traditional food-processing and newer dynamic sectors, such as textiles and metalworking. In 1945, for the first time in Argentina's history, industry accounted for a greater share of the gross domestic product (GDP) than agriculture.

A combined analysis of the main component evolution and the number of links between 1937 and 1954 reveals two parallel and simultaneous processes. The first can be defined as resilience among the traditional corporate elite. A metric that effectively captures this structural process is the main component, which remained stable between 1937 and 1954 and integrated more than 60% of companies. The increased number of multiple lines in the main component (see Figure 13.2) between 1944 and 1954 also implies stronger ties at the center, or core, of the network. This resilience was associated with the presence of an 'inner circle' of well-connected directors who were able to adapt to and survive (and even benefit from) state interventionism and industrialization policies, at least until the mid-1950s.

The identity of most central corporate actors in this period reveals how traditional local business groups defended, and even reinforced, their local positions. Brokers such as Enrique Roberts and Alejandro Drysdale, the two most central directors in 1954, successfully pursued an impressive networking strategy that enabled them to operate in and adjust to the political and economic setting created by Peronism, while at the same time keeping the clusters of the corporate network bound together. In particular, the Roberts business group used links with its controlled and affiliated firms' boards to incorporate large, traditional British and US companies into Argentina's corporate network (Bozzo and Mendoza 1974).

Another source of network cohesion came from some industrial firms consolidated during the Perón era, which benefited from ISI policies. These companies strategically relied on interlocking directorates to strengthen their collaboration and business control. For example, companies within the Italian-Argentine business network become more relevant in this period; *Banco de Italia y Rio de la Plata, Pirelli, Dalmine* and *Cia. De Fósforos Sudamericana* were among the top 10 firms, according to betweenness centrality measurements.

A second process was occurring alongside the one detailed previously: the progressive corporate elite was fading. Some ties that contributed to network cohesion were destroyed. For example, certain traditional alliances were severely undermined by the nationalization of firms that formerly provided connectivity to the network, such as electrical or railroad companies. By 1954, the network was showing signs of weakness, losing 105 links that had been in place in 1937; a 26% decrease in total ties occurred between 1937 and 1954 (see Appendix I and Figure 13.2). Other strong signs of a loss of cohesiveness include a decreasing average degree, from 6.9 in 1937 to 4 in 1954, a 6% drop in density and the loss of multiple directors between 1944 and 1954.

MNEs' changing role in the corporate network illustrates how the two parallel processes of change and resilience has taken place. Nationalization partly explains why the foreign utility firms lost their centrality in Argentina's corporate network (along with the reorganization of international financial markets in the second post-war period).[9] From 1946 to 1950, the role of MNEs changed significantly. Local firms accounted for 62% of the companies included in our sample, with multinationals dropping to second place (29% of the sample). This finding also supports the idea that the end of horizontal ISI was marked by diminished dependence on foreign capital, which altered the alliances between foreign and local business actors.

At the same time, we can observe the continuity of a model characterized by foreign companies' engagement in Argentina's corporate network using their connections and alliances with traditional Argentine business groups (such as the Robert Group). The few remaining foreign companies operating in nationalized industries continued to network even more actively at board level, as a defensive strategy, in an effort to adapt to a rather unfriendly setting. In 1954, three electrical subsidiaries controlled by the holding companies *Société Financière de Transports et d'Entreprises Industrielles* (SOFINA) and American & Foreign Power Company continued to hold relevant positions at the network's core (according to their eigenvector scores).

There is a limitation within our study concerning the more active role of the state during the Peronism period: the rankings in 1954 do not include complete data for state-owned enterprises (SOEs). We cannot, therefore, clearly establish the role played by SOEs during Peronism. However, the more active role of the state in development strategies is evident in the high centrality of *Banco Hipotecario Nacional*, a state-controlled financial institution, and the mixed-capital society, SOMISA (*Sociedad Mixta Siderúrgica Argentina*), which was created in 1947 to produce steel.

To summarize, the structural measures point to a fragmenting network. This disintegration process began at the periphery of the network, reaching the core of the corporate elite later. These findings support the argument that 1954 marked a transition in which fragmentation had just begun. Changes during the Perón era affected the Argentine corporate network's profile and cohesion (e.g., isolated and marginal firms increased), yet the resilience of the network's core remained. It is directly associated with the existence of an 'inner circle' of well-connected directors who were able to adapt to state interventionism and industrialization policies during the horizontal ISI stage. This relatively enduring cohesiveness requiring a socially interconnected elite that originated during the primary-export phase would fade away in the next period.

4. CORPORATE NETWORKS DURING THE 'VERTICAL' ISI PHASE

The period 1955–1970 featured a new phase in the development strategy. Along with many other countries in Latin America, horizontal ISI was superseded by a phase of 'vertical' ISI in Argentina by the mid-1950s. The emphasis was on internalizing all manufacturing of consumer goods, together with the backward integration of intermediate products and capital goods (Gereffi and Evans 1981; Ocampo and Ros 2011). Policy makers broadened the range of local production in an attempt to solve Argentina's endemic balance of payments deficit (Mallon and Sourrouille 1975).

The changing structure of interlocking directorates reflects these dramatic developments in the economy as a whole. Networks experimented with an almost complete replacement of interlocking directorates and central actors. The percentage of firms in the main component fell to 50%, with isolated and marginal firms increasing by 15% compared to 1954, when they reached almost 70%. Network density fell to 7% (even with the decline in the number of firms in the main component)—a clear sign of the corporate elite's diminishing cohesion.

As the resource dependence theory predicts, broken interlocks due to structural changes were not necessarily replaced by new links (Scott 1985). Instead, the network became less agglomerated and centralized, as measured by average degree and closeness centrality (see the 1970 structural measures in Appendix I). By 1970, the inner circle from the previous stage that consisted of foreign executives, business owners and members of the traditional elite disappeared (except for the Roberts business group) and was not replaced. Thus, the 1970 structure lacked an inner circle as strong as the one in the previous stages (see Figure 13.2).

In this development phase, the investments needed were more technologically sophisticated and capital intensive than those required by horizontal ISI. As a result, MNEs became central to Argentina's industrial development. Political shifts also paved the way for new types of participation for foreign capital.[10] New foreign players and the growth of MNEs that had already been established in Argentina changed the ownership structure of larger corporations. By 1970, around half (53%) of the non-financial companies in our sample were foreign; domestic private companies ranked second.

Board interlocks also were reshaped, largely as a result of the arrival of many multinationals, without simultaneous changes in Argentina's legal system. Six foreign-owned companies were among the twelve most central (by eigenvector) firms (one of which was a joint venture). In terms of betweenness and degree centrality, we find a similar share of foreign firms (see the website). In contrast, the SOEs seem to lack any active networking strategies (with the exception of SOMISA).[11] In this volatile political and economic context, overhauls of SOEs' boards and administrators were frequent, usually due to changes in economic policies or ruling interests. The insular behavior of SOEs could also have been fostered by the troubled institutional environment and the high turnover of their directors.

The isolation of SOEs did not mean that state policies had no impact on the Argentinean corporate network. In 1970, companies operating in sectors established as strategic by the government stood at the network's core. Two-thirds of the most central firms (by degree) were associated with sectors promoted by official industrial policies. Our data suggest that the largest companies in the most dynamic industries may have set out to strategically forge ties in order to advance their economic expansion plans. Similar trends have marked other countries. With the emergence of new industries, companies tend to foster cross-organizational links to secure resources, including information, capital and know-how (Powell et al. 2005). Moreover, state-owned banks provided the main source of industrial credit for the largest (local and foreign) firms in the economy.[12] Private banks did not play a significant role in the corporate network during this vertical ISI stage.

In this phase, characterized as it was by strong state intervention and dominated by MNEs, external directors prevailed. MNEs promoted—through the new, prevalent type of interlocking directorate—the inclusion of well-connected legal and financial advisors as directors: 12 of the top 16 directors by betweenness centrality were lawyers, engineers or certified public accountants. These actors knew how to successfully navigate the changing conditions created by political and economic instability, powerful labor unions, new economic regulations, stabilization-oriented economic plans and idiosyncratic credit allocation practices (Guillen 2000).[13]

5. CORPORATE NETWORKS IN THE 1990S: TOWARD FRAGMENTATION

By the early 1970s, vertical ISI alone proved incapable of resolving the problem of imbalanced economic relations. From a macro-economic perspective, Argentina underwent periodical crises with high inflation rates (and two hyperinflations[14]), alternating among populist, development, Keynesian and liberal policies, while enforcing orthodox and heterodox stabilization programs (Damill and Frenkel 1996). Constant changes in the 'rules of the game' derived from severe underlying political and social conflicts that translated into a succession of opposing civilian and military governments. During the 1980s, the Argentine economy performed at its worst in the post-World War II period.

In this context, the corporate network's main component suffered a substantial reduction, down to only 18% of Argentina's largest firms. This period shows the greatest percentage of isolated and marginal companies (82%). However, density was not negligible in the main component (12.3%) and the average degree of 3.9 resembled that of 1970. The network's main component may have, in fact, prevented its total disintegration (see Appendix I).

The military regimes and the democratic government elected in 1983 made a 'silent bet' on large local capital.[15] These policies did not provide protection for local capital in general, but they do seem to have provided greater incentives for the largest local business groups. Coupled with a troubled political and economic environment, several MNEs decided to withdraw from Argentina, a process that reconfigured the business alliances and contributed to the strengthening of the centrality of some new local business groups (Schvarzer 1983).

As a consequence, by 1990, the MNEs had lost their dominance, though we also note that the remaining MNEs engaged in an active networking strategy. The centrality of some foreign firms in 1990 (none of which were the same as the top centrality firms in 1970) can thus be largely explained by the type of interlocking directorates created by well-trained, well-connected Argentine managers in US companies who sat on the boards of other MNEs.

The changes in the profile of most central directors illustrates the alliances that prevailed in this capitalistic scheme, characterized by an active state that used inflation as a 'tax' to extract income from society, relying on public contracts as instruments to redistribute wealth to certain private-sector actors. As we have noted, an array of 'new', local, diversified business groups in assisted sectors increased in size and came to form the network's core. Previous literature in this area has emphasized how these groups benefited from investment and export promotion schemes, as well as market reserves, better access to public purchases, and contracts favored by state policies (Bisang 1999). We also find that some of them collaborated and developed active board relationships as part of their business strategies.

During the 1970s and 1980s, the state expanded its role as regulator, business owner and distributor (Belini and Rougier 2008). Our study includes information about most of the largest SOEs by 1990,[16] but it appears that the effect of SOEs on network structures was negligible. Just as in 1970, we detect a pattern of insular behavior by SOEs and a tendency to create few links with the private sector (local or foreign). SOEs in Argentina did not play a significant role in connecting firms, similar to the case in Italy (Rinaldi and Vasta, this volume).

Argentina's institutional uncertainty and turbulent environment became a key component in business behavior, because individual businesses were affected differently by the measures taken by successive governments or by a single government's successive economic ministers. In this troubled context, by 1990, big linkers had dropped to 1.6% and interlockers to 4.7%, implying an endogenous response to macroeconomic instability. However, this constant restructuring still did not lead to total disintegration. Corporate networks showed some flexibility, adjusting to a troubled, dynamic external environment. So, in a manner similar to 1970, firms that matched the type of capitalism that prevailed were able to survive and remain in the core of the network.

6. THE LIBERAL ERA: THE DISINTEGRATION OF CORPORATE NETWORKS, 2000

In the year 2000, Argentina's corporate network crumbled. The network's main component had disintegrated completely, leaving a collection of small, ownership-related clusters (the largest included only 5% of firms) and several isolated firms. At this stage, the few links that remained were facilitated by shared ownership.

Throughout the 1990s, Argentina undertook a wide range of market-oriented reforms, characterized by macroeconomic stabilization, financial liberalization, privatization and deregulation (Heymann and Kosacoff 2000). If industrialization and state intervention had been at the core of the previous development phase, the liberalization of market forces took on that role under the new paradigm (Ocampo and Ros 2011). As part of these reforms, the MNEs recovered—for the third time—their centrality in Argentina's economy, accounting for almost 70% of the top 100 companies in the 2000 sample.[17] Formerly large, diversified domestic groups lost their centrality, however.

The de-cohesion process was driven once again by external shocks, principally associated with ownership structure changes but also including the types of directors taken on. Most central firms' operations (according to both measures) matched the predominant foreign direct investment (FDI) trends of the 1990s, focusing on the service industries and public utilities privatized by the Menem administration. Resource-seeking flows targeted natural resources (e.g., Repsol, controlling companies like Astra and EG3 that formerly belonged to local groups). Most FDI into Argentina in the

1990s sought to purchase existing companies,[18] while mergers and acquisitions were common among domestic companies.

Few multiple board appointments took place in 2000; in other words, the massive transference of local firms did not promote local-international interlocks or reconfigured alliances between local and foreign capital (or among MNEs). Rather, the network was bound by weak ties. The small list of big linkers (1.9%) indicates that boards primarily appointed 'inside' directors. The central directors' profiles also suggest that the active market for corporate takeovers in the 1990s may have created an atmosphere conducive to diminished corporate (and elite) solidarity and uncooperative behavior (Davis and Thompson 1994).

Contrary to their previous practices, MNEs did not choose professionals or traditional MNE top managers as linkers. Their behavior might have been influenced by new regulations, or lawsuits, regarding directors' liability. By the end of the twentieth century, several sources refer to a growing concern among attorneys about their exposure when serving on boards. Tax authorities and labor courts contemplated extending liability for companies' tax and labor law violations to all board members (Loos 2010). These legal concerns may well have undermined the social status and prestige associated with multiple board memberships.

The process of the disintegration of the Argentinean interlocking directorates is not unique. Schifeling and Mizruchi (this volume) and Chu (2012) show that interlocking directorates in the US have suffered a process of de-cohesion and the disappearance of the inner circle of well-connected directors. In Argentina, however, the fragmentation process started prematurely and has been consistently stronger.

Thus, in the year 2000, we find extreme fragmentation in Argentina's corporate world. By this time, following a new (and radical) structural reconfiguration of local capitalism, uncooperative behavior prevailed. Business people became less prominent as linkers, reflecting the change in the corporate leaders' inner circle. We have proposed that the disappearance of the business (and social) elite in the network's core and the prevalence of inside directors in board appointments helps to explain the extreme fragmentation of Argentina's corporate world. Another important factor relates to the prominence of MNEs. In contrast to the claims of Stark and Vedres (2006) regarding Hungary, the largest MNEs in Argentina had no need to foster alliances with local firms in this liberal phase.

7. FINAL REMARKS

We have described the evolution of corporate networks in Argentina between 1923 and 2000. Our analysis emphasized how the economic and institutional environment in which firms are embedded affects their corporate network structure (Granovetter 1985). Interfirm relations are affected by both external and internal processes. The development model associated with the first global economy created resilient business networks with a high degree of interaction between local and foreign firms in Argentina. The sub-period of 1937 to 1944 was crucial in terms of integration and the creation of business coordination mechanisms through a highly connected core. These links survived until the end of the first stage of the inward development model (horizontal ISI). In contrast, during the 1990s, the so-called second global economy created a completely different network configuration in Argentina, characterized by a high degree of fragmentation and limited interconnections between local and international networks.

Over the long term, Argentina's corporate network experienced a progressive (but not linear) social capital destruction process (Bourdieu 1986; Burt 2000; Coleman 1988; Windolf 2002). This finding is meaningful, in that many studies of economic development suggest that the potential for economic transformation also depends on the business's capacity for collective action (Haggard, Maxfield, and Schneider 1997). If informal ties, as interlocking directorates, contribute to the creation of trust and reciprocity, the highly fragmented Argentinean business corporate networks would point to their incapacity to coordinate activities, which in the long run might, in combination with other factors, affect the pursuit of stable, long-term economic growth.

Another striking finding relates to the multiple, changing meaning of interlocking directorates in a historical perspective. During the first half of the twentieth century, interlocking directorates provided communication networks and coordination mechanisms between foreign companies (mainly, utilities and railroad companies) and traditional business elite members in a changing world. More active state intervention strengthened the 'axes of solidarity' between financial capitalists and diversified business groups (Brookfield et al. 2012). In the second half of the century, corporate networks exhibited great plasticity, undergoing substantial 'makeovers' in benchmark years, as a result of external shocks imposed by structural transformations undergone by local capitalism, as well as changes in the shape of the corporate leaders' inner circles. By the end of the twentieth century, interlocking directorates had lost their possible significance as a resource completely. We consider that these processes were directly associated with state-enforced economic policies—particularly the shifting roles of multinationals at different times. Therefore, our findings support our proposition that the character of the business community can be reshaped by state policies, which affects the character of government-business ties, as well as the nature of the corporate network.

NOTES

1. Tamara Van Hemelryck's excellent research assistance is gratefully acknowledged. We thank María Mercedes Dalla Vía, Florencia Prina and Natalia Bisang for their data collection assistance. Our gratitude also extends to our colleagues, who generously contributed to this study: José Armelini, María

Inés Barbero, Carlos Eschoyez, Norma Lanciotti, Graciela Mateo, Hugo Mondino, Patricia Olguín, Graciela Olivera, Andrés Regalsky, Cintia Russo, Elena Salerno, Jorge Waddell, Cristina Wirth and Jorge Yeroncich. We also thank the following institutions and their staff: Biblioteca de la Bolsa de Comercio de Buenos Aires, Inspección General de Justicia, Boletín Oficial de la República Argentina (Juan Ignacio Fernández and Natalia Yoma Auerbach), Banco Central de la República Argentina (Mariano Iglesias and Patricia León), Banco de la Provincia de Buenos Aires (Juan Pablo di Matteo), Biblioteca CDI-Ministerio de Economía de la República Argentina, Imprenta Provincial-Boletín Oficial de la Provincia de Santa Fe, Nuevo Banco de Santa Fe, Banco Residual and Fundación Banco de Santa Fe.
2. This approach considers important external constrains and policy regimes that govern the nexus between domestic and international markets. The models include trade and exchange rate policies, as well as regulations governing foreign direct investment and borrowing, which are the primary objects of conflict in domestic coalitions and bureaucracies (Haggard 1989). As Scott (1985) notes, the study of interlocks can illuminate the consequences of state interventions.
3. The interwar period proved a crucial phase for foreign investments. Both destinations and origins of foreign capital changed dramatically, and the US became Argentina's leading capital supplier.
4. Foreign direct investment (FDI) refers to an investment in a foreign firm that involves managerial control. Our definition of FDI thus includes three types of companies: typical multinationals that establish branch offices or affiliates abroad, free-standing companies specifically created to operate in the host economies, and foreign-owned companies incorporated in Argentina to conduct business unrelated to competitive advantages acquired in their homelands (Lanciotti and Lluch 2009).
5. The term 'business group' has no unique meaning. In this chapter, we adopt the definition provided by Khanna and Yafeh (2007), who view groups as sets of legally independent companies operating across (often unrelated) industries and bound together by persistent formal and informal ties.
6. Originally, the group was organized around the individual firm Roberts, Leng & Co. It was renamed Roberts, Meynell & Co. in 1936, which served as the representative of J. P. Morgan & Co. in Argentina.
7. Local currency devaluations, the introduction of exchange controls, and restrictions on foreign currency remittance all had negative impacts on foreign companies' returns in the 1930s.
8. For example, in 1937, amid contract renegotiations and high tensions, electrical companies greatly increased their centrality. See the Appendix on the website.
9. However, not all foreign utility companies were nationalized, and foreign companies were not formally discriminated once they had been granted operations permission.
10. This process climaxed during the Frondizi administration (1958–1962). Act 14,780, related to FDI, passed in 1958 with extremely favorable terms for MNEs.
11. We have information about seven of the largest industrial and public utility SOEs and ten state-owned banks in our database. We lack information about ENTEL and *Gas del Estado* because their annual reports did not provide information about their authorities or board composition.
12. Leading instruments included long-term facilities granted by *Banco Nacional de Desarrollo* (BANADE) and international financial institutions' loans (e.g., *Banco Interamericano de Desarrollo*), guaranteed by the state through BANADE (Barbero and Rocchi 2003; Rougier 2004).

13. These agents maintained low profiles in late 1960—intentionally so later, as political violence grew. During the late 1960s and early 1970s, foreign companies and executives were especially targeted by guerrilla groups that kidnapped prominent businesspeople, asking for large ransoms.
14. In 1986, Argentina's annual inflation rate climbed to 627%. It soared to a record high of 3,080% in 1989 (from December 1988 to December 1989, inflation almost reached 5,000%).
15. For example, in 1966, Dow Chemical submitted a project for a petrochemical hub in Bahía Blanca, but the plan caused so much resistance and debate—on account of Dow's foreign firm status—that the state decided to embark on the project on its own, partnering with national companies (López 2011).
16. Eighteen SOEs appeared in the top 100 ranking of *Revista Mercado*. We have data on 12. Some of these firms (e.g., *Gas del Estado, Fabricaciones Militares*) had a general manager, while others had initiated privatization processes and featured only an intervening actor.
17. The FDI legislation was amended in 1989 to repeal any remaining regulations. Argentina now imposes nearly no restrictions or differential rules on foreign companies' operations.
18. In the 1990s, FDI in Argentina (and around the world, except for Asia) tended to lean toward mergers and acquisitions of both public and private companies, which accounted for 60% of incoming flows in 1992–2000.

REFERENCES

Barbero, María Inés. 2011. "Los Grupos Económicos en la Argentina: Una Perspectiva de Largo Plazo (siglos XIX y XX)." In *El Impacto Histórico de la Globalización en Argentina y Chile*, edited by Geoffrey Jones and Andrea Lluch, 1–37. Buenos Aires: Editorial Temas.

Barbero, María Inés, and Fernando Rocchi. 2003. "Industry." In *The New Economic History in Argentina*, edited by Gerardo Della Paolera and Alan Taylor, 261–294. Cambridge: Cambridge University Press.

Belini, Claudio, and Marcelo Rougier. 2008. *El Estado Empresario en la Industria Argentina*. Buenos Aires: Manantial.

Bisang, Roberto. 1999. "La Estructura y Dinámica de los Conglomerados Económicos en la Argentina." In *Grandes Empresas y Grupos Industriales Latinoamericanos*, edited by Wilson Peres, 81–154. Siglo XXI/CEPAL: Mexico.

Bourdieu, Pierre. 1986. "The Forms of Capital." In *Handbook of Theory and Research for the Sociology of Education*, edited by John G. Richardson, 242–258. Westport, CT: Greenwood Press.

Boyd, Brian. 1990. "Corporate Linkages and Organizational Environment: A Test of the Resource Dependence Model." *Strategic Management Journal* 11 (6): 419–430.

Bozzo, Rubén, and Horacio Mendoza. 1974. "Grupo Roberts." *Realidad Económica* 18: 50–63.

Brennan, James. 2007. "Prolegomenon to Neoliberalism: The Political Economy of Populist Argentina." *Latin American Perspectives* 34: 49–66.

Brookfield, Jon, Sea-Jin Chang, Israel Drori, Shmuel Ellis, Sergio G. Lazzarini, Joran I. Siegel, and Juan P. von Bernath Bardina. 2012. "Liberalization, Network Dynamics, and Business Groups." In *The Small Worlds of Corporate Governance*, edited by Bruce Kogut, 77–115. MIT Press.

Burt, Ronald. 2000. "The Network Structure of Social Capital." In *Research in Organizational Behavior*, edited by Barry M. Staw and Robert I. Sutton, 345–423. New York: Elsevier.

Chang, Ha-Joon, and Peter Evans. 2005. "The Role of Institutions in Economic Change." In *Reimagining Growth*, edited by Gary A. Dymski and Silvana De Paula, 99–129. London: Zed Press.

Chu, Johan S. G., and Davis, Gerald F., Who Killed the Inner Circle? The Collapse of the American Corporate Interlock Network (September 11, 2013). Retrieved June 7, 2014. Available at SSRN: http://ssrn.com/abstract=2061113 or http://dx.doi.org/10.2139/ssrn.2061113.

Coleman, James S. 1988. "Social Capital in the Creation of Human Capital." *American Journal of Sociology* 94: 95–121.

Damill, Mario, and Roberto Frenkel. 1996. "Democratic Restoration and Economic Policy: Argentina 1984–91." In *Economic Policy and the Transition to Democracy: the Latin American Experience*, edited by Juan A. Morales and Gary McMahon, 49–111. London: IDRC-MacMillan Press.

Davis, Gerald F., and Mark Mizruchi. 1999. "The Money Center Cannot Hold: Commercial Banks in the U.S. System of Corporate Governance." *Administrative Science Quarterly* 44: 215–239.

Davis, Gerald F., and Tracy A. Thompson. 1994. "A Social Movement Perspective on Corporate Control." *Administrative Science Quarterly* 39: 141–173.

Gereffi, Gary, and Peter Evans. 1981. "Transnational Corporations, Dependent Development, and State Policy in the Semiperiphery: A Comparison of Brazil and Mexico." *Latin American Research Review* 16 (3): 31–64.

Gilbert, Jorge. 2001. "Empresario y Empresa en la Argentina Moderna. El grupo Tornquist 1873–1930." Unpublished M.A. thesis, Universidad de San Andrés.

Granovetter, Mark. 1985. "Economic Action and Social Structure: the Problem of Embeddedness." *American Journal of Sociology* 91: 481–493.

Guillén, Mauro. 2000. "Business Groups in Emerging Economies: A Resource-Based View." *Academy of Management Journal* 43 (3): 362–380.

Haggard, Stephan. 1989. "The Political Economy of Foreign Direct Investment in Latin America." *Latin American Research Review* 24 (1): 184–208.

Haggard, Stephan, Sylvia Maxfield, and Ben R. Schneider. 1997. "Alternative Theories of Business and Business–State Relations." In *Business and the State in Developing Countries*, edited by Sylvia Maxfield and Ben R. Schneider, 36–60. Ithaca, NY: Cornell University Press.

Heymann, Daniel, and Bernardo Kosacoff, eds. 2000. *La Argentina de los Noventa: Desempeño Económico en un Contexto de Reformas*. Buenos Aires: CEPAL-Eudeba.

Khanna, Tarun, and Yishay Yafeh. 2007. "Business Groups in Emerging Markets: Paragons or Parasites?" *Journal of Economic Literature* XLV: 331–372.

Kogut, Bruce. 2012. *The Small Worlds of Corporate Governance*. Cambridge, MA: MIT Press.

Lanciotti, Norma, and Andrea Lluch. 2009. "Foreign Direct Investment in Argentina: Timing of Entry and Business Activities of Foreign Companies (1860–1950)." *Entreprises et Histoire* 54 (1): 37–66.

Lluch, Andrea, and Erica Salvaj. 2012. "Fragmentación del Empresariado en la Época de la Industrialización por Sustitución de Importaciones (ISI) en la Argentina: Una Aproximación desde el Estudio de la Red Corporativa (1954–1970)." *Apuntes, Revista de Ciencias Sociales* XXXIX (70): 135–166.

Loos, Alexander. 2010. *Directors Liability: A Worldwide Review*. 2nd ed. Kluwer Law International BV. The Netherlands: International Bar Association Series.

López, Andrés. 2011. "Las Empresas Transnacionales en Argentina: del Modelo Agroexportador a las Reformas Estructurales." In *El Impacto Histórico de La Globalización en Argentina y Chile: Empresas y Empresarios*, edited by Geoffrey Jones and Andrea Lluch, 101–131. Buenos Aires: Editorial Temas.

Mallon, Richard D., and Juan V. Sourrouille. 1975. *La Política Económica en una Sociedad Conflictiva*. Buenos Aires: Amorrortu.
Maxfield, Silvia, and Ben R. Schneider, eds. 1997. *Business and the State in Developing Countries*. Ithaca, NY: Cornell University Press.
Mizruchi, Mark. 1996. "What Do Interlocks Do? An Analysis, Critique, and Assessment of Research on Interlocking Directorates." *Annual Review of Sociology* 22: 271–298.
Nollert, Michael. 2005. "Transnational Corporate Ties: A Synopsis of Theories and Empirical Findings." *Journal of World-Systems Research* XI (2): 289– 314.
Ocampo, Jose A., and Jaime Ros. 2011. "Shifting Paradigms in Latin America's Economic Development." In *The Oxford Handbook of Latin American Economics*, edited by Jose A. Ocampo and Jaime Ros, 3–25. Oxford: Oxford University Press.
Pfeffer, Jeffrey, and Gerald R. Salancik. 1978. *The External Control of Organizations: A Resource Dependence Perspective*. New York: Harper and Row.
Powell, Walter W., Douglas R. White, Kenneth W. Koput, and Jason Owen-Smith. 2005. "Network Dynamics and Field Evolution: The Growth of Interorganizational Collaboration in the Life Science." *American Journal of Sociology* 110 (4): 1132–1205.
Quennouëlle-Corre, Laure, and Youssef Cassis, eds. 2011. *Financial Centres and International Capital Flows in the Nineteenth and Twentieth Centuries*. Oxford: Oxford University Press.
Rougier, Marcelo. 2004. *Industria, Finanzas e Instituciones en la Argentina. La Experiencia del Banco Nacional de Desarrollo, 1967–1976*. Universidad Nacional de Quilmes: Bernal.
Schvarzer, Jorge. 1983. "Cambios en el Liderazgo Industrial en el Período de Martinez de Hoz." *Desarrollo Económico* 23 (October-December): 395–422.
Scott, John. 1985. "Theoretical Framework and Research Design." In *Networks of Corporate Power*, edited by Frans Stokman, Rolf Ziegler, and John Scott, 1–19. Cambridge: Polity Press.
Stark, David, and Balazs Vedres. 2006. "Social Times of Network Spaces: Network Sequences and Foreign Investment in Hungary." *American Journal of Sociology* 111 (5): 1367–1411.
Windolf, Paul. 2002. *Corporate Networks in Europe and the United States*. New York: Oxford University Press.

14 Between State Power and Familism
The Directorate Interlock Network in Taiwan throughout the Twentieth Century

Zong-Rong Lee and Thijs A. Velema

1. INTRODUCTION

The research literature on the economic development of East Asia and Taiwan has been dominated by two major theories concerning the analysis of markets: development theory, a concept from political economy, and a vision involving primordial social networks that emphasizes 'familism'. East Asian developmental state theory stresses the crucial role of the state in integrating and managing market forces to bring about successful economic development (Johnson 1982; Amsden 1985; Wade 1990; Evans 1995). The school of thought that takes Chinese 'familism' as the core factor in explaining economic growth downplays the importance of state power, while emphasizing social and cultural causes of East Asia's rapid economic growth (Hamilton and Biggart 1988). The prevalence of family businesses in Taiwan has been documented by scholars from different academic disciplines, and the prominence of family firms in the market has marked Taiwan as a typical case of *family capitalism* (Hamilton 1997). Although different schools of thought attribute Taiwan's economic development to the intervention of the state on the one hand, and to corporate networks on the other, few people have attempted to either integrate or compare the effectiveness of these two different perspectives. This raises a thought-provoking question. If markets, as current scholars indicate, are dominated by the social-structural mechanisms of networks, then, in a market in which state power intervenes heavily, how does state power interact with these social mechanisms? This is clearly a question that the existing literature does not answer in any great detail.

This question is particularly interesting because of the prominence of family businesses in Taiwan's economy and the turbulent development of the State of Taiwan. Just as many Asian countries experienced a period of foreign rule over either their entire territory or parts of it during the twentieth century; a foreign power imposed itself on Taiwan twice during the twentieth century. Japan gained control over the island after the Sino-Japanese war in 1895 and ruled until its defeat in World War II, while the nationalist Kuomintang (KMT) government imposed its rule over Taiwan after its retreat from Mainland China in 1949. While the island has gone through such disruptive political turmoil in the past century, family businesses are still the dominant force promoting economic progress. This study examines how the ruling state and cultural practices of 'familism' interplayed to shape the network of interlocking directorates in Taiwan throughout the twentieth century.

We envisage the politicized market area as a network, in which corporate and state actors are entangled in power relationships. We then map the intercorporate directorate networks between the state-owned and largest private firms in Taiwan at eight different years throughout the twentieth century. Our approach differs from other studies to the embeddedness of the public sector with private firms, which have mostly been based on the theory of embedded autonomy proposed by Peter Evans (1995). Our methodological approach is grounded in studies that focus on the interorganizational positions occupied by the state and private organizations (Laumann and Knoke 1987; Fernandez and Gould 1993; Heinz 1993; Padgett and Ansell 1993). This allows for the unpacking of state-business embeddedness into interorganizational meso-level measurements, and a more delicate understanding of the power relations between the state and the major corporations in an economy.

The empirical analysis in this chapter is based on a comprehensive dataset that includes major firms active in the pre-war colonial period, and all listed companies in the post-war period for eight benchmark years from 1941 to 2003 (i.e., 1941, 1962, 1969, 1982, 1988, 1992, 1998 and 2003). The information was retrieved from company directories published in different periods. In order to gauge the extent to which the public sector is related to private firms (especially for the post-war period), data on state-owned companies was also comprehensively covered. This was obtained through the Annual Report on State-owned Enterprise, published by the Ministry of Economic Affairs.[1]

We report descriptive statistics of the Taiwanese network of directorate interlocks in the eight selected years throughout the twentieth century in Table 14.1. Two factors stand out in all eight periods. First, following rapid economic growth, the number of firms increased throughout the second half of the twentieth century, with the appearance of new market actors becoming especially rapid after 1992. Second, throughout all eight periods, the network shows a relatively high number of multiple ties, which bind firms through more than one shared director. This is a very particular feature of the Taiwanese economy, as multiple ties are much higher than in other economies. In this chapter, we argue that the high level of multiple ties observed in Taiwan is a reflection of the dominant state and the cultural practices of 'familism', both of which help firms to navigate a highly politicized market and shape inter-firm relations with strong and trusted family ties.

Based on the data in Table 14.1, the Taiwanese twentieth century can be divided into three periods. Although each period has distinct characteristics,

Table 14.1 Descriptive Statistics Taiwan Directorate Interlock Network, 1941–2003

	Taiwan 1941	Taiwan 1962	Taiwan 1969	Taiwan 1982	Taiwan 1988	Taiwan 1992	Taiwan 1998	Taiwan 2003	Germany 1993	England 1993	France 1993	Switzerland 1995	Holland 1995	USA 1997
Number of firms	168	21	28	80	99	220	280	314	300	300	374	300	300	481
Number of directors	1326	411	551	1426	1667	2827	3038	3432	-	-	-	-	-	-
Average size board of directors	10.53	19.57	19.67	17.83	16.84	12.85	10.85	10.93	-	-	-	-	-	-
Interlocking directorates	1193	144	464	950	1308	1862	1404	2694	4228	696	2792	1267	1298	3428
Interlocking directorates dichotomized	864	100	228	570	878	1094	866	1650	3198	632	2224	982	1144	3196
Mean number of ties per firm	14.20	7.20	18.56	15.07	16.15	12.50	7.09	8.69	15.30	3.41	13.10	4.90	5.90	8.32
Mean number of reachable firms	10.29	5.00	9.12	9.05	10.80	7.34	4.37	5.32	11.60	3.10	10.40	3.80	5.20	7.60
Percentage of multiple ties	27.58	30.60	50.90	40.00	32.87	41.20	38.30	38.30	24.40	9.20	20.30	22.50	11.70	6.80
Percentage of firms in main component	89.0	95.2	89.3	76.3	76.8	60.5	62.5	98.4	89.7	63.0	52.9	80.1	72.0	83.0
Percentage of isolates	9.0	4.8	10.7	21.2	18.1	32.3	29.3	0.6	8.0	32.0	43.1	13.7	26.7	14.3
Percentage firms in particularistic ties	2.4	0.0	0.0	2.5	5.1	7.3	8.2	0.0	2.3	5.0	4.0	6.2	1.3	2.7
Mean degree centrality	7.82	51.10	35.30	25.80	24.10	17.50	6.10	3.78	8.00	1.53	13.20	49.00	78.00	4.60

Note:
a: Percentage of multiple ties = (interlocking directorates – Interlocking directorates dichotomized) / interlocking directorates
b: Particularistic ties = 1 – (percentage of firms in main component – percentage of isolates)
c: Mean number of ties per firms is only calculated over the non-isolated firms = (interlocking directorates dichotomized / companies with ties)
d: Mean number of reachable firms = (interlocking directorates dichotomized / number of firms)

Data on all Western industrialized nations is based on Windolf (2002) we also see continuity throughout the three periods. The first is the Japanese colonial period spanning the first half of the twentieth century. The colonial economy in 1941 is characterized by a high number of companies and directors, but a limited size of the average board of a company. Centrality is also relatively low in this period. Comparable figures are only reached again in the Taiwanese network in the 1990s. However, multiple ties and the share of firms in the main component in this period are relatively high, and remained so when the KMT took over after the war.

The second period is the era of widespread KMT state involvement, and runs from 1960 until the mid-1980s. Throughout this period, the level of multiple relations is very high, implying a very tightly linked and dense network. Even though almost all companies are linked in the main component in the 1960s, this percentage started to decline after 1969. The network became more exclusive over time, as a small core of tightly interlinked companies came to dominate the network. As we shall see, state-owned enterprises played an important role in this period, resembling corporatist economic systems. The dominant state, guiding economic growth, built a highly centralized network with a strong interlinked and exclusive core. In this network, public companies dominated and supervised the activities of other economic actors, while the state acted as 'patron' to the largest firms in the economy. The third phase of economic liberalization took root in the 1980s. The state gave up its dominant role in the economy, freeing up space for private companies and business groups to take over. During this period, the number of companies grew spectacularly, while the number of multiple relations declined. The main component came to include more firms, while centralization declined. The network in which the KMT state played such a dominant role dissolved over time.

In this chapter, we identify that during the Japanese colonial era, and the early period of KMT rule, the state was heavily involved in the network of interlocking directors, so as to influence economic development to its benefit. With the advent of liberalization and democratization in the 1980s, the Taiwanese state gave up its leading role in the network, allowing 'familism' to become the most important driver of the network of big business in Taiwan. We will discuss the role of the state in these three periods in the sections that follow, starting with the Japanese colonial period, after which the network under early KMT rule will be discussed. Following this, we will focus on the directorate interlock network in the period of liberalization starting in the 1980s. Section 7 concludes.

2. NETWORKS OF DIRECTORS UNDER COLONIAL RULE, 1940S

Taiwan became a Japanese colony after the first Sino-Japanese war of 1894 and 1895 and remained under Japanese rule until the end of World War II. The colonial period, spanning half a century, can roughly be divided into two periods. The first runs from 1895 to around 1930 and is characterized by the development of Taiwan's agricultural base (Ho 1984; Gold 1988a; Tu and Li 1999; Ka 2008). The colonial government developed Taiwan's agricultural base to ease the pressure on food prices and to free up labor for the industrial sector in Japan; it also developed the institutional, legal and technical environment needed for large-scale agricultural production. Taiwan produced various agricultural products for the Japanese market, but sugar was the most important.

The second period started around 1930 and ended with the surrender of the Japanese empire in 1945. Industrialization of the economy was a key priority for the colonial government in this period due to two factors (Gold 1988a; Tu and Li 1999). First, the militarization of Japan led the government to contribute to the Japanese war effort by developing industries that catered to the needs of the Japanese army. Military demand for various products became especially pressing after Japan invaded China in 1937. Second, the Southern Expansion Doctrine altered Taiwan's role in the empire, as Japanese possessions in the South Pacific were better situated for sugar and agricultural production. The colonial government wanted to industrialize the economy to compensate for agricultural production shifting to the South Pacific. These two periods left their mark on the colonial economy around 1941 in the form of a developed agricultural sector dominated by sugar producers and fledging industries in various fields. This economic situation provided the background in which the interlocking directorate network was formed.

The network of interlocking directorates is characterized by firms maintaining ties to many different companies, multiple ties between dyads of firms, a high level of inclusion and a low level of centralization. Table 14.1 shows the largest 168 companies employing 1,326 directors, with 1,193 interlocking directors. Some firms have more than 14 ties to other companies, with which they can reach a little over 10 firms. This means that between a quarter and a third of all ties are multiple ties—ties that link two firms through more than one director. Such a high frequency of multiple ties might indicate the presence of business groups—or *zaibatsu*—in the network, which coordinate the actions of member firms. If such groups were present, they are not sharply delimited. The network is very inclusive, with almost 90% of all firms connected to the main component. Isolated firms and dyads of companies make up a mere 10%. Moreover, a low level of centrality signals that the network is not particularly concentrated on one firm or group of firms, so that firms are relatively evenly connected.

The colonial government was involved in the composition of this inclusive and decentralized network by shaping the economic conditions in which the interlocking directorates developed in three ways. First, the government selected certain industries that it promoted through policies of improving the infrastructural, legal and financial environments. For example, the government played a crucial role in the development of

Japanese-owned sugar mills (Tu and Li 1999; Ka 2008). The government invested heavily in the infrastructure needed for the transportation of sugar cane to the sugar refineries and of refined sugar to markets in Japan. The Taiwan Bank was established to provide firms in selected industries with easy access to capital. This gave sugar mills the means to expand their operations rapidly, and to acquire non-Japanese sugar mills as their production grew.

From the 1930s onwards, the colonial government sought to develop industries that produced for the needs of the Japanese military by direct investments and encouraging companies to invest in such industries (Tu and Li 1999). The intensity of these efforts increased after 1937, when the Japanese invasion of China signaled the second Sino-Japanese war. Japanese military action in China, Southeast Asia and the Pacific further intensified the economic policy of the colonial government. The 1930s saw the establishment of firms in new sectors, such as textiles, electronics and chemicals. These firms grew rapidly and, by 1941, occupied central positions within the network, sharing directors with a large number of other firms.

Marginalizing certain unwanted producers and industries was a second way in which the colonial government shaped Taiwan's economy. The highly beneficial policies gave privilege to firms in Japanese hands, while indigenous entrepreneurs were deprived of such favorable opportunities. In most cases, Taiwanese firms would just simply not be recognized under Japanese merchant law (Gold 1988a; Kao 2005) and, consequently, not qualify for preferential treatment. Wealth and economic opportunities became increasingly concentrated in the hands of Japanese businesses, excluding the local Taiwanese population (see Myers and Saburo 1984; Morgan and Liu 2007). Many of the Taiwanese firms were forced out of existence or subsumed into Japanese-owned firms through mergers and acquisitions (see Tu and Li 1999).

Notwithstanding policies favoring Japanese businesses at the expense of Taiwanese commercial establishments, some Taiwanese managed to become successful entrepreneurs during the Japanese colonial period, laying the foundations of some of the family business groups that would dominate Taiwan's economy in the post-World War II era (Numazaki 1986; Gold 1988a; Chung 2006). Some of these entrepreneurs started out as small merchants and managed to grow their businesses, but most of them were landlords who developed their industrial assets based on their landholdings. Their success was built on collaborating with the colonial government, allowing them to become part of the colonial elite. By co-opting these landlords and entrepreneurs, the government prevented them forming an opposition against colonial rule. Moreover, their efforts now contributed to the economic and industrial development of Taiwan, and they served as examples for their compatriots, showing that it was possible for the Taiwanese to be successful in the Japanese colonial empire. Those entrepreneurs maintained their wealth in the colonial era, which gave them a strong position to continue their entrepreneurial endeavors after the war.

The third way in which the colonial government affected the interlocking directorate network was by making direct investments in the sectors it had selected for development and actively lobbying companies based in Japan and Taiwan to invest in those same industries. These lobbying efforts were mostly directed at the *zaibatsu*, the largest companies in Japan (Gold 1988a; Tu and Li 1999). To this end, the colonial government funded the Taiwan Development Company (TDC), which was responsible for investing in government-selected industries (Chu 2005). The TDC was one of the most central firms in the colonial economy. Sometimes, the TDC was the sole investor in a company, but much more often, it brought together a group of investors to fund a company. By 1941, the TDC held shares in nine other major companies. Its directors were involved in 11 other firms as shareholders and sat on the board of 33 other companies. Moreover, the TDC acted to build personal networks among business leaders, government officials and the military elite. The existence of the TDC allowed the government to exert considerable and direct influence on the colonial economy through investments in other firms and its directors' engagement in the activities of other firms, either through direct investments or by sitting on their boards. The colonial government successfully persuaded *zaibatsu* and other firms to develop their activities in Taiwan, giving them a considerable degree of influence in the colonial economy through their shareholder relations and directorate interlocks with other firms (Tu and Li 1999).

The activities and policies of the colonial government led to a network that involved many firms, but yet lacked a clear focal point or core. Sectors and industries were selected, but decisions about investments were still left to individual companies. The government actively searched for companies willing to invest in the colonial economy, but did not focus their search on one or two companies. On the contrary, the government sought to facilitate partnerships among several *zaibatsu* firms, and among the business world, the military and the government. As indicated earlier, it even founded and funded the Taiwan Development Company, with the sole purpose of building such coalitions. *Zaibatsu* jointly invested in particular firms and projects, assembling a network in which several bigger firms cooperated to develop the colonial economy. Through its activities in finding, encouraging and facilitating investments, the government played an indirect role in the formation of such an inclusive and decentralized network (Tu and Li 1999). This led to a network characterized by firms maintaining ties to many different companies, a high proportion of multiple ties and a very inclusive network with a low level of centralization. The continuity of many of the properties of this network after World War II implies that the early KMT state adopted a lot of policies that were similar to those of the colonial Government-General.

3. THE POLITICIZED INSTITUTIONAL ENVIRONMENT AND THE FORMATION OF POST-WAR INTERCORPORATE NETWORKS, 1960–1980

The Japanese colonial period in Taiwan came to an abrupt end with Japan's defeat in 1945. After the communists successfully battled the KMT, the government under Chiang Kai-Shek retreated from Mainland China to Taiwan in 1949. After the war, the national government received all the assets of Japanese companies and converted them into publicly owned businesses, forming an important foundation of the KMT's governance of Taiwan. Before the war, business owners in Taiwan, discriminated against by the legal system, could only consolidate their management interests by conspiring with the Japanese government. The custom of entrepreneurs cooperating with the state did not change in the slightest following the change in régime. Most post-war entrepreneurs, in the face of the KMT's monopoly of economic resources and political power, maintained their allegiance and deference. This characteristic also made its mark on newly established post-war companies.

The KMT party-state not only controlled basic industries, it also firmly controlled the financial system. The KMT government and the banks that moved with it from China to Taiwan seized the financial resources required to govern the economy (Amsden 1979; Chen 1993). The public sector's domination of private enterprise persisted for another 40 years. According to unofficial statistics, the turnover of the combined party-state, together with KMT party-owned companies, amounted to as much as 30% of Taiwan's gross national product (GNP) in 1990 (Chen et al. 1991).

In order to gain a foothold in Taiwan and to control the extreme imbalance of power in the overall economy between the public sector and the relatively weak private sector companies, the government actively patronized private industries (Chu 1989; Wang 1993). In keeping with the general thrust of such thinking, private companies were closely monitored. In the early 1950s, the KMT government was reliant on US economic and military assistance and political support. Because of the Cold War, the US needed examples of successful capitalist development, and the introduction of US assistance indirectly promoted the private sector. After the 1950s, under pressure from the US, the KMT government forged a favorable environment for private capital investment and withdrew some publicly owned companies from the light industrial sector (Gold 1988b, 184). This marked the beginning of the Taiwan government's support for private capital.

The power of a strong state shaped a peculiar institutional environment in which the interlocking directorate network emerged. Three elements were particularly important in this respect. First, the market was highly politicized: firms were selected, protected, sponsored and, in many cases, owned by the government (Wang 1988; Chu 1989; Wang 1993). Many state-owned enterprises operated as monopolist firms; other companies were constitutionally not allowed to enter their industries. In 1969, the government issued regulations allowing state-owned enterprises to invest in private companies, while maintaining stringent limits on the investments private firms could make. Investments by public firms gave the government considerable leverage and control over private firms (Liu 1992 [1974]; Lee 2007). The dominance and power of the government and state-owned enterprises was, in some ways, resembling the colonial government's policies of nurturing selected industries.

Second, the institutional environment was heavily regulated by the government. In the early period of economic development, Taiwan did not have an effective public market for corporate control; the modern form of corporation was virtually non-existent. According to a survey conducted in the mid 1950s (Liu 1968, 772), only 2% of all firms in Taiwan had the legal status of company or publicly traded company. Even though the government allowed firms to buy and sell shares from 1962 onwards, only a very small proportion of companies came under these regulations. Trade on the stock market was thus very limited. To make matters worse, the government often took private firms off the market, so many firms opted not to go public. In the face of this ineffective stock market, many firms stabilized capital flows and ownership through kinship and family ties, rather than through an erratic stock market.

A third element in this restrictive institutional environment was the regulation of company law, which, drafted right after World War II in 1946, aimed to promote market stability and economic security. By placing stringent limits on the size of investments in other firms, company law set to control the actions and expansion of firms. Businesses could invest only a quarter of their earnings in other firms. In 1970, the stringent regulation was loosened somewhat and firms were allowed to invest up to a third of their earnings; in 1980, 40%, with limitations abolished in 1990. Company law also placed limitations on the appointment of board members, which had a critical impact on the configurations of intercorporate networks in Taiwan. By law, only shareholders were eligible to sit on a company board. As a result, the origination of interlocking directorates indicates not only personal connections but also ties between owners involving a large amount of financial assets. The regulation was intended to align the legal responsibility of the governing body with invested financial interests. Such regulations were aimed at preventing a similar market collapse to that of which the KMT government had previously encountered in Mainland China before 1949. However, they also unintentionally generated a situation in which the appointment of trusted family members as directors prevailed because family owners were generally very reluctant to entrust their firms to outsiders. This also explains the unusually high frequency of multiple ties among firms clustered together (Lee 2009). Even though Taiwan's company law has been amended many times, the idea that only shareholders are eligible for directorships is still very much alive. Such regulations represent an important contrast between Taiwan's economic system and, for example, the Anglo-Saxon or Japanese model, where no limitation of such kind has been placed.

In such a highly politicized market environment, trust between companies was a major issue. Family firms became especially prominent, as trust in Chinese society is especially strong within kinship groups. Consequently, family firms played an important role in shaping the interlocking directorate network, as shared directorship and investments followed kinship lineages.

4. CORPORATE NETWORK AND CONTROL STRATEGIES BY THE STATE

In Taiwan's economy, the state powerfully controlled market activity. The KMT's governance, on many levels, adopted many elaborately designed network tactics. There were at least three important modes: the connecting of important companies, multiple network controls and the forging of a coherent core (Lee 2007). The following provides further explanation of each aspect.

Linking Important Companies

One of the most direct means by which the authoritarian state controlled companies was by holding shares in companies with important positions in the market. Figure 14.1 shows the shareholding relationships between publicly owned banks and private companies. As can be seen in the diagram, companies with shares held by publicly owned banks can be roughly divided into three categories, each category representing an important industry of the time. These three categories of firms can also be identified as the beginning of many of the biggest family business groups, which would come to dominate the Taiwanese economy for the remainder of the twentieth century. The first category consists of indigenous companies that inherited the profits of the Japanese colonial era. The second category of companies came from the textile industry (mostly of emerging entrepreneurs from China with close connections to KMT officials). The third category is formed by companies of emerging indigenous entrepreneurs in the petrochemical and heavy industries.

Among the indigenous companies that inherited the profits of the Japanese colonial period were the four companies: Taiwan Cement, Taiwan Pulp & Paper Corporation, Taiwan Industry Development Corp. and Taiwan Tea Corp. They were products of the land reform of 1953. Landlords were allocated shares from these four companies to compensate them for the requisitioning of land. Some of these former landlords were able to build up their family business emporium from this basis. The four conglomerates were the successors of great companies that had flourished during the Japanese colonial rule and the early years of KMT rule. In certain respects, these companies represented the incorporation of local

286 Zong-Rong Lee and Thijs A. Velema

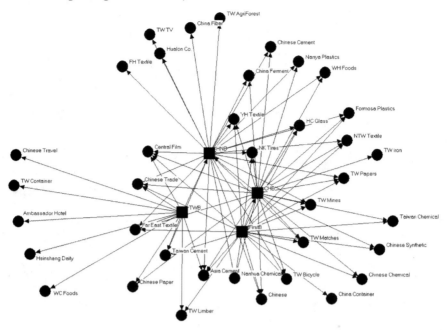

■ = publicly owned banks
● = privately owned companies

Figure 14.1 Shareholding Relationship between Early Taiwanese Publicly-Owned Financial Institutions and Large Private Companies in 1969

profit. Sometimes, the directors of these companies served concurrently as directors of other publicly owned companies or banks, symbolizing their eminence and esteem.

The second category of companies came from newly industrialized industries, such as textile. Most of the industrialists in this group moved with the KMT from Mainland China to Taiwan. The KMT government rewarded their loyalty by creating a friendly business environment for these companies (Gold 1988b). According to a survey of the 106 largest business conglomerates in the mid-1970s, textile companies were the core businesses (China Credit Information Service Ltd., 1976). The clear intercorporate links between the textile industry and the public sector illustrate an economic trait of the 1950s. Economic growth at that time largely resulted from the highly protected import-substituting industries producing everyday consumer goods—textiles and electrical appliances, for example. A third category of firms is formed by the petrochemical industry, the typical industry bringing together indigenous capitalists and foreign multinational companies.

Multiple Network Control

If the links between the KMT and major companies reflected the features of clientelism in the KMT's approach of governance, the multiple network control strategy illustrated the political concerns of the KMT régime as it faced a flourishing business community. It was relatively easy for important companies, such as Taiwan Cement, Formosa Plastics and many others, to obtain investment from the public sector, usually in the form of multiple investments from several state-owned firms. This implies that major private companies obtained state resources relatively easily, but, at the same time, they were monitored by multiple governance mechanisms. Group investment also enhanced the unity of each public sector institution, highlighting the state's consistent policy toward specific industries. Since the companies that accepted investments were mostly industry leaders, the result was that a group of successful public and private sector companies with outstanding reputations became intimately intertwined, invisibly affecting the formation of solid relationships between the state and business communities.

The Coherent Core

The various network methods to which we referred previously reveal a community comprising publicly owned and semi-publicly owned companies, which revolves around a core cluster comprising several publicly owned companies and banks. This core was formed collaboratively by such state-owned banks as the Bank of Taiwan (TWB), First Bank (FirstB), Hua Nan Bank (HNB) and Chang Hwa Bank (CHB), which each held shares in the others and were externally linked to other publicly owned companies. This organizational mode had already been established in the early years of KMT government and persisted in the same form for several decades. In some respects, this group resembled a defensive community: the KMT's economic power was founded within it in order to guard against any infringement of its 'commanding heights'. Scholars believed that the highly duplicated, intersecting share ownership illustrated how the KMT, through artful shareholdings, controlled the leveraging power of publicly owned banks in order to achieve the objective of industrial control through financial capital (Liu 1992 [1974], 284–326).

5. THE 'INNER CIRCLE' UNDER THE SHADOW OF STATE PATRONAGE

Scholars of business elites have proposed the idea of an 'inner circle' to describe the prominence of an elite circle of directors through multiple affiliations in formal organizations (Useem 1984). The clientelist nature of the interlocking directorate network in Taiwan is also apparent in the inner circle of the most connected directors, which consists of three groups (Lee 2009). First, the old landlord class from the colonial period, which was able to retain its prominent position after World War II (Gold 1988a; Numazaki 1992). Second, a group of new entrepreneurs arose, who either originated in Taiwan or were born in Mainland China and came with the KMT government to Taiwan in 1949 (Numazaki 1986). A third group comprised of a brokering social elite. The prominence of this group is apparent in panel 1 of Table 14.2, which shows that, from the 1960s until the 1980s, a relatively high percentage of the inner circle did not function as president of the board in any company in which they were active. These directors with no designated board role were crucial in tying the network together as they brokered relations between the government and the business world.

Political social capital was a crucial element in those constituting the inner circle. Many directors had a history of political involvement, acting as officials in local politics on the provincial level, or some even in the national government. In the 1960s, around a third of the inner circle had, at some point in their career, worked in politics (Lee 2009). Panel 1 of Table 14.2 also shows the prominence of directors who sat on the boards of state-owned enterprises. In the 1960s, between 80% and 90% of directors held positions in the boards of public firms. Even though this percentage dropped to just over 50% in the 1980s, the real drop only came in the 1990s.

The close relation that the inner circle of directors maintained with the political world is a further sign of the dominance of the government. Heavy state involvement resulted in a distinct quasi-corporatist network structure, with a highly centralized, close-knit and exclusive inner circle and a high level of multiple ties. The three groups of entrepreneurs patronized by the government—the landlords from colonial times, entrepreneurs loyal to the KMT, and the social elite brokers—were able to start and expand their businesses, laying the foundations for family business groups that would come to dominate Taiwan's economy in the later periods.

6. NETWORK TRANSFORMATION THROUGH A SHIFT FROM CONSOLIDATION TO PRIVATIZATION, 1990–2000

The 1980s were marked by the liberalization of Taiwan's institutional environment, a process that continued throughout the 1990s. Restrictions on company investments were finally abolished in a series of deregulation initiatives, opening up new opportunities for investment and company growth. State-owned enterprises were privatized and government-run firms became less prominent in the economy. Previously restricted sectors were opened up to private investors, allowing them to diversify their investment portfolios. Existing and newly established firms expanded rapidly in sectors such as banking, insurance, telecommunications, electricity, high-speed railways and oil refining. The market expanded and its force became more

Table 14.2 Directorate Interlocks in the Inner Circle of Directors and the Embeddedness of Public and Private Firms in the Directorate Interlock Network, 1962–2003

Panel 1: Characteristics of directorate interlocks formed by inner circle elite directors, 1962–2003[1]

Year	1962	1969	1982	1988	1992	1998	2003
Benchmark	3	3	4	4	5	5	6
Number of elite directors	13	21	21	24	20	15	24
Mean number of interlocks	3.23	4.33	5.57	5.67	6.25	5.53	6.37
Highest number of interlocks	5	9	12	19	13	9	10
Directors of public firms	11	17	11	12	12	4	5
Percentage directors of public firms	84.6	80.9	52.4	50.0	60	26.6	20.8
Mean number of public firms directorates	1.45	1.18	1.45	1.50	1.42	1.00	2.00
Number of board presidents	4	3	8	12	9	8	18
Percentage of board presidents	30.8	14.3	38.1	50.0	45.0	53.0	75.0

Panel 2: Embeddedness of public and private firms in the directorate interlock network, 1962–2003[2]

Year	1962	1969	1982	1988	1992	1998	2003
Number of firms	21	28	80	99	220	433	694
Number of public firms	9	6	11	18	22	30	36
Number of private firms	12	22	69	81	198	403	658
Interlocks among public firms	16	8	16	50	44	64	72
Interlocks between public and private firms	54	96	62	120	204	262	288
Interlocks among private firms	30	124	106	154	846	1336	2244
Density public firm interlocks	.444	.534	.290	.292	.174	.148	.114
Density public private firm interlocks	.500	.727	.081	.082	.046	.022	.012
Density of interlocks among private firms	.454	.536	.054	.048	.044	.016	.010

(*Continued*)

Table 14.2 (Continued)

Panel 3: Directorate interlocks of public and private firms, 1982–2003

Year	1962	1969	1982	1988	1992	1998	2003
Number of firms			80	99	220	433	694
Number of public firms			11	18	18	27	36
Number of private firms			69	81	202	406	658
Public firms mean directorate interlocks			7.91	8.77	5.61	7.84	6.36
Private firms mean directorate interlocks			7.53	8.88	4.92	3.59	3.61
Private firms with interlocks to public firms			16	26	48	60	71
Percentage private firms with interlocks to public firms			23.2	32.1	23.7	14.8	10.8

Note to panel 1: The benchmark forms the lowest number of interlocks for a director to be considered a member of the inner circle. For each period, this number is set to include the 20 to 30 most connected directors in the network, which form the inner circle. For instance, in 1962 there were 13 elite directors, with three or more directorate interlocks. The highest number of interlocks was 5, while on average, these directors maintained 3.23 interlocks. Eleven directors in the inner circle (84.6%) sat on the board of at least one government-owned public company. An average inner circle director sat on the board of 1.45 public firms. Four of the elite directors (30.8%) had the function of board president on at least one of the company boards they sat on.

Note to panels 2 and 3: Panels are based on the dichotomized network.

important, while the state-led corporatist economy declined. This had a profound effect on the interlocking directorate network.

Table 14.1 highlights the increase in market participants in the network. Between 1988 and 1992, the number of firms in the network doubled. In the decade between 1988 and 1998, the increase is fourfold. The average number of relations and the mean number of reachable firms declined in the same period. While the percentage of firms in the main component dropped between 1962 and 1988, it started to increase again in the 1990s. The network connecting firms through their directors became much more inclusive than in previous decades, but the connections between firms became much looser than before.

Liberalization also eroded the dominant positions occupied by state-owned enterprises during the 1960s and 1970s. Panel 2 of Table 14.2 shows that the interlocks maintained by public firms outnumbered those of private firms during this time. While interlocks between public firms grew from 16 to 72 between 1962 and 2003, interlocks between private firms exploded after liberalization, increasing from 154 in 1988 to 2,244 in 2003. The inner circle of the highest interlocking directors also became less dominated by public firm directors over time, as shown in panel 1 of the same table. While, in the 1960s, 80% of the most central directors were affiliated to a public firm, their share dropped to 50% in the 1980s and 20% in the new millennium. Interestingly, public firms still played an important role in the network well into the 1990s, when liberalization had already been in place for around a decade.

The decline of state-owned enterprises coincided with the rise of private firms from the 1980s onwards. As panel 2 shows, interlocks among private firms increased much more rapidly than interlocks among public firms or between public and private firms. The entire network became less dense over time, but the networks of private company directors became sparser much more rapidly than those of directors of state-owned enterprises or interlocking public and private firms. While network density of public and private firms was roughly equal in 1962 around .45, it decreased to .114 for state-owned enterprises, and plummeted to .01 for private firms. That state-owned enterprises had a much denser network than private companies indicates that during institutional reform, a group of interlinked public firms were able to retain their operations and maintain their internal cohesion within the network, as indicated earlier. Panel 3 shows that these firms maintained their average number of relations throughout the period of liberalization. However, the percentage of private firms interlocked with state-owned enterprises declines over time, showing that such relations became less important. Considered in this light, the evolution of the network and the decline of state-owned enterprises is perhaps more a consequence of the rise of private firms, rather than due to a decline of the government-run firm in Taiwan.

During the period of liberalization, an interlocking directorate network with very distinguished characteristics arose in Taiwan. From Table 14.1, it is clear that, first, the percentage of multiple ties in Taiwan is very high compared to corporatist economies such as Germany, the Netherlands or the US during the cartel period at the start of the twentieth century. Even Germany, with almost a quarter of all ties being multiple ties, does not come close to Taiwan's percentage of multiple ties in most years. Second, the average number of ties per firm increased from the 1960s to the start of the 1990s, but started to decline after 1992. In 2003, Taiwanese firms had a modest amount of ties, lower than those in corporatist countries but higher than those in Anglo-Saxon economies. Third, even though the Taiwanese network was highly centralized from the 1960s to the 1980s, the level of centralization dropped dramatically in the 1990s; the level of centralization in Taiwan is now comparable to that of the US. This contradicts earlier studies that argued that in smaller economies, an increase in the number of relations leads to a higher level of centralization in the interlocking directorate network (see Windolf 2002, 35).

Since liberalization, the state has receded from its dominant position in the network; it is no longer is a crucial player in shaping the network structure. This role has now been taken over by family business groups, in which cross-investments within the group are common, but investing in firms of other groups is less common, giving rise to a fragmented structure of loosely interlinked 'clans' of companies. Investments are stabilized and coordinated within the boundaries of family business groups as group members repeatedly invest and place directors on each other's board. This behavior results in a 'strong-tie' economy, in which clustered multiple ties are commonplace, and yet overall centralization is low.

Apart from this, by checking the ranking of most-connected firms over different historical periods, we can see that the directorate links appropriately reflect the characteristics of industrial development in Taiwan in the different eras (see Appendix I). We see the list of the most-connected firms unfold from the manufacturing sector, which was dominated in the early years by light industry, to the oil companies, which were added gradually, and service sector, which grew gradually in the 1980s, and, eventually, to the large number of electronics companies that emerged before the end of the 1980s. Although the financial industry has always been prominent, especially in the 1980s, it has not been particularly prominent in rankings of directorate networks. This shows that Taiwan's corporate networks do not completely conform to the 'financial hegemony' model, in which financial conglomerates make up the core (Windolf 2002; Stokman, Ziegler, and Scott 1985).

7. CONCLUSION

In this chapter, we began with an institutional perspective, emphasizing that corporate networks were deeply constrained by institutional power and social structures, and believing that the joint forces of state power and Chinese cultural 'familism' shaped the network of Taiwan's companies. Our empirical analysis clearly shows how the government exerted influence through intimate links with important companies, both in the colonial period and the early decades of the post-war era. Interestingly, both the Japanese colonial government and the KMT regime adopted similar strategies to exercise control over corporate behavior and intercorporate networks. Such similarity in network structures between pre- and post-war eras indicates strong path dependence and historical continuity in the state's involvement in market building and network formation.

The development of Taiwan's network of interlocking directorates since the 1980s mirrors the decreasing decline of the corporate network in many Western countries (Davis and Mizruchi 1999; Heemskerk 2007). Taiwan's network experienced a similar declining centrality, decreasing mean number of ties per firm, and diminishing reachability during the 1990s. However, Taiwan's experience differs from other countries in terms of the main actors who were driving the decline. While most analysts argue that the changing role of financial institutions caused the decentralization of the corporate network in many countries (see Mizruchi 2004), in Taiwan, the decline of state power and the tenacity of family businesses were the key forces behind this transformation. The impact of both is clearly visible in the features of the structure of the overall network. Comparing to the data from industrialized Western countries, the number of duplicate relationships in Taiwan is extremely high. This aspect reflects, on the one hand, the fact that private companies in Taiwan only deal with trusted partners in the intercorporate network, and on the other, the intimate involvement of publicly owned companies. This inadvertently leads to a relatively high proportion of particularistic network relationships. To our surprise, the high frequency of multiple ties among firms did not show signs of decline, even after the period of market liberalization, which may indicate the persistent force of strong ties based on kinship groups on the island.

The main argument in this chapter is that, in the process of market development, political power and markets often evolve concurrently and influence each other. In recent years, many scholars of economic sociology have begun to pay attention to questions of how the institutional environment shapes intercorporate networks (Stokman et al. 1985; Scott 1991, 1997; Gerlach 1992; Windolf 2002; Aguilera and Jackson 2003). Echoing this trend, this chapter attempts to integrate political perspectives and network research approaches by examining Taiwan's corporate networks. In this way, this chapter responds to organizational scholars' call to bring the state into intercorporate network research (Hage and Alter 1997; Todeva and Knoke 2003). Examining Taiwan's particular historical experience and corporate networks not only enables a reexamination of the applicability of existing theories, but also directly raises many interesting challenges to existing research paradigms. These clearly form a good basis for further research.

NOTE

1. For details about sources and procedures of our data collection, please refer to the Appendix.

REFERENCES

Aguilera, Ruth V., and Gregory Jackson. 2003. "The Cross-National Diversity of Corporate Governance: Dimensions and Determinants." *The Academy of Management Review* 28 (3): 447–465.

Amsden, Alice H. 1979. "Taiwan's Economic History: A Case of Etatisme and a Challenge to Dependency Theory." *Modern China* 5 (3): 341–379.

Amsden, Alice. H. 1985. "The State and Taiwan's Economic Development." In *Bringing the State Back In*, edited by Peter B. Evans, Dietrich Rueschemeyer, and Theda Skocpol, 78–106. Cambridge: Cambridge University Press.

Chen, Shih-meng, Chung-Chen Lin, C. Y. Cyrus Chu, Ching-hsi Chang, Jun-ji Shih, and Jin-Tan Liu. 1991. *Disintegrating KMT-state Capitalism (in Chinese)*. Taipei: Taipei Society.

Chen, Tun-jen. 1993. "Guarding the Commanding Heights: The State as Banker in Taiwan." In *The Politics of Finance in Developing Countries*, edited by Stephan Haggard, Chung H. Lee, and Sylvia Maxfield, 55–92. Ithaca, NY: Cornell University Press.

Chu, Te-lan. 2005. "Network Relations of the Taiwan Development Company Limited (1936–1945) (in Chinese)." *Taiwan Historical Research* 12 (2): 75–119.

Chu, Y.-H. 1989. "The Oligopolistic Economy and Authoritarian Political System (in Chinese)." In *Monopoly and Exploitation: A Political-Economical Analysis of Authoritarianism*, edited by M. Hsiao, C. C. Wu, and Y.-H. Chu., 139–160. Taipei: Taiwan Research Foundation.

Chung, Chi-Nien. 2006. "Beyond Guanxi: Network Contingencies in Taiwanese Business Groups." *Organization Studies* 27 (4): 461–489.

Davis, Gerald F., and Mark S. Mizruchi. 1999. "The Money Center Cannot Hold: Commercial Banks in the U.S. System of Corporate Governance." *Administrative Science Quarterly* 44: 215–239.

Evans, Peter B. 1995. *Embedded Autonomy: States and Industrial Transformation*. Princeton, NJ: Princeton University Press.

Fernandez, Roberto M., and Roger V. Gould. 1993. "A Dilemma of State Power: Brokerage and Influence in the National Health Policy Domain." *American Journal of Sociology* 99 (6): 1455–1491.

Gerlach, Michael L. 1992. *Alliance Capitalism: The Social Organization of Japanese Business*. Berkeley: University of California Press.

Gold, Thomas B. 1988a. "Colonial Origins of Taiwanese Capitalism." In *Contending Approaches to the Political Economy of Taiwan*, edited by Edwin A. Winckler and Susan Greenhalgh, 101–117. Armonk, NY: M.E. Sharpe.

Gold, Thomas B. 1988b. "Entrepreneurs, Multinationals, and the State." In *Contending Approaches to the Political Economy of Taiwan*, edited by Edwin A. Winckler and Susan Greenhalgh, 175–205. Armonk, NY: M.E. Sharpe.

Hage, Jerald, and Catherine Alter. 1997. "A Typology of Interorganizational Relationships and Networks." In *Contemporary Capitalism: The Embeddedness of Institutions*, edited by J. Rogers Hollingsworth and Robert Boyer, 94–126. New York: Cambridge University Press.

Hamilton, Gary G. 1997. "Organization and Market Processes in Taiwan's Capitalist Economy." In *The Economic Organization of East Asian Capitalism*, edited by Marc Orrú, Nicole W. Biggart, and Gary G. Hamilton, 237–295. Thousand Oaks, CA: Sage Publications.

Hamilton, Gary G., and Nicole W. Biggart. 1988. "Market, Culture, and Authority: A Comparative Analysis of Management and Organization in the Far East." *The American Journal of Sociology* 94: S52-S94.

Heemskerk, Eelke M. 2007. *The Decline of the Corporate Community: Network Dynamics of the Dutch Business Elite*. Amsterdam: Amsterdam University Press.

Heinz, John P. 1993. *The Hollow Core: Private Interests in National Policy Making*. Cambridge, MA: Harvard University Press.

Ho, Samuel Pao-San. 1984. "Colonialism and Development: Korea, Taiwan, and Kwantung." In *The Japanese Colonial Empire, 1895–1945*, edited by Raymond H. Myers and Mark R. Peattie, 348–398. Princeton, NJ: Princeton University Press.

Johnson, Chalmers A. 1982. *MITI and the Japanese Miracle: The Growth of Industrial Policy, 1925–1975*. Stanford, CA: Stanford University Press.

Ka, Chih-ming. 2008. "Agrarian Development, Family Farms and Sugar Capital in Colonial Taiwan, 1895–1945." *Journal of Peasant Studies* 18 (2): 206–240.

Kao, Shu-yuan. 2005. "The Government-General's Corporate Policies during Early Japanese Colonial Rule (1895–1923) in Taiwan (in Chinese)." *Taiwan Historical Research* 12 (1): 43–71.

Laumann, Edward O., and David Knoke. 1987. *The Organizational State: Social Choice in National Policy Domains*. Madison, WI: University of Wisconsin Press.

Lee, Z.-R. 2007. "Between the State Power and Chinese Familialism: Corporate Control and Intercorporate Networks in Taiwan Revisited (in Chinese)." *Taiwanese Sociology* 13: 173–242.

Lee, Z.-R. 2009. "Institutional Transition in Market Networks: An Historical Investigation of Interlocking Directorates of Big Businesses in Taiwan, 1962–2003 (in Chinese)." *Taiwanese Sociology* 17: 101–160.

Liu, Jin-Qing. 1968. "Taiwan's Enterprises." In *General Studies of Taiwan's Economy* (in Japanese), edited by Sasamoto Takeharu and Kawano Shigeto, 747-808, Tokyo: Ajia Keizai Kenkyujo.

Liu, J.-Q. 1992 [1974]. *An Economic Analysis of Post-war Taiwan (in Chinese)*. Taipei: Renjian public.

Myers, Ramon H., and Yamada Saburo. 1984. "Agricultural Development in the Empire." In *The Japanese Colonial Empire, 1895–1945*, edited by Raymond H. Myers and Mark R. Peattie, 420–452. Princeton, NJ: Princeton University Press.

Mizruchi, Mark S. 2004. "Berle and Means Revisited: The Governance and Power of Large U.S. Corporations." *Theory and Society* 33: 579–617.

Morgan, Stephen L., and Shiyung Liu. 2007. "Was Japanese Colonialism Good for the Welfare of Taiwanese? Stature and the Standard of Living." *The China Quarterly* 192: 990–1013.

Numazaki, Ichiro. 1986. "Networks of Taiwanese Big Business." *Modern China* 12 (4): 487–534.

Numazaki, Ichiro. 1992. "Networks and Partnerships: The Social Organization of the Chinese Elite in Taiwan." PhD dissertation, Michigan State University.

Padgett, John F. and Christopher K. Ansell. 1993. "Robust Action and the Rise of the Medici, 1400–1434." *American Journal of Sociology* 98 (6): 1259–1319.

Scott, John. 1991. "Networks of Corporate Power: A Comparative Assessment." *Annual Review of Sociology* 17: 171–203.

Scott, John. 1997. *Corporate Business and Capitalist Classes*. New York: Oxford University Press.

Stokman, Frans N., Rolf Ziegler, and John Scott, eds. 1985. *Networks of Corporate Power: A Comparative Analysis of Ten Countries*. Cambridge: Polity Press.

Todeva, Emanuela, and David Knoke. 2003. "Strategic Alliances and Corporate Social Capital." *Kölner Zeitschrift für Soziologie und Sozialpsychologie*: 345–380.

Tu, Zhaoyan, and M.-J. Li. 1999. *Taiwan under Japanese Imperialism (in Chinese)*. Taipei: Renjian Public.

Useem, Michael. 1984. *The Inner Circle: Large Corporations and the Rise of Business Political Activity in the U.S. and U.K.* New York: Oxford University Press.

Wade, Robert. 1990. *Governing the Market: Economic Theory and the Role of Government in East Asian Industrialization*. Princeton, NJ: Princeton University Press.

Wang, H.-R. 1988. "*Post-war Development of Private Capital (in Chinese)*." MA dissertation, National Taiwan University.

Wang, Jenn-hwan. 1993. "Taiwan's Political Transition and the Formation of New Government Business Relations (in Chinese)." *Social Studies Quarterly* 14: 123–169.

Windolf, Paul. 2002. *Corporate Networks in Europe and the United States*. New York: Oxford University Press.

15 Evolution of Corporate Networks in Twentieth Century Japan

Satoshi Koibuchi[*] *and Tetsuji Okazaki*[**]

1. INTRODUCTION

After operating an isolation policy for more than 200 years under *Tokugawa Shogunete*, Japan opened the country in the late nineteenth century. Following this, it showed steady economic growth until the 1980s, except the years just after World War II. This 'miraculous' growth of the Japanese economy has attracted the interest of many economists, economic historians and practitioners, not only because of the high speed of growth, but also because it was characterized by distinctive institutional and organizational features. These characteristics include a close government-firm relationship (industrial policy), long-term employment and pervasive corporate networks. It is the latter that is the focus of this chapter.

Our chapter seeks to investigate the structure of Japanese corporate networks and their change over time. We will achieve this in a consistent and comparative manner, and then relate them to the historical evolution of institutions in the Japanese economy.

To this end, we collected the directorship data of the 200 largest non-financial firms and the 50 largest financial firms, in terms of total assets, for the years 1911, 1928, 1937, 1957, 1973, 1982, 1992, 1998 and 2009, which are comparable to the data for the other countries in this volume. To this data, we apply the methodology of social network analysis. Our study is the first attempt to portray, comprehensively and comparatively, the structure and historical evolution of corporate networks in Japan through the whole of the twentieth century.

The remainder of this chapter is organized as follows. Section 2 briefly describes the data and samples. Section 3 presents the evolution of corporate networks in twentieth-century Japan, using the methodology of network analysis. In Section 4, we discuss the causes and implications of the changes in corporate networks over time, placing them in the broader context of the evolution of institutions. Section 5 concludes the chapter.

2. DATA AND SAMPLES

In order to obtain the asset data and information on directors and auditors for pre-war Japan, we used a series of company directories compiled by a major securities company, Osakaya Shoten (*Kabushiki Nenkan*). Because this source focuses on those companies with shares actively traded on the stock market, we supplemented the data for companies with closed ownership, such as the companies affiliated to major *zaibatsu*, with other sources, including *Ginko Kaisha Yoroku* by Tokyo Koshinjo, a credit bureau. With respect to the post-war period, the principal data source is a series of handbooks on the so-called *keiretsu* business groups by Toyo Keizai Shinposha (*Kigyo Keiretsu Soran*). As this source only covers the period from 1972 to 1999, we obtained the data for 1957 from *Jojogaisha Soran* by the Tokyo Stock Exchange, while the data for 2009 were collected from the annual reports of individual companies.

Using the dataset constructed from those sources, we identify the 200 largest non-financial firms and the 50 largest financial firms, in terms of total assets, for the aforementioned benchmark years. Then, for these firms, we construct a database of directors and auditors in order to explore the features and evolutions of Japanese corporate networks.

3. FEATURES OF THE JAPANESE CORPORATE NETWORK

The database of directors and auditors described in the previous section enabled us to identify the people who were simultaneously directors or auditors of more than one company. Those companies that shared at least one director, or one auditor, were regarded as being connected through director interlocking (Okazaki, Sawada, and Yokoyama 2005; Okazaki, Sawada, and Wang 2007; Okazaki and Sawada 2012). As we will show, such director interlocking formed extensive corporate networks, especially in the pre-war period.

Our basic data and statistics on corporate networks in Japan through the twentieth century are summarized in Appendix I. One striking feature shown in the table is a large change in the network structure during World War II. Before the war, corporate networks were very pervasive. Indeed, around 90% of the sample firms were connected to each other through director interlocking. It is also noticeable that, in the pre-war period, the networks become more coherent over time.

In the literature of network analysis, overall cohesion of the network structure is measured by 'density'—the ratio of observed lines between nodes to the maximum number of lines (n*(n-1)/2). In our work, the nodes represent firms. The degree of a node is the number of lines that intersect with it, and the average degree is the mean of the numbers of observed lines that our sample companies had. As shown in Appendix I, the total number of lines increased from 974 in 1911 to 1,236 in 1937, and the density increased from 0.031 to 0.040 in the same period. The multiple lines refer to those with two or more interlocking directors (see Appendix I). This measure indicates that the corporate network structure became stronger, as well as denser, over the pre-war period.

This trend ceased suddenly, however, during and just after World War II. Between 1937 and 1957, the percentage of connected firms declined from 94.4% to 52.8%. Density also declined in the same period from 0.040 to 0.005. The extent and density of the corporate networks continued to decline until the 1980s, after which the extent and density increased once again throughout the 1990s, although both were still substantially smaller than they were in the pre-war period (see Appendix I).

Another dimension with which the structure of a corporate network can be characterized is 'centrality'. Centrality concerns the extent to which certain firms play a central role in the network structure. One of the centrality measures is 'degree centrality', which is defined for each firm by the number of lines that the firm has. This is a simple measure that captures the importance of a firm in the network structure.

The top 10 firms in terms of degree centrality were the large hubs in the corporate network structure (see http://www.cgeh.nl/power-corporate-networks-comparative-and-historical-perspective). It is again noticeable that the period during and just after World War II represents a sudden watershed. In the pre-war period, the 'hub' firms had very large degree centrality. *Teikoku Seima*, *Tokyo Dento* and *Oji Seishi*, for example, which were the largest hubs in 1911, 1928 and 1937, had connections with 36, 39 and 43 firms, respectively. The largest hubs in the post-war period, however, had just 10–15 connections. The decline was rapid and severe.

If we consider the attributes of the large hub firms, we find that banks are not well represented throughout the pre-war period: no bank was listed in the top 10 firms in 1911, and just one bank was listed in both 1928 and 1937. Also, it is notable that none of the companies at the core of major *zaibatsu* were in the list with the exception of *Mitsui Ginko* in 1928 and 1937, and *Mitsui Shintaku* in 1937. *Zaibatsu* are the large business groups in pre-war Japan, which were characterized by a hierarchical organizational structure, family ownership and holding companies as the headquarters (Morikawa 1992; Okazaki 1999, 2001). It is therefore surprising that, in our data, we find that the firms at the center of the corporate network were non-*zaibatsu* firms. We will return to the reason for this finding. After the war, the importance of banks to the network grew over time. For example, though no bank features in the top 10 list until 1973, after this date, many banks are featured as top 10 companies.

4. CO-EVOLUTION OF CORPORATE NETWORKS AND ECONOMIC INSTITUTIONS

Several interesting findings concerning the features and changes in the corporate networks emerge from observing the data we highlight in the previous section. These features and changes, including very pervasive networks in the pre-war period and a sharp decline of networks over World War II, arguably reflect more general features and changes in the economic institutions in Japan.

The characteristics of the financial system in pre-war Japan are closely associated with the features of the corporate networks in that period. In a series of studies carried out since the 1990s, it has been shown that the pre-war Japanese economy had a large and active capital market and that the capital market played a central role in corporate financing. The function of the capital market was supported by an effective system of corporate governance, based on active boards of directors—internal mechanisms—as well as by the active market for corporate control—external mechanisms (Hamao, Hoshi, and Okazaki 2009; Hoshi and Kashyap 2001; Okazaki 1999, 2001, 2004). In this sense, the financial system in pre-war Japan can be classified as a 'market-based' system, at least in terms of Allen and Gale's (2000) taxonomy.

While it is true that there were a number of banks in pre-war Japan, many of them were controlled by non-financial firms or those firms' dominant shareholders; they were utilized as so-called 'organ banks'. These relationships gave rise to unsound related lending that, in turn, caused instability of the financial system in the 1920s. Indeed, many of the banks that were forced to close because of bank runs during the serious financial crisis in 1927 were those that had connections with industrial firms through director interlocking and ownership (Kato 1957; Okazaki, Sawada, and Yokoyama 2005; Okazaki 2007; Okazaki, Sawada, and Wang 2007; Yabushita and Inoue 1993; Yamazaki 2000). In this sense, banks were not leading players in the pre-war Japanese financial system, which is arguably the reason why they did not have a central position in the corporate networks, as was highlighted in the previous section.

The relatively minor position of *zaibatsu* is another remarkable feature of the pre-war network structure in Japan, as we mentioned in the previous section. To find the reason, one must investigate the key people in the network. Table 2E (see the website) shows the people who held the largest number of directorships and auditor positions—the 'big linkers'. We can identify four types of 'big linker' in pre-war Japan. The first type (shown as Type I in Table 2E on the website) is comprised of the owners of major *zaibatsu*. Zenzaburo Yasuda and Koyata Iwasaki were the owners of *Yasuda* and *Mitsubishi zaibatsu*, respectively. These 'big linkers' held director positions in the core firms of their own business groups. The second type (Type II) consists of the employed managers of the major *zaibatsu*. Principally, these are the directors of the holding companies, or the headquarters of *zaibatsu*. As such, they hold director and auditor positions in the core affiliated companies. The third type (Type III) is owners of medium-sized *zaibatsu*, including Asano and Okura. The fourth (Type IV) is non-*zaibatsu* large investors. They did not build tight-knit business groups, but instead invested in many companies to build substantial, but not dominant, shareholding. Based on this substantial shareholding, they obtained directorships and/or auditor positions. This type includes Shintaro Ohashi, Kaichiro Nezu and Eihachiro Tanaka.

One feature in Table 2E that is particularly noticeable and striking is how well represented the Type IV linkers are throughout the pre-war period. It can perhaps be seen as a more natural pattern because they invested in wide-ranging firms and were active players in the capital market. *Zaibatsu*, on the other hand, tended to concentrate their investments on their core affiliated companies in order to maintain a dominant shareholding position. However, it is also notable that the presence of Type II linkers—namely, the employed managers of major *zaibatsu*—increased over time. This trend reflects the organizational change in *zaibatsu*. Major *zaibatsu* expanded and diversified their businesses, especially during the early twentieth century, and in order to manage those businesses, they implemented considerable organizational reforms by the early 1920s. Specifically, they span off each of their various businesses, creating them as independent joint-stock companies that retained the holding company at the head of the *zaibatsu* as their headquarters. In order to maintain governance of the affiliated companies, the directors and executive staff of the holding companies also took positions on the boards of the newly created companies (Morikawa 1992; Okazaki 1999, 2001). It is these changes that are reflected in the increased presence of employed managers of the major *zaibatsu* in Table 2E. In addition, the expansion of directorship interlocking based on *zaibatsu* organizations explains the gradual increase of density.

The sharp change in the corporate network structure between the 1930s and 1950s that we have previously noted was due to the general transformation of the economic institutions in Japan that occurred during and just after World War II (Okazaki and Okuno-Fujiwara 1999). The pre-war Japanese economy had a market-based financial system. However, after the Sino-Japanese war broke out in 1937, the government thought that this system was not a suitable way to manage the economy and society during the war. For one thing, this system tended to exacerbate income inequality, with the possible consequence of making society more unstable in wartime. For another, the market-based financial system did not provide the most opportune environment in which the government could mobilize funds for itself and munitions industries. Finally, the corporate governance structure that was designed to protect the interests of investors was thought to impede munitions production, as under the official price system, these industries were not always profitable.

For these reasons, the government restricted the rights of investors, which resulted in a contraction of the capital market. Meanwhile, the banks were a convenient substitution for the role of the capital market, which resulted in a fundamental change to the market-based financial system. This change in the financial system and the corporate governance structure was reflected in a change in the corporate boards. As we have shown, the presence of large shareholders on the boards of firms declined, while directors who were promoted from within the companies increased (Okazaki and Okuno-Fujiwara 1999). In short, the financial system shifted from a market-based system to a bank-based one, in the sense of Allen and Gale (2000).

In addition, events just after World War II reinforced this shift in the base of the financial system. Japan was an occupied country. The US occupation authorities dissolved the *zaibatsu* as part of the economic reforms that were designed to eliminate the basis of militarism in Japan. Further, the property tax in 1947, as well as the hyperinflation that Japan experienced from 1945 to 1948, substantially damaged the assets of the wealthy, people who had previously been active players in the capital market. Indeed, what happened to the Japanese financial system in the 1940s has been called a 'great reversal' (Rajan and Zingales 2003).

Banks, which came to play a major role in the financial system during World War II, continued to perform this function. Indeed, banks were almost the only institutions to finance and govern the process of the reconstruction of the major Japanese industrial companies. One-to-one relationships between large firms and large banks, which had been formed under the direction of the government during the war, were maintained after the war was over and, subsequently, developed into the close tie called 'main bank' (Hoshi and Kashyap 2001). The 'main bank' relationship characterized the Japanese post-war financial system. In this configuration, each large firm has a certain 'main bank', which plays a major role in both the finance and governance of the firm. The 'main bank' did not supply a dominant portion of the funding, but it was the largest lender. Because of this status, it monitored and governed the firms to which it lent. The networks that are based on the 'main bank' relationships are sometimes known as '*keiretsu*', the original meaning of which, in Japanese, is 'affiliation' or 'group' (Aoki and Patrick 1994; Hoshi and Kashyap 2001).

The transformation of the institutions during World War II had a great impact on the nature of the corporate networks based on directorship interlocking. As the role of individual investors declined, it was mostly banks, and especially 'main banks', that took over the role of large shareholders in major firms. Alongside this distinctive feature of ownership structure, most of the directors of major firms were those who were promoted from within the company, employees and those who were dispatched from the 'main banks' and the firms that were large shareholders (Aoki and Patrick 1994; Hoshi and Kashyap 2001). Usually, a bank dispatched its employee, or employees, to a certain borrower to devote themselves to the duty of monitoring it. As this happened more frequently, the number of people who held multiple director positions declined. As a result, corporate networks based on interlocking directorships contracted in the post-war period. This is the explanation for the figures we highlighted in the previous section.

Given that main banks dispatched their employees to borrowers as directors, measuring corporate networks solely based on interlocking directorships may underestimate the 'real' corporate networks. To address this concern, we have employed additional data. For 1982, 1992 and 1998, the data on 'director dispatching' are available in *Kigyo Keiretsu Soran*. This data identifies cases where certain firms dispatched their employees to other firms as directors or auditors. Table 15.1 shows coherence measures that take account of director dispatching, as well as director interlocking during the post-war period. We found that the coherence measures are larger than those in the table of Appendix I, but at the same time, they are much smaller than those in the pre-war period.

Finally, as we have already mentioned, the extent and coherence of the corporate networks increased again during and after the 1990s. It is possible that this change reflects two things. First, the ban on 'pure' holding companies was lifted in 1997 as a part of the financial liberalization. Second, the Commercial Codes were amended in 2003, the purpose of which was to reform corporate governance. After the amendment, a new type of corporation—a 'corporation with committees'—was introduced. A 'corporation with committees' must establish nominating, audit and compensation committees in which more than half of the members are external directors—in other words, directors who have not previously been employed by the company. In many cases, these directors are appointed from the pool of reputable corporate executives, lawyers and scholars, which is currently not large in Japan. As a consequence, some people are appointed as external directors by many firms, which has effectively increased the number of interlocking directorships in recent years. So, while we see an increase in the number, which might look, on the face of it, like a return to the nature of the pre-war network structure, the *meaning* of the interlocking directorships has changed. It is now different from that in the pre-war period, when it was based on ownership, switching to one based on the employment of external directors from a limited pool and as required by corporate governance.

Table 15.1 Cohesion Measures Based on Director Interlocking and Director Dispatching

	Density	Degree centrality
1973	0.006	1.508
1982	0.007	1.644
1992	0.006	1.496
1998	0.009	2.144

5. CONCLUDING REMARKS

In this chapter, we collected the directorship data for Japan throughout the twentieth century, which are comparable to other countries in this volume, and explored the structure of the networks and their change over time. Some interesting findings have emerged. In pre-war Japan, there were very pervasive and dense corporate networks through director interlocking, which, in turn, was based on ownership. In other words, there were a number of large individual investors who held substantial portions of shares of many firms. The role of the major *zaibatsu* was not so prominent, principally because they concentrated on a limited number of core affiliated companies. Rather, it was large investors who did not build their own closed business group who were the 'big linkers' in pre-war Japanese corporate networks.

Also, it was revealed that there was a sharp break in the trend of corporate networks during World War II. The extent and density of corporate networks through director interlocking declined sharply in this period. This break reflects the general transformation of the economic institutions in Japan that occurred during and just after World War II. In particular, there were changes in the financial system and corporate governance structure that can be seen as the major causes bringing about the break in the evolution of corporate networks. The role of large investors, including *zaibatsu*, declined substantially, while banks came to play a central role in corporate finance and governance. This might be seen as banks 'substituting' for the role previously played by the *zaibatsu*. However, the so called 'main bank system' did not generate corporate networks through director interlocking. Instead, directorships were given to employees 'dispatched'—or nominated—by the banks to hold director positions in order to monitor borrowers.

NOTES

* Email: koibuchi@tamacc.chuo-u.ac.jp
** Email: okazaki@e.u-tokyo.ac.jp

REFERENCES

Allen, Franklin, and Douglas Gale. 2000. *Comparing Financial Systems*. Cambridge, MA: MIT Press.
Aoki, Masahiko, and Hugh Patrick, eds. 1994. *The Japanese Main Bank System: Its Relevance for Developing and Transforming Economies*. Oxford: Oxford University Press.
Hamao, Yasushi, Takeo Hoshi, and Tetsuji Okazaki. 2009. "Listing Policy and Development of the Tokyo Stock Exchange in the Prewar Period." In *Financial Sector Development in the Pacific Rim*, edited by Takatoshi Ito and Andrew Rose, 51–87. Chicago: University of Chicago Press.
Hoshi, Takeo, and Anil Kashyap. 2001. *Corporate Financing and Governance in Japan: The Road to the Future*. Cambridge, MA: MIT Press.

Kato, Toshihiko. 1957. *Honpo Ginko Shi Ron (On the History of Banks in Japan)*. Tokyo: University of Tokyo Press.
Morikawa, Hidemasa. 1992. *Zaibatsu: Rise and Fall of Family Enterprise Groups in Japan*. Tokyo: University of Tokyo Press.
Okazaki, Tetsuji. 1999. *Mochikabu Gaisha no Rekishi (History of Holding Companies in Japan)*. Tokyo: Chikuma Shobo.
Okazaki, Tetsuji. 2001. "Role of Holding Companies in Prewar Japanese Economic Development: Rethinking Zaibatsu in Perspectives of Corporate Governance." *Social Science Japan Journal* 4 (2): 243–268.
Okazaki, Tetsuji. 2004. "Holding Company and Bank: A Historical Comparative Perspective on Corporate Governance in Japan." *Seoul Journal of Economics* 17 (3): 383–401.
Okazaki, Tetsuji. 2007. "Micro-aspects of Monetary Policy: Lender of Last Resort and Selection of Banks in Pre-war Japan." *Explorations in Economic History* 44 (4): 657–679.
Okazaki, Tetsuji, and Masahiro Okuno-Fujiwara, eds. 1999. *The Japanese Economic System and Its Historical Origins*. New York: Oxford University Press.
Okazaki, Tetsuji, and Michiru Sawada. 2012. "Interbank Networks in Prewar Japan: Structure and Implications." *Industrial and Corporate Change* April: 463–506.
Okazaki, Tetsuji, Michiru Sawada, and Ke Wang. 2007. "The Fall of 'Organ Bank' Relationships During the Wave of Bank Failures and Consolidations: Experience in Pre-war Japan." *Corporate Ownership and Control* Vol. 5-1.
Okazaki, Tetsuji, Michiru Sawada, and Kazuki Yokoyama. 2005. "Measuring the Extent and Implications of Director Interlocking in Prewar Japanese Banking Industry." *Journal of Economic History* 65 (4): 1082–1115.
Rajan, Raghuram, and Luigi Zingales. 2003. "The Great Reversals: The Politics of Financial Development in the Twentieth Century." *Journal of Financial Economics* 69: 5–50.
Yabushita, Shiro, and Atsuhi Inoue. 1993. "The Stability of the Japanese Banking System: A Historical Perspective." *Journal of the Japanese and International Economies* 7 (4): 387–407.
Yamamoto, Kazuo. 2007. *Sumitomo Zaibatsu Keieishi (Business History of Sumitomo Zaibatsu)*. Kyoto: Kyoto Daigaku Gakujutsu Shuppankai.
Yamazaki, Hiroaki. 2000. *Showa Kin'yu Kyoko (Showa Financial Crisis)*. Tokyo: Toyo Keizai Shinposha.

Appendix I

DEFINITIONS

The reader will find in this Appendix the common definitions for the network indicators. These indicators refer to the dichotomized network. They have been chosen in order to make comparisons among countries and among different benchmarks possible. For every country, a table shows most of these indicators. The chapters in this volume refer to these indicators and definitions. Even more data information can be found on the website of the Centre for Global Economic History, http://www.cgeh.nl/power-corporate-networks-comparative-and-historical-perspective.

A. Structure of the Network

- *Connected firms* (number of and in % of total number of firms). Connected firms are firms that have at least one tie with another firm;
- *Isolated firms* (number of and in % of total number of firms). Isolated firms are firms that have no ties to other firms;
- *Marginal firms* (number of and in % of total number of firms). Marginal firms are firms with degree 1 or 2;
- *Isolated and marginal firms* (number of and in % of total number of firms);
- *Firms in main component* (number of and in % of total number of firms). "A component is a maximal connected sub-network" (De Nooy, Wouter, and Batagelj 2006, 318);
- Number of components.

B. Ties

- Total number of lines;
- *Number of multiple lines;*
- *Density.* "Density is the number of lines in a network, expressed as a proportion of the maximum possible number of lines" (De Nooy et al. 2006, 322);

- *Number of firms in 2 core.* "A *k*-core is a maximal subnetwork in which each vertex has at least degree *k* within the subnetwork" (De Nooy et al. 2006, 321).
- *Number of firms in 2-slice.* "An *m-slice* is a maximal subnetwork containing the lines with a multiplicity equal to or greater than *m* and the vertices incident with these lines" (idem).

C. Centrality/Cohesiveness

- *Diameter.* Diameter is the longest geodesics of the network; i.e., the length of the path between the two most distant nodes;
- *Average distance.* "The distance from vertex u to vertex y is the length of the geodesic from u to v" (De Nooy et al. 2006, 319);
- *Average degree.* "The degree of a vertex is the number of lines incident with it" (De Nooy et al. 2006, 63). The average degree of all vertices indicates the structural cohesion of a network;1
- *Degree centrality.* "The degree centrality of a vertex is its degree" (De Nooy et al. 2006, 319);
- *Closeness centrality.* "The closeness centrality of a vertex is the number of other vertices divided by the sum of all distances between the vertex and all others" (De Nooy et al. 2006, 318);
- *Betweenness centrality.* "The betweenness centrality of a vertex is the proportion of all geodesics between pairs of other vertices that include this vertex" (De Nooy et al. 2006, 318).

D. Distribution of Position over Individuals

- *Directors* (number of);
- *Interlockers* (number of). Interlockers are directors who have two or more positions in the network;
- *Big linkers.* Big linkers are directors who have three or more positions in the network;
- Interlockers as % of directors;
- Big linkers as % of directors;
- *Mandates (/Positions) held by interlockers* (number of and in % of total number of mandates/positions)
- *Mandates (/Positions) held by big linkers* (number of and in % of total number of mandates/positions)

TABLES

United States of America

Appendix UN1 A. Structure of the Network

		1962	1966	1974	1978	1982	1986	1990	1994	1999	2003	2005	2010
Number of firms	N	250	250	250	250	250	250	250	250	250	250	250	250
Average assets (million of 2003 dollars)		10996	13732	19740	18546	19858	22708	27236	32589	51904	76689	87606	83271
Continuing firms	%		88.8	76.8	76.8	61.6	82.4	75.2	79.6	66.8	69.6	78.0	72.8
Connected firms	N	238	238	237	243	240	245	246	243	236	228	227	221
	%	95.20	95.20	94.80	97.20	96.00	98.00	98.40	97.20	94.40	91.20	90.80	88.40
Isolated firms	N	12	12	13	7	10	5	4	7	14	22	23	29
	%	4.80	4.80	5.20	2.80	4.00	2.00	1.60	2.80	5.60	8.80	9.20	11.60
Marginal firms (degree = 1 or 2)	N	30	25	42	28	27	35	33	32	40	62	49	73
	%	12.00	10.00	16.80	11.20	10.80	14.00	13.20	12.80	16.00	24.80	19.60	29.20
Isolate and marginal firms	N	42	37	55	35	37	40	37	39	54	84	72	102
	%	16.80	14.80	22.00	14.00	14.80	16.00	14.80	15.60	21.60	33.60	28.80	40.80
Firms in main component	N	236	238	237	243	240	243	244	243	236	222	227	214
	%	94.40	95.20	94.80	97.20	96.00	97.20	97.60	97.20	94.40	88.80	90.80	85.60
Components	N	2	1	1	1	1	2	2	1	1	4	1	4

Appendix UN2 B. Ties

	1962	1966	1974	1978	1982	1986	1990	1994	1999	2003	2005	2010
Number of ties	2262	2292	1822	1914	2576	2402	2224	2250	1692	1370	1280	970
Number of multiple ties	382	400	272	242	330	312	296	226	166	122	84	48
Density	0.036	0.037	0.029	0.031	0.041	0.039	0.036	0.036	0.027	0.022	0.021	0.016
Size of 2-core	128	144	76	62	102	96	89	66	32	13	8	5

Appendix UN3 C. Centrality/Cohesiveness

	1962	1966	1974	1978	1982	1986	1990	1994	1999	2003	2005	2010
Diameter	7	8	7	8	7	7	6	7	8	11	8	10
Average distance	2.84	2.84	3.09	3.05	2.75	2.90	2.94	2.95	3.20	3.44	3.54	4.04
Average degree of full network	9.05	9.17	7.29	7.66	10.30	9.61	8.90	9.00	6.77	5.48	5.12	3.88
Average degree of main component	9.58	9.63	7.69	7.88	10.73	9.88	9.11	9.26	7.17	6.14	5.64	4.50
Closeness centrality	5.93	6.78	6.26	10.03	7.89	10.10	11.18	10.12	5.86	3.14	3.80	2.46
Betweenness centrality	204.2	207.9	233.8	241.1	200.7	223.1	229.6	229.6	244.4	239.4	260.2	276.8

Appendix UN4 D. Distribution of Position over Individuals

	1962	1966	1974	1978	1982	1986	1990	1994	1999	2003	2005	2010
Number of directors			532	582	647	614	573	536	504	421	2290	2401
Number of interlockers			176	168	234	232	213	211	150	110	419	364
Number of big linkers											101	64
(3+ positions)												
Interlockers as % of directors											18.3	15.2
Big linkers as % of directors											4.4	2.7

Note: Data for some variables and time points are missing due to the constraints of source data. Contact authors for additional details.

UNITED KINGDOM

Appendix UN5 A. Structure of the Network

		1904	1938	1958	1976	1983	1993	1997	2000	2010
Number of firms	N	250	250	187	250	218	251	250	250	247
Connected firms	N	173	202	141	189	174	202	225	218	227
	%	69.20	79.80	75.40	75.60	80.93	80.48	90.00	87.20	91.91
Isolated firms	N	77	48	46	61	41	49	25	32	20
	%	30.80	19.20	24.60	24.40	19.07	19.52	10.00	12.80	8.10
Marginal firms	N	87	64	56	54	64	67	63	88	60
	%	34.80	25.60	29.93	21.60	29.76	26.69	25.20	35.20	24.28
Isolated and marginal firms	%	64.80	44.80	55.38	46.00	48.84	46.22	35.20	48.00	32.39
Firms in main component	N	154	197	131	185	172	197	223	205	219
	%	61.60	78.80	70.10	74.00	80.00	78.49	89.20	82.00	88.66
Components	N	9	3	6	3	2	3	2	6	5

Appendix UN6 B. Ties

	1904	1938	1958	1976	1983	1993	1997	2000s	2010
Total number of lines	308	581	372	542	370	455	519	424	487
Number of multiple lines	39	133	51	35	26	14	12	14	53
Density	0.98	1.87	2.14	1.74	1.61	1.45	1.70	1.36	1.60
Number of firms in 2m-slice (or above)	50	115	62	52	36	23	24	25	67
Number of 2m-slices	15	21	15	17	12	9	12	11	15
No. of firms in largest 2m-slice	12	64	20	13	10	4	2	4	14

Appendix UN7 C. Centrality/Cohesiveness

	1904	1938	1958	1976	1983	1993	1997	2000	2010
Diameter	24	9	7	8	8	10	8	12	9
Average distance	10.15	3.44	3.12	3.26	3.72	3.98	3.86	4.4	4.15
Average degree of network	2.46	4.65	3.98	4.34	3.44	3.63	4.25	3.39	3.94
Average degree of main component	3.82	5.87	5.60	5.84	4.29	4.59	4.75	4.05	4.41
Network betweenness centrality %	4.68	10.79	5.91	7.64	13.50	6.70	5.46	7.22	4.62
Main component closeness centrality %	16.74	27.46	24.12	23.70	22.50	21.00	18.40	19.29	13.68

Appendix UN8 D. Distribution of Position over Individuals

	1904	1938	1958	1976	1983	1993	1997	2000	2010
Number of directors	2322	2170	2215	2682	2378	2258	2172	2218	1832
Number of interlockers	205	331	225	282	232	265	329	285	445
Number of big linkers	53	110	66	87	59	72	76	54	80
Interlockers as % of directors	8.82	13.52	10.19	11.75	9.76	11.74	15.15	12.85	24.29
Big linkers as % of directors	2.28	5.07	2.98	3.63	2.48	3.19	3.5	2.43	4.37
Number of board mandates	2596	2682	2515	3091	2686	2614	2597	2572	2368
Mandates of interlockers %	18.45	31.43	20.83	22.36	20.07	23.60	29.03	24.84	41.39
Mandates of interlockers N	479	843	524	691	539	617	754	639	980
Mandates of big linkers %	6.74	14.95	8.59	9.74	7.26	8.99	9.55	6.88	10.56
Mandates of big linkers N	175	401	216	301	195	235	248	177	250

312 *Appendix I*

GERMANY

Appendix UN9 A. Structure of the Network

		1896	1914	1928	1933	1938	1992	2010
Number of firms	N	211	250	250	250	250	252	251
Connected firms	N	156	236	244	245	245	237	171
	%	73.90	94.40	97.60	98.00	98.00	94.00	68.10
Isolated firms	N	55	14	6	5	5	15	80
	%	26.10	5.60	2.40	2.00	2.00	6.00	31.90
Marginal firms	N	61	27	10	14	14	31	74
	%	28.90	10.80	4.00	5.60	5.60	12.30	29.50
Isolated and marginal firms	%	55.00	16.40	6.40	7.60	7.60	18.30	61.40
Firms in main component	%	63.00	94.40	97.60	98.00	97.20	93.30	62.50
Components	N	9	1	1	1	2	2	8

Appendix UN10 B. Ties

	1896	1914	1928	1933	1938	1992	2010
Total number of ties	814	4572	10078	6888	6520	3032	752
Number of multiple ties	1018	6236	16676	10240	9632	4002	926
Percentage of multiple ties	20.00	26.70	39.60	32.70	32.30	24.20	18.80
Density %	1.84	7.34	16.19	11.07	10.47	4.79	1.20
Number of firms in 2-core	58	169	219	207	206	167	66

Appendix UN11 C. Centrality/Cohesiveness

	1896	1914	1928	1933	1938	1992	2010
Diameter	9	6	4	5	5	7	9
Average distance	3.46	2.42	1.97	2.17	2.17	2.69	3.84
Average degree centrality	3.90	18.30	40.30	27.60	26.10	12.00	3.00
Average closeness centrality (standardized)	30.00	42.40	51.60	47.10	46.90	38.30	27.10
Average betweenness centrality	102.50	157.90	115.30	139.30	138.00	184.70	138.50
Average betweenness centrality (standardized)	0.47	0.51	0.37	0.45	0.45	0.59	0.44

Appendix UN12 D. Distribution of Position over Individuals

		1896	1914	1928	1933	1938	1992	2010
Number of directors		1342	3103	5174	3867	3256		3585
Number of interlockers		198	604	1112	975	843		275
Number of big linkers		61	233	525	463	383		70
Interlockers as % of directors		14.80	19.50	21.50	25.20	25.90		7.70
Big linkers as % of directors		4.50	7.50	10.10	12.00	11.80		2.00
Number of board mandates		1665	4419	8169	6303	5401		3946
Mandates of interlockers N		510	1920	4107	3411	2988		636
Mandates of interlockers %		30.60	43.40	50.30	54.10	55.30		16.10
Mandates of big linkers N		236	1070	2933	2387	2068		226
Mandates of big linkers %		14.20	24.20	35.90	37.90	38.30		5.70

THE NETHERLANDS

Appendix UN13 A. Structure of the Network

Year		1903	1913	1928	1938	1958	1968	1983	1993	2003	2008
Number of firms	N	125	125	125	125	125	125	125	125	115	110
Marginal firms (M)	N	20	23	20	26	18	11	24	26	37	27
	%	16.00	18.40	16.00	20.00	14.40	8.80	19.20	20.80	32.20	24.50
Isolated firms (I)	N	22	20	10	18	12	11	13	13	17	42
	%	17.60	16.00	8.00	14.40	9.60	8.80	10.40	10.40	14.80	38.20
Isolated and Marginal firms	%	33.60	34.40	24.00	34.40	24.00	17.60	29.60	31.20	46.00	62.70
Firms in main component	%	78.40	84.00	90.40	82.40	88.80	91.20	88.00	88.00	85.20	50.00
Components	N	2	0	1	2	1	0	1	1	0	

Appendix UN14 B. Ties

Year	1903	1913	1928	1938	1958	1968	1983	1993	2003	2008
Total number of lines	402	416	587	439	599	573	436	371	236	80
Number of multiple lines	59	76	114	80	123	97	50	42	11	4
Firms in 2m-cores N	49	58	66	53	68	69	50	45	17	8
Firms in 2m-cores %	39.20	46.40	52.80	42.40	54.40	55.20	40.00	36.00	14.78	7.27
Density	5.19	5.37	7.57	5.67	7.73	7.39	5.63	4.79	3.60	1.33

Appendix UN15 C. Centrality/Cohesiveness

Year	1903	1913	1928	1938	1958	1968	1983	1993	2003	2008
Diameter	7	8	6	7	5	6	7	7	11	10
Average distance	3.03	2.96	2.5	2.85	2.47	2.46	2.83	2.86	3.65	4.60
Average degree	6.43	6.66	9.39	7.02	9.58	9.17	6.98	5.94	4.10	1.45
Degree centrality	5.19	5.37	7.57	5.66	7.73	7.39	5.63	4.79	3.60	
Closeness centrality	21.26	24.84	33.62	24.94	32.89	34.72	28.32	27.90	20.90	
Betweenness Centrality	1.01	1.12	1.00	1.02	0.94	0.98	1.15	1.17	1.70	

Appendix UN16 D. Distribution of Position over Individuals

Year	1903	1913	1928	1938	1958	1968	1983	1993	2003	2008
Number of directors	674	762	851	844	956	1023	977	948	861	870
Number of interlockers	154	167	182	153	177	190	178	169	110	68
Number of big linkers	53	65	80	65	79	74	65	59	43	7
Interlockers as % of directors	22.85	21.92	21.39	18.13	18.51	18.57	18.22	17.83	12.78	7.82
Big linkers as % of directors	7.86	8.53	9.40	7.70	8.26	7.23	6.65	6.22	4.99	0.80

Appendix I 315

SWITZERLAND

Appendix UN17 A. Structure of the Network

		1910	1929	1937	1957	1980	1990	2000	2010
Number of firms	N	100	100	100	100	100	100	100	100
Connected firms	N	85	90	89	91	94	91	89	76
	%	85.00	90.00	89.00	91.00	94.00	91.00	89.00	76.00
Isolated firms	N	15	10	11	9	6	9	11	24
	%	15.00	10.00	11.00	9.00	6.00	9.00	11.00	24.00
Marginal firms	N	23	22	15	17	12	19	29	37
	%	23.00	22.00	15.00	17.00	12.00	19.00	29.00	37.00
Isolated and marginal firms	N	38	32	26	26	18	28	40	61
	%	38.00	32.00	26.00	26.00	18.00	28.00	40.00	61.00
Firms in main component	N	82	90	89	91	94	88	82	70
	%	82.00	90.00	89.00	91.00	94.00	88.00	82.00	70.00
Components	%	17	11	12	10	7	11	15	28

Appendix UN18 B. Ties

	1910	1929	1937	1957	1980	1990	2000	2010
Total number of lines	267	356	384	432	428	351	199	115
Number of multiple lines	73	99	78	90	92	63	21	9
Density	5.30	7.10	7.70	8.60	8.60	7.00	4.00	2.30
Number of firms in 2-slice	59	61	61	55	57	43	28	16

Appendix UN19 C. Centrality/Cohesiveness

	1910	1929	1937	1957	1980	1990	2000	2010
Diameter	8	6	5	6	5	6	9	11
Average distance	3.0	2.8	2.5	2.5	2.5	2.6	3.7	4.3
Average degree	5.30	7.10	7.70	8.60	8.60	7.00	4.00	2.30
Degree centrality	5.40	7.20	7.80	8.70	8.60	7.10	4.00	2.30
Closeness centrality	23.40	30.40	32.70	34.90	36.90	30.60	19.10	11.10
Betweenness centrality	1.40	1.50	1.20	1.20	1.30	1.30	1.80	1.60

Appendix UN20 D. Distribution of Position over Individuals

	1910	1929	1937	1957	1980	1990	2000	2010
Number of directors	734	729	702	778	842	780	781	823
Number of interlockers	148	174	170	182	181	157	107	85
Number of big linkers	51	63	74	70	67	67	31	18
Interlockers as % of directors	20.20	23.90	24.20	23.40	21.50	20.10	13.70	10.30
Big linkers as % of directors	6.90	8.60	10.50	9.00	7.90	8.60	4.00	2.00
Number of mandates	970	1022	1000	1095	1153	1045	938	927
Mandates of interlockers %	39.60	45.70	46.80	45.60	43.10	40.40	28.00	20.40
Mandates of interlockers N	384	467	468	499	491	422	263	189
Mandates of big linkers %	19.60	24.00	27.60	25.10	23.10	23.20	12.00	5.90
Mandates of big linkers N	190	245	276	275	265	242	113	55

AUSTRIA

Appendix UN21 A. Structure of the Network

		1937	1949	1958	1967	1983	1992	1999	2008
Number of firms	N	125	125	125	125	125	125	125	125
Connected firms	N	111	87	115	117	90	83	99	82
	%	88.80	69.60	92.00	93.60	72.00	66.40	79.20	65.60
Isolated firms	N	14	38	10	8	35	42	26	43
	%	11.20	30.40	8.00	6.40	28.00	33.60	20.80	34.40
Marginal firms	N	20	21	12	13	23	19	28	19
	%	16.00	16.80	9.60	10.40	18.40	15.20	22.40	15.20
Isolated and marginal firms	N	34	59	22	21	58	61	54	62
	%	27.20	47.20	17.60	16.80	46.40	48.80	43.20	49.60
Firms in main component	%	85.60	68.00	92.00	93.60	70.40	63.20	70.40	58.40
Components	N	1	1	1	1	1	2	3	3

Appendix UN22   B. Ties

	1937	1949	1958	1967	1983	1992	1999	2008
Total number of lines	739	388	1025	911	465	339	420	212
Number of multiple lines	190	74	217	267	145	103	114	67
Density	9.53	5.01	13.23	11.76	6.00	4.37	5.42	2.74
Number of firms in 2-slice	79	45	75	76	48	39	51	41

Appendix UN23   C. Centrality/Cohesiveness

	1937	1949	1958	1967	1983	1992	1999	2008
Diameter	6	6	6	5	8	5	7	6
Average distance	2.39	2.68	2.24	2.28	2.57	2.51	2.66	2.81
Average degree	11.82	6.21	16.40	14.60	7.44	5.42	6.72	3.39
Degree centrality	16.80	7.78	21.84	22.37	11.60	8.00	10.42	5.58
Closeness centrality	4.81	2.34	8.25	9.82	2.52	2.03	2.36	1.74
Betweenness centrality	0.83	0.63	0.85	0.91	0.63	0.49	0.67	0.50

Appendix UN24   D. Distribution of Position over Individuals

	1937	1949	1958	1967	1983	1992	1999	2008
Number of directors	1188	1021	1286	1975	1300	1154	1247	1215
Number of interlockers	229	135	239	413	200	149	233	159
Number of big linkers	88	46	79	177	64	58	65	56
Interlockers as % of directors	19.30	13.20	18.60	20.90	15.40	12.90	18.70	13.10
Big linkers as % of directors	7.40	4.50	6.10	9.00	4.90	5.00	5.20	4.60
Number of mandates	1633	1252	1755	2847	1649	1415	1613	1454
Mandates of interlockers %	41.30	29.20	40.30	45.10	33.30	29.00	48.00	27.40
Mandates of interlockers N	674	366	708	1285	549	410	599	398
Mandates of big linkers %	24.00	15.00	22.10	28.60	16.80	16.10	21.10	13.20
Mandates of big linkers N	392	188	388	813	277	228	263	192

FRANCE

Appendix UN25 A. Structure of the Network

		1911	1928	1937	1956	1979	1990	2000
Number of firms	N	245	236	241	255	247	252	250
Connected firms	N	226	222	226	239	231	230	201
	%	92.20	94.90	93.80	93.70	93.50	91.30	80.40
Isolated firms	N	19	12	15	16	16	22	49
	%	7.80	5.10	6.20	6.30	6.50	8.70	19.60
Marginal	N	12	10	7	29	13	10	26
firms	%	4.90	4.30	20.90	11.40	5.30	4.00	10.40
Isolated and	N	31	22	22	45	29	32	75
marginal firms	%	12.70	9.40	9.10	17.60	11.70	12.70	30.00
Firms in main	N	226	220	224	235	229	230	190
component	%	92.20	94.00	92.90	92.20	92.70	91.30	76.00
Components	N	20	14	17	18	18	23	55

Appendix UN26 B. Ties

	1911	1928	1937	1956	1979	1990	2000
Total number of lines	2936	2956	3634	1776	2876	3134	1640
Number of multiple ties	532	582	862	310	644	592	282
Density (dichotomized network)	4.90	5.40	6.30	2.70	4.70	5.00	2.60
Density among financial firms (dichotomized network)	9.30	8.90	11.50	5.00	12.90	11.50	5.70
Density among non-financial firms (dichotomized network)	4.50	5.10	6.10	2.50	3.40	4.00	2.30
Number of firms in 2-slice	164	166	183	134	164	160	113

Appendix UN27 C. Centrality/Cohesiveness

	1911	1928	1937	1956	1979	1990	2000
Diameter (dichotomized network)	9	7	6	7	7	7	8
Average distance (dichotomized network)	2.74	2.62	2.4	3.30	2.74	2.63	3.01
Average degree (dichotomized network)	12.00	12.65	15.10	6.95	11.65	12.45	6.55
Average degree in main component (dichotomized network)	13.00	13.40	16.20	7.50	12.60	13.60	8.60
Degree centralization % (dichotomized network)	13.20	15.70	23.90	12.70	11.60	14.30	9.90
Closeness centralization % (main comp. only (dn))	23.60	23.20	30.90	26.90	22.50	24.20	26.40
Betweenness centralization % (dichotomized network)	4.80	4.90	6.10	9.60	3.60	3.60	4.70

Appendix UN28 D. Distribution of Position over Individuals

	1911	1928	1937	1956	1979	1990	2000
Directors	1578	1809	1816	1846	2050	2087	2005
Interlockers	437	474	549	424	446	438	331
Big linkers	186	219	253	149	213	213	130
Interlockers as % of directors	27.70	26.20	30.20	23.00	21.80	21.00	16.50
Big linkers as % of directors	11.80	12.10	13.90	8.10	10.40	10.20	6.50
Number of positions	2444	2756	2980	2538	2975	3010	2590
% of positions held by interlockers	53.30	51.60	57.50	44.00	46.10	45.30	35.30
% of positions held by big linkers	32.80	33.10	37.60	22.30	30.40	30.30	19.80

Appendix I
ITALY

Appendix UN29 A. Structure of the Network

		1913	1927	1936	1960	1972	1983	2001
Number of firms	N	250	250	250	250	250	250	250
Connected firms	N	229	235	231	233	226	217	179
	%	91.60	94.00	92.40	93.20	90.40	86.80	71.60
Isolated firms	N	21	15	19	17	24	33	71
	%	8.40	6.00	7.60	6.80	9.60	13.20	28.40
Marginal firms	N	27	32	29	21	45	63	70
	%	10.80	12.80	11.60	8.40	18.00	25.20	28.00
Isolated and marginal firms	N	48	47	48	38	69	96	141
	%	19.20	18.80	19.20	15.20	27.60	38.40	56.40
Firms in main component	N	229	234	223	229	222	209	153
	%	91.60	93.60	89.20	91.60	88.80	83.60	61.20
Components (exc. isolated firms)	N	1	3	5	3	3	5	12

Appendix UN30 B. Ties

	1913	1927	1936	1960	1972	1983	2001
Total number of lines	1484	2680	1693	1768	1270	637	420
Number of multiple lines	304	736	463	545	291	182	143
Density (x100)	4.77	8.61	5.44	5.68	4.08	2.05	1.35
Number of firms in 2-slice	158	187	177	188	161	133	95

Appendix UN31 C. Centrality/Cohesiveness

	1913	1927	1936	1960	1972	1983	2001
Diameter	7	6	6	7	7	9	11
Average distance	2.75	2.37	2.57	2.61	2.96	3.84	4.23
Average degree	11.87	21.44	13.54	14.10	10.16	5.10	3.35
Degree centrality (x100)	16.25	35.45	20.02	28.28	17.34	8.06	5.93
Closeness centrality	78.42	95.14	79.32	82.45	68.90	47.07	23.28
Betweenness centrality	0.06	0.08	0.07	0.09	0.06	0.09	0.08

Appendix UN32   D. Distribution of Position over Individuals

	1913	1927	1936	1960	1972	1983	2001
Total number of directors	1571	1827	1618	1932	2230	2108	1850
Number of interlockers	381	472	412	471	415	373	273
Number of big linkers	182	235	194	214	164	117	73
Interlockers as % of directors	24.25	25.83	25.46	24.38	18.61	17.69	14.76
Big linkers as % of directors	11.58	12.86	11.99	11.08	7.35	5.55	3.95
Number of mandates	2392	3024	2546	2933	3015	2678	2263
Mandates of interlockers %	50.20	55.20	52.60	50.20	39.80	35.20	30.30
Mandates of interlockers N	1201	1669	1340	1472	1200	943	686
Mandates of big linkers %	33.60	39.40	35.30	32.70	23.20	16.10	12.60
Mandates of big linkers N	803	1193	904	958	698	431	286

PORTUGAL

Appendix UN33   A. Structure of the Network

		1913	1925	1937	1957	1973	1983	1997	2010
Number of firms	N	125	125	125	125	125	125	125	125
Connected firms	N	71	85	73	84	80	23	64	76
	%	56.80	68.00	58.40	67.20	64.00	18.40	51.20	60.80
Isolated firms	N	54	40	52	41	45	102	61	49
	%	43.20	32.00	41.60	32.80	36.00	81.60	48.80	39.20
Marginal firms	N	39	44	42	58	53	23	36	37
	%	31.20	35.20	33.60	46.40	42.40	18.40	28.80	29.60
Isolated and marginal firms	N	93	84	94	99	98	125	97	86
	%	74.40	67.20	75.20	79.20	78.40	100.00	77.60	68.80
Firms in main component	N	66	53	54	48	43	3	56	68
	%	52.80	50.40	43.20	38.40	34.40	2.40	44.80	54.40
Components	N	2	4	3	7	7	3	1	2

Appendix UN34 B. Ties

	1913	1925	1937	1957	1973	1983	1997	2010
Total number of lines	120	198	117	102	101	15	92	129
Number of multiple lines	18	85	21	26	23	9	52	50
Density %	1.55	2.55	1.51	1.32	1.30	0.19	1.19	1.67
Number of firms in 2-slice	16	24	15	15	20	6	16	39

Appendix UN35 C. Centrality/Cohesiveness

	1913	1925	1937	1957	1973	1983	1997	2010
Diameter	14	8	8	13	8	2	8	9
Average distance	4.91	3.10	3.39	4.74	3.67	1.06	3.66	3.63
Average degree	1.92	3.17	1.87	1.63	1.62	0.24	1.47	2.06
Degree centralization	9.08	12.98	9.12	5.22	6.05	1.44	9.45	8.96
Betweenness centralization	9.43	6.01	7.33	6.88	4.21	0.01	10.84	10.49

Appendix UN36 D. Distribution of Position over Individuals

	1913	1925	1937	1957	1973	1983	1997	2010
Number of directors	445	545	512	537	675	583	790	945
Number of interlockers	63	95	69	74	82	20	77	108
Number of big linkers	19	28	15	16	10	3	21	26
Interlockers as % of directors	14.20	17.40	13.50	13.80	12.10	3.40	9.70	11.40
Big linkers as % of directors	4.30	5.10	2.90	3.00	1.50	0.50	2.70	2.80
Number of mandates	536	696	606	633	773	605	896	1085
Mandates of interlockers %	28.70	35.30	26.90	26.90	23.30	6.90	20.40	22.90
Mandates of interlockers N	154	246	163	170	180	42	183	248
Mandates of big linkers %	12.30	16.10	9.10	8.50	4.70	1.50	7.90	7.70
Mandates of big linkers N	66	112	55	54	36	9	71	84

Appendix I 323

BULGARIA

Appendix UN37 A. Structure of the Network

		1912	1929	1939	1945	1994	2005
Number of firms	N	125	125	125	125	125	125
Connected firms	N	95	111	107	108	34	41
	%	76.00	88.80	85.60	86.40	27.20	32.80
Isolated firms	N	30	14	18	17	91	84
	%	24.00	11.20	14.40	13.60	72.80	67.20
Marginal firms	N	31	28	24	32	33	41
	%	24.80	22.40	19.20	25.60	26.40	32.80
Isolated and marginal firms	%	48.80	33.60	33.60	39.20	99.20	100.00
Firms in main component	N	93	111	106	102	6	4
Components	N	2	1	1	3	12	17

Appendix UN38 B. Ties

	1912	1929	1939	1945	1994	2005
Total number of lines	284	360	377	313	23	24
Number of multiple lines	71	224	192	146	2	18
Density						
- for whole network %	3.70	4.60	4.90	4.00	0.30	0.30
- for ties within financial sector %	10.70	9.70	16.00	12.00	1.70	1.00
- for ties between industrial and financial sector %	4.90	6.20	5.60	4.60	0.40	0.10
- industrial sub-networks %	2.60	3.60	3.80	3.30	0.10	0.40
Number of firms in 2-core	74	99	95	84	3	3

Appendix UN39 C. Centrality/Cohesiveness

	1912	1929	1939	1945	1994	2005
Diameter	11	9	8	9	5	4
Average distance	6.90	4.40	4.40	5.10	5.00	4.00
Average degree						
- of network	2.30	2.90	3.00	2.50	0.20	0.20
- of main component	3.10	3.20	3.60	3.00	0.80	0.80
Degree centrality (normalized degree)	0.80	0.80	0.70	0.70	0.10	0.10
- network centralization by degree	3.00	3.60	2.60	2.30	0.90	0.70
Closeness centrality (normalized closeness)	2.80	5.90	4.80	3.90	0.80	0.80
Betweenness centrality (normalized betweenness)	1.20	1.40	1.30	1.30	0.00	0.00
- network centralization by betweenness %	9.50	7.20	6.70	8.50	0.10	0.00

324 *Appendix I*

Appendix UN40   D. Distribution of Position over Individuals

	1912	1929	1939	1945	1994	2005
Number of directors	1046	1339	1260	1192	572	816
Number of interlockers	101	204	157	125	26	45
Number of big linkers	38	66	58	45	1	1
Interlockers as % of directors	9.70	15.20	12.50	10.50	4.50	5.50
Big linkers as % of directors	3.60	4.90	4.60	3.80	0.20	0.10

FINLAND

Appendix UN41   A Structure of the Network

		1912	1927	1938	1974	1984	1994	2004
Number of firms	N	100	100	100	88	86	87	100
Connected firms	N	86	69	77	65	64	60	64
	%	86.00	69.00	77.00	73.86	74.42	68.97	64.00
Isolated firms	N	14	31	23	23	22	27	36
	%	14.00	31.00	23.00	26.14	25.58	31.03	36.00
Marginal firms	N	32	25	21	29	25	26	17
	%	32.00	25.00	21.00	32.95	29.07	29.89	17.00
Isolated and marginal firms	%	46.00	56.00	44.00	59.09	54.65	60.92	53.00
Firms in main component	%	75	64	75	67	65	63	64
Components	N	20	34	25	26	26	30	37

Appendix UN42   B. Ties

	1912	1927	1938	1974	1984	1994	2004
Number of ties	216	163	189	155	147	125	148
Number of multiple ties	37	27	38	30	41	13	9
Multiple ties (%)	17.13	16.56	20.11	19.35	27.89	10.40	06.08
Density (%)	4.40	3.30	3.80	4.10	3.90	3.30	3.00
Firms in 2-core (N)	47	28	41	36	33	15	17

Appendix UN43   C. Centrality/Cohesiveness

	1912	1927	1938	1974	1984	1994	2004
Diameter	8	9	9	9	7	7	8
Average distance	3.20	3.30	3.50	3.20	3.00	3.10	3.20
Average degree	4.30	3.30	3.80	3.50	3.30	2.90	3.00
Average betweenness centrality	1.40	1.20	1.20	0.90	1.60	1.00	0.70

Appendix UN44   D. Distribution of Position over Individuals

	1912	1927	1938	1974	1984	1994	2004
Number of directors	402	477	496	499	498	492	585
Number of interlockers (more than 3)	91	82	109	79	86	70	86
Number of big linkers	31	27	40	28	29	23	23
Interlockers (% of N)	22.64	17.19	21.98	15.83	17.27	14.23	14.70
Big linkers (% of N)	7.71	5.66	8.06	5.61	5.82	4.67	3.93
Mandates (N)	551	607	665	621	628	593	702
Mandates of interlockers N	239	212	274	201	216	171	204
Mandates of interlockers %	43.38	34.93	41.20	32.37	34.39	28.84	29.06
Mandates of big linkers N	121	102	140	99	102	77	78
Mandates of big linkers %	21.96	16.80	21.05	15.94	16.24	12.98	11.11

ARGENTINA

Appendix UN45 A. Structure of the Network

		1923	1937	1945	1954	1970	1990	2000
Number of firms	N	125	125	125	125	123	127	125
Firms in sample	N		59	85	58	48	49	56
previous year	%		47.0	68.0	46.0	39.0	39.0	45.0
Marginal firms	N	27	30	25	30	37	28	25
	%	21.00	24.00	20.00	24.00	30.00	22.00	20.00
Isolated firms	N	50	29	36	36	47	76	76
	%	40.00	23.00	28.80	28.80	38.00	59.00	60.00
Isolated and marginal firms	%	61.00	47.00	48.80	52.80	68.00	82.00	80.00
Firms in main component	%	47.00	64.00	63.20	66.00	50.00	18.00	5.00
Components (2m)	N	10	10	12	14	7	10	8

Appendix UN46 B. Ties

	1923	1937	1945	1954	1970	1990	2000
Total number of lines	263	405	344	300	236	180	169
Total number of lines (main component)	182	349	291	255	167	55	13
Total number of lines (main component dichotomized)	123	236	211	171	104	31	6
Number of multiple lines (main component)	59	113	80	84	63	24	7
Firms in 2m-cores N	23	45	52	44	18	24	21
Firms in 2m-cores %	18.40	36.00	42.00	35.00	15.00	19.00	17.00
Density (main component) %	9.10	13.00	10.74	7.10	6.60	17.80	53.30
Density (main component dichotomized) %	7.44	8.50	6.80	5.00	5.50	12.30	40.00

Appendix UN47 C. Centrality/Cohesiveness

	1923	1937	1945	1954	1970	1990	2000
Diameter	10	6	8	8	12	7	4
Average distance	4.11	2.80	3.15	3.90	4.30	3.20	2.10
Average degree	2.70	6.90	5.50	4.00	2.20	1.40	1.70
Average degree (main component dichotomized)	5.10	10.30	8.40	5.80	4.00	3.90	2.70
Degree centrality (main component dichotomized)	5.10	10.30	8.40	5.80	4.00	2.90	2.70
Closeness centrality (main component dichotomized)	25.42	36.28	33.30	26.60	24.70	32.00	50.30
Betweenness centrality (main component dichotomized)	5.57	2.36	2.79	3.60	5.46	10.70	26.70

Appendix UN48   D. Distribution of Position over Individuals

	1923	1937	1945	1954	1970	1990	2000
Number of directors	489	656	662	791	891	885	786
Number of interlockers	59	122	110	108	76	56	67
Number of big linkers	21	40	40	39	16	14	15
Interlockers as percentage of directors	12.00	18.60	16.60	13.60	8.50	4.70	8.50
Big linkers as percentage of directors	4.30	6.10	6.00	5.00	1.80	1.60	1.90
Number of mandates	588	873	852	955	991	957	871
% of mandates held by interlockers	26.90	38.90	35.10	28.50	17.80	13.40	17.50
% of mandates held by big linkers	14.30	20.20	18.70	14.03	5.70	4.60	5.50

TAIWAN

Appendix UN49   A. Structure of the Network

		1941	1962	1969	1982	1988	1992	1998	2003
Number of firms	N	168	21	28	80	99	220	280	314
Connected firms	N	153	20	25	63	81	149	197	309
	%	91.10	95.20	89.30	78.80	81.80	67.70	70.40	98.40
Isolated firms	N	15	1	3	17	18	71	83	5
	%	8.90	4.80	10.70	21.20	18.10	32.30	29.30	1.60
Marginal firms	N	33	7	1	16	19	52	84	52
	%	19.60	33.30	3.60	20.00	19.20	23.60	30.00	16.60
Isolated and marginal firms	N	48	8	4	33	37	123	167	57
	%	28.60	38.10	14.30	41.30	37.40	55.90	59.60	18.20
Firms in main component	N	149	20	25	61	76	133	175	309
	%	88.70	95.20	89.30	76.30	76.80	60.50	62.50	98.40
Components	N	18	2	4	19	21	79	90	6

Appendix UN50   B. Ties

	1941	1962	1969	1982	1988	1992	1998	2003
Total number of lines	1193	144	464	950	1308	1862	1404	2694
Percentage of multiple lines	27.58	30.60	50.90	40.00	32.87	41.20	38.30	38.30
Density	0.108	0.343	0.614	0.150	0.135	0.039	0.018	0.014
Number of firms in 2-core or 2-slice	134	17	25	55	66	118	128	286

Appendix UN51 C. Centrality/Cohesiveness

	1941	1962	1969	1982	1988	1992	1998	2003
Diameter	8	5	3	5	6	8	9	15
Average distance	4.20	2.02	1.72	2.32	2.32	3.09	3.99	5.81
Average degree	7.82	51.10	35.30	25.80	24.10	17.50	6.10	3.78
Degree centrality	6.16	23.81	30.16	9.02	9.05	2.27	1.11	1.68
Closeness centrality	4.52	34.27	21.65	4.65	3.82	1.05	0.86	11.73
Betweenness centrality	0.873	4.862	2.188	0.983	0.797	0.349	0.419	0.802

Appendix UN52 D. Distribution of Position over Individuals

	1941	1962	1969	1982	1988	1992	1998	2003
Number of directors	1326	359	424	1177	1097	2307	2783	2952
Number of interlockers	218	36	78	159	142	335	445	342
Number of big linkers	84	13	21	55	46	107	99	83
Interlockers as % of directors	16.44	10.03	18.40	13.51	12.94	14.52	15.99	11.59
Big linkers as % of directors	6.33	3.62	4.95	4.67	4.19	4.64	3.56	2.81
Number of mandates	1769	411	551	1445	1332	2839	3397	3424
Mandates of interlockers %	37.37	21.41	37.21	29.55	28.30	30.54	31.17	8.64
Mandates of interlockers N	661	88	205	427	377	867	1059	296
Mandates of big linkers %	22.22	10.22	16.52	15.15	13.89	14.48	10.80	23.77
Mandates of big linkers N	393	42	91	219	185	411	367	814

JAPAN

Appendix UN53   A. Structure of the Network

		1911	1928	1937	1958	1973	1982	1992	1998	2009
Number of firms	N	250	250	250	250	250	250	250	250	250
Connected firms	N	229	221	236	132	82	41	62	141	183
	%	91.60	88.40	94.40	52.80	32.80	16.40	24.80	56.40	73.20
Isolated firms	N	21	29	14	118	168	209	188	109	67
	%	8.40	11.60	5.60	47.20	67.20	83.60	75.20	43.60	26.80
Marginal firms	N	53	38	23	93	51	26	61	92	78
	%	21.20	15.10	9.20	37.20	20.40	10.40	24.40	36.80	31.20
Isolated and marginal firms	N	74	67	37	211	219	235	249	201	145
	%	29.60	26.80	14.80	84.40	87.90	94.00	99.60	80.40	58.00
Firms in main component	%	90.00	86.80	93.60	27.20	17.20	32.00	19.20	46.80	68.80
Components	N	24	32	16	139	185	158	175	116	73

Appendix UN54   B. Ties

	1911	1928	1937	1958	1973	1982	1992	1998	2009
Total number of lines	974	1106	1236	170	134	111	94	342	668
Number of multiple lines	123	290	247	14	8	12	2	30	20
Density	0.031	0.036	0.040	0.005	0.004	0.002	0.003	0.005	0.011

Appendix UN55   C. Centrality/Cohesiveness

	1911	1928	1937	1958	1973	1982	1992	1998	2009
Diameter	7	8	7	10	9	2	14	12	14
Average distance	3.02	3.02	3.01	4.32	3.37	1.07	5.16	5.12	4.55
Degree centrality	7.79	8.84	9.89	1.32	1.07	0.44	0.75	1.37	2.71
Closeness centrality	3.54	2.75	5.26	0.48	0.44	0.40	0.46	0.68	0.97

Appendix UN56 D. Distribution of Position over Individuals

	1911	1928	1937	1958	1973	1982	1992	1998	2009
Number of directors	1366	2056	2191	3747	NA	NA	NA	NA	3920
Number of interlockers	296	372	386	103	49	NA	NA	NA	232
Number of big linkers	113	160	155	17	9	NA	NA	NA	46
Interlockers as % of directors	21.67	18.09	17.62	2.70	NA	NA	NA	NA	5.92
Number of mandates	1912	2799	2957	3248	NA	NA	NA	NA	3095
Mandates of interlockers %	43.15	39.84	37.67	5.30	NA	NA	NA	NA	10.08
Mandates of interlockers N	825	1.115	1.114	172	NA	NA	NA	NA	312
Mandates of big linkers %	24.00	24.69	22.04	1.20	NA	NA	NA	NA	2.88
Mandates of big linkers N	459	691	652	39	NA	NA	NA	NA	89

NOTE

1. Average degree is a better measure of overall cohesion than density because it does not depend on network size, so average degree can be compared between networks of different sizes (De Nooy, Mrvar, and Batagelj 2006, 64).

REFERENCES

De Nooy, Wouter, Andrej Mrvar, and Vladimir Batagelj. 2006. *Exploratory Social Network Analysis with Pajek*. New York: Cambridge University Press.

List of Contributors

Thomas David is Professor of Economic and Social History at the University of Lausanne and Director of the College of Humanities at the Ecole Polytechnique Federale of Lausanne. His main research interests are corporate governance, networks, business and financial elites, and global health. He is currently writing a book on the Swiss economic elites during the twentieth century.

Susanna Fellman is Professor of Business History at the School of Business, Economics and Law, University of Gothenburg, Sweden. She worked previously at University of Helsinki, Finland, where she received her PhD. Her main research interests are the professionalization and modernization of management, and questions related to the evolution of the Nordic model of capitalism. Currently, she is working on a project on competition policy and cartels.

Álvaro Ferreira da Silva is Associate Professor of Business and Economic History at Nova School of Business and Economics. He presently serves as Associate Dean for Faculty Affairs and Research. His current research interests include business groups and corporate networks, and organizational issues in urban infrastructures.

Pierre François is Senior Researcher at the CNRS (Sciences Po/Centre de Sociologie des Organisations) and Professor at the Ecole Polytechnique. His research consists of an economic sociology of art worlds (music, contemporary art, poetry) and of a historical sociology of French capitalism.

Georgy Ganev is a program director for economic research at the Centre for Liberal Strategies in Sofia and an assistant professor at Sofia University's Faculty of Economics and Business Administration, where he teaches courses in introductory macroeconomics, money and banking, and new institutional economics. His interests are related to issues of macroeconomics and monetary theory and policy, political economy, transition, development and growth economics, new institutional economics and social capital. Currently, he is member of the board of the Bulgarian Macroeconomic Association.

Stéphanie Ginalski is Lecturer at the Institute of Economic and Social History, Lausanne University, and at the Swiss Federal Institute of Technology, Lausanne. Her main research interests focus on corporate governance, corporate networks, business elites and family capitalism.

List of Contributors

Valtteri Härmälä graduated from economic and social history at the University of Helsinki in 2012. He has previously studied youth, youth gangs and generational issues. He is currently working as an economist in Pellervo Economic Research PTT.

Martin Ivanov is Associate Professor and Senior Research Associate at the Institute of History at the Bulgarian Academy of Science. He has published on the economic history of Bulgarian and Southeast Europe, covering the period from 1870s to the present. His most recent work has been on GDP reconstruction, the Bulgarian Commercial Bank, business elite interlocking and economic reforms of centrally planned economies. Assoc. Prof. Ivanov served as National Archivist of Bulgaria (2011–13) and is chief adviser to the President of Bulgaria on education and culture (2013–).

Satoshi Koibuchi is Associate Professor of Finance, Faculty of Commerce, Chuo University, Tokyo, Japan. His areas of focus are corporate finance, financial system and macroeconomics. Koibuchi received his MA and PhD in economics from the University of Tokyo, and BA in economics from Waseda University. Before joining Chuo, he was Assistant Professor at Chiba University of Commerce, Japan and a visiting scholar at School of International Relations and Pacific Studies, University of California, San Diego.

Philipp Korom is a research fellow at the Max Planck Institute for the Study of Societies, Cologne. His habilitation research focuses on explanations for the widening disparities in the distribution of wealth. Other research interests are economic sociology, sociology of elites and intellectuals, and social network analysis.

Zong-Rong Lee received his PhD in sociology at the University of Chicago in 2005 and has since joined Academia Sinica, where he is currently an associate research fellow for the Institute of Sociology. His main research interest focuses on sociological understanding of individual and corporate market behaviors from the social network perspective. His recent research projects include the kinship network analysis among Taiwanese business groups and the dynamic analysis on intercorporate networks in post-war Taiwan from the institutionalist approach.

Claire Lemercier is a research professor in history at CNRS and a member of the Center for the Sociology of Organizations (Sciences Po, Paris). Among her research interests are the relationships between the State and businesses in nineteenth and twentieth century France and historical applications of social network analysis (and quantitative methods, generally).

Andrea Lluch is an associate researcher at the National Council of Scientific and Technical Research of Argentina (CONICET) and Professor at Universidad Nacional de La Pampa (Argentina). She is also a researcher at CEHDE-Universidad de San Andrés (Argentina). She was a research fellow at the Harvard Business School for the years 2007 and 2009. She was the Harvard-Newcomen Postdoctoral Fellow for 2006–2007. Her main current business research interests are in the history of direct foreign investment, family businesses and corporate networks in Argentina during the twentieth century.

André Mach is Senior Lecturer in Comparative Political Economy at the Institute of Political and International Studies (University of Lausanne). His areas of specialization include comparative political economy, economic sociology, elite sociology, industrial relations, corporate governance, interest groups, Swiss politics, and impact of globalization on national politics and policies.

Mark S. Mizruchi is the Barger Family Professor of Organizational Studies, Professor of Sociology, and Professor of Business Administration at the University of Michigan. He works in the areas of economic, organizational and political sociology, as well as on the methods of social network analysis.

Pedro Neves is Assistant Professor at ISEG—School of Economics and Management, Universidade de Lisboa. His research centers on the Portuguese business history of the nineteenth and twentieth centuries. Currently, he participates in research projects concerning the Lisbon Stock Exchange, business groups and corporate networks.

Tetsuji Okazaki is Professor of Economic History at the University of Tokyo. He currently serves as Vice-President of the International Economic History Association (IEHA). He has published extensively on the Japanese and comparative economic history in major journals, including *Journal of Economic History*, *Economic History Review* and *Explorations in Economic History*.

Kari-Matti Piilahti, PhD, is Adjunct Professor at the University of Helsinki. He specializes in economic and family history. In recent years, he has studied the structural change of the Finnish business elite in the nineteenth and early twentieth centuries.

Alberto Rinaldi is Assistant Professor of Economic History at the University of Modena and Reggio Emilia. He has published extensively on the Italian contemporary economic history, focusing in particular on industrial districts, trade, economic growth and the structure of the corporate system. His works are published in leading international journals, such as *Explorations in Economic History*, *Business History* and *Enterprise & Society*.

Erica Salvaj is a management and strategy professor at Universidad del Desarrollo (Chile). She has published several articles and chapters on corporate governance, strategy and social networks in major journals, including *Harvard Business Review*, *Business History Review* and *Corporate Governance: an International Review*. Professor Salvaj was a GCEE Fellow at Babson College (2012) and has been a visiting professor at Universidad Torcuato Di Tella (Buenos Aires) since 2009.

Todd Schifeling is a PhD candidate in the sociology program at the University of Michigan. He has published his research on how corporate networks shape employment during recessions in the *American Journal of Sociology*. His dissertation examines the proliferation of market niches over time, and how this relates to society and markets.

Gerhard Schnyder is a senior lecturer in comparative management at King's College, London. His work focuses on the institutional, political and historical contingency of national corporate governance systems and firm-level corporate governance practices. His most recent publications include "Ordoliberal Lessons for Economic Stability: Different Kinds of Regulation, Not More Regulation",

Governance (with Mathias Siems) and "Logics of action and models of capitalism: Explaining bottom-up non-liberal change", *Swiss Political Science Review* (with Julien Etienne).

Frans N. Stokman is Honorary Professor of Social Science Research Methodology, University of Groningen. His main fields of specialization are models of and strategic intervention in collective decision making, social network analysis, policy networks and local energy cooperatives.

Michelangelo Vasta is Professor of Economic History at the University of Siena, Department of Economics and Statistics. He has published extensively on the Italian contemporary economic history, focusing in particular on innovation, education, trade and the structure of the corporate system. His works are published in leading international journals such as *Economic History Review*, *Explorations in Economic History*, *Business History* and *Enterprise & Society*.

Thijs Velema is a PhD candidate in sociology at National Taiwan University, interested in social networks and status processes in institutional fields. His doctoral dissertation examines how social networks and status influence the actions of organizations and the careers of individuals within European professional football. He has published on co-authorship networks in Taiwanese academia.

Gerarda Westerhuis works as a researcher and lecturer at the Department of History and Art History (Utrecht University) and at the Department of Finance, Rotterdam School of Management (Erasmus University). Recently, she started a new research project (veni grant) entitled, "Unraveling the origins of a banking crisis: changing perceptions of risk and managerial beliefs in Dutch banking, 1957–2007". Her main research interests are banking, financing, corporate governance, networks and financial elites.

John F. Wilson is Director of Newcastle University Business School, where he is also professor of strategy. He has published extensively on British and international business history, including studies of the Co-operative Group, Ferranti, Manchester Business School and BP. In addition, he has written textbooks on British business and management history, as well as edited *Business History* for 10 years.

Paul Windolf is Professor Emeritus of Sociology at University of Trier, Germany. His areas of research include economic sociology, corporate networks and financial markets.

Index

People

America: chapter 2 (31–47); the Americans 17; Anglo-American countries 5; bank 77, 225; big business 222; CEO 119; corporate network 120; corporations 77; elite 121; industry 76; Latin 258, 260–1, 266; North 213; occupation 17; politicians 66; scholars 5
Amsterdam 220; elites 94; Exchange 94
Anglo-Saxon 149; brand of capitalism 62; corporate governance 7; economies 51, 291; heritage 7; investment funds 119; model 155, 285; view 8
Argentina 2, 15, 18–21, chapter 13 (257–75); corporate network 19
Asia 119, 273; corporate networks 6; countries 5, 68, 276; East 276; economies 69; investment funds 119; Southeast 281
Austria 2, 5, 17–19, chapter 7 (125–45); banks 225

Belgium 5, 260–1
Berlin 71, 96, 220; Berliner Handelgesellschaft 81; Wall 226
Bucharest 220
Buenos Aires 261–2, 272
Bulgaria 2, 14–15, 17, 21, chapter 11 (213–32)

Canada 7

Europe 5, 8, 131, 210, 224, 261–2; Central 226; companies 260–1; continental 5, 11; countries 5, 117, 164, 192, 210, 222; economy 193–4; European Economic Community 193, 206; European Roundtable of Industrialists 155; European Single Market 182; great power 130; integration 20, 97, 206; Organization for European Economic Cooperation (OEEC) 133; periphery 214, 226; scholars 5; Southeast 213; states 138; view 8; Western 37, 125, 137, 213

Finland 2, 14–16, 18–19, 21, chapter 12 (233–53); network 15
France 2, 5–7, 15, 18–20, 73, chapter 8 (149–68), 169, 175, 205, 233; army 73; banks 225; financial institutions 111; list of largest firms 193; network 15; occupation zones 133; part of the country 112

Germany 2, 4–5, 7, 12, 14–18, 22, 49, 56, 62, chapter 4 (66–85), 94–5, 100, 109–10, 113, 125, 131, 152, 175, 181, 184, 212, 226, 233, 291; banks 61, 95, 110, 125, 225; boards system 216; capital 141; companies 110, 120; corporate governance system 107; financial institutions 111; German-type *Kreditbanken* 214; German-type universal banks 171, 174, 179, 183; investments 220; investors 111; Germanization 17, 125, 130, 132; industry 17; *Konzern* 56;

occupation 156; *Reich* 132; Supreme Court 14; war economy 17, 132

Italy 2, 5–7, 14, 16–20, 134, chapter 9 (169–88), 205, 209, 269; bank 221; banking group 126; investments 220; Italian-Argentine business network 265; network 14

Japan 2, 15, 17–18, 68–9, 276, 280–2, chapter 15 (296–304); *amakaduri* 154; army 280–1; businesses 281; colonial period 279, 281, 283, 285; companies 18, 283; corporations 69; defeat 18, 283; Empire 280–1; firms 69, 281; government 283, 292; invasion 281; merchant law 281; military action 281; model 285; militarization of 280; Sino-Japanese war 276, 279, 281; society 68

London 96, 220

Manchester 220

Netherlands, The 2–5, 14–19, 21, 23, chapter 5 (89–106), 164, 175, 181, 184, 224, 291; banks 17; origin 260
New York 1, 71, 77, 96, 220; First National Bank of 32; National City Bank of 76

Pacific 281; South 280
Paris 15, 96, 149–50, 153, 156, 159, 163, 220; Banque de l'Union parisienne 158; Parisian firms 153–4, 157, 161, 163; Parisian headquarters 153
Portugal 2, 14–20, 134, 167, chapter 10 (191–212)

Rotterdam 220

Sofia 220, 224
Soviet: occupation zones 133; the Soviets 133; trade 244, 246; Union 19, 233, 246

Spain 7, 169
Sweden 221, 233, 238, 244, 246; Astra AB 54; network 15; Swedish-speaking 235, 239–40, 242
Switzerland 2, 5, 7, 14–15, 18–19, 21, 56, 67, 73, 91 chapter 6 (107–24), 141, 151, 164, 175, 181, 184, 224

Taiwan 2, 17–19, chapter 14 (277–95)
Tokyo 297–8
Trieste 220

UK 7, 14–15, 18–20, 22, 154, 175, 221–2, 251, chapter 3 (48–65); companies 264; corporate network 14; list of largest firms 193; occupation 74; Zeneca group PLC 54
US 2, 4–5, 7–8, 11, 14–19, 22, 51, 66–8, 73–82, 94, 100, 109, 119, 221–2, 250, 270, 283, 291; bank 61, 75–7; case 20; Clayton Act 79; companies 264, 268; Congress 1; firms 4; models 164; network 20, 72, 74; occupation 74, 80, 301; Standard Industrial Classification 58; *see also* America

Vienna 130–1, 133; Stock Exchange 127

Zurich 112

Persons, Enterprises, and Organizations

ABN AMRO 97–8, 102
Accumulatoren Fabrik 70
AKU 94
Allianz 70
Alpine Montangesellschaft 131–2, 135, 137
American & Foreign Power Company 265
Anlagewerte 110
Annual General Meetings (AGMs) 114
Astra 270
Astrazeneca 54
Austrian Federal Highway (ÖBB) 138

Index   337

Austrian Freedom Party (FPÖ) 127
Austrian People's Party (ÖVP) 127, 139
Austrian Social Democratic Party (SPÖ) 139

Baker, G.F. 32
Baker, W.E. 34–5
Banca Commerciale 14, 178
Banco de Angola 195
Banco de Buenos Aires 262
Banco de Fomento Nacional 201
Banca d'Italia 178
Banco Hipotecario Nacional 265
Banco Italia y Rio de la Plata 262, 265
Banco Nacional Ultramarino (BNU) 195, 197, 199, 201
Banco Uruguayo 262
Bank Austria 126, 138–9
Bank of Taiwan 287
Banque de l'Union parisienne 158
Barnes, R.C. 35
BB 197
BBI/BCCI 204
BCP 207
Benac, A. 155
Berov, L. 220
BES 207
Biggart, N. 69
Bjorneborgs Mekaniska Verstad (BMV) 249
BNP 162
Bodencreditanstalt 131
Bolloré groupe 161
BPA 204
BPI 207
BPSM 202
Brandeis, L. 1
Brauerei Schwechat 135
British Zeneca Group PLC 54
Bulgarian National Bank 217
Bulgaska Tugrovska Banka (BTB) 220, 224–5
Bunting, D. 32
Burovs 217
BZ Bank 118

Caiwa Geral de Depositos 200
Caoutchoucs de Padang 161
Cardenas, J. 7
Carter, J. 38
CGD 207
Chang Hua Bank (CHB) 287
Chase Manhattan Bank 41

Chemical National Bank 41, 75
Chicago National 75
Chiesi 179
Chu, J.S.G. 35, 120, 270
CNE 202
Colli, A. 183
Colpan, A. 201
Cometna 202
Committee for Economic Development (CED) 37
Commission Peters 103
Compagnie du Cambodge 161
Companhia dos tobacos de Portugal (CTP) 197, 199
Companhia Uniao Fabril (CUF) 196, 202, 204
Conseil d'Etat 154
Conyon, M. 7
Creditanstalt (CA) 125–6, 131, 134–5, 137, 140
Creditanstalt-Wiener Bankverein 131, 133
Credit Bank 221
Crédit National 154, 156
Credito Italiano 14, 178
Crédit Suisse 110, 117, 119
CSConf 202
CSM 202

Dalmine and Cia 265
David, T. 50
Davis, G.F. 34–5, 42, 120
De Fosforos Sudamericana 265
Democrazia Cristiana 180, 182
De Nooy, W. 54
Department of the Interior 38
Despres, R. 156
Deutsche Bank 70, 76–7, 132
Dougan, B. 119
Dresdnerbank 131
Dritsas, M. 127
Drysdale, A. 264
Durand, P. 156
Durand, R. 156
Durand electricity groupe, 157

Ebner, M. 118
ECL 202
Ecole nationale d'administration (ENA) 154–5
Ecole Polytechnique 154–5
EDP 207
EDP Renovaveis 207

EG3 270
Ehrnrooth, G. 248
Eihachiro Tanaka 300
Elanto 249
Elektrobank 110
Elia, S. 263
ELIN 137
Enel 180
Enso-Gutzeit 239
Enson puuhiomo 242
Ente Nazionale Idrocarburi (Eni) 171
Environmental Protection Agency 38
Equitable Trust Company 75
Evans, P. 277

Fennema, M. xv, 89
FIMBAG 138
Fina 204
Financieel Adresboek 91
Finmeccanica 179
First Bank (FirstB) 287
First National Bank of New York 32
Fiskqrs 248
Fonsecas, Santos & Viana (FSV) 197, 199
Forenings-banken i Finland-Suomen Yhdyspankki (SYP) 239, 244, 246–7
Formosa Plastics 287
Fortune 35
Fraser, D. 38
Friedrich Krupp AG 76–7

G. A. Serlachius 243
German Corporate Governance Code 74, 80
Gerschenkron, A. 179, 213
Geshovs 217
GKB-Bergbau 138
Goldschmidt, J. 73
Gösser 135
Göstq Serlachius 243
Grand Marnier 163
Granitoid 221
Granovetter, M. 1
Grantion 219
Griff, C. 60
Griten, W.C.L. van der 99
Gubidelnikov 217
Gut, R.E. 119

Hall, P. 6, 68
Hamilton, G. 69
Hankkija 249

Heemskerk, E.M. 89
Hellema, H.J. 98
Helmers, H.M. 89, 97
Hikino, T. 201
Hilferding, R. 1, 75, 107, 213
Home Savings 75
Hua Nan Bank (HNB) 287

IBM 42
Instituto per la Ricostruzione Industriale (Iri) 171

J.P. Morgan & Co. 32, 41
Jensen, M.C. 39
Johnson, L. 36
José Henriques Totta (JHT) 197, 201

Kaichiro Nezu 300
Kajaani 244
Kansallis-Osake-Pankki (KOP) 239, 244–7
Katz, R. 69
Keskusosuuskunta Liha OK 249
Kogut, B. 7
Kommerzialbank 138
Kotz, D. 75
Koyota Iwasaki 299
Kratzer, J. 192
Kuhn, Loeb & Co. 32
Kuomingtang (KMT) 276, 279, 282
Kurt And & Co. 249

Lafond, H. 158
La Hénin 160
Lampe, J. 213
Länderbank 131, 133–5, 137–8
Laumann, E. xv
Lenzing 132
Le principali società italiane 172
Leykam-Mürztaler Papier u. Zellstof 134
Louis XIV 149
Lubbers, R. 101

Maatschappij tot Financiering van National Herstel (Dutch Recovery Bank) 98
Maclean, M. 191
Manne, H.G. 39
Mannesmann 70
Marathon Oil 42
Marx, K. 55
Maschinenfabrik Andritz 134
Meckling, W.H. 39
Mediobanca 180

Mercier, E. 152
Mercurbank 131
Mestrallet, G. 155
Meynell 263
Mintz, B. xv, 75
Mitsui Ginko 298
Mitsui Shinataku 298
Mizruchi, M.S. 33, 36, 42, 153, 270
Morawetz, I. 135
Morgan, J.P. 32
Motor-Colombus 110

Nakane, C. 68
Napoleon 149
Naroden Sgovor 222
Natan, J. 220
National Association of Manufacturers (NAM) 37
National City Bank of New York 32, 76–7
National Labor Relations Board 38
Nederlandsche Handel-Maatschappij (NHM) 95
Niederösterreichische Escompte-Gesellschaft 131
Nixon, R. 36
Nokia Oy 244–5, 248
Nordiska Forenings-banken-Pohjois maiden Yhdyspankki (PYP) 239–40, 242; *see also* Forenings-banken i Finland-Suomen Yhdyspankki (SYP)
Notizie statistiche sulle principali società italiane per azioni 172

Occupational Safety and Health Administration 38
O'Farrell 263
ÖIAG 135, 137
Oji Seishi 298
OMV 127, 137
Organisation for Economic Co-operation and Development (OECD) 61
Organisation for European Economic Cooperation (OEEC) 133
Osakaya Shoten (Kabushiki Nenkan) 297
Österreichische Kontrollbank 137
Österreichische Kraftwerke 132
Österreichisches Credit-Institute 131

Pappi, F. xv
Peron government 264, 266

Petrosul 202, 204
Peyerimhoff, H. de 152
Philips 94
Pirelli 265
Pohjola 244, 248
PT 207
Pujo Committe 1

R&S-Mediobanca 172
Rae, G. 225
Raffeisen bank 139
Raffeisen Oberösterreich 139
Raffeisen Zentralbank (RZB) 139
Rauma-Repola 244
Reagan, R. 10, 19, 38, 100
Reichswerke Göring 132, 140
Renault 156
Repsol 270
Ritter, E.R. 35
Rive Reine conference 119
Roberts, E. 263, 264
Roy, W. 32
Royal Dutch Shell 94

Sacor 202, 204
Schiff, J.H. 32
Schijf, H. 89
Schnyder, G. 107–8
Schoeller-Bleckmann 132
Schwartz, M. xv, 75
Scott, J. 5, 49, 60
Semperit 134
SFSIE 110
Shintqro Ohashi 300
Shipilov, A. 7
Siemens 70
Siemens-Schukert-Werke 132
Silverberg, P. 73
Sociaal-Economische Raad (SER) 99, 100
Socialist Party (Italy) 180
Sociedad Mixta Siderurgica Argentina (SOMISA) 266, 267
Società Bancaria Italiana 14, 178
Société de banque suisse (SBS) 110, 116–18
Société Financière de Transports et d'Entreprises Industrielles (SOFINA) 265
Société Générale 162
Solmssen, G. 73
Sonae 207
Sonap 202, 204
Sonarep 202

Soskice, D. 6, 68
Standard Chartered 54
Standard & Poor's 35
Steyr-Daimler Puch 134–5
Stichting van de Arbeid 99
Stillman, J. 32
Stokman, F.N. xv, 5
Stopansko Razvitie 222
Streeck, W. 69
Swedish Astra AB 54
Sweezy, P. 4
Swiss Army 119
Swiss Bankers Association (SBA) 114, 119

Tabaksblat, M. 103
Taiwan Cement 285, 287
Taiwan Development Company (TDC) 282
Taiwan Industry Development Corp. 285
Taiwan Pulp & Paper Corporation 285
Taiwan Tea Corp 285
Tampella 240
Tarr, J. 75
Teikoku Seima 298
Telecom Austria 138
Thatcher, M. 10, 19, 100
Tokwo Dento 298
Treibacher Chemische Werke 134

Unicredit 126
Unilever 94
Union des banques suisses (UBS) 110, 116–18
United Auto Workers 38
United States Steel Corporation 32, 76–7
United Tobacco Factories 219
Universale Bau 134
UPM-Kymmene 248
Urho Kekkonen 244
US Chamber of Commerce (USCC) 37
US Congress 1
Useem, M. 31
US Standard Industriel Classification (SIC) 58

Van Oss Effectenboek 91
Van Tienhoven 96
Veen, K. van 192
Verbundgesellschaft 135, 138
Verdam, P.J. 100
VEW 137

VIAG 132
Voest-Alpine (VOEST) 132, 137, 140
Vontobel 118

W. Gutzeit & Co Oy 242
W. Rosenlew & Co Ab 249
Wartsila 248
Westerhuis, G. 50
Wiener Bank-Verein 131
Windolf, P. 49, 163, 204
Wirtschafts-Trend-Zeitschriftenverlagsgesellschaft 127

Yasuda and Mitsubishi 299
Yhdistyneet Villatehtaat Oy 242
Yoo, M. 34–5

Zentralsparkasse 138
Zenzaburo Ysuda 299
Ziegler, R. 5, 135

Themes and Topics

acquisition 4, 39–40, 43, 119, 132, 138, 142, 201, 239; merger and acquisition 40, 160, 162, 193, 200, 270, 273, 281; wave of 34, 39, 44; *see also* merger
agency 4, 22, 39, 126
Anschluss 17, 126, 130, 132
Aryanisation 17, 125, 132
asset 8, 77, 126, 130–1, 133, 192–3, 204, 216, 223–6, 283, 297, 301, 307; financial 41, 284; industrial 281; management 117, 119; net 50; total 18, 32, 91, 126–7, 171, 179, 183, 296
average: centrality 161; degree 9, 13, 16–17, 20, 35, 51–2, 57, 91–2, 96–8, 111, 153, 157–63, 174, 194–9, 206, 237, 260, 263, 268, 298; density 58–9, 237; distance 34–6, 43, 51–2, 91–2, 109, 174, 262; income 82; indegree 75; number of directors 195; number of members 219–21; number of positions 73, 173; number of relations or ties 51, 260, 290–1; outdegree 76–7; path length 7; size; ties 117

bank xv, 10–11, 15, 18, 36, 49, 56–7, 66, 75, 80, 90, 94, 101, 104, 114–15, 131, 152, 157, 160,

Index

162, 169, 180, 201, 205, 224, 244, 259, 283, 286, 298–9, 301, 303; Austrian 126; British/UK 60–1; central 102, 141, 156–8, 225; centrality 18, 49, 58, 60, 62, 77, 112, 115–16, 161; commercial 32, 41–3, 45, 98, 101, 140, 207, 239, 242, 244, 249, 262; control 3–4, 22, 63, 107–8, 112–13, 115, 120; cooperative 98, 238; crisis 16, 73, 89, 96, 246; dominance/domination 4, 56, 60–1, 130; Dutch 17, 95, 97, 101–2; German 61, 66, 72, 75–7, 79–80, 107, 110, 125, 171, 174, 183, 225; hegemony 48–9, 75; and industry/industrial companies 4, 6, 14, 16, 56, 76, 89, 96, 107, 111–13, 115, 117, 120, 126, 131–2, 134, 140, 180, 195, 209, 233–5, 242–3, 249; investment 32, 41–3, 45, 77, 80, 90, 101, 137, 158, 160, 184, 201, 207, 247; main 301; merchant 261; nationalized 135, 142; power of 3, 75, 112, 130; regional 139; role of 3, 14, 17, 22, 107, 248; private 118; secrecy 111; sector 16, 20, 49, 63, 96, 107, 126, 138, 162, 178, 193, 201, 207, 226, 244; strategy of 16, 20, 63, 101, 90, 115–16, 131, 181, 184; Swiss 108, 110–11, 113, 117, 119; universal 16, 54, 76–7, 95, 125, 131, 139, 171, 174, 178–80, 183; US 77; withdrawal of 36; *see also* board, director, family, international, law, manager, state
banker xv, 1, 3, 14, 33, 76, 78, 80, 94, 96–7, 104, 107, 120, 131, 245; position of 68, 75, 103; private 113.
betweenness centrality 9, 35, 52–3, 110, 178–9, 185, 224, 228, 261–3, 265–7
big linkers 4, 9, 16, 21, 23, 55–6, 74, 77, 80, 93, 97, 104, 116, 132, 151–6, 158–60, 164, 177–8, 197, 199, 205, 209, 234–6, 243, 246, 250–1, 263, 269–70, 299, 303, 306; German 73; very big linker 55–6, 61–3

blockholder 7, 113, 115
board: of bank, 14, 63; member/membership xvi, 15, 23, 82, 103, 110, 117, 141, 242, 251; position 4–5, 16, 40, 45, 72–4, 80–1, 97, 103–4, 158, 164, 172, 246, 248, 250–1; size 42, 102, 117, 164, 235, 237, 251, 270, 284; *see also* director, interlock
bureaucracy 18, 213, 244; *see also* state
business elite 5, 12, 55, 215–18, 221, 223, 229, 236, 287; British 251; Bulgarian 213, 218, 222–3, 227; cohesion 14–15, 56; Dutch 89; Finnish 251; group of 12; inner circle of 5; members 4, 61, 216, 227, 230; national 21; portions of the 23; pre-communist 214; pre–World War II 214; Swiss 113, 119–21; traditional 271
business group 8, 10–11, 15, 18, 22, 56, 62, 68–9; Argentina 260–2, 264–6, 268, 271–2; Austria 126, 135; Bulgaria 219; France 149–50, 155–6, 160, 165–6; Japan 297–300, 303; Portugal 199, 201–5, 207, 209; Taiwan 279–81, 285, 288, 291–2; United States 37; *see also* chaebol; zabaitsu
businessman/businessmen 19, 151, 152, 154–5, 158, 163, 172, 181–2, 204, 216, 217–18, 221, 225, 236–7, 239, 240, 242, 243; *see also* business elite, business group

capital 4, 11–12, 20, 22, 32, 94, 96–7, 99, 110, 137, 140, 181, 196, 205, 225–6, 239, 247, 267, 281; accumulation 215; concentration of 33; equity 73, 76–7, 91; finance/financial 3, 60, 75, 89, 107, 287; flow 200, 246, 284; industrial 3, 75; investment 3, 6, 110, 133, 283; patient 68, 77; share 14–15, 113, 121, 127, 131, 150, 153, 157, 160–3, 180–1, 258; stock 238; supplier 4, 101; working 95; *see also* foreign, market, social capital
capitalism 14, 55, 61, 81, 193, 196, 236, 246, 261, 269; British 48–9, 54, 56, 62; Bulgarian

214–15, 217, 229–30; competitive 33, 66; cooperative 33, 66–7; coordinated 156; family 276; finance/financial 48, 60; French 149–50, 154, 157, 160, 166; Italian 169–71, 180; local 257, 270–1; managerial 48; modern 3–4; monopolistic 220; organized 66, 79, 109, 115; political 169, Portuguese 191; primary-export 259; Rhineland 69, 155; state capitalism 10, 138, 147, 166; varieties of (VOC) 6–7, 67, 149, 169–70, 191, 210, 234
capitalization 32, 101, 118, 164, 181
cartel/cartelization 4, 10, 11, 14, 15, 17, 33, 54, 58–60, 66–9, 71–2, 74, 78–80, 111, 114, 150, 155–6, 162, 200, 204, 291; *see also* law
centrality 42, 57, 68, 153, 159, 174, 178, 223, 234, 240, 265, 268–9, 279, 292, 298, 306; measure 50, 52, 178–9, 298; *see also* average, bank, betweeness centrality, closeness; degree; eigenvector
CEO 40–1, 43, 45, 75, 82, 119, 158, 217, 235–7, 239, 241, 243–8, 251–2
chaebol 68–9
clique 161, 166, 194, 199, 202, 206, 220–1, 223, 228, 259
closeness 52–3, 153; centrality 35, 52, 174, 266; score 52
cluster 195, 197, 199, 202, 204, 209, 219, 220, 221, 228, 230, 264, 269, 287
coalition 12, 127, 180, 182, 191, 209, 224–5, 263, 272, 282
cohesion 3–4, 10, 14–15, 18, 22, 35, 39, 52, 89, 126, 172, 197, 221, 291; class 11, 15, 19, 56, 62, 108, 112–13, 121, 152, 191, 251, 257; de-cohesion 269–70; group 68; national 107; of the network 9, 16, 32, 53, 116, 130, 172, 174, 177, 181, 193, 199, 202, 207, 209, 260, 264–6, 297, 302, 306; political 251; social 4, 69, 71, 113, 120
Cold War 17, 283
colonization/colonial/colony 17, 93, 132, 160, 195–7, 199–200, 209, 277, 280, 285; company 161, 197, 199, 204; economy 279–82; enterprise 22, 209; firm 15, 94, 194, 197, 200, 202; government 18, 280, 282, 292; period 277, 279–80, 283–5, 288, 292; *see also* economy; elite; firm; government; state
communication 3–4, 10–11, 22, 37, 61, 138, 178–9, 191, 264, 271
communism/communist 10, 17, 159, 214, 217, 222, 226, 283; party 15, 17, 73, 214, 226; post-communism 21, 215, 227–30
company: network 48, 55, 60, 107–8, 113, 116–17, 120, 238; stock company 4, 133, 216, 222; foreign 110, 119, 127, 248, 250, 260, 263, 265, 271–3; *see also* state; bank
comparison 2, 8–9, 17, 23, 51, 63, 80, 89, 127, 150, 164, 184, 191, 215, 218, 240, 305
competition xv, 3, 10–11, 16, 22, 62, 117, 134, 162, 182, 200, 204; anarchic 66; free 66; global xvi, 37–8; international 34; law 58; regulation of/regulated 67, 69, 78–9; restrict(ed) 4, 33, 191
component xv, 182, 269; k-components 135; main 33, 35, 43, 54, 61, 92–3, 108, 113, 129–30, 135–6, 154, 157, 161, 173, 195, 197–200, 202, 206, 257, 259–64, 266, 268–9, 278–80, 290; secondary 202, 206; separate 159; small 130, 153
concentration 7, 33, 76, 116, 118, 125, 156, 166, 197, 199; camp 214; deconcentration 17, 74; ownership 170
connection 20, 21, 40, 44, 93, 97, 120, 155, 158, 195, 199, 221–2, 227–30, 240, 243–44, 250–1, 265, 284, 290–9; connectivity 34–5, 38, 40, 43, 49, 51, 53, 62, 128, 135, 174, 180, 182–3, 214–5, 222, 228–31, 257, 265; direct connection 133; disconnection 92, 102, 177–8, 181; family 217; few 21, 43, 90, 119, 249; interconnection 8, 111, 135, 177, 184, 202, 204, 206, 271; international 261; political 12,

114, 119, 229, 233, 264, 285; *see also* family
control xvi, 1, 3, 6, 7, 12, 14, 16, 22, 53, 56, 62, 68, 71, 107, 112, 115, 125, 134, 162, 180–1, 223, 261, 265; corporate 284, 299; exchange 262, 272; function 63, 104, 151, 251; hierarchy of 128; management/managerial 192, 272; model 10; moral 4; mutual 49; network 287; oligopolistic 60; over the economy 127, 138; ownership and 10, 18, 48, 60, 103, 205; price 200; *see also* bank; state
cooperation 16, 19, 43, 67, 69, 98, 113, 121, 204
coordinated market economy (CME) 2, 6–7, 67, 107, 169, 250,
coordination 4, 10, 15, 19–20, 22–3, 58, 60–3, 66–7, 74, 79, 113, 115, 120, 125–6, 128, 169, 204–5, 209, 258, 264, 271; *see also* elite
core 18, 56, 130, 132, 135, 138, 150–51, 155, 213, 217, 221, 235, 257, 260–3, 279, 282, 285, 287, 298; core-periphery 20, 155, 161, 165; company/firm 249, 299, 303; group 251; hard 160; m-core 53, 92, 305; of the network 19, 21, 153–4, 156, 159–60, 163, 223, 240, 246, 259, 264, 266–9
corporate governance 7, 67, 74, 81, 107, 113, 120, 170, 299–303; code 74, 80, 103–4; movement 61–3
corporate network 1–2, 4–8, 10, 48, 66–8, 70–1, 82, 96, 107, 114, 125, 129, 137–8, 191–2, 242, 257–8, 276, 283–5, 298–302; American 31–3, 35–6, 43–4, 120; Argentina 261–7, 269, 270–1; Austrian 126, 128, 140; British 49, 53, 61; decline of 16–17, 20–21, 31, 36, 44, 74, 90, 101, 120, 140, 175, 178, 181, 184, 292; Dutch 89, 91–3, 97, 103; emergence of 13–15, 19–20, 196–9, 206, 209; Finnish 234–5, 239, 247; functions of 3, 20; German 69, 72, 74, 79–80, 83; intercorporate network 12,

48, 125–6, 140–2, 277, 283–5, 292–3; Italian 171–5, 177–84; Japanese 295, 297, 303; national xiii, xvi, 14–15, 18, 21–2, 90; Portuguese 193, 195–7, 204, 206–7, 209–10; structure 9, 11, 12, 17–18, 20; Swiss 108–11; Taiwan 292–3
corporatism/corporatist 17, 37, 99, 104, 155, 192, 194–6, 207, 243, 279, 288; economy 290–1; institutions 19, 195, 200–1, 204–5, 209
cosmopolitan 23
creditor 10–11, 77
culture 15, 77, 97, 102, 155, 171, 239

debt/debtor 3, 6, 14, 32, 68, 76–7, 80, 90, 127, 180, 182, 225, 264
decartelization 17, 74, 80
degree 42, 51, 63, 81, 132, 185, 197, 237, 240, 242, 263, 297; centrality 9, 98, 110–11, 131, 142, 161, 174, 178–9, 185, 223–4, 240, 267, 278, 298, 302; cumulated 56–7; of economic development 10, 22; of fragmentation 271; highest 97; of homophily 159; of interaction 271; of interlocks 248; mean 160, 278; outstanding 152; score 42; *see also* average degree; indegree; network; outdegree
density 9, 19, 38, 51, 59, 68–70, 79, 150, 155, 160, 165, 175, 193, 221, 228, 260, 262, 268, 297–8, 302, 305; decline/decrease 20, 96, 158, 161, 237, 247, 265; intra-sectoral 58–9, 78–9, of interlocks 157, 289; of network/corporate network 14–16, 18, 21, 31–5, 40, 43, 51–3, 58, 72–4, 78, 80, 90, 108–9, 120, 174, 199, 206, 209–10, 214, 233–4, 263, 266, 291, 303; of ties 21, 161, 166, 202, 204; *see also* average
depression 8, 22, 32, 262; Great Depression 15–16, 96, 131, 171, 180, 192, 194–5, 200–2, 215, 217, 258
diameter 35, 174
directors 1, 3–4, 9–10, 12–13, 15–16, 21, 23, 32–3, 43–5, 49, 51, 53,

55, 61–3, 67, 70, 73, 75, 80, 82, 90–1, 97, 100–4, 112, 116, 120–1, 132, 142, 150–1, 153, 156, 158, 163, 172, 191, 195, 214, 216–17, 222, 227–30, 263, 267, 280, 284, 286, 288, 290–2, 297, 301; appointment of 205; bank 70, 75–6, 80, 102; board of 18, 48, 50, 60–1, 67, 107–9, 118, 181, 233, 235–6, 245, 247, 299; central 262, 264, 268, 270, 290; characteristics of 32; choice of 154; circle of 287–9; company 4, 297; composition of 239; connected 33, 237, 262, 264, 270, 288; director-general 132; directorship 4, 7, 33, 40, 130–1, 171, 177–8, 180–4, 195, 205, 226, 242–3, 246–7, 284, 296, 299–300, 303; distribution 55; Dutch 90, 96; elite 289–90; executive 1, 75–7, 108, 156, 216, 226, 242; external 82, 267, 302; Finnish-speaking 239; foreign 21, 102, 113, 118–19, 164; French 151; groups of 104; high-status 150, 164–6; independent 164; individual 55, 234; inside 270; interlocking 279–80, 290, 298; Jewish 16, 73; joint 181; managing 90–1, 95–6, 98, 103–4, 236, 243, 251; multiple 67, 128, 243, 248, 263, 265, 302; network of 23, 94, 279; non-executive 1, 62, 91, 94, 156, 205; outside 40, 62; percent of 93, 197; profile of 257, 263; rewarded 164; selected 217; shared 31, 61, 109, 153, 260, 277, 281, 285; single 128, 173; supervisory 91, 96, 98–100; Swiss 118; top 98; types of 263, 269; *see also* average; ties
directory 82, 277, 297
disintermediation 101
distance 21, 34–6, 43, 51–3, 91–2, 109, 174, 262, 306

economy 3, 12, 18, 31, 36, 40, 44, 121, 125–7, 130–2, 138, 149, 151, 181, 182, 199–201, 206, 225, 228, 236, 238, 243, 257–8, 262, 266–7, 277, 279–80, 283, 288, 292; Agrarian 224, Argentine 260, 268–9 Austrian 125, 127–33, 137, 141, Bulgarian 220, 227, 229, colonial 279, 280, 282, corporatist 200, 290, Dutch 90, 93–4, European 193, Finnish; French 152, 156, 246–7, 250, German 66–7, 73, global 69, 260, 271, hidden/black 229–30; internationalization of/ globalization of 16–17, 74, 109, Italian 184, Japanese 297, 299, 300; local 17, 132, mature 69, mixte 125, 134, 140, moral 66, national 15, 71, 183; new 81, political 19, 22, 276, Portuguese 194–5, 200; state 10; socialist 215; war 17, 132; Swiss 108, 112, 120; Taiwan 276–7, 281, 285, 288; world 5, 19; *see also* coordinated market economy (CME), liberal market economy (LME), manager, market
education 12, 44, 67, 118, 154, 191
eigenvector 260–1, 267; centrality 263; score 265
electricity 132–3, 138, 152, 156–7, 172–4, 179–80, 183, 195–6, 202, 204, 207, 219–20, 252, 263, 288
elite 11–12, 130, 155, 221, 223, 230, 258; American 121; Amsterdam 94; Bulgarian 21; club 217; cohesion 120, 152; colonial 281; consolidation 221; coordination 23; corporate 37–8, 44, 89, 102, 264–6; economic 23, 73, 164, 217, 249; families 149–50; French 154; group 219; interconnected 266; members 217, 222, 227, 263, 271; military 282; network 121, 249; political 12, 19, 218, 223, 230, 244, 249; qualifications of 217; recruitment 23; regional 112; reproduction 154; schools 155–6, 164; social 270, 288; sociology of 22; solidarity 270; Swiss 109, 113, 119–20; traditional 263, 266; transnational 23; unification of 221; wealthy 97; *see also* business elite; directors
employee 9, 12, 19, 67–8, 94, 97, 99–100, 118, 131, 200, 301–3

family 94, 155–6, 163, 218, 226, 231, 242, 246, 250, 261, 276; bank 199; business group 149, 201, 281, 285, 288, 291, 292; capitalism 276; connections 217; firm 10, 22, 98, 113, 163–4, 194, 245, 249, 260, 262, 276, 285; ownership 234, 298; ties 1, 11, 277, 284; *see also* shareholder

finance/financial; center 96, 107–8, 110; companies 3, 48, 56, 97, 107–8, 111, 120, 225, 233, 267; firms 8, 32, 34, 50, 102–3, 110, 159–61, 169, 193–5, 296–7, 318; hegemony 3, 292; institution/institutions 1, 32, 34, 41, 44, 49, 60, 76, 111, 119, 132, 213, 221, 272, 286, 292; sector 8, 10, 16, 48, 56–8, 61, 76, 79, 108, 111, 116, 120, 159–60, 173, 201, 205–6, 219, 225–6, 323; system 111, 138, 233–4, 247, 283, 299–301, 303; *see also* asset, capital capitalism, foreign, market

financialization 5, 8, 90, 101, 160, 165

firms: colonial 15, 94, 194, 197, 200, 202; domestic 5, 260, 270; family 10, 22, 98, 113, 163–4, 194, 245, 249, 276, 285; industrial 68, 70, 75–7, 89, 95, 107–8, 112–13, 117, 120, 159, 240, 248, 252, 262, 264, 299; (inter)connected 53, 109, 129–30, 197, 202, 240, 249, 298, 305, 307, 309, 316, 318, 320–1, 324, 327, 329; isolated 82, 92, 129–30, 153, 173, 183, 260, 262, 269, 280, 305, 307, 309, 313, 318, 320–1, 324, 326–7, 329; joint-stock 8, 227; marginal 108–9, 129, 173–4, 183, 195, 209, 259, 266, 305, 307, 309, 312–13, 316, 318, 320–1, 323–4, 326–7, 329; non-financial 10, 41–2, 49–50, 56, 58, 63, 76–8, 102, 154, 161, 193–4, 259, 297, 299, 318; public 5, 19, 157, 205, 284, 288, 289–90, 291; *see also* company, core, foreign

Foreign Direct Investment 10, 269, 272–3

foreign/foreigners 15, 19, 90, 102, 110, 112, 118–20, 199, 217; capital 111, 201, 229, 239, 246–7, 258, 260, 265, 267, 270, 272; company/firms 110, 119, 127, 163, 193, 219, 225, 229, 248, 250, 257, 263–5, 367–8, 271; financial market 15, 119; influence 15, 110, 120, 160; investors/investments 115, 119, 141, 165, 197, 220, 260–1, 263; occupation 17, 276; overforeignization 110; ownership 228, 230, 239, 248, 250; sales 97; *see also* directors, international

fragmentation 44, 219, 220–1, 247–9, 259, 266, 268, 270–1

globalization xvi, 2, 5, 7–8, 13, 19–22, 74, 90, 93, 96, 185, 248

governance 155–6; *see also* corporate governance

government 4, 10, 16–17, 19–20, 267–9, 271, 296; Austrian 131, 133–4, 137–41; Bulgarian 223; coalitions 182; colonial 18, 280–2; Dutch 100; fascist 171; French 149; German 73; Indonesian 97; Italian 170; Japanese 300–1; Kuomintang 276, 283–92; ownership 140; Peron 264; Portuguese 201, 205; right-wing 160; Socialist-Communist 159; US 31, 33, 26–9, 43–4; Vichy 158; *see also* state

hegemony 3, 5, 48–9, 75, 161, 292
hierarchy 3, 90, 128, 150, 153, 164, 214
holding, 5, 78, 80, 114, 125, 131, 132, 135, 138, 139, 141–2, 171, 180–2, 185, 205, 209, 264, 298, 300, 302, state-owned 16, 180–2
homophily 153–4, 157, 159, 161–2

ideology 40, 117, 120, 137, 139, 215
indegree 63, 75–7
indicator 2, 8–9, 50, 54, 56, 116, 127–30, 153, 159–60, 166, 172, 174, 194, 197, 214, 224, 305
industrialization 11, 13, 18, 77, 94–5, 98, 171, 192, 215, 226, 236, 258–9, 262, 264, 266, 269, 280

Industrial Revolution; second 2, 13, 171, 180; third 182–3; *see also* network
inner circle 5, 113–14, 217–19, 222–3, 249, 257, 262, 264, 266, 270–1, 287–90
institutions 12, 21, 68–9, 79–81, 226, 296; corporatist 19, 195, 201, 204–5, 209; Dutch 102; financial 1, 32, 34, 41, 44, 49, 60, 76, 111, 132, 213, 221, 261, 266, 292; economic 65–7, 191, 299–300, 303; investors 101, 119, 161; national 2, 13, 22; public sector 298; *see also* politics, shareholder
insurance 80, 112, 119, 121, 172, 206–7, 229, 288; companies 1, 3, 32–3, 57, 108, 111, 117, 126, 139, 156, 160, 179–80, 182, 202, 205, 233, 235, 244, 248–9
integration 108, 112, 120, 151, 183, 193, 195–7, 200, 214–15, 223, 257; dis-integration 20, 116, 202, 204, 210, 259, 266, 268–70; European 20, 97, 206; global 81; network 19, 55, 58–60, 109, 196
interconnection. *See* connection
interdependence 2, 8, 68, 260
interlocking directorate 3, 5, 11, 15, 18, 20–4, 48, 50, 56, 78, 107, 109, 111, 115, 119–20, 126–8, 130–1, 134, 140, 149, 152, 160, 191–2, 196, 206–7, 209, 213, 257–8, 260–8, 270–1, 276–80, 282–5, 287–92, 297
interlocks xv–xvi, 4, 10–11, 17–21, 23, 32, 57–8, 74, 79, 89, 96–7, 103, 108, 111, 113, 116, 120–1, 128, 139, 149–58, 162, 207, 213, 223, 225, 233, 240, 248, 251, 290; banking 104; board 1, 89, 257, 267; corporate/corporation/firm 3, 5, 40–3; cross-industry 32; decline in 16, 238; directed 75; double 174; functions of 10–11, 61, 164, 263; interlockers 55–6, 63, 93, 160, 164, 197, 227–8, 240, 244–5, 263; interlocking directorship; 50, 171, 177–8, 180–1, 183–4, 226, 233–4, 242, 248, 302; intra-sector 59–60, 62, 78; local-international 270; multiple 161, 164, 242, 248, 251; role of 234; ties 44, 62, 201, 205, 209, 258; *see also* interlocking directorates
international 34, 60, 90, 102, 108; actors 120; business networks 261; companies 119; connections 261; expansion 118; financial system 111; institutes 139; investors 101, 114, 131; markets 137, 247, 260, 265; shareholders 101
internationalization 10, 13, 20–1, 90, 104, 108, 119–20, 139, 141, 183; bank system 140; economic 7, 16–17, 109; economic elites 164
interwar 15, 69, 99, 111–13, 121, 130, 154–5, 159–60, 184, 194, 220, 239, 242–3

Keynes/Keynesian 19, 37, 101, 137, 268

labor 11–12, 17, 20, 22, 36, 37–9, 44–5, 99, 205, 252, 270, 280; cost 205; force 132, 134; labor lines; 53, 92, 128, 174, 261, 297–8; multiple labor lines 128, 174, 261, 264, 298; organized 20, 32, 36, 37; regulation 170; union 36, 267
laissez faire 10, 93, 98
law 10, 16–17, 18, 22, 73–4, 79, 100, 134, 158, 164, 201, 206; accounting10; anti-trust 18, 58, 60, 62, 74, 82; bank secrecy 111; banking 10, 16, 180, 201; cartel 71; company 110, 114, 133, 216, 251, 284; competition 58; corporate/corporation 10, 15–16, 99–100, 110, 114, 169; incorporation 152; labor 38, 270; nationalization 133, 180; professor 99–100; stock corporation 114–15; trade 60
lawyer 112, 267, 302
leader/leadership 11, 34, 37, 43–4, 152, 177, 222–3, 243, 257, 270–1, 282, 287
legislation/legal 14, 33, 36, 38, 71, 130, 191–2, 200–1, 213, 218, 224, 238, 244, 267–8, 280, 283; antitrust 74, 230; restrictions 33

legitimacy 5, 15, 39, 153, 182
liberalism 10, 196, 238; qualified 238
liberal market economy (LME) 193, 246, 248, 250
linker: 251, 300; big 4, 9, 16, 21, 23, 55–6, 61–2, 73–4, 77, 80, 93, 97, 104, 116, 132, 151–2, 154, 156, 158, 160, 164, 177–8, 184, 197, 199, 205, 234, 236, 243, 246, 248, 250–1, 263, 269–70, 299, 303
loan 4, 10, 14, 16, 61, 68, 75, 77, 80, 95–8, 101, 104, 113, 118, 131, 180, 244

manager/management: 1, 4, 9, 19–23, 33–4, 39–40, 43, 67, 71, 73–8, 80, 90–1, 99–101, 103, 113, 115–19, 127, 131, 134, 154, 171, 181–2, 191, 214–7, 219, 227, 233–40, 242–3, 245, 250, 260–2, 268, 270, 283, 300; of the economy 215; managerial entrenchment 21, 21, 90–1, 104; manageralism 230; owner-manager 98; *see also* capitalism, control
mandate 61, 117–18, 120; *see also* position
market xvi, 4, 20, 39, 41, 60, 79, 81, 130, 140, 162, 182, 200, 204, 225, 258, 260, 262, 268, 270, 276–7, 281, 283, 285, 290; capital 11, 18, 41, 97–8, 101, 118, 134, 299–301; capitalization 101, 118, 164; domestic 60, 169, 183, 201, 264; economy 125, 192–3, 200, 215–16, 230; exchange 66, 74; export 163; failure 10; financial 6, 10, 15–16, 48, 61, 69, 74, 77, 81, 98, 109, 193, 243, 246, 261, 265; free 67, 81, 93; international 137, 247, 272; labor 11; liberal 62; liberalization 293; non-market 6, 218, 224; order 66–7; political/politicized 171, 282–3, 285; product 11; stock 101, 169, 194, 244, 246, 284, 297; structure 66; *see also* liberal market economy (LME), coordinated market economy (CME)

mean 40, 53, 109, 117, 160, 194, 290, 292, 298
merger 11, 14, 33, 40, 54, 97, 102, 116, 118–19, 126, 131, 139, 150, 156, 160, 162, 193, 199–200, 205–6, 245, 248, 270, 281; *see also* acquisition
methodology 7, 50, 215, 220, 226–7, 230, 235, 259, 296
modernization 17, 67–9, 95, 132, 152, 197, 213–14, 236
monopol/monopoly 3, 14, 66, 127, 134, 156, 158–9, 165, 169, 183, 197, 220, 230, 239, 283
multinational (MNE) 8, 19, 21, 22, 94, 119, 183, 185, 249, 251, 258, 260, 262–263, 265, 267–72, 286

nation/nation state xvi, 68
nationalization 18, 20, 110, 125, 133, 139, 172–4, 179–80, 183, 192–6, 200, 204–6, 209–10, 214–15, 222, 265
Nazi 17, 132, 140, 264; regime 16, 73
neoliberal/neoliberalism 19, 81
network xvi, 1, 3, 12–13, 19, 31, 33–5, 43, 51–3, 55–6, 59, 67, 73, 80, 90, 92, 98, 102, 104, 111, 130, 150, 157, 159, 193, 199, 240, 250, 279, 306; (social) network analysis xv, 1, 17, 23, 50, 91, 107–8, 126, 171–2, 178, 183, 192, 199, 226, 230, 234, 237, 263, 265, 296–7, 306; business 5, 192, 215, 220, 222, 224, 229–30, 234, 248, 261, 265, 271; cohesive 20; connectivity 34–5, 43, 49, 128, 230; degree 40; depth 20, 54, 61, 102; ego-network 70–1; indicator 8–9, 194, 197; interlock (ing) 34, 36, 39–43, 51, 62, 151–4, 157, 160, 165, 214, 257, 276–9, 282, 291–2; interpersonal 9; kinship 249; national xv–xvi, 20, 71, 73–4, 108, 110–13, 118, 248; policy xv; power xv; segmentation 204; social xv, 11, 21, 51, 69, 220, 228–30, 276; specialist 79, 154–6, 164–5; (infra)structure 53, 61, 76, 126, 137, 155, 158, 162, 164, 173, 179, 202, 237, 269, 288, 292, 297–300, 306; sub-network 92, 174, 257,

305, width 20, 54, 61; *see also* cohesion, company network, control, core, corporate network, density, directors, elite, integration, international, politics, transnational
node 9, 34, 51–3, 55, 135, 297

oligarchy/oligarchic 12
openness 10
outdegree 63, 75–7
owner/ownership 4, 7, 9, 11, 14, 18–19, 21, 31, 34, 39, 43, 48–9, 60, 74, 90–1, 94–5, 98, 103, 125, 140, 156, 159–60, 169–70, 180–1, 205, 238, 244–5, 258, 261, 267, 269, 284, 287, 297, 299–303; public 138; state/governmental 207, 209, 230; structure 119, 301

pantouflage/pantoufleur 154–5, 158, 160, 164–6
performance 6, 8, 13, 39, 69, 80, 103, 133–4, 137, 213, 257
periphery/peripheral 20–1, 109, 135, 150, 153–5, 157, 159, 161–3, 164, 178, 193, 213, 224, 226, 257, 266
poison pill 4
politics/political 9, 14, 16, 22, 36, 119, 149, 170, 218, 223, 229, 242–3, 288; change 156; conflict 268; connections/connectivity 12, 158, 214, 229, 264; crisis 69; economy 19, 22, 67, 276; elite xv, 12, 19, 217–18, 223, 230, 244, 249; environment 9, 243, 268; influence 155, 199; instability 204–5, 267; institution 1, 69; network 225; party 18, 134, 181–2, 222–3, 229; power 153, 283, 293; regime 9, 192; *stability* 111, 139, 151; *see also* capitalism, cohesion, market
politician 1, 3, 12, 66, 99, 112, 134, 216–18, 222, 233, 242
position 4–5, 9–12, 14–18, 23, 40, 56, 72–5, 80, 93–104, 114, 134, 156–8, 164, 172–4, 242–5, 248, 250–1, 265, 277, 288, 302–3; *see also* mandate
power center xv–xvi

practice 11, 31, 33, 40, 44, 51, 60, 96, 100–2, 117, 120, 150–1, 158, 164–5, 184, 191, 216, 223–30, 267, 277
privatization 19–21, 101, 125–7, 137–41, 162, 171, 173, 175, 182, 184–5, 192–3, 195, 206–7, 227–9, 269, 288

reform 33, 38, 58, 60, 215, 222, 226–7, 258, 269, 288, 291, 300–2
regulation 21, 37–8, 41, 67, 74–7, 81, 103, 110–14, 120, 162, 169, 193, 218, 236–8, 243–6, 263, 267, 270, 284, 288
reputation 6, 77, 100, 155, 191, 196, 263, 287

selection 67, 215, 263
service 20, 32, 41, 43, 59, 115, 119, 173, 207, 224, 236, 249, 269, 292
shareholder 11–12, 31, 39, 62, 67, 95, 98, 111, 115, 137, 140, 181, 195, 200, 204, 225, 245, 282, 284; activism/activist 61, 117; family 163; historical 113; institutional 49, 101; interests 12, 90, 99; large 301; majority 114–15, 138; meeting 99–100, 114, 134, 262; minority 19, 117, 120, 169, 181; protection 169–70; return 40; right 103–4; structure 138–9; value 21, 39–40, 43, 90, 101–3, 108, 116–18; *see also* international
slice: m-slice 35, 53–4, 174, 237, 305
social capital 218, 225, 271, 288
social group 5, 114
small world 7
stakeholder 9, 11–12, 22, 99, 215
state 6, 10, 11, 14, 16, 22, 36–7, 44, 66, 69, 76, 98–101, 126–7, 130–1, 133, 137–8, 140, 149–50, 152, 154–5, 169, 180–1, 195, 204, 207, 213, 238, 263, 268, 276–7, 279, 283, 285, 293; administration 223; bank 207; bureaucracy 18, 244; capitalism 10, 138, 166; company 18–19, 233–5, 238–9, 244–5; control 159, 209; economic policy 20; industry 137; intervention/interventionism 7, 10, 17, 19,

39, 115, 125, 163, 169, 184, 200–1, 204, 206, 259, 262, 264, 266–7, 269, 271; monopoly 158–9, 165; ownership 18, 205, 207, 209, 238; participation 18, party-state 283; power 276, 292; protection 169; regulation 77, 218; state-led industrialization 258; state-owned bank 138, 142, 169, 262, 267, 272, 287; state-owned enterprise (SOE)/firms 8, 10, 16, 22, 125, 133, 137, 157–61, 163, 166, 170, 173, 177–9, 185, 194–5, 200, 205–6, 209, 214, 217, 226, 242, 252, 265, 277, 279, 283–4, 287–8, 290–1; state(-owned) holding 16, 141, 171, 180–2; subsidy 126, welfare 67; *see also* elite, holding

status 3, 15, 21, 150–66

stockholder 36, 29, 75

strategy 12, 20, 116–18, 131, 137, 180–4, 229, 240, 242, 258, 260, 262–6, 268, 287

structural break 16, 22–3, 49, 126

takeover defense 4, 12, 19, 91, 98, 103

ties 1, 19–21, 35, 39–42, 44, 48, 51, 58, 61–3, 108–13, 120, 154–7, 161, 166, 172, 174, 182–4, 199–207, 218, 244, 257–8, 263–5, 270, 282; capital 196, 209; directed 75; directorship 7, 31; family 1, 217, 277, 284; friendship 261; government-business 271; informal 271; inter-group 18; intra-group 18; intra-sectoral 72, 79; multiple 70, 134, 150, 183, 277, 279–80, 284, 288, 291–3; personal 10–11, 98, 116, 128, 135, 139; social 69; transnational 5

top executives 3, 158

trade 18–19, 94–6, 194, 197, 200, 207, 233, 236, 238–40, 243–4, 246; freedom of 66; union/association 60, 67, 204

transaction costs 4, 69, 213, 218, 258

transnational/transnationalization 23, 107, 116, 118, 141; elite 23; network 22–3, 119; ties 5

Transport/transportation 15, 32, 37, 154, 156–7, 195, 197, 199, 202, 204–5, 207, 209, 239, 244, 260, 281

trust 6, 100, 218, 223, 236, 243, 245–6, 271, 277–85, 293; trust/companies 3, 33, 76, 158, 214, 233

war: World War I 14, 151, 238; World War II 13, 17, 128, 132, 150, 165, 214, 236, 262, 276, 297, 299, 301, 303

woman 23

worker 19, 39, 43, 137, 204, 264

zaibatsu 17, 280, 282, 297–301, 303